Managing
Supply Chain
Microsoft Dynamics AX 2009

Other books by Scott Hamilton

Managing Information: How Information Systems Impact Organizational Strategy (with Gordon B. Davis), Business One Irwin (1993), an APICS CIRM textbook

Maximizing Your ERP System, McGraw-Hill (2003)

Managing Your Supply Chain Using Microsoft Navision, McGraw-Hill (2004)

Managing Your Supply Chain Using Microsoft Axapta, McGraw-Hill (2004)

Managing Your Supply Chain Using Microsoft Dynamics AX, Printing Arts (2007)

Managing Your Supply Chain Using Microsoft Dynamics AX 2009

Scott Hamilton, Ph.D.

ISBN 978-0-9792552-2-9

To my son, Martin

Contents

Preface

The target audience for *Managing Your Supply Chain Using Microsoft Dynamics AX 2009* consists of those individuals involved with supply chain management in manufacturing and/or distribution firms. In particular, it is focused on those implementing or considering Microsoft Dynamics AX 2009[1] as their ERP system. My involvement with this target audience and Dynamics AX provided the motivation for writing this book. There were three motivating factors.

First, I would have liked a guidebook when I was learning Dynamics AX. Something that explained how it all fit together to manage key business processes in manufacturing and distribution. Something that gave me a mental framework for putting together the details learned through hands-on experience, user documentation, and training courseware. Many within the target audience are also faced with learning Dynamics AX.

The second motivating factor involved a desire to facilitate system implementation and on-going usage. My efforts to train and consult with firms implementing an ERP system like Dynamics AX often involve explanations about improved business processes and effective system usage to solve critical problems. These firms often want a vision of how an integrated ERP system could help achieve this, with practical suggestions that simplify and improve processes and system usage. This book represents a baseline of knowledge about how Dynamics AX solves common and unique business problems.

The third motivating factor involved a desire to assist those providing services related to Dynamics AX. They are charged with providing knowledgeable service across all interactions with their customers and suggesting solutions to business problems. This book reflects my experience in working alongside these people serving the marketplace of manufacturers and distributors. Our working relationship typically involved training and joint efforts at selling, consulting, and customer support.

This book focuses on the latest version (AX 2009) of Dynamics AX. Two previous editions of this book explained version 3.0 and version 4.0 of

---

[1] Dynamics AX is a registered trademark of Microsoft Corporation.

Dynamics AX.[2] This edition covers the new functionality incorporated into AX 2009, and reflects several years of additional experience. The prior research for writing the third edition built on my previous efforts for understanding Dynamics AX and the target audience. For example, my previous efforts covered the available training courses and hands-on exercises, the computer-aided instruction materials, the on-line documentation, white papers, independent analyses, presentations at various conferences, face-to-face meetings with current users, talking with knowledgeable experts at partners and Microsoft, and consulting engagements with firms implementing Dynamics AX. The same efforts were undertaken for the third edition. Most importantly, my learning process was supplemented by thousands of hands-on simulations to understand how the system really worked and how it solves the business problems of various environments.

In terms of understanding the target audience, the prior research involved gaining an in-depth knowledge of various types of operations and the management team responsible for those operations. In this respect, the prior research built on my experiences as MIS manager and manufacturing manager implementing various ERP systems in several firms, and face-to-face consulting engagements with over a thousand manufacturing and distribution firms.[3] These engagements primarily focused on supply chain management and effective ERP system usage. Each engagement required interviews with the management team to gain an in-depth understanding of how they currently run (and want to run) their business, and facilitative discussions about ways to improve operations and system effectiveness. These engagements covered the spectrum of operations, company size, levels of ERP expertise, terminology, geographies, and cultures across six continents. Each engagement required explanations that accounted for these variations in the target audience.

Other venues have also provided opportunities to understand the target audience and attempt to provide meaningful explanations through teaching and written materials. These other venues included teaching training seminars, conducting executive seminars, software user group presentations, MBA classes at several major universities, and classes for vocational-

---

[2] *Managing Your Supply Chain Using Microsoft Axapta* covered version 3.0, and *Managing Your Supply Chain Using Microsoft Dynamics AX* covered version 4.0. These previous editions are available on Amazon.com.

[3] Syntheses of these consulting engagements and related case studies have been published in two previous books. *Managing Information: How Information Systems Impact Organizational Strategy* (Irwin, 1993, with Gordon B. Davis) was one of the textbooks for the Certificate in Information Resource Management by the American Production and Inventory Control Society (APICS). *Maximizing Your ERP System: A Practical Guide for Managers* (McGraw-Hill, 2003) focuses on supply chain management in manufacturing firms.

technical colleges and APICS certification. Attempts to provide written explanations have included my responses to hundreds of RFPs (requests for proposals) related to ERP systems, as well as writing software user manuals, books, and scholarly articles based on field research and secondary research.[4] In particular, the written explanations include my contributions to the AX 2009 user documentation related to product costing and quality management. Written explanations also include a previous book, *Managing Your Supply Chain Using Microsoft Navision* (now called Dynamics NAV), and previous books on Dynamics AX.

The opportunities to consult with firms implementing or considering Microsoft Dynamics AX have supplemented the foundation of prior research. Each engagement has broadened the ability to provide meaningful explanations about improving business processes and system usage. Other opportunities to learn and work with software extensions (developed by Microsoft partners and independent software vendors) have also broadened my understanding of how Dynamics AX works. The case studies reflect some of these consulting engagements and software extensions.

A critical issue in writing this book involved the choice of topics, and the sequence and level of detail for explaining these topics. The topics focus on key software functionality that supports the dominant business practices in manufacturing and distribution environments. The topics reflect those use cases actually tested and proven to work; not all use cases could be tested or proven. The linear presentation sequence was shaped by what worked most effectively in previous writing, teaching, and consulting efforts for the target audience. The presentation employs a baseline model of operations to simplify the explanatory approach. Variations in this baseline model—such as custom products, batch/serial tracking, project-oriented operations, service-oriented operations, and multisite operations—are covered using an anchor-and-adjustment approach to the explanations. The explanations are segmented into basic and advanced considerations, and include scenarios and case studies illustrating different types of business practices.

A second critical issue in writing this book involved the evolving nature of software package functionality. The standardized functionality covered in this book reflects the AX 2009 version. It is the author's intention to publish new editions as new releases become available, along with additional case study examples.

---

[4] Examples of relevant articles range from "Requirements of Smaller Manufacturers for Computer-Based Systems" (published in the *APICS Quarterly*, Winter 1984) to "Trends Affecting Manufacturers and ERP" (published in *TechnologyEvaluation.com*, October 2003). More academic-oriented articles include an annual summary of MIS doctoral dissertations since 1973 (published in the *MIS Quarterly*).

The book reflects my interpretation of how to use Microsoft Dynamics AX 2009. Errors of omission and commission, and any misunderstandings, are hopefully minimized.[5] Corrections and suggestions are welcome, as well as additional case study examples. Please send to **ScottHamiltonPhD@ aol.com**. The intended goal is to provide an overall understanding of how it all fits together so readers can accelerate their learning process about managing their supply chain activities.

Each day of writing was started with the following prayer:

> Creator of all things, give me a sharp sense of understanding, a retentive memory, and the ability to grasp things correctly and fundamentally. Grant me the talent of being exact in my explanations, and the ability to express myself with thoroughness and charm. Point out the beginning, direct the progress, and help in the completion.

Many people helped in completing this book, especially Jan DeGross in editing and typesetting, and Deb Skoog and Robyn Voges in printing the book. Invaluable feedback was obtained from reviewers, especially Mark Hermans, John Holbrook, Frans Hoogenraad, Brian Lounds, Russell Mascarenhas, Alex Rejon, Robert Rudd, Frank Stephens, Jim Sutorus, Einar Ulfsson, Bob Vanderslice, and Haiyan Zhao. My writing efforts were supported by my wife Cindy and my son Martin. This book is dedicated to Martin, who has inspired me in many different aspects of life and faith.

---

[5] The book is for information purposes only. The author, publisher, and Microsoft make no warranties, expressed or implied, in the presentation of information.

Chapter 1

Introduction

Most manufacturing and distribution businesses opt for a software package as the foundation for managing their supply chain activities. The package's standardized functionality provides the basic framework for supporting variations in business processes, with unique requirements covered by varying degrees of customization. Learning the standardized functionality represents a critical activity for system selection, implementation, and ongoing usage by individuals within these firms.

An individual's learning process usually builds on training courseware and user documentation. In many cases, these provide a detailed viewpoint expressed in software-specific terminology and a screen-by-screen field-by-field walk-through approach. It makes an overall understanding difficult and requires time-consuming efforts to piece the details together into a mental framework. Most people can accelerate their learning process with a mental framework of how the system fits together to run a business, expressed in generally accepted terminology. The mental framework—in combination with hands-on experience, user documentation, and training courseware—reduces the learning curve, and an overall understanding leads to more effective system usage.

This book addresses the need for an overall understanding of the current release of one ERP system: Microsoft Dynamics AX (formerly known as Axapta).[1] It focuses on using Dynamics AX 2009 for managing supply chain activities in manufacturing and distribution environments.

The targeted reader includes those individuals implementing or considering Dynamics AX as their ERP system as well as those providing sales and implementation services. Firms involved with a system selection process may be considering Dynamics AX as a candidate package, and this book can help reduce selection risks, evaluate system fit and needed customizations, and provide a vision of an integrated system. The book can help businesses involved in implementing and using Dynamics AX by accelerating the

---

[1] Dynamics AX is a registered trademark of Microsoft Corporation.

		Distribution or Manufacturing Firm	Solution Provider
	Overall Goal	Improve firm performance through effective supply chain management systems	Improve firm performance through effective customer service
System Implementation Life Cycle	System Selection	Reduce selection risk Evaluate system fit and needed customizations Provide vision of an integrated system	Accelerate learning process Reduce new employee ramp-up time Improve solution-selling techniques Improve training and consulting efforts Support gap/fit analyses Improve customization capabilities
	Implementation	Accelerate learning process Reduce implementation costs and time Reduce user resistance to change	
	On-Going Operation	Suggest changes to improve system usage Revitalize a wayward implementation	

Figure 1.1 Reasons for Reading Book

learning process, reducing implementation time and costs, and reducing user resistance to change. It suggests changes that can improve system usage and revitalize a wayward implementation. For firms providing sales and services related to Dynamics AX, this book can accelerate the employee learning process for providing knowledgeable customer service in sales, support, and professional assistance. Figure 1.1 summarizes these reasons for reading the book.

A Baseline Model of Operations

The book employs a baseline model of operations to simplify explanations. The baseline model focuses on standard products (identified by an item number) that must be tracked by bin locations within a warehouse, where one or more warehouses belong to a site. Each site typically represents a physical location, and the multisite functionality within Dynamics AX supports financial reporting by site, site-specific standard costs for an item, and site-specific bills and routings for a manufactured item.[2] Examples of warehouses within a site could include separate warehouses for raw material, finished goods, floor stock inventory for production, and/or service parts

---

[2] Dynamics AX supports three basic approaches for modeling physical sites, as described in Figure 13.2. The book's baseline model focuses on the two approaches involving the new multisite functionality introduced in AX 2009.

inventory. Several policies can be site- or warehouse-specific, or reflect a company-wide policy. These policy variations are summarized in Figure 2.1 (Company-Wide Versus Site/Warehouse Information), Figure 2.2 (Planning Data for Purchased Items), Figure 3.6 (Planning Data for Manufactured Items), and Figure 13.2 (Planning Data for Transfer Items). Chapter 9 provides further explanation about sites, warehouses, and bin locations and their related policies.

The baseline model of operations also focuses on a single company with one or more autonomous physical sites. Multisite operations requiring coordination of material movements between sites and companies are covered separately in Chapter 13. Other major variations to the baseline model include project-oriented and service-oriented operations, which are covered separately in Chapter 12 and Chapter 14. The book employs the baseline model to explain the key business processes involved in supply chain management, and the typical variations in each process. This baseline model reflects an explanatory approach and not a system limitation.

Design Factors Shaping System Usage

ERP system usage is shaped by several design factors related to the user interface, system functionality, and customization tools. For example, consistency and symmetry in the user interface and functionality make an ERP system easier to learn and use. The design factors shaping usage of Microsoft Dynamics AX are covered throughout this book and summarized in the concluding chapter. The interested reader may want to read the last chapter first. However, five design factors require up-front attention. These factors include terminology, a role-centered viewpoint, web-based applications, the primary engine for coordinating supply chain activities, and standardized versus customized functionality.

Terminology   One design factor involves the terminology used to describe system usage. The system-specific terminology for functions, window titles, and field labels has been used as much as possible to explain system functionality. However, alternative phrasing or common synonyms are sometimes used to clarify understanding. Common terminology makes it easier for beginner users to understand system functionality. The explanations refer to the system-specific terminology when using common terminology. The Appendix contains illustrations of Microsoft Dynamics AX

Area	Representative Roles	Typical Tasks	Typical KPIs (Key Performance Indicators)	Relevant Book Chapters
Engineering	Engineering Manager & Engineers	Create/maintain items Define bills of material & routings Configure custom products	BOM accuracy Routing accuracy	2- Purchased Material 3- Manufactured Items 4- Custom Product Manufacturing
Engineering	Cost Accountant	Establish standard costs Track actual product costs	Purchase/production variances Profitability	5- Product Costing
Supply Chain Management	Operation Manager & Production Manager	Manage operations/production	Production performance Delivery Performance Profitability	2- Distribution Items 3- Manufactured Items 4- Custom Product Manufacturing 5- Sales & Operations Planning 11-Production Order Processing
Supply Chain Management	Production Scheduler & Master Scheduler	Schedule production orders Manage capacity		
Supply Chain Management	Purchasing Agent	Create/maintain purchase orders Handle requisitions & RFQs	Vendor performance Purchase variances	2- Purchased Material 6- Sales & Operations Planning 8- Purchase Order Processing
Supply Chain Management	Purchasing Manager	Handle agreements, blanket POs		
Supply Chain Management	Warehouse Manager	Manage warehouse workers	Delivery performance Receiving performance Inventory levels & accuracy	9- Inventory & Warehouse Mgt 13- Multisite Operations
Supply Chain Management	Warehouse Worker & Shipping/Receiving	Handle outgoing shipments Handle incoming receipts		
Quality	Quality Manager & Inspectors	Define testing requirements Report inspection results	Quality performance	10- Quality Management
Sales	Order Processor & Sales Representative	Handle sales orders & quotes Configure custom products	Delivery performance	4- Custom Product Manufacturing 6- Sales & Operations Planning 7- Sales Order Processing
Sales	Sales Manager	Manage sales reps Forecast sales	Sales rep performance Sales performance	
Sales	Customer Service Manager & Service Technicians	Monitor service activity & levels Perform service work orders	Service performance	14- Service Order Processing
Project	Project Manager & Project Team Members	Create/maintain projects Track time/expenses/material Track project activities	Project cost performance Project schedule performance	12-Project Oriented Operations
Exec	CEO & CFO & COO	Define S&OP game plans Track actual versus game plans	Profitability Key ratios: return on assets, etc. Sales/schedule/cost performance Quality performance	6- Sales & Operations Planning

Figure 1.2 Role Centered Viewpoint

terminology and synonyms. It also defines the significance of several key terms—such as posting and journals—that are essential for understanding system functionality.

Role Centered Viewpoint   A role centered viewpoint reflects the typical departments and positions involved in running a company. This book focuses on the roles involved in supply chain management within a manufacturing/distribution company, and the related roles in engineering, quality, sales, customer service, projects, and executive management. Figure 1.2 summarizes some representative roles, the typical tasks and KPIs (key performance indicators) for each role, and the relevant book chapters for each role.

The book does not cover the roles related to finance, human resources, and marketing, although it does cover some customer relationship management (CRM) aspects of marketing such as quotations, sales orders, and service orders. In addition, it does not address internal IT roles involved with administration and customization of Dynamics AX.[3]

Dynamics AX incorporates a role centered viewpoint through the explicit definition of roles and role centers.

❖ *Definition of Roles.* The definition of a role (termed a *user group*) includes the users assigned to the role. For example, a role could represent a given type of job (as illustrated in Figure 1.2), or the approvers for purchase requisitions within a department (as described in the Chapter 8 section on the approval process for purchase requisitions).

❖ *Definition of Role Centers.* A role center page provides an overview of information pertaining to a role. The overview information may include key forms/reports, a list of activities, and key performance indicators (KPIs). Each user within a company is assigned to a user profile, and a role center is specified for each profile.

A role center page contains Web parts that represent individual pieces of displayed information; the content and layout can be personalized. The typical Web parts on a role center page include:

– Frequently used forms, reports, and list pages (termed *quick links*).

– Visual representations of workload (termed *cues*) comprised of filtered views of forms or list pages, such as a list of overdue activities.

– Work lists that display alerts, workflow items, and activities that need attention.

– Reports and key performance indicators based on information within the AX database or online analytical processing (OLAP) cubes.

– Business overview information that summarizes comparative measures versus goals across various time periods.

A role centered viewpoint is also implicitly embedded within the structure of the user documentation. That is, user documentation about applications and business processes reflect various functional areas (and associated roles) that are termed the customer model. For example, the user documentation that covers setting up and maintaining supply chain management includes the following major sections:

---

[3] See *Inside Dynamics AX 4.0* (by Arthur Greef, Michael Fruergaard Pontoppidan, and Lars Dragheim Olsen, Microsoft Press, 2006) for in-depth explanations about the development environment using MorphX and the X++ programming language. This book includes suggestions for system customizations and extensions, integration of XML documents, and use of the Enterprise Portal.

❖ *Design and Engineering*, which covers items, bills of material, work centers, routings, and standard costs.

❖ *Operations*, which covers forecasts, master planning, purchasing, production, warehouse operations, receiving, and shipping.

❖ *Customer Service*, which covers service objects and tasks, service agreements, repair management, and customer returns.

Web-based Applications The Enterprise Portal provides a Web-based application framework that allows users to interact with data in Dynamics AX through a Web browser. You can create new content for the Enterprise Portal, and also modify existing content. Most additions and changes can be made using resources in the Application Object Tree (AOT)[4] in combination with Windows SharePoint Services. More advanced applications and modifications can be created by using Visual Studio and the development framework for Enterprise Portal.

Web Modules are the resources in the AOT that define the overall structure and top-level navigation for Enterprise Portal. That is, they define the sites and subsites in Windows SharePoint Services that make up an Enterprise Portal installation. The main Enterprise Portal site contains several role center pages that are customized for each role in the company. The first page the user sees when opening Enterprise Portal is the role center to which they are assigned. In addition, the main Enterprise Portal site contains several subsites. Each subsite is referred to as a module site. These module sites have names such as Sales, Purchasing, and Project. They represent distinct areas in which users can perform tasks in the Enterprise Portal. Examples of these enterprise portal applications include customer self service (described in Chapter 7), vendor replies to purchasing RFQs (described in Chapter 8), and technician reporting of service orders (described in Chapter 14).

Primary Engine for Coordinating Supply Chain Activities The primary engine for coordinating supply chain activities consists of a *master scheduling task*. The master scheduling task uses information about demands and supplies and a set of master plan policies to calculate net requirements for material and capacity (termed a set of master plan data). The system

---

[4] In Microsoft Dynamics AX, there is a three-tier infrastructure with a database server, an application object server (AOS), and a client. The database server contains the table data. The AOS is used to execute application objects, such as queries and classes. Application objects in the user interface, such as forms and reports, run on the client computer.

supports multiple sets of master plan data for simulation purposes, and generates suggested schedules for purchasing, production, and distribution. The *forecast scheduling task* represents a second coordinating engine when forecasted demands are applicable. One or more sets of forecasted demands can be defined and uniquely identified by a forecast identifier. This forecast identifier is assigned to each sales forecast or purchase forecast for an item. The forecast scheduling task calculates forecasted demand and gross requirements for material and capacity based on several policies, such as the specified set of forecast data and planning horizon. The single term *planning calculations* refers to the combination of master scheduling and forecast scheduling tasks. The single term reflects generally accepted terminology. A master schedule generally refers to stocked items while a final assembly schedule (or finishing schedule) refers to make-to-order items. The master scheduling task applies to both stocked and make-to-order items. Chapter 6 provides further explanation of planning calculations and use of the master scheduling and forecast scheduling tasks.

Standardized Versus Customized Functionality A final design factor involves standardized functionality versus customizations. A focus on out-of-the-box or standardized functionality provides a baseline for learning how the system manages supply chain activities in different environments. However, Dynamics AX is highly customizable, and independent software vendors (ISVs) have developed significant extensions. The general idea is that standard functionality meets 80% to 90% of a firm's requirements while customizations and independently developed extensions meet the remaining needs. The book employs case studies to illustrate typical customizations and ISV extensions.

Key Business Processes

Manufacturing and distribution companies have many similarities in their supply chain activities and ERP system requirements. In addition, many manufacturers operate as a distributor, selling purchased products or coordinating replenishment across their distribution network. Many distributors also operate as a manufacturer, performing light assembly, repairs, or installations. Some companies are in the midst of switching products from purchased to manufactured, or vice versa. Therefore, an overall understanding often requires consideration of both environments. The starting point for an overall understanding consists of several key business processes built on a common database. A key aspect of the common database involves item information about a firm's saleable products. For simplicity's sake, the item information can be viewed from the two perspectives of a distributor and a manufacturer. A product costing perspective applies to both distribution and manufacturing environments.

❖ *Distribution Items and Purchased Material.* Saleable products consist of purchased material in a distribution environment. These items are typically stocked in advance of sales orders but may be purchased to order.

❖ *Manufactured Items.* A manufacturing environment also purchases material and then produces manufactured items either to stock or to order or both. The transformations from purchased material to manufactured item are minimally defined by bill of material information, with the processing steps and resource requirements optionally defined by routing information. Manufactured items can be categorized into standard and custom products. Whereas a standard product has predefined bill and routing information, a custom product typically involves the definition of components (and routing operations) to meet a customer's specifications. For example, the components can be defined by an option selection or a rules-based configurator approach.

❖ *Product Costing.* Product cost information supports valuation of an item's inventory transactions using a standard cost or actual cost method. Actual cost methods include weighted average, LIFO, and FIFO. Standard costs provide the basis for identifying variances in purchasing and manufacturing. Product costs for a manufactured item can be calculated using its bill of material information, and optional routing and overhead information.

Several business processes can be identified for supply chain management in manufacturing and distribution environments. Three of these business processes revolve around sales orders, purchase orders, and production orders. Quality management concerns apply to each process.

❖ *Sales Order Processing.* The sales order process typically starts with sales order entry and finishes with shipment and invoices. It requires definition of customers, and involves related activities such as quotes and customer returns and the larger context of managing customer relationships.

❖ *Purchase Order Processing.* The purchase order process typically starts with purchase order entry and finishes with receipts and vendor invoices. It requires definition of vendors, and involves related activities such as purchase requisitions, requests for quotes and vendor returns, and the larger context of managing vendor relationships. Coordination of purchasing activity focuses on suggested actions to replenish inventory to meet demand.

❖ *Production Order Processing.* The production order process starts with creation of the production order and finishes with a completed product. Coordination of production activity focuses on production schedules and suggested actions to replenish inventory or meet demand.

❖ *Quality Management.* The broad viewpoint of quality management concerns every aspect of supply chain management. In particular, it involves the enforcement of materials management policies about batch and serial tracking, receiving inspection, and product testing. It also involves the tracking of quality problems, and the use of work flow tools for managing business processes

Three additional business processes apply to all environments: sales and operations planning, inventory and warehouse management, and inventory movement across multisite operations.

❖ *Sales and Operations Planning.* One of the most critical business processes involves running the company from the top. This business process requires balancing sales demand against the ability of operations to supply product, and it is commonly termed the sales and operations planning (S&OP) process. It starts with the definition of all demands for the firm's products, and formulates S&OP game plans that drive supply chain activities to meet those demands. The nature of each game plan depends on the environment. An S&OP game plan can be expressed as master schedules for stocked items and/or finishing schedules for make-to-order items.

❖ *Inventory and Warehouse Management.* Inventory and warehouse management involves receipts and issues in supporting the above-mentioned business processes. For example, warehouse management involves receiving and put-away for purchase orders, and picking and shipment for sales orders. It also involves handling internal inventory adjustments, transfers, and physical inventory counts. These activities taken as a group represent a key business process.

❖ *Multisite Operations.* Some multisite operations involve transfers between locations. Transfer orders coordinate movements between sites in a single company, while intercompany purchase orders and sales orders coordinate movements between sites in multiple companies. Multisite operations often require other forms of coordination, such centralized engineering or consolidated financial reports.

Two business processes reflect the unique environments of project-oriented operations and service-oriented operations.

❖ *Project-Oriented Operations.* Some companies have project-oriented operations, with material and capacity requirements tied to specific projects.

❖ *Service-Oriented Operations.* Service-oriented operations involve service orders. The service order process starts with the creation of the service order and finishes with a completed service. The service order may be generated from service agreements that define periodic requirements such as monthly maintenance. Coordination of service activity focuses on service schedules, and on the material and labor to meet service order demands.

This simple mental framework provides an organizing focus for further explanation. The book's chapters cover the common database information about purchased items, manufactured items, custom product manufactured items, and product costs, and the above-mentioned business processes.

This format enables readers to focus on just distribution or manufacturing. For example, a single-site distributor can focus on the database for distribution items (Chapter 2) and their costs (Chapter 5), and their key business processes for planning, sales, purchasing, inventory, and quality (Chapters 6 through 10). A single-site manufacturer can focus on the database for purchased material (Chapter 2), manufactured items (Chapter 3 and 4) and product costs (Chapter 5), the basic business processes (Chapters 6 though 10), and the additional business processes involving production (Chapter 11). The final chapter summarizes the design factors shaping system usage in distribution and manufacturing environments.

Each chapter provides a basic overview of critical information and variations in business processes supported by standard functionality within Dynamics AX. Each chapter also includes an executive summary and case studies that highlight use of standardized and customized functionality.

Summary of Case Studies Used Throughout the Book

Case studies illustrate how standardized functionality applies to different types of environments, especially the flexibility to model variations in business processes. They also illustrate customizations and ISV extensions that go beyond standardized functionality in solving business problems. The book's case studies are drawn from six representative environments (one distribution company, four manufacturing companies, and one catchall company) as described below.

Company A: All-and-Anything The All-and-Anything company consists of several businesses that have been acquired. Each business operates autonomously and produces a unique set of products.

Company B: Batch Process The Batch Process company manufactures two major product lines involving liquids and solids. It purchases materials and builds product to stock.

Company C: Consumer Products The Consumer Products company manufactures electrical products and other products for the consumer marketplace. It purchases materials and builds product to stock.

Company D: Distribution The Distribution company represents a wholesaler carrying two major product lines—one for consumer products and another for industrial products—that are purchased and then sold from stock.

Company E: Equipment The Equipment company manufactures industrial and medical products. Some standardized products are built to stock; other products are configured and built to customer specification from stocked subassemblies.

Company F: Fabricated Products The Fabricated Products company builds custom products to customer order using metal and plastic raw materials.

Case studies for the catchall company (Company A) represent common problems or different environments. Figure 1.3 summarizes the case studies by chapter and company, and each cell indicates the relevant case number used in the book. In addition, each chapter includes scenarios that represent additional case studies, such as the scenarios for sales and operations planning (Chapter 6) and project-oriented environments (Chapter 12).

		A	B	C	D	E	F
	Focus	All-and-Anything	Batch Process	Consumer Products	Distribution	Equipment	Fabrication
Chapter	Type of Products	Miscellaneous	Liquid & Solid	Electrical & Other	Industrial & Consumer	Industrial & Medical	Metal & Plastic
2	Purchased Material	1. Variable Min/Max	2. Batch-Specific Costing	3. Document Handling	4. Item Variants	5. Replacement Parts	
3	Manufactured Items	6. Virtual Manufacturing 7. CAD Integration	8. Authorized Recipes 9. By-Products	10. Printed Circuit Boards 11. Item Variants in Bills	12. Kit Items 13. Light Assembly	14. Revision Levels and ECOs 15. Engineering Bills versus Production Bills	16. Cut-to-Size Material 17. By-Products
4	Custom Product Manufacturing	18. Custom Windows 19. Custom Store Fixtures			20. Custom Surgical Kit	21. Overhead Crane 22. Auto-create Product Structure Skeleton	23. Plastic Bags 24. Plastic Assembly
5	Product Costs	25. Convert from Actual to Standard Costs	26. Calculate Item Sales Prices	27. Simulate Impact of Cost Changes	28. Material-Related Overheads	29. Calculate Sales Price for a Sales Quotation	30. Costing for Precious Metal Components
6	Sales & Operations Planning	31. S&OP Simulations 32. Aggregate Forecasts by Item Group	33. Component Forecast	34. Kanban Coordination 35. S&OP Process Improvements	36. Statistical Forecasting	37. Planning Bills 38. Manual MPS	39. Manual Forecast Consumption 40. S&OP for One-Time Products
7	Sales Order Processing	41. Automotive Tire Outlets 42. Commissions and Rebates	43. Reserved Material by Batch	44. Mobile Order Entry 45. RMAs for Serialized Items	46. Rules-Based Pricing 47. Drop Shipments	48. Tiered Pricing for Year-to-Date Quantity	49. Sales Quotations & Collaborative Selling
8	Purchase Order Processing	50. Vendor Performance	51. Conditional Releases	52. Buyer Action Messages	53. Supplier Coordination via E-commerce		54. Multiple Subcontractors
9	Inventory and Warehouse Mgt	55. UPS Integration	56. Consolidated Picking List	57. ASNs and Bar-Coded Labels	58. Data Collection System	59. Stockroom Action Messages	
10	Quality Management	60. Batch Attributes	61. Regulated Manufacturing	62. Instrument Calibration	63. Inspection Frequency	64. Quality Metrics	
11	Production Order Processing	65. Plant and Fleet Maintenance		66. Orderless Production		67. Customer-Supplied Parts	68. APS Integration
12	Project-Oriented Operations	69. New Product Development Project		70. Professional Service Projects		71. Engineer-To-Order Equipment	
13	Multi-Site Operations	72. Modeling Transfers via Production Orders	73. Master Scheduling across Companies	74. Home Furniture Outlets	75. Van Deliveries of Dairy Products	76. Multiple Plants Build Same Item	
14	Service Orders	77. Planning Calculations for Service Parts		78. Repair Department	79. Installation Services	80. Equipment Maintenance Services	

Companies

Figure 1.3 Summary of Case Studies

Chapter 2

Distribution Items and Purchased Material

Information about material items provides the foundation for managing supply chain activities in distribution and manufacturing environments. A comprehensive common database about item information must satisfy requirements stemming from multiple stakeholders to avoid the problems associated with multiple nonintegrated files. The stakeholders include sales, purchasing, warehouse management, quality, and accounting, as well as engineering and production for manufactured items. Other stakeholder considerations include customers, vendors, industry standards, intercompany coordination, international operations, and web-based applications. The multiple stakeholders often have differing requirements concerning item identification and item attributes.

Item identification and descriptive information represent some of the basic issues for many firms implementing an ERP system for supply chain management. For example, the item identification issues often arise from efforts to replicate a company's current scheme, or to account for capabilities within the ERP software package. The basic issues also include the effective use of item planning data to support supply chain coordination, and recognizing company-wide versus site/warehouse information for items. These basic issues are reflected in the eight sections within this chapter.

1. Item identification for material
2. Additional considerations about item identification
3. Descriptive information about material items
4. Company-wide versus site/warehouse information for items
5. Planning data for purchased material
6. Costing and financial reporting for purchased material
7. Alternative approaches to an item's purchase price
8. Alternative approaches to an item's sales price

This chapter focuses on purchased items, whereas the next two chapters focus on manufactured items. This chapter includes a comprehensive explanation of planning data for material (such as coverage codes, action messages, and coverage groups), so that subsequent chapters only cover unique aspects of planning data for manufactured items (Chapter 3) and transfer items (Chapter 13). This chapter also introduces alternative approaches for handling costing, sales prices, and purchase prices. Subsequent chapters provide more detailed explanation about costing (Chapter 5), sales (Chapter 7), and purchasing (Chapter 8).

Item Identification for Material

Item identification for a standard product typically consists of an item number. Some environments require identification based on the item number and additional field(s) such as a configuration ID and/or variant code. This section introduces these alternative approaches to item identification, and the policies embedded in the dimension group assigned to an item.

Item Number The item number provides a unique internal identifier for each material item.[1] An item number can be manually or automatically assigned. A new item's information can be created from a template.[2] An existing item number can be changed or deleted when no inventory exists for the item. Changing (aka renaming) an existing item number will result in automatic updates to related information, such as changing the item number on existing sales orders and purchase orders.

Item Number and Variant Code Such as Color and Size An alternative approach to item identification involves the combined identifiers of an item number and variant code. Color and size reflect the two out-of-the-box names for these variant codes; they can easily be renamed, and additional variant codes can be created. For simplicity's sake we will refer to these color and size fields as variant codes. The variant code can be represented by a single field or by two fields, and variant codes (or combinations of var-

---

[1] The field size for item number (20 characters) and other fields can be easily changed using the extended data type capabilities.

[2] A template can be created from an existing item and multiple templates can be defined. The user can then select a template when creating a new item. The template concept applies throughout the system for creating new records.

iant codes) must be user defined. Item variants represent an alternative to using separate item numbers. Item variants normally apply to a purchased item but they can also apply to a manufactured item. The system treats an item with a combined identifier exactly like one identified by just an item number, with several major exceptions.

❖ *Costing of a Variant.* You can choose whether the variants have the same cost or a different cost, as defined by the item policy *use combination cost price.* For example, each variant can have a different standard cost.

❖ *Transfers of a Variant.* The transfer journal transaction enables you to transfer one variant of an item to another variant, much like you would transfer inventory from one warehouse to another warehouse. For example, with an item number that represents an animal or plant, and a variant code that represents the item's age, you can transfer a one-year old variant to a two-year old variant. In contrast, a transfer order does not allow you to change the variant code.

❖ *Manufactured Item with Variants.* All variants of a manufactured item reflect the same bill and routing. An item number and variant code can be specified as a component, but the parent cannot be the same item number.

The significance of the combined identifier (of item number and variant code) is reflected in all supplies and demands; it can be optionally reflected in purchase prices and sales prices. Further explanation of item variants will be limited to special cases, such as Case 4 and Case 11.

Item Number and Configuration ID   Another approach to item identification involves an item number and a configuration ID. Each new configuration ID must be user defined. There are two options for using the combined identifier of an item number and configuration ID. The first option is termed a *non-configurable item*, and the configuration ID acts exactly the same as a variant code field. The second option is termed a *configurable item*, which allows two additional capabilities: (1) a unique bill and routing can be created for an item's configuration ID, and (2) the item's bill of material (BOM) can serve as a bill of options (with option selection rules) for creating a unique bill and routing via option selection. Once an item's configuration ID has been created, it can be forecasted and stocked just like items identified by an item number.

A configuration ID is sometimes used to reflect packaging variations of the same item (such as box, carton, or barrel), where the bill of material for each predefined configuration specifies the item quantity and the packaging components. Chapter 4 provides further explanation about configurable items and their applicability for handling custom product manufacturing.

Significance of Item and Inventory Dimensions

The basis for item identification is embedded in the policies defined for the dimension group assigned to an item. The dimension group defines two sets of policies termed the *item dimensions* and *inventory dimensions*.

❖ *Item Dimensions*. The item dimensions indicate whether additional fields will be used for item identification, such as a variant code or configuration ID. The policies also determine whether trade agreements concerning sales prices and purchase prices are based on the item number, or the item number and the additional field(s).

❖ *Inventory Dimensions*. The inventory dimensions define several policies concerning inventory stocking locations (site, warehouse, and bin), quality management (batch and serial number tracking), and warehouse management (tracking inventory by serialized container). In particular, the site and warehouse dimensions indicate whether company-wide or site- and warehouse-specific information will be used for inventory replenishment, financial tracking, and trade agreements about sales prices and purchase prices.

Item Numbers for Indirect Material Direct material items within distribution and manufacturing environments have unique item numbers, and the company's sales and operations planning (S&OP) game plans drive replenishment. Similarly, indirect materials such as replacement parts for maintenance, repair, and operations (MRO) purposes typically have unique item numbers. The unique item number provides the basis for sourcing and agreement information, and tracking usage and purchase history.

Indirect materials that represent workplace items (such as office supplies, furniture, and computer-related items) do not typically have a unique item number. In order to buy these items within Dynamics AX, you create and use generic item numbers (aka category items) that represent various categories of nonstock or expense items. When buying a category item, the user enters descriptive text and the vendor's item number to define what is being purchased, and an optional G/L account number associated with purchasing an expense item. A category item does not require tracking of physical or financial inventory, which should be reflected in the policies of the dimension group assigned to the item.

The concept of a non-inventoried item is that it can be issued or received without tracking inventory. It often represents a workplace or expense item such as office and production supplies, consulting or engineering time, or anything that does not require inventory tracking. Several guidelines apply to the definition of non-inventoried items.

❖ *Item Type.* A non-inventoried item is typically designated as a service item or a purchased item. The two item types of *service* and *item* are treated exactly the same with two major exceptions: planning calculations do not generate planned orders for service items, and service items cannot have a standard cost inventory model.

❖ *Dimension Group Policies.* A separate dimension group should be defined for non-inventoried items, where the inventory dimensions may include the site and warehouse. The financial and physical inventory does not need to be tracked.

❖ *Inventory Model Group Policies.* A separate group should be defined, where the policies reflect an actual costing method and no tracking of financial and physical inventory.

❖ *Item Group and G/L Account Number Assignment.* A separate item group should be defined, where the G/L account numbers reflect the nature of the non-inventoried item. Multiple item groups may need to be defined to differentiate the financial impact of transactions for various non-inventoried items. An item's financial dimension can also be used to differentiate the financial impact.

❖ *Coverage Group.* A separate coverage group should be defined with a reordering policy of manual.

The system treats a non-inventoried item just like any other item, other than the lack of inventory tracking. For example, trade agreements, purchase orders, and sales orders can apply to a non-inventoried item.

Additional Considerations about Item Identification

A common problem with item information involves differing requirements for units of measure and alternate identifiers. The system supports several variations for each of these two basic issues.

Unit of Measure (UM) Variations   Unit of measure codes must be pre-defined, such as pieces, each, box, and kilogram. The abbreviation UM (aka UOM) will be used for simplicity's sake. Each item requires one UM for costing and inventory purposes. This is termed the *inventory UM*, but it will also be referred to as the *base UM*. An item's base UM is reflected in its inventory balances and planning calculations, costs and cost roll-up calculations, and inventory transaction quantities reported through inventory journals and production order receipts.

You can optionally specify a default UM for purchasing purposes and another default UM for sales purposes. Most companies find a single unit of measure sufficient. In these cases, the single unit of measure should also be assigned as the item's default UM value for purchase orders and sales orders to make system usage easier.[3]

❖ *Default UM for Sales Purposes.* The order quantity modifiers (such as minimum, multiple, maximum, and standard order quantity) for sales order purposes are expressed in the default sales UM. The default sales UM and these order quantity modifiers are reflected in a manually entered sales order line item. In addition, the default sales UM applies to the company-wide sales price for the item.

❖ *Default UM for Purchasing Purposes.* The order quantity modifiers for purchase order purposes are expressed in the default sales UM. The default purchase UM and these order quantity modifiers are reflected in a manually entered purchase order line item. In addition, the default purchase UM applies to the company-wide purchase price for the item.

Some environments require more than one UM for an item, such as selling or buying an item in different units of measure. The system supports UM variations in the following six areas, but each UM must be authorized for the item:

---

[3] The item's default UM for purchase orders and sales orders serves a secondary purpose for defining a company-wide standard purchase price and standard sales price. However, trade agreement information (about an item's purchase price and sales price) can be expressed in a different UM regardless of the default UM.

❖ *Sales Orders.* A sales order line item can specify any authorized UM for the item, where the sales quantity and price reflect the specified UM. Shipment quantities are reported in the specified UM.

❖ *Purchase Orders.* A purchase order line item can specify any authorized UM for the item, where the purchase quantity and price reflect the specified UM. Receipt and return quantities are reported in the specified UM.

❖ *Trade Agreements.* An item's prices (and line discounts) can be specified for any of its authorized UM in sales trade agreements and in purchase trade agreements. As a related issue, the minimum quantity for including a supplementary item also reflects a specified UM for the item.

❖ *Forecasts.* An item's sales forecast and purchase forecast can specify any of its authorized UM.

❖ *Bill Component and Picking List Quantities.* The component quantity in a bill of material can be expressed in any authorized UM for the item. With production orders, the component's issue quantity is reported in the specified UM. With orderless production reporting (via the BOM journal), the component's auto-deduct quantity always reflects the item's base UM.

❖ *Display of Inventory Balances.* An item's inventory balances are displayed in terms of its base UM; the system does not retain identification of a different receiving UM once material goes into inventory.

The item's base UM represents an authorized UM for the item. Any other UM must be authorized before it can be used for the item. An authorized UM means it has a UM conversion factor that ties it back to the item's base UM. The UM conversion factors can apply to all items, such as standard UM conversions between kilograms, grams, and milligrams. Standard UM conversions can be user-defined, such as 10 pieces per box and 4 boxes per carton. However, some items may require definition of an item-specific UM conversion factor, such as nine pieces per box. When entering transactions, the system displays an item's authorized UMs in the drop-down list for the UM field.

Alternative Item Identifiers for Sales and Purchasing Purposes   An internal item number can be associated with other item identifiers for sales and purchasing purposes. These are termed *external item numbers*. Each external item number can be mapped to one internal item number and have a separate description.

❖ *Sales Purpose.* The external item number can be specified for a single customer to reflect a customer item number, or for a group of customers to reflect a catalog item number or an industry standard.

❖ *Purchasing Purpose.* The external item number can be specified for a single vendor to reflect a vendor item number, or for a group of vendors to reflect an industry standard.

Company Item Number for Intercompany Sales and Purchases A company item number provides item identification for viewing inventory balances across multiple companies. It is also used with intercompany sales orders and purchase orders, thereby supporting different item identification schemes within each company. Each company item number (and description) must be defined independently, and then assigned to the relevant item on the item master within the database for each company. As an alternative, you can select an existing item number (with an assigned company item number) in one company, and then automatically create the item in other selected companies (with the same item number or a different item number).

Alternative Identifier for Electronic Transactions (External Code) Electronic exchange of documents with customers and vendors is supported by various methods such as Microsoft Biztalk. These documents include sales orders and purchase orders. As part of the setup for each type of document, the item identification can be based on the internal item number, the external item number (described above), or another identifier termed an external code. The external code must be mapped to an internal item number, and it may represent an industry standard such as the UPC (Universal Product Code) number or EAN (European Article Number) identifier.

Alternative Identifier for GTIN (Global Trade Item Number) The GTIN number reflects a standardized 14-digit identifier for a specified format (such as EAN/UCC-8), which can be mapped to the internal item number and a specific UM.

Alternative Item Identifier for Bar Coding Purposes The bar code for an item requires an explicit mapping between the internal item number and the bar code digits, even when the bar code digits are exactly the same. The mapping also defines the bar code size and type (such as EAN13 or EAN128/UCC128). If required, the system supports two different bar code identifiers for the same item: one for scanning and one for printing purposes.

Descriptive Information about Material Items

So far the explanation of material items has focused on item identification. Several types of descriptive information can be defined for an item, including the item description fields, documents, physical dimensions, and measurement information.

Item Description   An item's description consists of two fields: a single 30-character field (that can be expanded) and a second field for unlimited descriptive text. This descriptive text automatically carries forward to sales order and purchase order line items. Language-specific item descriptions can also be defined for both fields.

Document Handling Capabilities   The document handling capabilities allow entry of extended text using a document type of note. Other document types include Word files, Excel spreadsheets, and images. One or more documents can be defined for an item, and each one flagged for internal or external purposes. A note document can be explicitly copied to a sales order or purchase order line item; it does not automatically carry forward. Form setup policies for each type of form (such as a sales order confirmation) determine whether a note document (designated for external purposes) should be printed on the form.

Dynamics AX supports user-defined names for document types, such as names for different note documents. This capability can be creatively used to classify different types of note documents, such as notes related to material handling or quality, and to selectively print the type of note document.

Physical Dimensions   An item's net weight and volume are used to calculate total weight and volume on sales orders and purchase orders. In addition, the total net weight for a manufactured item can be calculated based on its components.

Measurement Information   Measurement information about an item includes depth, width, height and density. A manufactured item's measurements can be used in a formula to calculate component quantity requirements, as described in Chapter 3.

Company-Wide Versus Site/Warehouse Information for Items

The basic item information about item identification, inventory UM, and description represents company-wide information. Other aspects of an item can reflect company-wide information, or site- and warehouse-specific information, as summarized in Figure 2.1. For example, an item's company-wide information includes quality management policies about batch/serial tracking, and the costing method for standard versus actual costing. However, an item's standard costs can only be maintained as site-specific information, whereas an item's actual costs can be tracked by site and warehouse.

A manufactured item (produced in more than one site) can have a company-wide bill of material that applies to all sites and/or a site-specific bill of material. However, the routing for a manufactured item must be site-specific, and work centers must be site-specific. You specify planning data for a purchased item as company-wide information that acts as default values which can be overridden on a site- and warehouse-specific basis. You can also specify sales and purchase trade agreement information at the appropriate

	Type of Information	Company-Wide	Site-Specific	Warehouse-Specific
Basic	Item Identifier	Yes	N/A	
	Inventory UM			
Quality	Batch/Serial Tracking			
	Quarantine for Received Items			
Costing	Costing Method (Standard vs Actual)			
	Standard Cost for Item	N/A	Yes	
	Actual Cost for Item		Yes[1]	
Mfg	Bill of Material for Manufactured tem	Yes	Yes	N/A
	Routing for Manufactured Item	N/A	Yes	
Planning	Primary Source of Supply (Make/Buy)	Specify Act as Default	Override[2]	
	Coverage Group (Set of Policies)			
	Preferred Vendor			
	Purchasing Lead Time			
Price	Purchase Price Trade Agreement	Yes[3]		
	Sales Price Trade Agreement			

Note: The information level reflects the item's dimension group fields for (1) tracking financial inventory, (2) coverage planning, and (3) trade agreements.

Figure 2.1 Company-Wide Versus Site/Warehouse Information

level. The appropriate information level reflects policies embedded in the dimension group assigned to an item. This brief explanation is intended to introduce the concept of company-wide versus site/warehouse information.

Planning Data for Purchased Material

Planning calculations suggest planned purchase orders based on an item's planning data. Most of the planning data reflect an item's company-wide policies, which can be overridden to reflect the site- and warehouse-specific policies for the item. Maintenance of an item's planning data involves several forms within standard Dynamics AX: the Item Detail form, the Default Order Settings form, the Site-Specific Order Settings, and the Item Coverage form. Figure 2.2 summarizes the planning data for purchased items, and highlights the company-wide versus site/warehouse policies as well as the forms for data maintenance. The figure also indicates various types of replenishment limitations for a purchased item. Further explanation covers each aspect of planning data within Figure 2.2.

	Company-Wide Policies	Site-Specific Policies	Site/Warehouse Coverage Planning Policies
Relevant Inventory Dimensions (For Coverage Planning Policies)	Specify		
Primary Source of Supply (Make/Buy)			
Preferred Vendor			
Coverage Code (Reordering Policy)		N/A	Override
Action Message Policies	Specify (Act as Defaults)		
Coverage Group (Set of Policies)			
Purchase Lead Time		Override	
Order Quantity Modifiers for Purchasing			N/A
Minimum Quantity	N/A		Specify
Buyer Responsibility	Specify		
Stop Purchasing Activities for an Item	Specify	Override	
Limit Item Purchases to a Single Site	Specify Site		N/A
Limit Purchases to a Single Site/Warehouse		Specify Warehouse	

Use Items form or Default Order Settings   Use Site-Specific Order Settings form   Use Item Coverage form

Figure 2.2 Planning Data for Purchased Items

Relevant Inventory Dimensions for Coverage Planning Policies An item's replenishment logic can reflect a company-wide, site, warehouse, or bin location viewpoint, as defined by its coverage planning policies (embedded in the Dimension Group assigned to the item). Coverage planning does not apply to inventory dimensions for batch, serial, or pallet. The book's baseline model (described in Chapter 1) assumes that site, warehouse, and bin locations will be used, and that coverage planning will apply to sites and warehouses.

Primary Source of Supply (Make/Buy) The make/buy code for a purchased item (with an Item Type of *Item*) specifies a company-wide policy on the primary source of supply, so that planning calculations generate planned purchase orders. If needed, the item's primary source of supply can be overridden for a given site/warehouse as part of the item coverage policies, where the policy is termed *change planned order type*. For example, the item may normally be transferred from another warehouse rather than purchased, so that the planned order type would be transfer, and you would specify the source warehouse. Chapter 13 provides further explanation of planning data for transfer items in a multisite operation.

Some environments need to internally produce a purchased item, typically on an intermittent basis. In this case, the item should be designated as a manufactured item (with an Item Type of *BOM*) to support the use of bill/routing information and production orders. The item also needs to be flagged so that cost roll-up and planning calculations normally treat it as a purchased item. These policies are termed the *stop explosion checkbox for cost calculation* (specified in the calculation group assigned to the item) and the *stop explosion checkbox for item coverage* (specified for the item). Chapter 3 explains manufactured items and Chapter 11 explains production orders for manufactured items.

Preferred Vendor An item's preferred vendor can be specified as a company-wide policy. If needed, it can be overridden as part of the item's coverage policies for a given site/warehouse. However, the preferred vendor field should be left blank to support automatic vendor assignment on planned purchase orders based on trade agreement information for lowest price or delivery lead time.[4]

---

[4] A company-wide policy (defined in the master planning parameters) determines whether the planning calculations will use the trade agreement information to suggest a vendor for purchased items, and whether price or delivery lead time serves as the basis for suggesting a vendor.

Logic Basis	Coverage Code and its significance	Planning Parameters		
		Primary Parameters	Order Quantity Modifiers**	Safety Stock Inventory Plan
Order Point	**Min-Max** Suggested order quantity achieves maximum inventory quantity subject to order quantity multiple	Minimum Quantity* Maximum Quantity	Multiple	N/A
MRP	**Period** Suggested order quantity covers multiple demands within reorder cycle subject to order quantity modifiers	Coverage Period	Minimum Multiple Maximum	Minimum Quantity
Order Driven	**Requirement** Suggested order quantity covers one demand subject to order quantity modifiers		Minimum Multiple Maximum	Minimum Quantity
Manual Planning	**Manual** No suggested orders	N/A		

*Minimum Quantity represents a site/warehouse-specific safety stock quantity, and differs from the order quantity modifiers for a minimum.

**Three different sets of order quantity modifiers can be defined for an item: for sales orders, purchase orders and for production orders. Planned transfer orders use the order quantity modifiers related to production orders.

Figure 2.3 Reordering Policy (Coverage Code)

Coverage Code (aka Reordering Policy)

The reordering policy represents a key part of the buyer's decision-making logic about generating planned purchase orders. It is embedded within the coverage group assigned to an item, but its importance merits a separate explanation. The four reordering policies include min-max (time-phased order point logic), period (period lot-sizing logic), requirement (order-driven logic), and manual. Each method can be characterized by its primary planning parameters, order quantity modifiers, and inventory plan, as shown in Figure 2.3 and summarized below. The left-hand column of Figure 2.3 characterizes each policy in terms of its underlying logic, such as order point or period lot-sizing logic.

❖ *Min-Max (also known as Order-Up-To).* When an item's projected inventory falls below its *minimum quantity*,[5] the planning calculations suggest an order quantity that achieves the item's *maximum quantity*, subject to an order quantity multiple. The values for minimum and maximum quantity can be specified using a fixed or variable approach. A variable approach,

[5] A setup policy determines how planning calculations treat the due date for the minimum quantity. The due date can be viewed as today's date (when the planning calculations are performed), or as a future date based on the item's lead time or coverage time fence.

for example, can specify a different quantity for each month to reflect seasonality or trends.

Time-phased order point logic using min-max represents a simple and easy-to-administer method for replenishing stocked material. In addition, the variable min/max quantities can be used to anticipate changing demand patterns. An implied inventory plan reflects the extent to which an item's minimum quantity exceeds typical demand over lead time.

❖ *Period (also known as Period Lot Size).* When an item's projected inventory reaches zero (or its minimum quantity), the planning calculations suggest an order quantity that covers demands over the *coverage period,* subject to order quantity modifiers. A coverage period reflects the frequency of replenishment or reorder cycle, such as weekly or monthly.

The warehouse-specific minimum quantity represents an explicit inventory plan or safety stock for an item. An implied inventory plan reflects the extent to which the period lot size and order modifiers (for minimum and multiple) inflate the suggested order quantity so that it exceeds the requirements.

❖ *Requirement (also known as Order-Driven or Lot-for-Lot).* The planning calculations suggest an order quantity that covers each individual demand, subject to order quantity modifiers. As noted above, the minimum quantity and order modifiers represent explicit and implied inventory plans respectively.

❖ *Manual.* The system does not suggest orders, but does calculate net requirements to support manual planning efforts.

Action Message Policies Action messages represent a key tool for coordinating an item's supply chain activities. Action message policies are embedded within the coverage group assigned to an item, but their importance merits a separate explanation. Planning calculations can generate two types of action messages termed actions and futures, as shown in Figure 2.4 and explained below.

❖ *Actions Message.* An actions message indicates a suggestion to advance/ postpone an order's delivery date, to increase/decrease an order quantity, or to delete an order. Suggested advancement of an existing order reflects the item's rescheduling assumption, so that the system suggests expediting rather than a new planned order to cover a requirement. Actions messages are displayed for each planned order, and are also summarized on the Actions form.

	Message	Significance	Message Filters		
			Tolerance	Suppress	Horizon
Actions	**Advance**	Expedite the order to an earlier date	Advance Tolerance (in days)	Yes/No	Actions Look-Ahead Horizon (in days)
	Postpone	De-expedite the order to a later date	Postpone Tolerance (in days)	Yes/No	
	Increase	Increase order to a suggested quantity	N/A	Yes/No	
	Decrease	Increase order to a suggested quantity		Yes/No	
	Delete	Delete order because the requirement has been changed or cancelled		N/A	
Futures	**Delay**	Projected completion date does not meet requirement date	N/A	Yes/No	Futures Look-Ahead Horizon (in days)

Figure 2.4 Suggested Action Messages

❖ *Futures Message.* A futures message indicates that the projected completion date for supply chain activities (based on realistic scheduling assumptions) will cause a delay in meeting a requirement date such as a sales order shipment. Actions messages are displayed for each planned order, and are also summarized on the Actions form.

Message filters can eliminate unnecessary suggestions about actions and futures, as shown in the right side of Figure 2.4. Message filters about actions, for example, include the ability to suppress a message, a look-ahead horizon to limit the number of messages, and tolerances that eliminate unnecessary messages to advance or postpone a scheduled receipt.

Coverage Group (Set of Policies) The coverage group assigned to an item contains the coverage code, action message policies, and other policies that represent a model of the buyer's decision-making logic about planned purchased orders and existing orders. The previous subsections explained the coverage code and action messages; this section covers the other policies. The company-wide policy for an item's coverage group can be overridden for a given site/warehouse.

❖ *Planning Horizon and Related Time Fence Policies.* The planning horizon for requirements calculations generally extends several months (e.g., 6 to 12 months) beyond the cumulative lead time to obtain the product. This planning horizon should be reflected in several time fence policies, including the forecast plan and coverage time fences.

❖ *Policies for Automatic Firming.* The system can automatically create purchase orders from planned purchase orders within a specified time horizon termed the *firm time fence.* With automatic firming, planned purchase orders with suggested vendors can be grouped into multiline purchase orders based on grouping preferences, such as a multiline purchase order reflecting the same vendor and weekly time period.

❖ *Use of a Frozen Period.* The frozen period (termed a *freeze time fence*) for a purchased item represents the shortest possible turnaround time to obtain material with a new purchase order. When the required date falls within the freeze time fence, planning calculations will place the new planned order at the end of the frozen period.

❖ *Safety Margin.* A safety margin represents paperwork preparation time, which means a longer purchase lead time since the order must be placed earlier than normal. Although it can be expressed as three different values, the system only uses the sum as the safety margin.

❖ *Calendar.* Most environments will use the shop calendar assigned to each warehouse for planning calculation purposes. Some environments require a calendar assigned to items, such as a 24/7 operation for selected products that can be received and shipped at any time.

Definition of Calendars

Each calendar has a unique user-defined identifier. A calendar identifies working and non-working days, and the specified hours of operation during working days, for a specified range of dates. A base calendar can be defined and then used as a template for other calendars. After defining the identifier for a new calendar, the working times must be calculated for a specified date range using a working time template. A calendar can be assigned to different entities, such as a warehouse, work center, vendor, or customer.

Purchase Lead Time An item's purchase lead time can be specified as a company-wide policy (as part of the item's default order settings for purchase orders). If needed, it can be overridden as part of the item's site-specific order settings, or as part of the item's coverage policies. The item's purchase lead time can also be specified in purchase price trade agreements. These options provide increasing levels of specificity. Planning calculations use the highest possible specificity as the basis for an item's purchase lead time. Each delivery lead time is defined in terms of calendar days unless explicitly flagged as working days.

Order Quantity Modifiers for Purchasing   Planning calculations suggest a planned purchased order quantity subject to order quantity modifiers for a minimum, maximum, and multiple. The system also provides a soft warning during purchase order entry when the user enters a quantity that does not meet these criteria. With a reordering policy of period or requirement, planning calculations suggest planned orders that account for order quantity modifiers.

❖ *Minimum.* The minimum represents the smallest suggested order quantity.
❖ *Multiple.* The suggested order quantity will always reflect the multiple, even if it exceeds the maximum.
❖ *Maximum.* The maximum represents the largest order quantity, so that planning calculations suggest multiple planned orders to cover requirements exceeding the maximum.

Some situations require a fixed order quantity, perhaps reflecting considerations about batch tracking, transportation, production, or some other factor. Using the same values for maximum and multiple means that planning calculations can generate multiple planned orders for the fixed quantity.

Standard Order Quantity for Purchasing   The item's standard purchase order quantity is used as a default when manually entering a purchase order line item. The company-wide value can be overridden for a given site/warehouse.

Inventory UM and Default Purchase UM   The planning calculations and planned purchase orders for an item reflect its inventory UM, whereas firming up a planned purchase order results in a purchase order for the item's default purchase UM.

Minimum Quantity   The minimum quantity represents an item's inventory plan or safety stock for a given site/warehouse, and normally reflects average demand over lead time. Considerations about the minimum quantity include the interpretation of its requirement date, automatic calculation based on historical data, and use of a variable minimum quantity by time period.

❖ *Requirement Date for Minimum Quantity.* The requirement date for the minimum quantity typically reflects a future date that accounts for the item's lead time. The system supports other bases of the requirement date, such as today's date, as defined in the warehouse-specific coverage data for an item.

❖ *Automatically Calculating the Minimum Quantity.* The minimum quantity can be automatically calculated based on historical data, using either average issues during lead time or a desired service level reflecting the standard deviation. The calculation requires at least three months of historical data. Using the calculation capability (termed the *item coverage* or *safety stock journal*) involves four steps: identifying the items and historical date range, calculating the proposed minimum inventory, reviewing and possibly overriding the proposed minimum, and updating the minimum quantity. The projected impact on inventory value can be viewed prior to updating the minimum quantity. The calculations can help identify items that have less than the minimum inventory level; correcting this situation can reduce potential stock outs.

❖ *Using a Variable Quantity for Minimum or Maximum Quantity.* The variable quantity approach reflects different quantities by time period such as months. The variable quantity for each period is expressed as a multiplier (such as 1.5 or .75) of the minimum quantity. Each pattern of time periods and multipliers is termed a *Minimum/Maximum Key,* and must be user-defined. A separate key can be assigned to the item's minimum quantity and to the item's maximum quantity as part of the warehouse-specific planning data. Each pattern typically has a specified starting date (such as January 1, 20XX) to model seasonality or trends in demands across the calendar year. The variable quantity approach pro-vides flexibility in modeling changing demand patterns in comparison to a fixed quantity.

Buyer Responsibility The concept of buyer responsibility provides an organizing focus for communicating the need to synchronize supplies with demands. The concept of buyer responsibility is typically based on the buyer group field; an alternative basis could be the item group field. User-defined buyer groups can be assigned to an item or vendor. Planning calculations generate planned orders identified with the buyer group, so that a buyer can selectively view planned orders for which they have responsibility. By assigning the buyer group to items, the process of firming planned purchase orders can generate multiline purchase orders containing items that have been assigned the same buyer group.

A purchase order header contains a buyer group that applies to all purchase order line items. Hence, a buyer can selectively view action messages about existing orders for which they have responsibility.

Replenishment Limitations for a Purchased Item Enforcement of replenishment limitations can stop purchases of an obsolete item, or limit purchases to the single site (and warehouse) that actually buys the item.[6]

❖ *Stop Purchasing Activities for an Item.* Certain situations require stoppage of all purchasing activities for an item, such as an obsolete or unsafe purchased material. The purchasing stop flag can be specified as a company-wide policy, and optionally overridden for a specific site. The purchasing stop flag means that an item's existing purchase orders cannot be received, and that new purchase orders cannot be created for the item. The stopped flag does not impact planning calculations, so that planned orders will still be generated. Note that a different stopped flag can also be specified for a purchase order line item, rather than stopping all purchase activities for the item.

❖ *Limit Item Purchases to a Single Site.* When a purchased item is only purchased by a single site, you can specify a mandatory limitation in order to avoid item purchases by other sites. The site acts as a default value when manually creating a purchase order line item for the item. The policy does not limit transfers to other sites.

❖ *Limit Item Purchases to a Single Site and Warehouse.* When a purchased item is only purchased by a single warehouse within a site, you can specify the mandatory limitation in order to avoid item purchases by other warehouses. The site and warehouse act as default values when manually creating a purchase order line item for the item. The policy does not limit transfers to other warehouses.

Maintaining an Item's Coverage Data An item's coverage data must be specified for each relevant site/warehouse that requires stock replenish-

---

[6] A separate set of policies can be specified for sales order purposes (to stop or limit sales of an item) and for manufacturing purposes (to stop or limit manufacturing replenishment of an item).

ment. An item stocked in three warehouses, for example, would require three records for its item coverage data. An item's coverage data can be maintained by accessing it from the Items form, or from the Item Coverage Setup form. In either case, you can directly maintain the records, or use a wizard to create new records for selected sites/warehouses (which can then be directly maintained). Use of the Item Coverage Setup form provides several advantages.

- View items without any item coverage records, thereby making initial data maintenance easier.
- View a subset of items by filtering on item group or buyer group, or the currently assigned coverage group or dimension group.
- Use the default settings (of a selected record of one item's coverage data) as the copy basis for initially creating a new record for selected items without data.
- Delete the item coverage data records for selected items, so that you have a fresh start at maintaining the data.

Costing and Financial Reporting for Purchased Materials

So far the explanations have focused on item master information related to supply chain coordination, such as item identification and planning data. Other item master policies determine the costing method, G/L account number assignment, and financial dimensions associated with items.

Costing Method for Purchased Material   Item costs provide the basis for valuing inventory transactions. An item's costs can be based on a standard costing or actual costing method (such as FIFO, LIFO, and weighted average cost), as defined by the costing method policy embedded in the Inventory Model Group assigned to the item. Chapter 5 provides further explanation for maintaining standard costs or actual costs for an item.

Item Group and the G/L Accounts for Inventory Transactions   The Item Group assigned to an item defines the G/L account numbers impacted by the item's inventory transactions. The item group can serve other purposes including forecasting for a group of items and filtering for items, planned orders, and action messages.

Financial Dimensions for an Item   The financial dimensions represent the organizational segments of the G/L account number assigned to a transaction. The system supports up to 10 user-definable financial dimensions, such as department, cost center, purpose, customer type, or product line. One or more financial dimensions can be assigned to an item, which will be inherited by any item-related transaction. On a sales order line item, for example, the financial dimensions could reflect the customer type and product line, where the product line value gets inherited from the item.

Financial dimensions also provide the basis for business analytics, and thereby represent a unique type of item attribute. Financial dimensions can be assigned to other entities such as customers, vendors and salesmen to support multidimensional reporting. Examples of multidimensional reporting include sales analysis by product group and customer group, and profit-and-loss analysis by site in a multisite operation.

Alternative Approaches to an Item's Purchase Price

An item's purchase price can be defined several different ways. A single company-wide purchase price (and default purchase UM) represents the simplest approach. The item's purchase price can be manually entered (on the item master) or automatically calculated based on the last purchase invoice. These approaches to a standard purchase price are summarized in Figure 2.5 and described below. Figure 2.5 also identifies other alternatives to an item's

Approach to Purchase Price		Factors	Significance for Purchase Order Price
Standard Purchase Price	Manually Entered	None	Company-Wide Purchase Price
	Updated by Last Purchase Invoice		
Trade Agreement	Purchase Price Trade Agreement	Vendor Unit of Measure Quantity Breakpoints Effectivity Dates Delivery Lead-time	Company-Wide or Site/Warehouse Price
Source Document	Purchase Requisition	N/A	Inherit Price From Source Document
	Accepted RFQ Reply		
	Blanket Purchase Order		
	Copy a Purchase Order		

Figure 2.5 Alternative Approaches to Purchase Process

purchase price, such as purchase price trade agreements and a blanket purchase order. These alternatives involve additional constructs beyond the item master, and the chapter on purchase order processing (Chapter 8) provides further explanation.

Standard Purchase Price and UM   An item's standard purchase price is expressed for the item's default purchase UM. The item's standard purchase price and default purchase UM act as defaults on purchase orders when other sources of pricing information do not exist. When the item's purchase price must be expressed with more than two decimal places (such as $.00123 per unit), the price unit field can be used to express the purchase price for a different quantity (such as $1.23 per thousand units).

Standard Purchase Price and Miscellaneous Charges   The concept of a miscellaneous charge typically reflects setup fees, freight, or other special surcharge related to the purchase of an item. For example, a miscellaneous charge can be related to an item's standard purchase price, and either included in the purchase price or shown as part of the total amount owed for a purchase order line item. When miscellaneous charges are included in the total amount owed, the system does not provide descriptive information on purchase documents about why the amount is higher than the purchase price. The system supports several other approaches for handling the concept of miscellaneous charges on a purchase order, as described in Chapter 8.

Alternative Approaches to an Item's Sales Price

An item's sales price can be defined several different ways. A single company-wide standard sales price (and default sales UM) represents the simplest approach. The item's standard sales price can be manually entered (on the item master) or automatically calculated. These approaches to a standard sales price are summarized in Figure 2.6 and described below. Figure 2.6 also identifies other alternatives to an item's sales price, such as sales price trade agreements and a blanket sales order. These alternatives involve additional constructs beyond the item master, and the chapter on sales order processing (Chapter 7) provides further explanation.

Standard Sales Price and UM   An item's standard sales order price is expressed for the item's default sales UM. The item's standard sales price and

Approach to Sales Price		Factors	Significance for Sales Order Price
Standard Sales Price	Manually Entered	None	Company-Wide Price
	Calculated based on Item's Standard Purchase Price	Markup % or Contribution Ratio	
	Calculated based on Item's Inventory Cost		
	Calculated based on Bill and Routing for Manufactured Item	Markup % & Inventory Cost for Purchased Items, Markup % for Work Centers and Overheads	
		Markup % & Trade Agreements for Purchased Items Markup % for Work Centers and Overheads	
Trade Agreement	Sales Price Trade Agreement	Customer or Customer Group Unit of Measure Quantity Breakpoints Effectivity Dates Delivery Lead Time	Company-Wide or Site/Warehouse Price
Source Document	Sales Quotation	N/A	Inherit Price From Source Document
	Blanket Sales Order		
	Copy a Sales Order		

Figure 2.6 Alternative Approaches to Sales Prices

default sales UM act as default values on sales orders when other sources of pricing information do not exist. When the sales price must be expressed with more than two decimal places (such as $.00123 per unit), the price unit field can be used to express the list price for a different quantity (such as $1.23 per thousand units). The item's standard sales price can be manually entered (on the item master) or automatically calculated.

An item's standard sales price can be automatically calculated based on the item's standard purchase price or inventory cost. As changes occur to the item's standard purchase price (or inventory cost), the system automatically recalculates the item's standard sales price. This calculation is termed a *price update* approach, and it reflects a specified markup percentage or contribution ratio. A standard sales price based on an inventory cost of $10, for example, would be $11 using a 10% markup. It would be $11.11 using a 10% contribution ratio.

The standard sales price for a manufactured item can be calculated based on a cost-plus-markup approach for its purchased components and routing operations, as described in Chapter 5. The calculation can also update the item's inventory cost. If applicable, the price update approach (described above) can then be used to automatically calculate the item's standard sales price based on the calculated inventory cost.

Standard Sales Price and Miscellaneous Charges   The concept of a miscellaneous charge typically reflects setup fees, freight, or other special surcharge related to sales of an item. For example, a miscellaneous charge can be related to an item's standard sales price, and either included in the sales price or shown as part of the total amount owed for a sales order line item. When miscellaneous charges are included in the total amount owed, the system does not provide descriptive information on sales documents about why the amount is higher than the sales price. The system supports several other approaches for handling the concept of miscellaneous charges on a sales order, as described in Chapter 7.

Suggestions for a Single-Site Company

Many firms operate as a single-site company, especially smaller firms. Therefore only one site needs to be defined within Dynamics AX, where the site will contain one or more warehouses.   The following suggestions for modeling a single site company include topics that will be covered in future chapters.

❖ *Relevant Inventory Dimensions.* Inventory will be tracked by site, warehouse, and bin, but the site should be used in coverage planning. This approach takes advantage of site-related functionality, and anticipates the potential for other sites. The sales and purchase trade agreements should reflect a company-wide policy.

❖ *Item Planning Data.* Specify the single site as the mandatory default for inventory, sales, and purchasing purposes.

❖ *Forecasts.* Enter forecasts for the single site.

❖ *Standard Costs for Items.* Enter a site-specific standard cost for purchased items, or calculate for manufactured items.

❖ *Labor and Overhead Costs.* The cost records for labor rates (cost categories) and overhead formulas can be company-wide or site-specific.

❖ *Bill of Material for Manufactured Items.* Each master BOM and BOM version can be company-wide or site-specific.

❖ *Routing Data for Manufactured Items.* Each master routing and routing version must be site-specific. The site must also be specified for work center groups.

❖ *Customer and Sales Order Information.* Each customer's preferred ship-from site should identify the single site, which acts as a default value on sales orders and quotations.

❖ *Vendor and Purchase Order Information.* Each vendor's preferred ship-to site should identify the single site, which will act as a default value on manually entered purchase orders.

Case Studies

Case 1: Variable Min/Max Quantities
The All-and-Anything company used the capabilities for variable minimum and maximum quantities to model daily usage rates that varied over time. Using the min-max reordering policy, planning calculations suggested replenishment based on the variable minimum and maximum quantities.

Case 2: Batch-Specific Costing
The Batch Process company produced a food product line—bottles of mustard—from purchased batches of different types of mustard seeds. The purchased seeds required batch tracking, with quality and taste attributes associated with each batch. An actual costing method applied to the purchased seeds, with batch-specific costing identified as an inventory dimension policy. The manufacturing process involved mixing batches of mustard seeds into a paste that was packaged in various bottle types with different labels and cases. The batches of purchased material could be tracked to a daily production run, and the batch number assigned to each case and bottle represented the daily production run. This manufacturing date served as the basis for indicating shelf life.

Case 3: Document Handling
The Consumer Products company required several types of item-related documents to support the engineering and quality functions. These documents include CAD drawing files, word documents with testing specifications, and scanned images. These documents were linked to item master information through the document handling capabilities.

Case 4: Item Variants in Wholesale Distribution
The Distribution company carried several product lines involving item variants, ranging from t-shirts (with color and size variants) to industrial hardware (with variants for lengths, finish, and head type of bolts and screws). Authorized variants were defined for each item, and each variant had site/warehouse-specific planning data. The sales prices were different for each item variant and UM. For example, a lower price was offered for buying t-shirts in dozens. The sales trade agreement information included the item variant code and sales UM to reflect these variations.

Case 5: Replacement Parts for Sold Equipment The Equipment company stocked and sold purchased material that served as replacement parts for previously sold equipment. These purchased materials were also used in manufacturing the equipment. A separate warehouse was defined for the service parts function, and each replacement part had two authorized warehouses—one for manufacturing and one for the service parts function. The service parts function had site/warehouse-specific planning data to support customer service objectives.

Executive Summary

Information about purchased material represents the heart of a distribution environment, and a significant portion of the cost of sales for most manufacturing environments. Item identification and descriptive information represent some of the basic issues in system implementation and usage. Company-wide and site/warehouse-specific viewpoints apply to item information, especially the item's planning data. Alternative approaches for item costing, purchase prices and sales prices must be considered. Several case studies highlighted variations in distribution environments, such as item variants, batch-specific costing, and variable min-max quantities.

Chapter 3

Manufactured Items

The product structure for a manufactured item is defined by bill of material and optional routing information. Bill of material (BOM) information defines the product design for a manufactured item, and provides the basis for product costing, material planning, material usage reporting, batch and serial tracking, and tracking progress through stages of manufacturing. Routing information defines the process design for a manufactured item, and provides the basis for calculating value-added costs, determining capacity requirements, scheduling production activities, reporting actual work performed, and tracking progress of production activities.

There are two basic approaches—a standard product approach and a custom product approach—to defining product structure information for manufactured items.

❖ *Standard Product Approach.* The standard product approach reflects a predefined bill of material and routing, and typically applies to manufactured items with repeat requirements that are built using a make-to-stock or make-to-order production strategy. This chapter focuses on the standard product approach.

❖ *Custom Product Approach.* The custom product approach reflects a make-to-order production strategy and unique bills of material, typically defined in the context of a sales order or quotation. An item number serves as the starting point for defining the unique BOM/routing information using option selection or a rules-based configurator. Chapter 4 covers these custom product approaches.

The concepts of a *Master BOM* and a *Master Routing* are used to define product structure information. Each master BOM has a unique identifier and specifies material components. Each master routing has a unique identifier and specifies operations. The master BOM and routing can be defined independently from any parent item, and their identifiers subsequently assigned to manufactured items to define product structure. The assignments are termed *BOM Version* and *Route Version*, respectively, and multiple versions can be assigned to a manufactured item. An item's BOM version can be site-specific or company-wide, whereas an item's routing version must be site-specific. A separate breakout box summarizes how the BOM version and route version define the product structure for a manufactured item.

Each manufactured item and its components must be defined in the item master. Item information for purchased material was covered in the previous chapter. This chapter covers information that uniquely applies to a manufactured item and its components, and consists of eight major sections.

1. Item information for manufactured items and components
2. Master BOM and BOM versions
3. Component information
4. Work centers and work center groups
5. Master routing and route versions
6. Routing information for an internal operation
7. Subcontracted production using an outside operation component
8. Maintaining BOM and routing information
9. Planning data for manufactured items

Summary of Product Structure Information

Product structure information consists of bill of material (BOM) and routing information, as exemplified in Figure 3.1 for End-Item #1. In this example, the identifiers for the master BOM A1 and the master routing A are assigned to End-Item #1, since these define the components and operations to produce it. The assignments of a master BOM and master routing are termed a BOM version and a route version respectively. The master BOM A1 contains the component Intermediate #2 and other components. The master routing A contains three operations, where each operation consists of an operation number, a work center, and a master operation identifier. A master operation must be predefined, such as the master operation TEST41 performed at the testing work center. In a similar fashion, the master BOM B1 and master routing B are defined and assigned to Intermediate #2.

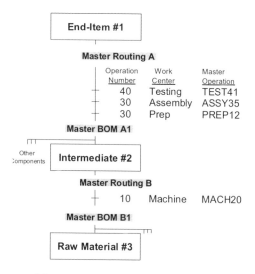

Figure 3.1 Summary of Product Structure Information

Item Information for Manufactured Items and Components

Designation of a manufactured item enables planning and costing calculations to recognize the item's BOM and routing information. An Item Type of *BOM* designates a manufactured item. The previous chapter explained item information for purchased material, including item identification, unit of measure variations, alternate identifiers, descriptive information, and company-wide versus site/warehouse information. This previous explanation about purchased items also applies to manufactured items, so it will not be repeated here. However, there are some aspects of item master information that uniquely apply to manufactured items and components, as described below.

Item Identification Considerations for Manufactured Items Any stage in the manufacturing process that can be stocked (or sold or purchased complete) requires an item number. While routing operations are generally used to reflect various steps in the manufacturing process, the stocking level consideration may mandate a separate item (with its own bill of material) for a given step. A production environment requiring an outside operation, for example, often employs one item number for each unfinished item sent to the subcontractor and a separate item number for the completed item. The approach to outside operations also requires a separate item number to identify the purchased service. Finally, a phantom component requires an item number.

The item identification for a manufactured item could include variant code(s) such as color and size, but there are several caveats with this approach. First, a bill of material and routing can only be specified for an item number; they cannot be specified for an item number and variant code. Second, a BOM component can be specified with an item number and variant code(s). You can also specify a BOM version that applies to this component. However, an item number and variant code cannot be a BOM component of the same item number.

Another facet of item identification involves revision level significance. An item's revision level generally represents a level of documentation, and several terms (such as engineering change level) refer to the same concept. The significance of an item's revision level differs among manufacturers. One viewpoint considers revision level to be different versions of an item's bill or routing, and the item's revision levels are interchangeable. Dynamics AX supports this viewpoint. Another viewpoint considers revision level as a unique identifier (in combination with the item number) that differentiates supplies, demands, and costs for an item. Dynamics AX supports this second viewpoint by embedding the revision level in the item number, or by using the configuration ID to represent a revision level. Case 14 describes alternative approaches to revision level significance.

Document Handling for Manufactured Items The document handling capabilities support different types of documents (such as drawings, images, and Word files) which can be attached to an item number; a master BOM, BOM version or BOM component; and to a master routing, route version, routing operation, or a master operation.

Default Values When Adding a Component The component information in a bill of material includes the item's unit of measure, component type, and planned scrap information expressed in terms of a fixed scrap amount and/or variable scrap percentage. The values for these component fields can be defaulted from the item master information for the component. For example, the item may always represent a phantom component type when it is included in a bill of material, so that the item's default value for its component type could be specified as phantom.

Auto-Deduction Policy Component material can be manually issued to a production order, or auto-deducted from inventory based on the item's auto-deduction policy (termed the *flushing principle*). The flushing principle determines whether the trigger for auto-deduction will be based on the started quantity for an operation, or the reported-as-finished quantities for a production order. Hence, a flushing principle of *Start* represents a forward flushing approach to auto-deduction, whereas a flushing principle of *Finish* represents a backward flushing approach. The flushing principle can be specified for a component within the bill of material, which would override the item's flushing principle.

Auto-deduction is closely tied to production order processing, where the started and report-as-finished quantities can trigger auto-deduction. In addition, the production order policies can override the item's auto-deduction policy. Chapter 11 provides further explanation about auto-deduction of material components in the context of production order processing.

Other Attributes of Manufactured Items Other attributes of a manufactured item include its net weight, production group, production pool, and property.

❖ *Net Weight.* The net weight of a manufactured item can be manually specified, or updated based on a calculation of its components' net weights. Use the cost roll-up calculation (termed the BOM calculation) to calculate and update the item's net weight.

❖ *Property.* The user-defined property assigned to a manufactured item provides the basis for sorting and filtering production orders. For example, the property could reflect a similar production characteristic.[1]

❖ *Production Group.* The user-defined production group assigned to a manufactured item provides the basis for sorting and filtering production orders. In addition, the production group can define the basis for assigning G/L account numbers related to manufacturing activities for the item (such as reporting work center time or a finished quantity) when assignment is based on the production group.

❖ *Production Pool.* The user-defined production pool assigned to a manufactured item provides the basis for sorting and filtering production orders. For example, a production pool could reflect the planner responsibility for manufactured items.

---

[1] The property assigned to a manufactured item only provides reference information. In contrast, the property assigned to an operation provides the basis for block scheduling of production orders as described Chapter 11.

Special Cases for Manufactured Items The special cases include handling kit items and treating a manufactured item as a purchased item.

❖ *Handling Kit Items.* A kit item can be sold complete or as separate components. For handling a sold complete situation, the item must be flagged (using the *auto-report as finished* field) so that posting the sales invoice auto-deducts the item's components. The sales price reflects the kit item. For handling a kit item sold as separate components, the sales order line item (for the kit item) must be exploded into its components, thereby generating a new sales order line item for each component. The sales price on each line item reflects the component's sales price.

❖ *Treating a Manufactured Item as a Purchased Item.* Some situations involve a manufactured item with BOM information that should be treated as a purchased item. The typical situations include a purchased item that is occasionally manufactured, or a manufactured item that is now being purchased. Two item-related policies prevent cost calculations and planning calculations from using the item's BOM and routing information. These policies are termed the *stop explosion* flag for cost calculation (specified in the calculation group assigned to the item) and the *stop explosion* flag for item coverage (specified for the item).

Master BOM and BOM Versions

A master BOM defines the components in a bill of material. The identifier for a master BOM (termed the *BOM Number*) can be manually or automatically created. Manual creation should be used when the master BOM identifier needs to be meaningful. Examples of a meaningful identifier include the parent item number, the drawing number, or a customer item number plus revision level. You can define components after creating the identifier, and also assign the master BOM to the relevant item number(s) for manufactured items. Each assignment is termed a *BOM Version*, and a manufactured item can have multiple BOM versions.

Creating and Assigning a Master BOM There are two basic approaches for creating and assigning master BOMs.

- Create a master BOM and its components, and then assign it to the relevant item number(s).[2] There is an approval step for the master BOM, and a separate approval step for each assignment (BOM version).

- Create a master BOM and its components for a specific manufactured item, which means the master BOM is automatically assigned to the item. There is a single approval step. The master BOM can still be assigned to other manufactured items, and each assignment requires a separate approval step.

Approved and Active BOM Versions A master BOM and a BOM version must be approved, as described above. Only an approved BOM version for a manufactured item can be marked as active. The active BOM version for a manufactured item will normally be used in planning and cost calculations. However, other approved BOM versions can be used in selected situations to override the active BOM version, such as specifying an approved-but-not-active version for a manufactured component, or when creating a production order.

Company-Wide Versus Site-Specific BOM Versions A master BOM can be assigned to a manufactured item and a specific site, thereby defining a site-specific BOM version. A BOM version can also be company-wide (designated by a blank site).[3] The primary difference is that planning calculations will use a site-specific BOM version (if it exists) based on the site of the item's requirements. If a site-specific BOM version does not exist, the planning calculations will use the company-wide BOM version for the manufactured item (if it exists). The planning calculations will generate an error message if an appropriate BOM version does not exist. A slight secondary difference concerns the options for defining the warehouse source of a component item. The section about component information (and Figure 3.3) provides further explanation about the warehouse source of component inventory.

---

[2] The assignment of master BOMs to a manufactured item can be assisted by an attribute (the item group) assigned to each master BOM. Based on this attribute, the drop-down list of master BOMs can display the subset with an item group that matches the manufactured item.

[3] An additional note is that a master BOM can be designated as site-specific or company-wide (designated by a blank site), and a company-wide master BOM can be assigned to a manufactured item as a company-wide BOM version or as a site-specific BOM version.

A Master BOM and BOM version can only span one site, so that a component cannot be sourced from a warehouse in a different site. It may be necessary to employ replenishment logic to transfer a component to the desired warehouse.

Rationale for Multiple BOM Versions   A manufactured item can have multiple active BOM versions that reflect different sites, nonoverlapping validity periods, and/or different quantity breakpoints. Other BOM versions may be approved but not active, typically to model an alternate bill of material. A BOM version may not yet be approved, typically because the component information has not yet been completely defined. Hence, a manufactured item may require multiple BOM versions for several reasons.

❖ *BOM Variations Between Sites Producing the Same Manufactured Item.* The site-specific BOM versions can reflect variations in component requirements. In addition, a site-specific BOM version may apply to production at one site, and a company-wide BOM version may apply to production at the other sites.

❖ *Planned Engineering Changes with Effectivity Dates.* The multiple BOM versions can represent planned engineering changes to a manufactured item, where each BOM version has a different validity period. For example, a manufactured item may have two BOM versions—one valid to date X and the other valid from date X+1—to indicate planned engineering changes.

❖ *Variations Due to Production Order Quantities.* The multiple BOM versions can represent quantity-sensitive formulations, where each BOM version has a different production quantity breakpoint.

❖ *Alternate Bills of Material.* Additional BOM versions can represent alternate formulations for producing the manufactured item. In this case, the BOM version can be approved (but not active), and specified for a sales order line item or for a manufactured component, or for a manually created production order. Planning and costing calculations employ the specified BOM version rather than the active BOM version.

A manufactured item can have multiple active BOM versions that reflect different sites, nonoverlapping validity periods, and/or different quantity breakpoints. An item can also have approved-but-not-active BOM versions.

Component Information

The critical information for a component (termed a *BOM Line*) consists of the component type, component item, and required quantity. Other component information includes the effectivity dates, operation number, and the warehouse source for the component.

Component Type and Component Item The component type (termed a *BOM Line Type*) indicates whether the component is treated as a normal item or a phantom item. Two other component types—production and vendor—support make-to-order and buy-to-order logic. Each component type has a different impact as described below.

❖ *Item (or Normal).* Planning calculations employ netting logic to suggest a planned order to satisfy requirements, such as a planned purchase or production order (for a purchased or manufactured component respectively). These orders are not directly linked to the production order for the parent item.

❖ *Phantom.* A phantom component type only applies to a manufactured item. The requirements for a phantom component are passed (or blow-through) to its components and routing operations. The impact of blow-through logic becomes obvious in an order-dependent bill and routing for a production order (termed the *Production BOM* and the *Production Route*). Planning calculations ignore the phantom's on-hand inventory and scheduled receipts in the netting logic, and suggest planned orders for the phantom's components to satisfy requirements.

❖ *Production.* A production component type only applies to a manufactured item, and represents a make-to-order production strategy with direct linkage between production orders. That is, a scheduled production order for the parent automatically generates a linked production order (also termed a *sub-production* or *reference order*) for each component with a component type of production. Planning calculations ignore the component's on-hand inventory and scheduled receipts in the netting logic for a production component type.

A multilevel bill containing production component types at each level will be represented by multiple linked production orders, as illustrated in Figure 3.2. Linkage with a sales order reflects the generation of a production order from the sales order.

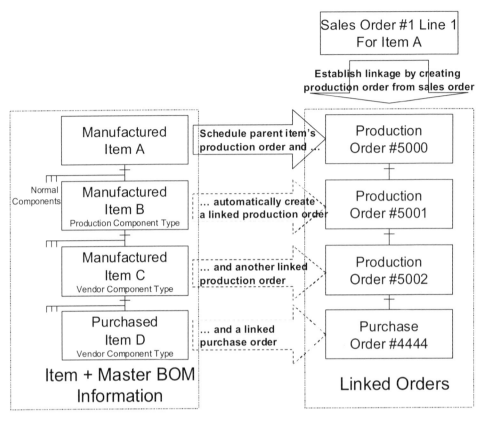

Figure 3.2 BOM Information Versus Linked Production Orders

The system indicates linkage via the reference fields in each production order, and linked orders can be scheduled separately or synchronized. Netting logic does not apply to the order quantity for these linked orders, since the system assumes they are being produced just for the parent item.

❖ *Vendor.* A vendor component type applies to either a manufactured item or a purchased item. It supports make-to-order logic and linkage capabilities similar to the production component type, as illustrated in Figure 3.2 and explained below.

○ *Manufactured Item.* This provides linkage just like the production component type. As a minor difference, this type of production order is labeled vendor rather than standard. For example, a production order type of vendor could indicate subcontract manufacturing will be used for one or more outside operations.

○ *Purchased Item.* This represents a purchased-to-order material or service, and provides linkage between a purchase order and production order. That is, a scheduled production order for the parent automatically generates a linked purchase order for each purchased component with a component type of vendor. The vendor component type for a purchased item has one other unique feature: a preferred vendor can be defined for the component. When automatically generating a linked purchase order, the system assigns the component's preferred vendor (if defined) or the item's preferred vendor to the purchase order.

An outside operation component represents one case of the vendor component type. The Dynamics AX approach to modeling subcontracted production involves a separate outside operation component to specify the value-added costs and indicate a purchase requirement. The section on routing information provides guidelines for handling subcontracted production using an outside operation component.

Specifying an Approved-But-Not Active BOM Version or Route Version for a Manufactured Component

The planning calculations for a normal manufactured component consider its active BOM version (and route version), with netting logic that considers the component's available supplies.[4] Specifying the active BOM version (or route version) for a manufactured component has the same effect. However, specifying an approved-but-not-active BOM version (or route version) for a manufactured component will override consideration of the active version in planning calculations. In addition, you can choose whether the netting logic should recognize or ignore the component's available supplies.

If the component's specified BOM version represents a unique requirement (so that netting logic should ignore available supplies), then the planning calculations should generate a planned production order to cover the entire required quantity. You define this policy (termed the *BOM Version Requirement*) as part of the Coverage Group assigned to the item.

---

[4] Netting logic always ignores the manufactured component's available supplies for a component type of production, vendor, and phantom.

This policy also applies to sales orders for a manufactured item, where you specify the item's approved-but-not-active BOM version on a sales order line item. That is, the policy determines whether planning calculations will account for or ignore the item's available supplies.[5] This logic makes sense in a make-to-order environment involving different approved-but-not-active BOM and route versions. Chapter 4 explains how a product model can generate an approved-but-not-active BOM version (and route version) for a modeling-enabled item, and automatically specify these versions on a sales order line item.

Component Required Quantity A component's required quantity normally reflects the amount needed to build one parent item, expressed as a variable consumption amount in the component's inventory UM. This quantity can be entered as a fraction or decimal, with a limit of four decimal places. Some environments require variations in expressing the component's required quantity, as described below.

❖ *Component Quantity UM.* The component's UM initially defaults to the value specified for the item (the bill of material UM); this can be overridden with another UM authorized for the item.

❖ *Component Quantity with More than Four Decimal Places.* The component's required quantity is typically expressed for building one parent item. It can also be expressed for building more than one parent item, such as the quantity per 100 or per 1000 parent items. This provides one approach for handling required quantities that must be expressed with more than four decimal places, such as expressing a required quantity of .123456 kilograms as 12.3456 kilograms per 100 parent items.

❖ *Fixed Component Quantity (Constant Consumption).* The component's required quantity can be a fixed amount rather than a variable amount.

❖ *Component Quantity and its Rounding-Up Policy.* The component's required quantity can be rounded up to a specified multiple, such as 1.00 to represent a whole number. This rounded-up quantity impacts cost roll-up calculations, planning calculations, and the order-dependent bill. The additional component requirements stemming from the specified multiple represent excess consumption or scrap.

---

[5] When using a modeling enabled item in a custom products environment, the netting logic always ignores the item's available supplies, regardless of the item's policy concerning the BOM Version Requirement.

❖ *Negative Component Quantity for a By-Product Component.* A negative quantity for a component represents a by-product component. Cost roll-up calculations subtract the cost for a by-product component. Planning calculations recognize the scheduled receipt for a by-product component. The order-dependent bill for a production order includes the by-product component, and a by-product component can be manually added to the order-dependent bill. A by-product component in the order-dependent bill can be received into inventory from the production order (via the picking list journal). Differences between standard and actual by-product receipts are treated as a variance.

❖ *Component Quantity based on a Formula and Measurements.* A special case of component required quantity involves a calculation formula and measurement information, such as height, width, depth, and density. Measurement information must be specified for the parent item and the relevant component(s). The approach is most easily explained using an example, such as a cut-to-length steel rod (with a base UM of feet) used in different lengths for different products. In this case, two pieces of steel rod are required to build each parent item.

  ○ *Component Quantity Formula and Measurements.* With the formula "height × constant," the component quantity of 2 pieces represents the constant while the value of 1.0 (in the height field) indicates use of the height measurement.

  ○ *Parent Item Measurements.* Each parent item requires a different length (such as 3.125 or 8 feet), as specified in the parent's height measurement. Hence, the formula actually consists of "parent height × component height × constant" for calculating total linear footage requirements. The formula would be $3.125 \times 1.0 \times 2.0 = 6.25$ linear feet in this example.

With a calculation formula approach, the component's rounding-up policy takes on special significance. In the just cited example, let's assume the cut-to-length component of 8-foot lengths is taken from 10-foot steel rod, so that the multiple is 10 and requirements are rounded to increments of 10.

The formula approach supports the use of a common master BOM that can be assigned to multiple manufactured items. The required quantities for cut-to-size components are dependent on measurement information about each parent item. Measurement information about the parent

item and its cut-to-size component act as default values on a production
order and its order-dependent bill respectively.

❖ *Planned Scrap for a Component.* A component's planned scrap can be
expressed as a percentage or a fixed amount or both. You can optionally
designate an item's planned scrap factors on the item master, meaning the
values act as defaults when adding the item as a component. Other
approaches can be used to identify planned scrap as described in the
following breakout box.

Approaches for Identifying Planned Manufacturing Scrap

Planned manufacturing scrap can be expressed for components and for
routing operations. The planned scrap percentage and/or fixed amount for
a component result in increased requirements. The planned scrap percentage
for an individual operation results in increased requirements for its total time
and units, and for related material components. An operation's scrap
percentage has a cumulative effect on previous operations in a multistep
routing, and the system automatically calculates an accumulated scrap
percentage for each operation. Each order-dependent bill and routing inherit
the scrap factors from the master BOM and routing, and these can be
overridden on the production order. These scrap factors are included in
planning and cost roll-up calculations.

Operation Number When routing data exists, the operation number
assigned to a routing operation can also be assigned to relevant components.
This ensures that material due dates reflect the operation start date, material
requirements reflect the operation scrap factors, and auto-deduction of
material components can be tied to the started quantities for specified operations. The system assumes that material components with a blank operation
number are required for the first operation. The scheduling logic normally
assumes a component is required at the start of its assigned operation
number, unless it has been explicitly flagged as required at the end.

The assigned operation number (for a material component) provides the
starting point for determining the work center that requires the material, and
for supporting work center consumption logic about the warehouse source of
component inventory.

		Option #1	Option #2	Option #3
		Specified Warehouse In Master BOM	Use Item's Default Inventory Warehouse	Assign Warehouse Using Work Center Consumption Logic
Master BOM Information		Only for Site-Specific BOM	Applies to Site-Specific or Company-Wide BOM	
Key Fields	Component Warehouse	Specify Warehouse	None	None
	Component's Work Center Consumption Policy	No	No	Yes
	Operation Number For the Component	N/A	N/A	Specify Operation Number
Additional Information Required		N/A	Item's default inventory warehouse for the required site	Route version for the manufactured item, with a work center operation for the specified operation number
				Work center assigned to a production unit
				Picking warehouse assigned to the production unit
Impact on the Component's Warehouse in the Production BOM for a Production Order		Inherit the component's specified warehouse	Inherit the item's default inventory warehouse	Inherit the picking warehouse associated with the work center

Figure 3.3 Options for a Component's Warehouse Source

Warehouse Source of a Component A component's warehouse source indicates where to pick the item for a production order. There are three basic options for defining the component's warehouse source, as summarized in Figure 3.3 and explained below.

❖ *Specify the Component Warehouse in the Master BOM.* The first option only applies to a site-specific BOM version, and the specified warehouse must belong to the site. After creating a production order for the manufactured item, the Production BOM inherits the component's specified warehouse.

❖ *Use the Component Item's Default Inventory Warehouse.* The second option does not specify a component warehouse, and requires additional information about the item's default inventory warehouse for each site (as defined in the site-specific order settings). After creating a production order, the Production BOM inherits the component's default inventory warehouse for the required site.

❖ *Assign the Component's Warehouse Using Work Center Consumption Logic.* The third option does not specify a component warehouse, but it does specify a work center consumption policy and an operation number for the component. This option requires additional information in order to connect the component's operation number to a work center operation in the manufactured item's routing. In addition, the work center must be assigned to a production unit that defines the associated picking warehouse. After creating a production order, the Production BOM inherits the picking warehouse associated with a work center requiring the component.

The third option provides the greatest flexibility for indicating the warehouse source for a component, but also requires routing data. The second option can be used when routing data has not been defined. If no information has been entered for the three options, then the component's warehouse on the Production BOM will be blank.

Effectivity Dates for a Component   A component's valid-from and -to dates indicate planned changes to a master BOM. Phasing out an existing component on date X and phasing in a new component on date X+1, for example, would indicate a planned replacement.

Position Information for a Component   A component's position information provides reference data that can serve different purposes. For example, it can represent a sequential counter of components, often tied to the find number on drawings. It can identify a grouping of components, such as the material needed for an operation (when routing data does not exist), the delivery area for a group of picked components, or a group representing related parts in the production process. The position field also provides one approach for handling reference designators.

Order-Dependent Bill of Material (Production BOM)   An order-dependent bill of material (termed a *Production BOM*) refers to the components attached to a production order. Changes to an order-dependent bill do not affect the master BOM. Creation and maintenance of an order-dependent bill reflect several rules.

- Creation of a production order for a manufactured item also creates an order-dependent bill.
- The order-dependent bill initially reflects the master BOM and the delivery date (or a specified BOM date) assigned to the production

order. The user can optionally override the master BOM (or the BOM date) when manually creating a production order, or use the copy function to update this information after order creation.
- The order-dependent bill contains components of a phantom.
- The user can modify the components in an order-dependent bill at any time prior to reporting the production order as finished or ended.
- A material item can be issued to a started production order even when the component does not exist on the order-dependent bill. The issued component will be automatically added to the order-dependent bill with a zero required quantity.

Work Centers and Work Center Groups

A work center group consists of one or more work centers, where a work center represents an internal resource (such as a machine, person, or tool) or an external vendor that performs a routing operation. Definition of the work center group precedes definition of a work center within the group, and a group must contain at least one work center. The group's information can act as default values when creating related work centers. A routing operation can be specified for a work center or a work center group. The suggested approach depends on several factors described in the Routing Information section.

The attributes of a work center group and work center are almost identical, and both provide several default values when specified for a master operation. Figure 3.4 illustrates how work center information provides default values when creating a master operation. For example, the run time and setup time within a master operation initially default to the values defined for the work center assigned to the master operation. These default values can be overridden within the master operation.

The arrows within Figure 3.4 also illustrate how the master operation values act as the defaults when the master operation is specified as an operation in a master routing. These values can be overridden. Likewise, the master routing provides default values on the production route for a production order, and these values can be overridden.

Work Center Identification   A work center group has a unique identifier and description, and each work center within the group has a separate identifier and description. The exact same work center such as a specific machine in two different places must be identified with two different identifiers.

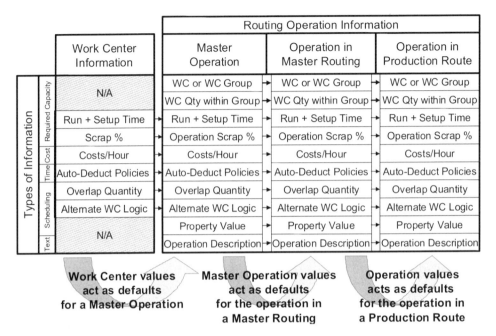

Figure 3.4 Work Centers and Default Values for Operations

Other considerations will also shape work center identification, such as the need for secondary resources or variations in cost structures. You can view a human resource work center as an individual employee or as a work group with similar skills.

Types of Work Centers The type of an internal work center can be a machine, human resource, or tool. The internal work center types provide reference information, and do not impact scheduling or costing.

❖ *Machine.* A machine type of work center may represent a single machine, a manufacturing cell, an assembly line, or a tightly linked group of machines. The work center capacity for a single machine is typically expressed as one.

A machine work center may also be used to model a miscellaneous area comprised of a mixture of personnel and equipment performing various operations. This provides the basis for defining routing operations, and an approximation of costing, capacity planning, and scheduling considerations. The work center capacity provides an approximation of how many operations can be concurrently processed within the miscellaneous area.

❖ *Human Resource or Personnel.* A human resource may represent a specific person (with optional assignment of the employee number) but it typically represents a labor pool of people with similar skills. Examples of skills include machine operators and quality inspectors. The work center capacity for a labor pool provides an approximation of how many operations can be concurrently processed, and typically reflects the average head count when there is a one-to-one relationship between people and operations.

❖ *Tool.* The need for defining a tool as a work center typically reflects a critical scheduling constraint on performing work by machines or labor pools. Examples of tools include a reuseable fixture, die, mold, room, or other constraining resource.

An external work center has a work center type of vendor, and a designated vendor. Each subcontractor performing outside operations can be defined as an external work center. Definition of an external work center is similar to an internal work center, but with several major exceptions. First, costs are not typically specified for the external work center. Second, the calendar for the external work center should reflect the vendor's hours of operation, so that scheduling logic can calculate the turnaround time at the subcontractor. Third, a corresponding warehouse must be defined when components or finished items are stocked at the vendor. However, an external work center and a separate routing operation are not required to support subcontracted production. A separate section explains subcontracted production using an outside operation component.

Assigning a Site to a Work Center Group   A work center group must be assigned to one site, and the site applies to all work centers within the group. Stated another way, a work center group cannot contain work centers from different sites. As a related issue, a master routing cannot have work center operations that span more than one site.

You can optionally assign a warehouse (and even a bin location) to a work center and work center group, but this only represents reference information. If specified, the assigned bin location must represent a location type for production input.

Production Unit for a Work Center Group   A production unit provides a grouping of work center groups. It can be optionally assigned to one or more work center groups; the assignment applies to all work centers within a group. The production unit provides the basis for filtering information on forms and printed documents, and for viewing aggregate capacity requirements for all work centers within the production unit.

A production unit can also be assigned a picking warehouse to support work center consumption logic in determining the warehouse source of a component, as described in the previous section on "Component Information." Information about the picking warehouse (and the work centers) assigned to a production unit are used in the work center consumption logic, so that a component will inherit the picking warehouse associated with the work center that requires the component.

Work Center Available Capacity A work center's available capacity is defined by two basic factors: the hours of operation and the capacity per hour.

❖ *Hours of Operation.* The calendar assigned to a work center defines the hours of operation (such as 7:00 a.m. to 4:00 p.m.) for each calendar day. Exceptions to this calendar of daily working hours can be specified for the individual work center, or for all work centers using the assigned calendar.

❖ *Capacity per Hour.* A single work center working on one task at a time has a capacity of 1.00 during working hours. However, a work center sometimes represents a number of people or machines, where more than one task can be performed at the same time. The average number of concurrent tasks is termed the *work center capacity.* With a capacity of 5, for example, up to 5 different operations can be scheduled concurrently for each hour of operation.

The system calculates a work center's available capacity based on the user-initiated function to compose working times. The system also calculates available capacity for a work center group based on the sum of available capacities of its related work centers.

Available and Required Capacity Based on Run Dates

The concept of run rate typically applies to a machine. A run rate per hour represents a different way to express available capacity (such as 5000 cycles per hour) and a different way to identify capacity requirements for operations (such as 5 cycles per unit).

❖ *Available Cycles per Hour at a Work Center.* The work center's *capacity* field defines the available cycles per hour. An optional capacity unit provides reference information about the run rate, such as strokes per hour, meters per hour, or pounds per hour.

❖ *Required Cycles per Unit for a Work Center Operation.* An operation's required capacity (termed *consumption calculation*) is expressed in cycles per unit rather than time per unit. This approach employs a formula type of *capacity* (rather than *standard*) for consumption calculation, and a *factor* defining the required cycles per unit. For example, a factor of 10 means that 10 cycles will produce 1 unit, whereas a factor of .5 means that 1 cycle produces 2 units. The operation's run time will be calculated based on the required cycles per unit and the work center's available cycles per hour.

The concept of using run rates to define an item's required capacity can be extended to handle the quantity produced by a mold and die. This quantity is termed the *batch quantity*. For example, a work center that represents a mold may require 2 cycles to produce a batch quantity of 10 items. In this case, you define the work center's *batch capacity* as 10. In the operation, you define a formula type of *work center batch* for consumption calculation, and a *factor* of 2 for the required cycles per batch.

Infinite Versus Finite Available Capacity for a Work Center A work center's available capacity can be designated as finite or infinite for scheduling purposes. An infinite capacity viewpoint means that scheduling logic ignores existing loads when scheduling a given production order, but still considers constraints related to hours of operation and concurrent task capabilities to calculate operation durations. An analysis of work center load versus capacity can be used to identify overloaded periods, so that manual adjustments can be made to loads or available capacity.

A finite capacity viewpoint means that scheduling logic considers current loads and the concurrent task capability for each work center when scheduling a given production order. The finite scheduling viewpoint includes consideration of several other factors, such as the maximum percentage of available capacity that can be scheduled. Finite capacity considerations can be included or ignored when scheduling individual production orders.

Designating Bottleneck Work Centers for Finite Capacity Planning Purposes The optional designation of a bottleneck work center can improve performance of planning calculations, where finite capacity planning on the bottleneck resource will only be run when needed. Additional master plan policies must be defined for the use of bottleneck scheduling and for three time fence policies (the finite capacity time fence, the backward capacity time fence, and the bottleneck capacity time fence).

Work Center Efficiency The time requirements expressed in routing operations can be factored up or down based on the work center efficiency percentage. The work center's efficiency percentage acts as a default in the work center's assigned calendar; the efficiency for selected working times (such as the late night hours) can then be manually overridden in the calendar.

Work Center Costs The costs associated with a work center can be expressed in terms of hours for setup and processing time, and in terms of piece rates for output units. Different costs can be associated with setup time, processing time, and output units. This cost information is embedded in the cost categories assigned to the work center, and the cost categories also determine how costs will be segmented into cost groups by cost rollup calculations. The costs associated with setup, processing, and output units are normally included in the estimated and actual costs for a manufactured item. However, some cases require selective exclusion of these costs, as expressed by policies embedded in the routing group assigned to a work center. Chapter 5 provides further explanation of product cost calculations.

Time Reporting and Auto-Deduction Policies The time associated with processing and setup, and the output units, can be manually reported or auto-deducted as indicated by three different *Automatic Route Consumption* policies. These auto-deduction policies are embedded in the routing group assigned to a work center. Chapter 11 provides further explanation about production orders and the use of auto-deduction for time reporting.

Using the Alternate Work Center Concept (via Task Groups)

An alternate work center (or work center group) can be automatically considered by detailed scheduling logic when there is insufficient capacity available at the primary work center to meet the due date. The concept of an alternate work center is implemented via a *task group* that defines one or more alternate work center or work center group, listed in descending preference order. In addition, the scheduling logic can optionally consider work center capability versus the required capability for an operation (called the *work center requirement*).

An example concerning presses will help illustrate how to handle alternate work centers and requirements. Let's say we have three work centers that identify a 2-ton press, a 5-ton press, and a 10-ton press. The first step is to define a task group (let's call it *presses*) that includes the same three work centers with a requirement of 2, 5, and 10 respectively. The task group is then assigned to each of the three work centers as the basis for suggested alternates. At this point, scheduling logic considers the requirement specified for an operation (such as 4) in selecting an alternate work center that can handle a requirement value of 4 or more. Hence, only the 5-ton and 10-ton presses would be considered as alternate work centers.

There are other methods for handling the concept of alternate work centers. For example, the use of a work center group in a routing operation enables scheduling logic to consider all work centers within the group as interchangeable. Another example involves the use of different master routings that identify the alternate work centers, and manually assigning the desired version to a production order. An alternate work center can also be manually assigned in the order-dependent routing for a production order.

Block Scheduling via Properties   Block scheduling represents one approach to scheduling similar operations together, and involves the use of properties in two ways. First, a property must be assigned to a specified block of working time within the work center's calendar.[6] Second, a property must be assigned to operations. Scheduling logic can then schedule operations with the same property to the designated block of time, thereby minimizing setups for similar operations.

Summarized Information for a Work Center   A work center's statistics summarizes available capacity, actual reported time, and a capacity utilization percentage for the current accounting period, current year to date,

---

[6] Block scheduling requires that the work center must be flagged as having a finite property, and that production orders must be scheduled based on a finite property.

and the preceding year. A work center's load window summarizes available capacity, expected load, and a capacity utilization percentage for various time increments, such as months and weeks. It also provides drill down to the production orders causing the expected load.

Aggregate Capacity and Loads for a Work Center Group The aggregate capacity for a work center group is based on the sum of available capacity for the related work centers. The aggregate load for the work center group includes routing operations that specifed the work center group or a related work center. An analysis of aggregate load versus capacity can help anticipate overloaded periods.

Master Routing and Route Versions

The definition and use of master routings are similar to master bills of material. The identifier for a master routing (termed a *Route Number*) can be automatically or manually created. Manual creation should be used when the master routing identifier needs to be meaningful, such as the item number for an item-specific routing or a process specification for a common routing. You can define operations after creating the identifier, and also assign the master routing to the relevant item number(s) for manufactured items. Each assignment is termed a *Route Version*, and a manufactured item can have multiple route versions.

Creating and Assigning a Master Routing There are two basic approaches for creating and assigning master routings.

- Create a master routing and its operations, and then assign it to the relevant item number(s).[7] There is an approval step for the master routing, and a separate approval step for each assignment (route version).
- Create a master routing and its operations for a specific manufactured item, which means the master routing is automatically assigned to the item. There is a single approval step. The master routing can still be assigned to other manufactured items, and each assignment requires a separate approval step.

---

[7] The assignment of master routings to a manufactured item can be assisted by an attribute (the item group) assigned to each master routing. Based on this attribute, the drop-down list of master routings can display the subset with an item group that matches the manufactured item.

Approved and Active Route Versions   A master routing and a route version must be approved, as described above. Only an approved route version for a manufactured item can be marked as active. The active route version for a manufactured item will normally be used in planning and cost calculations. However, other approved route versions for an item can be used in selected situations to override the active route version, such as specifying an approved-but-not-active version on a sales order line item or a manufactured component, or when creating a production order.

Site-Specific Route Versions   A master routing can be assigned to a manufactured item and a specified site, thereby creating a site-specific routing version.[8] The routing operations must reflect work centers within the site. Planning calculations will use the site-specific route version based on the site of the item's requirements.

Rationale for Multiple Route Versions for a Manufactured Item   A manufactured item can have multiple active route versions that reflect different sites, nonoverlapping validity periods, and/or different quantity breakpoints. Other route versions may be approved but not active, typically to model an alternate production process. A route version may not yet be approved, typically because the routing information has not yet been completely defined. Hence, a manufactured item may require multiple route versions for several reasons.

❖ *Routing Variations between Sites Producing the Same Manufactured Item.* The site-specific route versions reflect variations in the work centers and operations for producing the item.

❖ *Planned Engineering Changes with Effectivity Dates.* The multiple route versions can represent planned engineering changes to the production process, where each route version has a different validity period. For example, a manufactured item may have two route versions—one valid to date X and the other valid from date X+1—to indicate planned engineering changes.

❖ *Variations Due to Production Order Quantities.* The multiple route versions can represent quantity-sensitive formulations, where each route version has a different production quantity breakpoint. For example, the route version can reflect use of a faster manufacturing process for a large production order quantity.

---

[8] A master routing has an implied site, since its operations reflect work centers within a single site.

❖ *Alternate Routings.* Additional route versions can represent alternate processes for producing the manufactured item. In this case, the route version can be approved (but not active), and specified for a sales order line item or a manufactured component, or for a manually created production order. Planning calculations employ the specified route version rather than the active route version.

A manufactured item can have multiple active route versions that reflect different sites, nonoverlapping validity periods, and/or different quantity breakpoints. An item can also have approved-but-not-active route versions.

Routing Information for an Internal Operation

The critical information for an internal operation consists of an operation number, a master operation identifier, the work center, and time requirements. A master operation provides default values for information about an operation, so that further explanation starts with an understanding of the master operation concept.

Master Operation A master operation (termed *Operation*) has a unique identifier, and each routing operation must specify a master operation identifier. The master operation provides default values (such as the time requirements and the work center) for the operation's information subject to applicability rules. Using a master operation as the source of default values can simplify routing data maintenance in some situations, but it introduces an additional level of system complexity.

A common starting point involves defining all master operations that will use a given work center. A master operation can have one or more sets of information that serve as default values, where each set has applicability rules. For example, a set of data (such as time requirements and the work center) for a master operation may only apply to (or be related to) a group of items. An additional set of data can be defined with applicability rules for another group of items. Each set of data is termed an *Operation Relation* for the master operation. The applicability rules for each set of data are defined in terms of characteristics about the manufactured item (such as a specific item number, an item group, or all items) and master routing (such as a specific master routing identifier or all master routings). These applicability rules reflect decreasing levels of specificity.

When manually adding an operation to the routing version for an item, the user can enter the master operation identifier and the system automatically assigns default values based on the applicability rules. No default values are assigned when nothing applies, and the system automatically creates an additional set of data (i.e., an additional operation relation) for the specified item number and master routing. In cases where multiple sets of data may apply, the system uses the most specific set of data possible.

Operation Number   The operation number provides a unique numeric identifier for each operation within a routing, and the basis for scheduling a serial routing. The system automatically assigns new operation numbers in increments of 10 but this operation number can be overridden. The use of operation numbers has several scheduling implications.

❖ *Identifying Material Components Required for an Operation.* Assigning the operation number to the required material components allows the planning calculations to synchronize material due dates with the operation start date. It also provides the basis for auto-deduction based on the started operation quantity, and the basis for calculating the impact of operation scrap percentages on material requirements. A component's assigned operation number is also used to support work center consumption logic for determining the source warehouse for the component.

❖ *Indicating the Next Operation and Last Operation.* Scheduling logic requires additional information about the next operation number, especially to model a nonsequential or parallel routing. In particular, a value of 0 (zero) in the Next Operation field indicates the last operation in a routing and only one operation can be designated as the last operation.

❖ *Indicating a Secondary Resource for an Operation.* Using the same operation number and a priority of secondary indicates a secondary resource for an operation. Operation priority is covered in the next paragraph.

Primary Versus Secondary Resources (Operation Priority)   Each operation requires a primary resource, specified as a work center or a work center group. Most production environments can be modeled using operations with just a primary resource.

Some production environments have operations requiring one or more secondary resources, such as the people and tools for running a machine. The operation's primary resource represents the pacing or bottleneck resource that determines operation duration. The same operation number must be assigned to the secondary operation(s), and time requirements cannot be specified for a secondary operation since it is not the pacing resource. Operations with the same operation number are termed *simultaneous operations.*

Indicating the Type of Linkage between Operations The type of linkage between operations affects scheduling logic, where the link type can be hard or soft. After completion of an operation, for example, you can indicate the next operation must start immediately (a link type of hard) or at anytime (soft). A soft link type means that scheduling logic allows a time gap between ending the operation and starting the next operation. As another example, you can indicate that secondary resources for an operation must start at the same time as the primary operation (a link type of hard). A link type of blank indicates no linkage between operations.

Work Center Each operation requires a designated work center or work center group. The following breakout box provides several guidelines concerning which approach should be used.

Guidelines for Using a Work Center or Group in a Routing Operation

Several factors must be considered in choosing whether to designate a work center or a work center group for performing an operation. A key factor involves the scheduling method, and Chapter 11 explains the detailed (job) and rough-cut (operation) scheduling methods. Only the detailed scheduling method can assign work to specific work centers within a group. The following guidelines assume use of the detailed scheduling method, with illustrations based on machines:

Work Center Use of the work center assumes the operation can only be performed at one machine. The operation identifies the machine-specific times and costs. When coupled with alternate work center logic, specifying a work center indicates the preferred machine while the operation's task group indicates a prioritized list of alternate machines. The detailed scheduling method considers the alternate work centers (and their machine-specific times and costs) when the due date cannot be met, and assigns an appropriate machine.

Work Center Group   Use of the work center group can apply to machines or people. With machines, specifying a work center group assumes the operation can be performed on any machine within the group, and the machines have similar run times and cost structures. The operation identifies the average times and costs for all machines within the work center group. The detailed scheduling method assigns a specific machine (within the group) to an operation. However, the run times and cost structures still reflect the work center group and not the assigned machine.

With people, the work center group typically identifies a group of individuals with interchangeable skills. An operation's work center quantity indicates the number of people (or crew size) required to perform an operation. The alternate work center approach can be used to indicate different run times based on different crew sizes.

Work Center Quantity   The work center quantity only applies when the routing operation is for a work center group. It indicates the number of work centers required to perform the operation, and is best illustrated by a work center group for human resources containing work centers that represent individual people. For example, a run time requirement of 3 hours and a work center quantity of 2 people would be interpreted as a total load of 6 hours (for the work center group). The detailed scheduling method creates a load of 3 hours for 2 different work centers (people).

Time Requirements   Time requirements are normally expressed in hours (up to two decimal places) and consist of the run time per unit and optional setup time. Several additional considerations may apply to the time requirements.

* *Run Time per Unit.* The run time can be expressed for a different quantity, such as the run time per 100 units. This provides one approach for handling more than two decimal places in the run time hours.
* *Setup Time.* The setup time represents a fixed time for producing an item regardless of order quantity or sequencing considerations.
* *Expressing Time Elements in Hundredths of an Hour.* The time requirements for all time elements in an operation can be expressed in a fraction of an hour, such as tenths or hundredths, based on an operation-specific conversion factor. This provides another approach for handling more than two decimal places in the time elements.

❖ *Other Time Elements for Scheduling Purposes.* Other time elements can be used for scheduling purposes, such as the number of hours for queue time before and after the operation, and the transit time to the next operation.[9] The next operation can also start before operation completion based on the overlap quantity.

Scrap Percentage   The planned scrap percentage for an operation affects the required runtime and the materials tied to the operation. The system automatically calculates and displays an accumulated scrap percentage for each operation in a routing with multiple operations.

Cost Data for an Operation   The cost data for an operation defaults from the assigned work center or work center group, and can be overridden. Chapter 5 provides further explanation of cost data and cost calculations.

Reporting Operation Time   The auto-deduction policies for an operation default from the assigned work center or work center group, and can be overridden.

Operation Description   The operation description consists of unlimited free-form text, and the optional use of documents such as a Word file or an image.

Order-Dependent Routings (Production Route)   An order-dependent routing (termed a Production Route) refers to the routing operations attached to a production order. Changes to an order-dependent routing do not affect the master routing, and typically reflect an alternate operation. The previously described rules for creation and maintenance of an order-dependent bill also apply to an order-dependent routing. However, time can only be reported when the operation sequence exists in the order-dependent routing.

Subcontracted Production Using an Outside Operation Component

The Dynamics AX approach to modeling subcontracted production involves a separate component (with a vendor component type) of the manufactured

---

[9] The time elements associated with a routing operation can be selectively considered (or activated) for detailed scheduling purposes based on the policies embedded in the routing group assigned to the operation.

item to specify the value-added costs and indicate a purchase requirement. The separate component will be called the *outside operation component*. The following guidelines suggest the simplest way for handling subcontracted production using an outside operation component and no routing data.

Item Information   Each outside operation component requires a unique item number representing the combination of outside operation and parent item. The item's critical attributes include item type (service), item group (with relevant G/L account numbers), inventory model group (with no posting of physical/financial inventory), calculation group and cost group (to segment subcontracted production costs), coverage code (requirement), and flushing principle (auto-deduct upon finish). The item's unit of measure typically reflects the parent item UM (such as piece), and the item's cost reflects the cost per unit. Other item information may apply, such as the preferred vendor and lead time (reflecting the turnaround time to send supplied material and receive completed items), and purchase price trade agreement information.

Bill of Material Information   The simplest approach involves a parent item representing the completed product and components that must be supplied to the subcontractor.[10] The additional outside operation component must have a component type of vendor so that the purchase order will be linked to the production order. The preferred vendor and operation number can be specified for the component. Each component supplied to the vendor should have the same operation number. This simple approach does not require routing information.

A more complex approach is required when employing routing data. The outside operation component should be associated with an operation number, and scheduling implications must be considered to account for turnaround time. In the BOM version, the outside operation component should be flagged as a requirement at the end of the operation.

Identifying the Suggested Vendor for an Outside Operation Component   Information about the suggested vendor can be specified in three places—the external work center, the component, and the item—representing decreasing levels of specificity. The system uses the most specific infor-

---

[10] The parent item may be a component of another item. Its component type can be normal or vendor, depending on the need for linkage.

mation possible when automatically creating the purchase order. The system prevents automatic purchase order creation when a suggested vendor does not exist in any of the three places.

Identifying a Production Order That Involves Subcontracted Manufacturing The Subcontractor Work form displays scheduled production orders with a linked purchase order that represents the subcontracted operation. The form displays information about purchase order status, and enables the user to update production order status via the start task and report-as-finished task. Chapter 12 explains production orders and production order status.

When routing operations are defined for subcontracted work, the Operations List can also be used to view production orders and then filter on the master operations associated with subcontracting. You can also update production order status via the start and report-as-finished tasks.

An order can be designated with a production order type of vendor (rather than standard), but this provides only reference information for filtering purposes.

Coordinating the Production Order and Purchase Order A purchase order will be automatically created after updating the status of the parent item's production order (to a status of at least estimated). The purchase order must be received and invoiced upon completion of the outside operation, and the production order must be reported as finished.

Coordinating Supplied Material There are four basic variations of coordinating supplied material: as a kit that is picked or transferred, or as stocked material at the subcontractor that is purchased or transferred.

❖ *Kit That Is Picked for a Production Order.* The supplied material is issued to the subcontractor using the picking list journal for the production order (and a specified operation).

❖ *Kit That Is Transferred to the Subcontractor.* The supplied material is issued via transfer orders, and stocked at the warehouse representing the subcontractor.

❖ *Stocked at Subcontractor via Purchases.* The supplied material is stocked at the warehouse representing the subcontractor, typically via purchase orders with deliveries sent to the warehouse.

❖ *Stocked at Subcontractor via Transfer Orders.* The supplied material is stocked at the warehouse representing the subcontractor, typically via transfer orders from another warehouse.

Each variation of supplied material has special considerations, such as the warehouse for components, auto-deduction policies, and coverage policies by warehouse. The kit approach can employ a special version of the printed pick list (termed a *vendor delivery note*) only when a routing operation has been defined for the subcontracted production. The printed information indicates the delivery address for the vendor.

Handling the Completed Parent Item The major variations for handling the parent item include the following:

❖ *Parent Item Returned.* The site and warehouse specified on the production order indicate where to place the returned parent item after completion of the outside operation.
❖ *Parent Item Stocked at the Subcontractor.* The site and warehouse specified on the production order reflect the subcontractor.
❖ *Parent Item Sent to the Next Subcontractor.* The site and warehouse specified on the production order reflect the next subcontractor. As an alternative approach, the production order output could be placed in the first subcontractor warehouse and then transferred to the next subcontractor warehouse.

Maintaining BOM and Routing Information

BOM and routing information can be maintained using several approaches, such as planned engineering changes, the copy function, mass changes to components, and a graphical tool. The analyses of BOM and routing information include multilevel and where-used viewpoints.

Managing Planned Engineering Changes Planned engineering changes to an item's bill of material can be identified using three different approaches: the date effectivities for a component, the date effectivities for a BOM version, and the specified BOM version for a manufactured component. Figure 3.5 illustrates these three approaches to planned engineering changes.

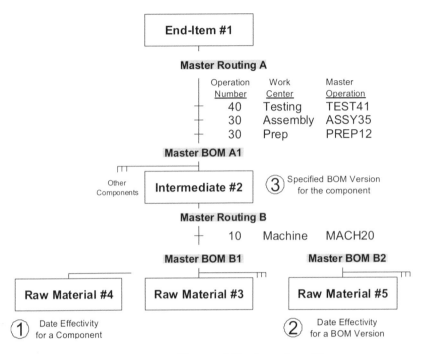

Figure 3.5 Three Approaches to Planned Engineering Changes

The first approach employs date effectivities for a material component in a master BOM, such as the new component Raw Material #4 in master BOM B1 that becomes effective on a specified date. A second approach employs date effectivities for BOM versions, such as phasing out the assignment of master BOM B1 and phasing in the assignment of master BOM B2 assigned to Intermediate #2.

The third approach employs a specified BOM version for a manufactured component, where the item's BOM version is approved but active. The master BOM A1 for producing End-Item #1, for example, can specify that the component Intermediate #2 should be produced using master BOM B2. This third approach can build on the use of component date effectivities to phase in and phase out specified BOM versions for a manufactured component. The previous section about component information explained the use of an approved-but-not-active BOM version and route version for a manufactured component.

Planned engineering changes to an item's routing can be identified using two approaches: the date effectivities for a routing version, and the specified routing version for a manufactured component. With a date effectivity approach, the specified date on a production order determines which routing version, BOM version, and components will be used as the basis for requirements.

The approval status and active status for a BOM version or routing version provide one approach for indicating whether information has been completed or is still under development. However, some firms must work with partially defined bill of material information to calculate requirements for long lead-time materials or to perform preliminary calculations for cost or sales price. This means the partially defined BOM version must be approved and active in order to be recognized by planning and cost roll-up calculations.

You can discontinue use of a master BOM or master routing by removing its approval. Removing the approval status or the active status on a BOM version, or phasing out the effectivity, provides a selective approach to discontinued use.

Copying Components to a Bill of Material   A copy function can be used to add components to master BOMs and order-dependent bills. For a master BOM, components can be copied from another master BOM as of a specified date. Alternatively, the components can be copied from the order-dependent bill associated with a specified production order. You determine whether the components will add to or replace the existing components. Hence, the copy function can be used multiple times to generate incremental additions.

The copy function also works for an order-dependent bill of material. The copy-to information identifies the specified production order number, and the copy-from can be another production order or a master BOM.

Copying Operations to a Routing   A copy function can be used to add operations to master routings, and works much like the copy function for bill of material information. Operations can be copied from another master routing, or from the order-dependent routing associated with a specified production order. You determine whether the operations will add to or replace the existing operations, and whether the applicability rules will be updated for master operations.

The copy function also works for an order-dependent routing. The copy-to information identifies the specified production order number, and the copy-from can be another production order or a master routing.

Mass Changes to BOM Components Based on Where-Used Information   Where-used information provides the basis for a mass replace and a mass add function for maintaining components (via the periodic task *Change BOM Item*). For example, the user can select an item to be phased out, view the affected bills of material (and selectively eliminate them from the update), and indicate when the existing item should be phased out and when a new item should be phased in.

Graphical Tools for Maintaining Master BOM Information   The Bill of Material Designer (BOM Designer) provides a graphical tool for maintaining component information about active BOM versions. It is also termed the *composed-of tree*.   The form displays a multilevel indented bill of material in graphical format, and also displays the item master data. You can add components from the item master via drag-and-drop capabilities. Master routing data is also displayed (but not maintained) so that components can be associated with operation numbers. This graphical tool is employed in other contexts, such as displaying the BOM information during sales order entry.

Analyzing BOM and Routing Information   Analysis tools for master BOM and routing information include multilevel bill of material reports, and a multilevel costed bill with routing information (via the BOM calculations). The analysis tools also include where-used inquiries about a component item, a master BOM, a work center, a master routing, and a master operation. For example, the work center where-used information identifies usage by master operations, production routes, and task groups.

There are two other types of where-used inquiries that reflect information about existing production orders and batch/serial number tracking. The first type includes single- and multilevel pegging to the sources of demand and supply. The second type includes forward and backward batch tracking and serial tracking throughout the product structure.

Planning Data for Manufactured Items

Planning calculations suggest planned production orders based on the planning data for a manufactured item. Much of the planning data reflect an item's company-wide policies, which can be overridden to reflect the site- and warehouse-specific policies for the item. Figure 3.6 summarizes the planning data for manufactured items, and highlights the company-wide

	Factors	Company-Wide Policies	Site-Specific Policies	Site/Warehouse Coverage Planning Policies
Planning Data for Manufactured Items	Relevant Inventory Dimensions (For Coverage Planning Policies)	Specify		
	BOM Version	Specify as Company-Wide	Specify as Site-Specific	N/A
	Route Version	N/A	Specify as Site-Specific	
	Primary Source of Supply (Make/Buy)	Specify (Act as Defaults)	N/A	Override
	Coverage Code (Reordering Policy)			
	Coverage Group (Set of Policies)			
	Default Order Settings: Production Lead Time (When routing data does not exist)		Override	N/A
	Default Order Settings: Order Quantity Modifiers for Production (Minimum, Multiple, Maximum)			
	Minimum Quantity	N/A		Specify
	Planner Responsibility	Specify		
Replenishment Limitations	Default Order Settings: Stop Production Activities for an Item	Specify	Override	N/A
	Default Order Settings: Limit Item Production to a Single Site	Specify Site		
	Limit Production to a Single Site/Warehouse		Specify Warehouse	

Use Items form or Default Order Settings form   Use Site-Specific Order Settings form   Use Item Coverage form

Figure 3.6 Planning Data for Manufactured Items

versus site/warehouse policies as well the forms for data maintenance.[11] The figure also indicates various types of replenishment limitations for a manufactured item. Further explanation covers each aspect of planning data within Figure 3.6.

Relevant Inventory Dimensions for Coverage Planning Policies

An item's replenishment logic can reflect a company-wide, site, warehouse, or bin location viewpoint, as defined by its coverage planning policies (embedded in the Dimension Group assigned to the item). Coverage planning does not apply to inventory dimensions for batch, serial, or pallet. The book's baseline model (described in Chapter 1) assumes that site, warehouse, and bin locations will be used, and that coverage planning will apply to sites and warehouses.

---

[11] Similar planning data information is defined for purchased items (see Figure 2.2) and transfer items (see Figure 13.4).

BOM Version   The BOM versions for a manufactured item can be site-specific or company-wide. Planning calculations will use an item's site-specific BOM version (if it exists) based on the site of the item's requirements. If a site-specific BOM version does not exist, the planning calculations will use the company-wide BOM version (if it exists).

Route Version   Planning calculations will use an item's site-specific route version (if it exists) based on the site of the item's requirements.

Primary Source of Supply (Make/Buy)   The make/buy code for a manufactured item (with an Item Type of *BOM*) specifies a company-wide policy on the primary source of supply, so that planning calculations generate planned production orders. If needed, the item's primary source of supply can be overridden for a given site/warehouse as part of the item's coverage policies, where the policy is termed *change planned order type*. For example, the item may normally be transferred from another warehouse rather than manufactured, so that the planned order type would be transfer, and you would specify the source warehouse. Chapter 13 provides further explanation of transfer orders in a multisite operation.

Coverage Code (aka Reordering Policy)   The reordering policy represents a key part of the planner's decision-making logic about creating new production orders. The four reordering policies include min-max (time-phased order point logic), period (period lot-sizing logic), requirement (order-driven logic), and manual. Chapter 2 described these reordering policies.

Coverage Group (Set of Policies)   The coverage group assigned to a manufactured item contains the coverage code, action message policies, and other policies that represent a model of the planner's decision-making logic about planned production orders and existing orders. Chapter 2 explained these policies for purchased material (especially the action message policies), and the explanation also applies to manufactured items. However, there are several policies for manufactured items that merit additional explanation.

❖ *Planning Horizon and Related Time Fence Policies.* The planning horizon for a manufactured item must extend beyond its cumulative manufacturing lead time in order to provide visibility on the requirements for purchased items, and to anticipate potential capacity constraints. This planning horizon should be reflected in the time fences for coverage, explosion, capacity, forecast, and futures. The planning horizon should also be reflected in the ATP time fence policy for the manufactured item.

❖ *Assignment of Production Order Status after Firming a Planned Production Order.* Firming a planned production order can result in a status of created estimated, scheduled, released, or started. Several factors influence the choice of an assigned status. As a typical approach, the scheduled status should be assigned so that planning calculations recognize material and capacity requirements for the production order, and the planner can subsequently start the production order at the appropriate time.

❖ *Policies for Automatic Firming.* Automatic firming (based on the firm time fence) can be employed when planned production orders do not require review and changes.

❖ *Use of a Frozen Period.* The frozen period (termed a *freeze time fence*) for a manufactured item represents a management policy about making changes to the near-term schedule. Changing the schedule within the frozen period typically creates headaches and inefficiencies, especially when setups and sequencing have been established.

Production Lead Time   A manufactured item's lead time can reflect a variable or fixed elapsed time, where a variable time can be calculated based on routing information. An item's fixed production lead time (expressed in days) can be specified as company-wide value, and overridden for a site/warehouse.[12]

Order Quantity Modifiers for Production   Planning calculations suggest a planned production order quantity subject to order quantity modifiers for a minimum, maximum, and multiple. The system also provides a soft warning during manual creation of a production order when the user enters a quantity that does not meet these criteria.

Standard Order Quantity for Production   The item's standard production order quantity is used as a default when manually creating a production order. The item's company-wide value can be overridden for a given site/warehouse. The standard order quantity can also be used in cost calculations to amortize constant costs, as described in Chapter 5.

---

[12] Override the company-wide production lead time as part of the item's site-specific order settings, or as part of the item's coverage policies.

Minimum Quantity   The minimum quantity represents an item's inventory plan or safety stock for a given warehouse. Chapter 2 explained the considerations about a minimum quantity, such as automatic calculation based on historical data, and the use of a variable minimum quantity by time period.

Planner Responsibility   The concept of planner responsibility provides an organizing focus for communicating the need to synchronize supplies with demands. The concept of planner responsibility is often based on the production pool or the buyer group assigned to a manufactured item. For example, planning calculations generate planned production orders identified with the buyer group, so that a planner can selectively view and mark planned orders for which they have responsibility. In addition, production orders inherit the item's production pool thereby enabling the planner to selectively view orders for which they have responsibility.   Changes to the order status of production orders can be based on the production pool, and a planner can selectively view action messages by production pool.

Replenishment Limitations for a Manufactured Item   Enforcement of replenishment limitations can stop production of an obsolete item, or limit production to the single site (and warehouse) that actually produces the item.[13]

❖ *Stop Production Activities for an Item.* Certain situations require stoppage of all production activities for an item, such as an obsolete or unsafe product. The concept of a production stop flag is implemented via the field labeled the inventory stop flag. It can be specified as a company-wide policy, and optionally overridden for a specific site. The inventory stop flag means that an item's existing production orders cannot be received, and that new production orders cannot be created for the item. It actually enforces even more restrictive limitations, since it prevents any further receipts or issues. The stop flag does not impact planning calculations, so that planned orders will still be generated.

❖ *Limit Item Production to a Single Site.* When a manufactured item is only produced at a single site, you can specify a mandatory limitation in order to avoid production by other sites. The site acts as a default value when manually creating a production order for the item. The policy does not affect transfers to other sites.

---

[13] A separate set of policies can be specified for sales order purposes (to stop or limit sales of a manufactured item).

❖ *Limit Item Production to a Single Site and Warehouse.* When a manufactured item is only produced at a single warehouse within a site, you can specify the mandatory limitation in order to avoid item production by other warehouses. The site and warehouse act as default values when manually creating a production order for the item. The policy does not affect transfers to other warehouses.

An item's coverage data can be maintained by accessing it from the Items form, or from the Item Coverage Setup form. In either case, you can directly maintain the records, or use a wizard to create new records for selected sites/warehouses (which can then be directly maintained). Use of the Item Coverage Setup form provides several advantages, such as viewing items without any item coverage records, viewing a filtered subset of items, and deleting coverage data information so that you can enter new information.

Case Studies

Case 6: Virtual Manufacturing   One division of the All-and-Anything company was moving toward virtual manufacturing with outsourcing of almost all production activities. Items were either purchased complete or subcontracted, with supplied material linked to the outside operation. The components provided by the subcontractor were identified in the bill of material, but flagged as not included in cost roll-up calculations (and also flagged for no inventory tracking in their dimension group). With the subcontracted approach, the supplied material and finished goods inventory were stocked at the vendor's location. Purchased material was shipped directly to a subcontractor and sales orders were shipped directly from a subcontractor. Supplied material was auto-deducted based on reported completions and replenished based on site/warehouse-specific planning data. In some cases, the completed units were transferred back to a company warehouse for further processing (such as final assembly and test) before sales order shipment.

Case 7: CAD Integration   The All-and-Anything company required integration between its computer-aided design (CAD) package and information about items, bills and routings. For standard products, this involved importing information from the CAD package into the master BOM and viewing the CAD drawing via the document handling capabilities. They used a rules-based configurator to define the bill for a custom product and calculate a quoted price and estimated costs. This configuration information could then be used by their CAD package to generate 3D models (for viewing) and 2D layout drawings, and cut lists for assisting production personnel in completing the work. This integration helped reduce the elapsed time to prepare sales quotes, the man-hours to define drawings and bills, and the cost of errors (including production rework, field installation services, and customer confidence).

Case 8: Authorized Recipes in Process Manufacturing The Batch Process company produced batches of bulk chemical and immediately put them in various bottles with labels and packaging material for each bottle. They had several authorized recipes for each product that reflected variations in batch size, which were modeled using different BOM versions with quantity breakpoints. The planning calculations used the BOM version that matched the quantity for a planned production order. The BOM version could also be manually overridden when creating a production order.

Case 9: By-Products in Pharmaceutical Products The Batch Process company produced a pharmaceutical product where the production process resulted in several by-products of lower potency. Each by-product was a different item number, and could be packaged and sold as a different item. The master BOM identified each planned by-product as a negative component. The component quantity expressed a ratio (such as .15) indicating the expected by-product output relative to the parent item output.

Case 10: Printed Circuit Boards The Consumer Products company produced electrical products that required assembly of printed circuit boards from components. Critical components, boards, and end-items required batch tracking and serialization of end-items. Using customized BOM functionality, the engineering function identified approved vendors for components and specified reference designators for placing components on printed circuit boards.

Case 11: Item Variants in Bills The Consumer Products company purchased apparel in various colors and sizes, and then packaged them together (such as a 24 pack) with a mix of colors and sizes. They used item variants to identify the purchased apparel, and a manufactured item for each package (such as the 24 pack). Variants of the purchased items were specified as components of the manufactured item.

Case 12: Kit Items   The Distribution company sold unassembled kits of material, where a separate item (and associated master BOM) defined each kit's components. Two types of kits could be sold. One type of kit was priced and sold as a single item, and posting the sales invoice auto-deducted the item's components. Another type of kit was priced and sold as separate component items. Each sales order line for a kit item was exploded into its components, thereby creating multiple line items with separate prices that were shipped and invoiced separately.

Case 13: Light Assembly   The Distribution company performed light assembly for both make-to-stock and make-to-order products, such as repackaging purchased materials and painting/finishing items to customer specification. With stocked items, they used an order-less approach to reporting completed units that auto-deducted components. With make-to-order items, a production order was created from (and directly linked to) the sales order line item. Customer specifications were identified on the order-dependent bill and routing, which sometimes required a sales price recalculation.

Case 14: ECOs and Revision Levels   The Equipment company was considering different alternatives for handling Engineering Change Orders (ECOs) and revision levels. They required workflow capabilities for an ECO approval process, revision levels for purchased items (reflecting documentation changes), and revision levels for manufactured items (reflecting bill, routing, or documentation changes). The new revision level for a manufactured item, for example, could reflect a nonsignificant change (such as a new BOM version) or a significant change that required a new identifier for the item. One of the alternatives employed an additional field (an item dimension) to identify a revision level[14], whereas another alternative embedded the revision level in the item field.[15]

Case 15: Engineering Bills Versus Production Bills   The engineering department wanted to define a separate engineering bill and then convert it into a production bill of material. They defined a separate BOM version for the engineering bill, and used the approved status to indicate it was ready for use by production. The scheduler defined a cut-over date for the new BOM version that considered current inventories and other factors.

---

[14] See **www.columbusit.com** for further information about their ECO module.
[15] See **www.ERPSolutions.biz** for further information about their ECO module.

Case 16: Cut-to-Size Raw Materials in Fabricated Products The Fabricated Products company needed to express bill requirements in terms of the number of pieces of cut-to-size raw materials, such as steel rod and sheet metal, but did not want to create item numbers for each unique size. They solved the problem using the calculation formula and measurements for a component's required quantity. One example involved sheet metal purchased in pounds, costed and stocked in 5×10 sheets, and with component requirements expressed in square feet. Each parent item produced from the sheet metal required different height and width measurements, but only one master BOM to calculate the required square footage in sheet-size increments (50 square feet). This approach also identified purchasing and stockroom picking requirements for the raw materials, and provided cut-to-size instructions for production.

Case 17: By-Products in Fabricated Products Manufacturing The Fabricated Products company produced plastic parts where the production process for plastic resulted in reusable scrap (identified by a unique item number) that could be melted down in subsequent runs. The reusable scrap represented a by-product that was identified in the master BOM as a negative quantity, and received into stock as a result of a production order.

Executive Summary

Modeling supply chain activities for a manufactured item involves item master, bill of material, and optional routing information. A master BOM defines the components to build a manufactured item, and a master routing defines the work center operations to build an item. An item may have multiple BOM versions and route versions to support site-specific variations, planned engineering changes, and alternate formulations. The case studies illustrated variations in manufacturing environments, including virtual manufacturing, by-products, authorized recipes, cut-to-size material, and the use of engineering versus production bills of material.

Chapter 4

Custom Product Manufacturing

The nature of custom product manufacturing can differ significantly, ranging from a one-time engineer-to-order item to a configure-to-order item built from predefined options. One approach to modeling a custom product involves creation of new item numbers and their master BOM/routing information, just like the standard products approach described in the previous chapter. Another approach employs a project to define requirements and track actual consumption for the product design, as described in Chapter 12. Dynamics AX supports two additional approaches for modeling a custom product. These are commonly referred to as option selection approach (via a configurable item) and a rules-based product configurator approach (via a modeling-enabled item).

❖ *Option Selection Approach (aka Configurable Items).* The item number for a configurable item serves as the starting point for defining related configuration IDs, typically in the context of entering a sales order or quotation. The item's BOM version defines a bill of options, and an option selection process defines the components for a specific configuration ID. The item's route version defines the common operations for producing a configuration. Each configuration is uniquely identified by the item number and configuration ID, and its components and operations provide the foundation for calculating total costs, a suggested sales price, and a capable-to-promise delivery date. A configuration's component can be another configurable item, thereby supporting a multi-level custom product.

Once an item's configuration ID has been created, the system treats it almost like a standard product. For example, an item's configuration ID can be forecasted and have sales trade agreements, and inventory can be tracked through a distribution network. The primary difference with a standard product approach is that a configuration's bill of material cannot be directly maintained.

❖ *Rules-Based Product Configurator Approach (aka Modeling-Enabled Items).* The item number for a modeling-enabled item serves as the starting point for using a rules-based product configurator, typically in the context of entering a sales order or quotation. Each configurator is termed a product model. A product model defines a user dialogue and the logic for creating bill and routing data based on user responses. It automatically creates a new master BOM and master routing, and assigns these to the modeling-enabled item. In the context of sales order entry, for example, it also assigns the newly created master BOM and routing to the sales order line item. These are termed the sub-BOM and sub-route. The newly created master BOM and routing provide the foundation for calculating total costs, a suggested sales price, and a capable-to-promise delivery date. A component can be another modeling-enabled item with a specified sub-BOM and sub-routing, thereby supporting a multilevel custom product.

A product model can alternatively create a new item as an output, and assign the newly created master BOM and routing to the new item. The system treats the new item just like any other standard product, including the maintenance of bill and routing information.

The explanation of custom product manufacturing starts with the option selection approach. The chapter's explanation of the option selection approach consists of seven major sections.

1. Item information for a configurable item
2. Master BOM for a configurable item
3. Master routing for a configurable item
4. Using the option selection process
5. Maintaining a configuration's components and operations
6. Considerations about the bill of options and option selection
7. Modularizing the bills to support option selection

The rules-based product configurator approach will then be covered, with an initial focus on handling option selection environments to enable an apples-to-apples comparison with the option selection approach. The chapter's explanation of the product configurator approach consists of five major sections.

1. Item information for a modeling-enabled item
2. Usage of a product model

3. Basic steps to defining a product model
4. Considerations about defining a product model
5. Considerations about using a product model

The chapter concludes with several guidelines about using the different approaches to handle custom products.

Option Selection Approach

The option selection approach employs the master BOM to define a bill of options for a configurable item. An option selection process can then be used to define an item's configuration ID and its components, typically in the context of configuring a line item for a sales order or quotation. Several guidelines apply to the definition of item information, the master BOM and routing, the option selection process, and data maintenance.

Item Information for a Configurable Item

A configurable manufactured item is defined on the item master just like any other manufactured item, with two major differences. First, the dimension group assigned to the item must include configuration as an item dimension. This means each configuration will be uniquely identified by the combination of the item number and a configuration ID. Second, the item must be designated as configurable. A configurable item has three other characteristics that differ from standard manufactured items.

❖ *Master BOM Information.* The master BOM assigned to a configurable item represents a bill of options, with each component designated as common or optional based on the configuration group assigned to the component.

❖ *Master Routing Information.* The master routing assigned to a configurable item represents the common routing operations performed on all configurations of the item.

❖ *Costing Information for Each Configuration ID.* An item master policy (termed the *use combination cost price* field) determines whether each configuration ID will have a separate inventory cost, or all configurations will have the same inventory cost.

The next two sections provide further explanation about master BOM and routing information in the context of option selection for a configurable item.

Master BOM for a Configurable Item

The master BOM assigned to a configurable item (aka the *BOM version*) represents a bill of options that provides the basis for option selection. The definition and maintenance of this master BOM information is exactly the same as other master BOMs, as described in the previous chapter. For example, each BOM version can be site-specific or company-wide, and there are several options for the warehouse source of a component.[1] There is one exception: the user-defined configuration groups can be assigned to relevant components for option selection purposes. The assigned configuration group represents a required option in the option selection process, since you must select one component from each configuration group to configure a custom product.

The custom equipment manufacturing example shown in Figure 4.1 will be used to explain configuration groups within the master BOM, and the impact on the option selection process. The configurable item Custom Equipment has three required options for a base unit, a color, and a control, which are identified by three configuration groups.

Configuring the equipment in this example involves a required option for the base unit (basic or deluxe) that must be built from a second-level power unit option (high or low) and some other materials. Both base unit options have a component type of production, so that the production order will be linked to the production order for assembling the equipment. Configuring the equipment involves another required option for paint color (designated as a component type of vendor since it is performed as an outside operation) and an optional option for an extra control. Every configuration includes a set of common parts, where the component has been designated as a phantom component type. This equipment example illustrates different component types in the master BOM, in addition to the concept of required, optional, and common options.

---

[1] If a configurable item can be produced at different sites, a company-wide BOM version should be used when the same bill of options applies to these sites, and a site-specific BOM version should be used when the bill of options varies by site. The options for a component's warehouse source are summarized in Figure 3.3.

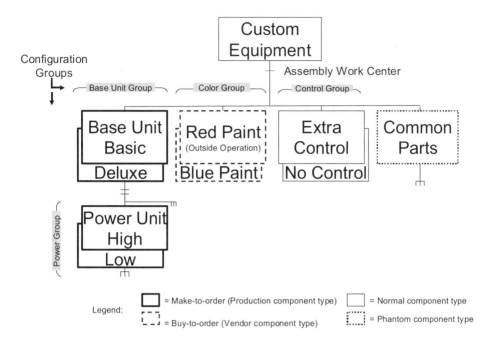

Figure 4.1 Option Selection Example

❖ *Required Option.* A component representing a required option has a value specified for its configuration group, such as the Base Unit Group and the Color Group in Figure 4.1. Two or more components can be assigned the same configuration group, and the option selection process forces the user to select one option within the group.

❖ *Optional Option.* A component representing an optional option also has a value specified for its configuration group, such as the Control Group in Figure 4.1. However, one component will represent the null choice, where the null-choice component typically reflects a non-inventoried item with a zero quantity required. The Extra Control item in Figure 4.1 represents an optional option, and the No Control item represents the null-choice component.

❖ *Common Option.* A common component has a null value for its configuration group. The system does not display a common component during the option selection process, and automatically includes it in a configuration's components.

The equipment example in Figure 4.1 also illustrates a multilevel custom product configuration, where a component can be another configurable manufactured item. In this example, the base unit configuration consists of a power unit (high or low), so that the bill of options for a base unit includes components assigned to the configuration group Power Group.

The component quantity for each component within a bill of options will act as the default value when you select the component during the option selection process. You cannot enter a component quantity during option selection.

A graphical view of a configurable item's bill of options uses an indented bill format to display each component within its assigned configuration group. This graphical view is termed a *configuration tree*.

Master Routing for a Configurable Item

The master routing assigned to a configurable item (aka the *Route Version*) represents the common operations performed on every configuration. In the equipment example shown in Figure 4.1, the route version includes one operation for the assembly work center. The definition and maintenance of this master routing information is exactly the same as other master routings, as described in the previous chapter. There is one exception: you can maintain the routing data for an item's specific configuration ID (after creating a configuration). This routing data initially reflects the common operations within the master routing.

Routing operations cannot be selected as part of the option selection process to define a configuration, but you can maintain the routing data for an item's specific configuration ID (as mentioned above). Alternatively, you can select phantom components with routing operations, so that the order-dependent routing for the production order contains the phantom's operations. The system automatically reassigns the phantom's operation numbers in the order-dependent routing (aka the *Production Routing*).

Using the Option Selection Process

Option selection involves a two-step process. The first step defines a configuration's components via a selected option from each configuration group. The second step requires user assignment of the item's configuration ID. The first step is termed the *Configure Item* dialogue; the second step is termed the *Configuration Creation* dialogue.

The two-step option selection process applies to the parent item, and (in a multilevel configuration) must be repeated for each component representing a configurable item. Completion of the two-step process results in automatic creation of the configuration's components and routing operations. Alternatively, the user can select an existing configuration ID (during the first step) rather than going through the option selection process.

The option selection process can be initiated from several places: when entering a line item on a sales order, sales quotation, or service order; when manually creating a production order; or from the item master.[2] Each starting point involves several considerations as described below.

❖ *Create Configuration from a Sales Order Line Item.* The user initiates the two-step option selection process by starting from the configuration field on a sales order line item for the configurable item. After completing the two-step process, the system automatically places the item's configuration ID in the sales order line item.

    The sales order price defaults to the item's standard price, and can be manually overridden. However, the user can optionally calculate the configuration's cost and sales price (via the *Order-Specific BOM Calculation* function), and transfer the sales price to the sales order line item. Chapter 5 explains order-specific BOM calculations. The user can also calculate a capable-to-promise delivery date (via the *Explosion Inquiry*), and transfer it to the confirmed ship date on the sales order line item. Chapter 7 explains how to make delivery promises for a sales order line item.

❖ *Create Configuration from a Sales Quotation Line Item.* The user initiates the two-step option selection process by starting from the configuration field on a sales quotation line item for the configurable item. The order-specific BOM calculation of a cost and sales price for a quotation works just like a sales order. A capable-to-promise delivery date cannot be calculated.

❖ *Create Configuration from a Service Order Line Item.* The option selection process for a service order line item works just like the process for a sales order line item. Chapter 14 describes service order processing.

❖ *Create Configuration when Manually Creating a Production Order.* The user initiates the two-step option selection process by starting from the configuration field when manually creating a production order for the

---

[2] The context of sales orders and production orders will be further explained in Chapters 7 and 11, so this section only describes the aspects related to option selection.

configurable item. After completing the two-step process, the system automatically returns the configuration ID so that you can create the production order. The configuration's components and operations provide the initial values for an order-dependent bill and routing.[3] Chapter 11 explains production orders and the calculation of related costs and a completion date.

❖ *Create Configuration from the Item Master.* The two-step option selection process can be initiated from the item master by setting up a configuration. A separate BOM Calculation process can be used to calculate each configuration's cost and sales price, and update the item master data, as described in Chapter 5.

An existing configuration ID (for a configurable item) can be selected when entering a line item, or when manually creating a production order.

Maintaining a Configuration's Components and Operations

The configuration's components and operations resulting from option selection often require manual maintenance, especially when predefined options only comprise part of the product.

Routing Maintenance A configuration's routing operations can be manually maintained on the route version for the configurable item. You need to specify the configuration ID of the configurable item in order to maintain the configuration's routing data. A configuration's routing data initially reflects the common operations.

Component Maintenance A configuration's components cannot be directly maintained, such as manually adding components or changing a component's quantity. The configuration's components can be viewed for a sales order line item using the composed-of tree, but component maintenance on the composed-of tree will update the master BOM rather than the configuration's components.

---

[3] The system does not synchronize these two sets of data—for the configuration and the production order—so that changes in one set (such as the configuration's components) do not automatically update the other (such as the order-dependent bill). A manual approach can be taken to synchronize the data, such as deleting a production order and then re-creating it with the latest configuration information.

As an alternative approach for component maintenance, you can reuse the setup configuration dialogue as if you were creating a new configuration, and override a selected option. When overriding a selected option, the system will prompt for a new configuration ID when required.

Considerations about the Bill of Options and Option Selection

Information about components in the master BOM affects the behavior of option selection. It also affects the calculation of costs and prices for a configuration.

Sequences and Names for Groups During Option Selection   Proper sequencing of configuration groups can make option selection an easier and more logical process. The system normally sequences groups based on the group identifier. However, a user-defined sequence (termed the *configuration route*) can be defined for the master BOM. As part of the group sequencing information, the user can define a 30-character name (rather than the 10-character group identifier) that is displayed as a prompt during option selection.

Displayed Options Based on Date Effectivities   The system enforces the availability of options during option selection based on the date effectivities of the BOM version and the components. With respect to component date effectivities, the option selection process only displays options (within a configuration group) that are in effect as of the delivery date for a sales order line item, thereby supporting the introduction of a new group or the discontinuation of an out-of-date group. The system only displays a group if there is at least one option in effect.

Providing a Null Choice Within a Configuration Group   Since the option selection process forces the user to select one option within a configuration group, a non-inventoried component can represent the null choice within the configuration group. It typically has a zero quantity and zero cost. It may optionally provide cost or markup information for BOM calculation purposes.

Basic Configuration Rules Affecting Option Selection   Option selection is affected by two basic configuration rules defined for a component in the master BOM. One rule provides automatic selection, while the other rule prevents selection.

❖ *Automatic Selection.* When the component is selected, the system automatically selects an option within another configuration group.
❖ *Prevent Selection.* When the component is selected, the system prevents selection of an option within another configuration group.

These basic rules can help speed up the option selection process via automatic selection and avoiding incorrect selections. A change in configuration rules does not affect existing configurations.

Direct Linkage Between a Production Order and a Sales Order Line Item for a Configuration After creating a configuration during sales order entry, the user can create the production order to ensure linkage with the sales order line item. The nature of direct linkage was covered in Figure 3.2, and Chapters 7 and 11 provide further explanation of direct linkage between a production order and sales order. Direct linkage can also apply to the production orders for configurable components in a multilevel configuration.

Multilevel Option Selection and Sequences Option selection is performed for each configurable item, so that a component representing a configurable item involves another level of option selection. A multilevel configured item affects the sequencing of option selection, since the system displays option selection at deeper levels before it returns to the originating level. The group sequencing information only applies to option selection on a given level in the bill of material.

Calculating the Total Cost and Sales Price for a Configuration The approach for calculating a configuration's cost and sales price will vary slightly based on the starting point. For example, the calculations for a configuration on a sales order and sales quotation are termed an order-specific BOM calculation; they do not require a specified costing version and do not update item master data. The BOM calculations affecting item master data must specify a costing version. Chapter 5 explains the difference between order-specific BOM calculations and BOM calculations.

Assigning a Configuration ID When Option Selection Results in Identical Configurations After completing the first step of the two-step option selection process, the system automatically recognizes when the selected options match those of an existing configuration ID. It automatically assigns the existing configuration ID, and does not display the second step that would allow assignment of a new configuration ID. This logic makes sense when option selection results in 100% definition of a configuration's components, since it prevents duplicate identifiers and enforces a smart part number. This logic does not make sense in some situations, such as when option selection results in a partial definition of a configuration's components, and additional components must be manually maintained. By indicating the system should ignore identical configurations, the system always displays the second step of the option selection process. The user can then assign a unique configuration ID or select an existing configuration ID.

Predefining Configurations via Option Selection   For some items, it makes sense to define all possible configurations via option selection and then turn off the configurable policy. For example, there may be a limited number of configurations, the assigned configuration IDs represent a smart part number, or further configurations must be prevented. This means that users (such as sales order entry personnel) cannot create new configurations via option selection and must select from a list of predefined configurations.

There is one special case where the item starts with the configuration policy turned off, so that you only create configuration IDs for the configurable item. The configuration ID acts like a variant code in providing a unique identifier.

Modularizing the Bills to Support Option Selection

Many manufacturers with multiple variations of similar products can benefit from modularizing their bills to support option selection. There are warning signals for needed modularity: an explosive growth in the numbers of items and bills, overly complex bills of material, a perceived need for negative component quantities, difficulties in anticipating demands, and longer-than-necessary delivery lead times. Bill modularization leads the way for a custom products approach to defining and selling products via options.

Bill modularization starts with a detailed understanding of the product structure. One starting point involves "deconstructing" the product variations to identify common and unique items, and then restructuring the bill to reflect the new groupings of common and unique options. This typically results in disentangling an overly complex bill, isolating the unique items for usage late in the production process, and the use of phantoms for groups of common components. Another starting point involves lead time analysis of the multi-level product structures to identify the highest possible stocking level that supports the desired minimum delivery lead time. The stocking level may be stated in the new groupings of common and unique options, typically leading to a reduction in the number of items to forecast.

Bill modularization typically impacts routing operations. Final assembly operations can be assigned to the master routing for the configurable end item. Operations can also be embedded in the master routings for phantom components.

When bill modularization and a custom product approach replace a standard products approach, there are many implications for other aspects of the business. It requires changes to items and bills, item planning parameters, and the approach to sales and operations planning. It also requires changes to manufacturing documentation and drawings, sales literature and product pricing, order entry and delivery promises, paperwork (such as acknowledgments, packing lists and invoices) and sales analysis.

Rules-Based Product Configurator Approach

The rules-based product configurator capabilities embodied in the Product Builder provide one approach to defining the product structure for a custom product. Each rules-based configurator is termed a product model. A product model defines the prompts in a user dialogue and the logic for creating bill and routing data to produce a custom product. A product model can be assigned to one or more manufactured items designated as modeling-enabled. This section starts with item master information for a modeling-enabled item, and then describes the definition and usage of a product model.

Item Information for a Modeling-Enabled Item

A modeling-enabled item is defined on the item master just like any other manufactured item, with one major difference. The item must be designated as modeling enabled.

Several other item master polices only apply to modeling-enabled items, and these policies impact the user dialogue when using the configurator. For example, the item-related policies determine whether to automatically start the configurator after entering a sales order line item.

Usage of a Product Model

There are several starting points for using an item's product model, as shown in the bottom half of Figure 4.2. A sales order or sales quotation line item for the modeling-enabled item typically serves as the starting point for capturing customer specifications. A similar starting point could be a web-enabled application for customer self-service. A production order may serve as the starting point for internal production purposes. A purchase order line item can also serve as a starting point when purchasing a custom product. Further explanation focuses on the sales order context.

The inputs and outputs of a product model provide one way to understand how to define it. From an input perspective, the product model provides a user dialogue that captures responses to prompts for data. For example, the response could be a selection from an enumerated list of possible outcomes, or the entry of an integer for a quantity or length. The prompts for data (termed modeling variables) are grouped together (termed variable groups), and optional validation rules can apply to the responses, as shown in Figure 4.2.

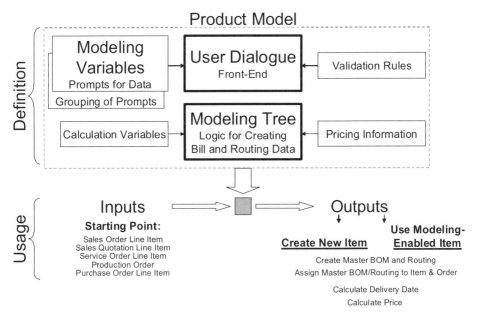

Figure 4.2 Definition and Usage of a Product Model

From an output perspective, use of a product model automatically generates a new master BOM and routing based on the inputs. There are two basic variations of output.

❖ *Create New Item.* The system automatically creates a new item, and assigns the newly created master BOM and routing to the new item and the sales order line item. With automatic item number creation, the item number reflects a user-defined format that can include responses to prompts, fixed information, and a sequential counter.[4] The new item inherits the same item master information as the original modeling-enabled item.

❖ *Use Modeling-Enabled Item.* The system automatically assigns the newly created master BOM and routing to the modeling-enabled item and the sales order line item. Each assignment represents an additional BOM version and routing version for the modeling-enabled item.

Each product model has a policy determining whether the output reflects a new item or use of the modeling-enabled item. The system can create multiple sets of output (e.g., multiple new items) for a multilevel custom product, where the product model reflects a modeling-enabled item that has a component that is also modeling-enabled. Each modeling-enabled component requires a separate product model.

The user can manually maintain information about the newly created master BOM/routing (and new item number), just like any other master BOM/routing (and item). The ability to manually maintain this information is important when use of the product model only results in a partially defined product structure.

As part of the output, the system can calculate the sales price based on the bill/routing information (via the BOM calculation), or based on pricing information embedded in the product model.[5] A subsequent section in this chapter provides further explanation of the pricing information embedded in a product model. An additional output includes the calculation of a delivery date based on the bill/routing information. The system can automatically calculate the sales price and delivery date without the need for a user-initiated task.[6]

---

[4] Automatic creation of a new item reflects the item dimensions of the modeling-enabled item. As a result, the system can create a new configuration ID and/or variant code(s) along with the new item number.

[5] A company-wide policy (embedded in the Product Builder parameters) determines which basis will be used for calculating the sales price of a custom product created from product models.

[6] Two company-wide policies (embedded in the Product Builder parameters) determine whether the user needs to initiate calculation of a price and delivery date, or whether the system calculates them automatically without user intervention.

At the end of the user dialogue, the user can accept the delivery/price calculations and the system automatically populates the sales order line item with the delivery date and sales price. The user can modify responses within the user dialogue prior to acceptance. The user can also reuse the product model to modify responses after acceptance, as long as it's done before generation of a production order for the sales order line item.

Basic Steps to Defining a Product Model

Several basic steps apply to the definition of every product model, starting with the creation of a product model identifier and ending with the assignment of the product model identifier to a modeling-enabled item. An example will be used to explain the basic steps. Option selection represents one class of custom product environments addressed by the use of product models, so that the equipment example in Figure 4.3 will be used to illustrate the basic steps.

The example in Figure 4.3 closely parallels the previous example shown in Figure 4.1, thereby providing the basis for comparing the two custom product approaches. The product configurator capabilities can handle more than option selection situations, as explained in subsequent sections and illustrated by case studies at the end of the chapter.

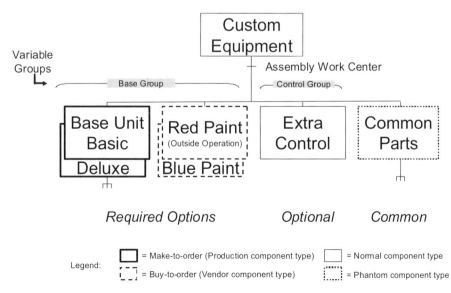

Figure 4.3 Option Selection Example

The six basic steps to defining a product model are summarized below. You can optionally use a Product Model Wizard that structures these same steps.

Step 1: Create a Product Model Identifier The first step consists of defining a product model number and description. A product model generally corresponds to a product line of manufactured items with similar manufacturing characteristics. For example, the custom equipment in Figure 4.3 represents one product line, and another type of equipment would require a unique product model.

Step 2: Create Prompts for the User Dialogue The user dialogue consists of one or more prompts for data. Each prompt is termed a *modeling variable*, with the grouping of prompts based on *variable groups*. Figure 4.4 illustrates the variable groups and modeling variables for the equipment example shown in Figure 4.3. This simplistic example contains only two groups, and the base group contains only two prompts for the base unit and the color. Grouping is normally employed when an item requires many modeling variables.

Each group and modeling variable must be predefined prior to usage in a product model, as described below.

Product Model for Custom Equipment

Variable Group	Modeling Variable and descriptive prompt	Mandatory	Enumerated Outcome
Base	BaseUnit What base unit do you want?	X	Basic Deluxe
	Paint What paint color do you want?	X	Blue Red
Control	XControl Do you want the extra control?		Extra Control

Figure 4.4 Product Model Example for a Basic User Dialogue

❖ *Variable Group.* A variable group provides a logical grouping of prompts within the user dialog. After defining variable groups, the relevant groups must be associated with a specific product model. The user can then define the hierarchy and sequence of groups that will appear in the user dialogue.

❖ *Modeling Variable.* Each variable consists of a user-defined identifier, a description that serves as the prompt, and a data type. For simplicity's sake the equipment example only uses one data type that supports selection from a predefined list of possible outcomes. This data type is termed *enumerated text*. The user specifies the possible outcomes after creating the variable, such as blue and red for the color variable.

A prompt may involve other different types of responses, as indicated by the data type for the modeling variable. Other data types include whole numbers (*integer*) and decimal numbers *(real)* for quantity responses, a yes/no response *(Boolean)*, and text for descriptive responses such as an operation or invoice description. A data type can also be information within the Dynamics AX database, which involves specifying the table and the desired field. This *table* data type can provide a list of values for option selection purposes, and therefore represents one alternative to the enumerated text approach. Each prompt can have help text (that will be displayed at the bottom of the screen during the user dialogue), and different language texts for the prompt and help text.

The user dialogue is affected by several additional policies associated with each prompt.

- Multiple prompts within a group can be sequenced in the user dialog.
- A prompt can be display only, editable, or hidden. It can also be mandatory, which means a null response is not allowed.
- A prompt can have a default value.
- Selected values within a prompt's enumerated text can be excluded based on the response to another prompt.

Some product models require a calculation variable that does not display as a prompt in the user dialogue, but is used in the modeling tree. There are several types of calculation variables that serve different purposes. A simple variable, for example, must be defined to hold calculation data such as the multiplication of length and width to determine area. A system variable, for example, can be used to include information about the sales order line item (such as quantity) in the modeling tree. Other calculation variables provide information about any of the extended data types (such as the customer identifier), tables, and classes.

Step 3: Define the Modeling Tree The modeling tree provides a mapping between the responses to user dialogue prompts and the desired output of BOM and routing information. It also provides a graphical representation of the X++ code that will be executed when using a product model. The mapping for the equipment example, for instance, involves a series of statements such as "if the response for the <u>paint</u> modeling variable equals <u>blue</u>, then the bill of material should include the blue-paint <u>component</u>." This example could be stated with three types of elements (termed nodes) in the modeling tree—a switch node, a case node, and a BOM node—as illustrated in Figure 4.5.

Information about a BOM node reflects the typical component information described in Chapter 3, such as the component quantity and component type. The other modeling tree entries in Figure 4.5 define the switch node for the BaseUnit and XControl modeling variables, and the associated case nodes and BOM nodes. A subsequent section describes the other types of nodes in a modeling tree.

Type of Node	Meaning
Switch Node	If the response for the *Paint* modeling variable
Case Node	equals *Blue*
BOM Node	then add *component* Blue-Paint
Case Node	equals *Red*
BOM Node	then add *component* Red-Paint
Switch Node	If the response for the *BaseUnit* modeling variable
Case Node	equals *Basic*
BOM Node	then add *component* Base-Unit-Basic
Case Node	equals *Deluxe*
BOM Node	then add *component* Base-Unit-Deluxe
Switch Node	If the response for the *XControl* modeling variable
Case Node	equals *Extra Control*
BOM Node	then add *component* Extra-Control

Figure 4.5 Example of Modeling Tree Nodes

Step 4: Define Policy for Creating a New Item   The output of a product model can be a new item number in addition to the new master BOM/routing information. The user-defined format can include responses to prompts and fixed information, thereby providing one approach to a smart part number. In our example, the automatically created item number could be Equip-Deluxe-Red-001, which reflects the responses (for Deluxe and Red), a fixed prefix (Equip), separators (-), and a counter. When creating a smart part number, the value for each response should be as short as possible, thereby shortening the number of characters in the newly created item number.

Step 5: Compile the Product Model   The compilation creates an executable version of the product model, and also detects errors in the modeling tree. Once compiled, the product model can be used in test mode to verify that the user dialogue works correctly.

Step 6: Assign the Product Model to an Modeling-Enabled Item
A product model is assigned to a modeling-enabled item, or to multiple modeling-enabled items that share the same configurator and manufacturing characteristics. An approval process parallels the approval process for master BOMs and BOM versions. That is, the product model must be approved, and assignment to a modeling-enabled item must be approved and flagged as active. At this point, a user can configure a custom product using the product model from any of the starting points such as a sales order line item.

Considerations about Defining a Product Model

Some basic guidelines should be considered when defining a product model. Bill modularization represents a basic guideline. Other considerations include planned changes to an item's product model, the sequence of prompts, a multilevel custom product, validation rules, and the calculation of a sales price.

Planned Changes to an Item's Product Model   Planned changes to an item's product model may stem from several reasons, such as a change in the user dialogue and/or modeling tree to reflect changes in the product design. Planned changes can be indicated via the effectivity dates for product models assigned to the item; the assignments must be approved and active. The system uses the current date (rather than the delivery date) to determine which product model is in effect.

The sales order starting point allows the user to manually override the version of an item's product model for configuration purposes. That is, you can specify an approved-but-not active version of the product model on the sales order line item.

Sequences of Prompts During the User Dialogue   Proper grouping and sequencing of the prompts can make the user dialogue an easier and more logical process. The variable groups can be sequenced and reflect a hierarchy of groups. The modeling variables within a group can also be sequenced.

Handling a Multilevel Custom Product   A multilevel custom product reflects a modeling-enabled item with one or more components that are also modeling-enabled items. There are three basic guidelines for handling a multilevel custom product.

- The user dialogue for the top-level product model must contain all prompts (modeling variables) employed by lower-level components.
- A separate product model must be created for each modeling-enabled item that represents a lower level component. The values for the modeling variables employed in the product models for a lower-level component are flagged as inherited.
- The modeling tree for the top-level product model must contain a BOM node that identifies the item number for a first-level modeling-enabled component. Similarly, the modeling tree for a first-level component must contain a BOM node identifying the item number for a second-level modeling-enabled component. The same guideline applies to each level in a multilevel custom product.

Each product model creates a master BOM and routing, which are then used to define the sub-BOM and sub-route in the component information.

Validation Rules Affecting the User Dialogue   Validation rules apply to the user's responses to prompts (modeling variables) or to calculated values (calculation variables). These validation rules can be defined for a specific product model (termed a local rule). Validation rules for modeling variables can also be defined for multiple product models (termed a global rule). Calculation variables only apply to a specific product model, so a global rule cannot be defined for a calculation variable. This explanation focuses on local validation rules for a specific product model. There are three types of validation rules.

❖ *Constraint Rule Type.* A constraint rule defines an exception condition which must not exist, such as excluding selection of an outcome. In the equipment example, for instance, the red paint option could be excluded when the deluxe base unit option is specified. In addition, you can prevent the display and/or editing of a prompt. In the equipment example, for instance, the display of the extra control prompt can be prevented when the basic base unit is specified.

❖ *Action Rule Type.* An action rule defines what happens based on a true or false condition. In the equipment example, for instance, the selection of a deluxe base unit can result in an action to automatically include the extra control.

❖ *Formula Rule Type.* A formula rule defines a fixed or calculated value for a calculation variable.

These validation rules can help simplify and speed up the product configuration process and avoid incorrect selections.

Calculating the Sales Price for a Sales Order   The system supports two basic approaches to calculating a sales price for a modeling-enabled item. A company-wide policy determines whether it will be a cost-plus-markup approach or a rolled-price approach. The cost-plus-markup approach reflects an order-specific BOM calculation, as described in Chapter 5. The rolled-price approach reflects pricing based on user responses, with pricing information embedded in the product model. The following guidelines apply to the rolled price approach.

– The standard sales price for the modeling-enabled item represents the default price, and the baseline for calculating a price.

– An additional amount can be defined for each response. Entering the response adds a positive amount to (and subtracts a negative amount from) the standard sales price. Alternatively, a percentage can be defined for a response, which means a percentage is added (or subtracted) to the standard sales price.

- The system automatically calculates and displays a running total sales price based on each response.

Using a Variable Quantity for a Component in a BOM Node A component's required quantity can reflect a variable rather than a fixed value, where the variable may reflect a user response to a prompt (a modeling variable) or a calculation variable. In the equipment example, for instance, the component quantity for the extra control could reflect a user response to an additional modeling variable for an integer. The concept of a variable field value can be applied to almost any field related to a component, such as the item number and operation. Other examples include the fields in a routing operation such as the run-time quantity or work center.

Reusing the Information about Previously Created Master BOMs and Routings The system can automatically detect whether a product model generates the same output as a previously created master BOM and routing, so that it can reuse the information rather than create a new master BOM/routing. The user can optionally override this logic for a given product model output so that the system does create a new master BOM/routing.

Copy a Product Model Information about an existing product model can be copied into a new product model. This copy feature reduces the time to develop a new product model, especially when it represents a slight revision of an existing product model.

Importing and Exporting a Product Model The X++ code associated with a product model can be exported into a DEF and a DAT file. Conversely, a DAT file containing X++ code can be imported into a product model.

Where-Used Information A where-used report indicates the product models (or the modeling-enabled items) using several types of data, including the modeling variables, master operations, work centers, items, master BOM identifiers and master routing identifiers.

Types of Nodes in a Modeling Tree A modeling tree consists of nodes of different types and reflects a graphical representation of the X++ code underlying a product model. Three types of nodes—a switch node, case node, and BOM node—were used in the above-mentioned equipment example. Other commonly used nodes include the following:

❖ *Route Node.* A route node is similar to a BOM node, but defines the information for a routing operation rather than a material component. For example, a route node could be used to define the common routing operation shown in Figure 4.3.

❖ *Default Route Node.* A default route node specifies a master routing identifier, so that all of its routing operations will be included. This provides an alternative approach for handling a group of routing operations since they do not have to be individually defined in the modeling tree.

❖ *Default BOM Node.* A default BOM node specifies a master BOM identifier, so that all of its components will be included. This provides an alternative approach for handling a group of components (such as the common parts on the equipment example) since they do not have to be individually defined in the routing tree. These components act as the starting point for additional components, therefore a default BOM node must be at the top of the modeling tree.

❖ *Simple Node.* A simple node is used for simple calculations, typically using information about modeling variables and/or calculation variables.

❖ *Table Node.* A table node is used for fetching values for a field in a table, such as a table in the database or a user-defined table. The set of field values can be optionally limited to a specified range, and the set viewed as a list of choices in the user dialogue.

❖ *Code Node.* A code node specifies the user-defined X++ code that represents the body of a method for a Dynamics AX class.

Each node in a modeling tree represents one way to create X++ code. The X++ code for a product model can also be manually entered and maintained.

Composed-Of Information   A composed-of report summarizes the variables and X++ code related to a product model (or a modeling-enabled item).

Considerations about Using a Product Model

Some basic guidelines can be considered when using a product model. These considerations include how to manually maintain bill/routing data and the user dialogue format.

Maintaining Information about Components and Routing Operations   The output of a product model includes a master BOM and routing, and these can be manually maintained just like any other master BOM and routing. After using a product model (in the context of a sales order) to create a master BOM, the composed-of tree provides an additional approach to maintaining the master BOM.

Format of the User Dialogue   The user dialogue can be displayed in either a tab format or a tree format. The tab format only applies when the dialogue involves less than three levels of prompts.

Customer Self Service for a Product Model   A web form can be generated for a product model, so that selection of a modeling-enabled item for the shopping cart will result in the user dialogue.

Using a Specified Product Model during Sales Order Entry   Some situations involve multiple product models assigned to a modeling-enabled item. The user can specify an approved-but-not-active product model on the sales order line item, rather than using the active product model.

Direct Linkage Between a Production Order and a Sales Order Line Item for a Custom Product   After completing product model usage during sales order entry, the user can create the production order to ensure linkage with the sales order line item. The nature of direct linkage was covered in Figure 3.2, and Chapters 7 and 11 provide further explanation of direct linkage between a production order and sales order. Direct linkage can also apply to the production orders for modeling-enabled components in a multilevel configuration.

Automatic Deletion of Master BOM and Routing Information   Some custom product environments involve the creation of many quotations (or sales orders) that are not built. When product model usage does not create a new item, deletion of the sales order line item automatically results in the deletion of the newly created master BOM and routing.

Guidelines for Choosing the Appropriate Approach

Product structure information can be defined using a standard product or custom product approach. Many products could be modeled using either approach and the approach may change over time. A custom product with limited combinations of options, for example, could be modeled as several item numbers or as several predefined configuration IDs. A standard product may evolve into many variations, which can be modeled as options of a custom product.

Choosing between the two custom product approaches involves several considerations. The option selection approach is typically limited to the class of custom product environments involving predefined options for 100% of the configuration. In particular, the component quantity for a selected option cannot be manually overridden, and a configuration's bill of material cannot be manually maintained, although a configuration's routing can be manually maintained. The options reflect a one-to-one correspondence to items and modularized bills of material. Since the option selection process displays a list of item numbers to the user, the user must be comfortable with the internal item identification.

An option selection environment can also be modeled using the product configurator approach, as illustrated by this chapter's examples. The definition of a product model for an option selection environment involves slightly more work than the configurable-item approach. The user dialogue displays a list of enumerated text (rather than item numbers), and the approach does not necessarily require a one-to-one correspondence with modularized bills. The user can specify a quantity for an option. The product model generates master BOM/routing information (and even new item numbers) that can be maintained just like a standard product.

The product configurator can handle other types of custom product scenarios, ranging from the simple to the complex. In particular, it can dynamically create master BOM and routing information that reflects user-defined calculations and the responses to user-defined prompts. The case studies illustrate other types of custom product scenarios.

Case Studies

Case 18: Window Configurations
A manufacturer of custom windows employed a rules-based product configurator for each product line. With a window product line, for example, the user dialogue captured information about the dimensions, glass type, casing, and other key attributes. The modeling tree defined the rules for generating the master BOM and routing to build the window, including the calculation of glass and wood

component quantities and routing operation times. The product model also calculated the sales price.

Case 19: Store Fixture Configurations   A manufacturer of store fixtures employed a rules-based product configurator to identify the desired options for horizontal racks and vertical supports in a customized store fixture. This involved a two-level custom product, since a customized rack consisted of various subassemblies, and the rack went into a customized store fixture.

Case 20: Surgical Kit Configuration   One product line at the Distribution company involved a customer-specified kit of components that represented surgical items. For example, a surgical kit was configured based on the requirements to perform a surgery at a hospital. A master bill defined the possible options, and the sales order entry function used the option selection process to identify the desired components in the surgical kit. A customization enabled users to enter the quantity for a selected option. The sales price for a surgical kit reflected the selected components and the cost-plus-markup approach embedded in the BOM calculation.

Case 21: Auto-Create Product Structure Skeleton for a Custom Product   One product line at the Equipment company involved building customized machines to customer specifications. Every customized machine had a unique identifier, and its product structure consisted of the same type of customized subassemblies (such as a power unit, a horizontal table, and a vertical column) with unique item identifiers. Each customized subassembly required several unique components with long purchasing lead times, and subassembly production was initiated prior to receipt of these unique components. Substantial engineering time was required to define the unique item identifiers, initiate purchases of the long lead time components, and ultimately define each machine's product structure (with unique components correctly placed in subassembly bills of material). Any delays in these engineering efforts impacted the purchasing and production activities, and the delayed definition of the product structure information made it difficult to coordinate requirements. As a solution approach, the company employed the product configurator to autocreate the unique item numbers and the product structure skeleton, with the unique purchased components correctly placed in the subassembly BOMs. The solution approach resulted in significant reductions in engineering time and the number of delays.

Case 22: Overhead Crane Configuration   One product line at the Equipment company involved a customized overhead crane for moving heavy material around a factory floor. The user dialogue in the product model identified usage characteristics, such as maximum load weight, mounting height, and the factory floor dimensions. The modeling tree translated the usage characteristics into the required materials and operations to produce the customized overhead crane.

Case 23: Customized Plastic Bags   One product line at the Fabricated Products company involved customized plastic bags, such as bags for grocery stores and retail stores. The plastic bags were produced on a single machine from plastic pellets, and various ink colors were used to print logos on the bags. A rules-based configurator captured customer requirements (via the user dialogue) and generated a new item number and the master BOM/ routing information (via the modeling tree). BOM calculations suggested a sales price, and sales price trade agreements were defined for ongoing sales of the bag.

Case 24: Customized Plastic Assembly   One product line at the Fabricated Products company involved customized plastic assemblies that reflected a two-level custom product. Plastic components were produced to custom specifications, and then assembled into a customized plastic product. The user dialogue in a product model captured the customer specifications, and product models provided a mapping to the required materials and operations. The two-level custom product enabled warehouse personnel to find the customized plastic components that were prepared for final assembly.

Executive Summary

The nature of custom product manufacturing can differ significantly, ranging from special one-time items to an assemble-to-order product built from predefined components. In addition to the standard product approaches, Dynamics AX provides an option selection approach and a rules-based product configurator for handling custom products. The option selection approach applies to a configurable item that employs a configuration ID in its identifier. The master BOM represents a bill of options consisting of optional and common components, and the option selection process can define a new configuration ID and its associated components and routing.

The product configurator approach applies to modeling-enabled items. Each configurator is termed a product model. A product model consists of a user dialogue that captures responses to prompts, and a modeling tree that defines the logic for creating a master BOM and routing based on the responses. Both approaches are typically used in the context of a sales order or quotation, but they can also be invoked for a manually created production order. Several case studies illustrated how to handle custom products for windows, store fixtures, surgical kits, overhead cranes and plastic bags.

Chapter 5

Product Costing

Product cost information supports valuation of an item's inventory transactions using a standard cost or an actual cost method. Actual cost methods include weighted average, LIFO, and FIFO. Standard costs provide the baseline for identifying variances in procurement and manufacturing. Product costs for a manufactured item can be calculated using its bill of material (BOM) information, and optional routing and overhead information. These calculations can also be used to project future costs, simulate the impact of cost changes, analyze cost reduction opportunities, analyze profitability, and calculate an item's suggested sales price.

An explanation of product costing can be organized around several major variations in business practices, as summarized in Figure 5.1. The basic variations reflect distribution and manufacturing environments. A purchased material item in a distribution environment (described in Chapter 2) can be valued at standard or actual cost, often reflecting a replenishment strategy of buy-to-stock or buy-to-order respectively. A manufactured item that represents a standard product (described in Chapter 3) is typically valued at standard cost, whether the replenishment strategy is make-to-stock or make-to-order. A BOM calculation function is used to calculate a manufactured item's standard cost, and to optionally calculate its sales price. A custom product manufactured item (described in Chapter 4) is typically valued at actual cost, although some its components may reflect standard products valued at standard cost. A custom product is typically produced to meet customer specifications for a specific sales order, and it reflects an engineer-to-order or configure-to-order replenishment strategy. In many cases, an order-specific BOM calculation function can be used to calculate the order's cost and sales price, and transfer the calculated sales price to the sales order.

The primary variations in product costing displayed in Figure 5.1 provide an organizing focus for further explanation. The chapter consists of the following major sections.

1. Standard costs for purchased material
2. Standard costs for manufactured items and BOM calculations
3. Converting items to a standard cost model

Primary Variations	Distribution		Manufacturing	
	Purchased Material		Standard Product	Custom Product
Typical Costing Method	Standard Cost	Actual Cost	Standard Cost	Actual Cost
Requirement for Item Cost Records	Yes	No	Yes	No
Use Cost Records for Labor and Overhead	N/A		Yes	
Approach to Cost-Rollup Calculation			Use BOM Calculation to calculate an item's standard cost	Use BOM Calculation to calculate an item's planned cost
Approach to Sales Price Calculation			Use BOM Calculation to to calculate an item's sales price	
Approach to Order-Specific Calculation			Generally N/A	Use Order-Specific BOM Calculation to calculate an order's cost and sales price, and transfer sales price to sales order

Figure 5.1 Primary Variations in Product Costing

4. BOM calculation of a manufactured item's planned cost
5. BOM calculation of a manufactured item's suggested sales price
6. Order-specific BOM calculations
7. Actual costing

Use of a standard cost method requires the definition of item cost records within a costing version, as shown in Figure 5.1. Manufacturing environments typically require additional cost records associated with labor and overhead, whether they employ a standard or actual cost method. An understanding of costing versions and cost records provides the foundation for further explanation, as summarized in the following breakout box.

Summary of Costing Versions and Cost Records

Standard costing employs one or more sets of cost data (termed *Costing Versions*) that contain item cost records about each item's standard cost. A costing version typically represents a user-defined time period such as a year or a quarter. For example, three costing versions could represent the three different time periods for years 2008, 2009, and 2010. Figure 5.2 displays these three costing version examples which will be used throughout the explanation of standard costing. These examples represent some common approaches to using costing versions.[1]

---

[1] There are many creative approaches for using costing versions. For example, the user documentation describes a two-version approach to maintaining standard costs.

Identifier of Costing Version	Costing Type	Purpose of Costing Version
Std-2008	Standard Cost	Contains item cost records for 2008, plus cost records for labor and overhead formulas
Std-2009	Standard Cost	Contains item cost records for 2009, plus cost records for labor and overhead formulas
Std-2010	Standard Cost	Contains item cost records for 2010, plus cost records for labor and overhead formulas
Simulated-Cost	Planned Cost	Contains selected cost records for simulation purposes and item cost records generated by BOM calculations
Sales-Price	Planned Cost	Contains item sales price records generated by BOM calculations

Figure 5.2 Examples of Costing Versions

The concept of an annual time period is reflected in the first three costing versions displayed in Figure 5.2, all of which have a designated costing type of standard cost. In the examples within this section, we assume an implementation cutover date during 2008, so that the costing version *Std-2008* contains the initially loaded item cost records. The examples within this section also reflect time progression into late 2009, which means that the costing version *Std-2009* will contain item cost records that must be prepared beforehand, and activated on January 1, 2009.

Several aspects of a costing version only apply to manufacturing environments. For example, the costing version for *Std-2008* can also contain the cost records related to labor (termed *Cost Categories*) and overhead formulas (termed *Indirect Cost Calculation Formulas*). These cost records will be used in calculating a manufactured item's cost. The costing version *Simulated-Cost* will be used to simulate the impact of cost changes on a manufactured item's calculated cost. The costing version **Sales-Price** will contain the item sales price records that have been calculated for manufactured items.

A costing version has two blocking policies that constrain the ability to enter and activate cost records. For example, these blocking policies can help enforce a frozen standard cost after all cost records within the costing version have been entered and activated. As another example, the blocking policies for the costing version *Simulated-Costs* should allow entry of cost records, but prevent activation.

Standard Costs for Purchased Material

When using a standard cost valuation method, an item's receipts and issues are valued using the item's active standard cost. Variances capture the differences between this standard cost and the actual cost of transactions. The standard costs for a purchased item are defined by item cost records within a costing version. Each item cost record is uniquely identified by five key fields. An understanding of these key fields provides the starting point for explaining how to maintain an item's standard cost across time.

Key Fields in an Item Cost Record The standard cost for a purchased material item is defined by an item cost record within a costing version containing standard costs. The key fields and other fields in an item cost record are summarized in Figure 5.3 and explained below.

❖ *Item Identifier.* The item identifier normally consists of an item number. When the item identifier includes a configuration ID or variant code such as color and size, an item-specific policy (termed *use combination cost price*) determines whether item cost records can be maintained for the various combinations of the item identifier. Chapter 2 described the variations in item identifiers, and Chapter 4 described configurable items.

	Field	Significance of the Field
Key Fields in Item Cost Record	Item Identifier	The identifier indicates the item number
	Costing Version	The costing version can contain standard costs or planned costs; this costing type affects the calculation policies for a manufactured item's calculated cost.
	Site	A standard cost item requires an item cost record for each site that stocks the item. Transfers between sites can result in a variance when standard costs differ.
	Effective Date	Initial entry of an item cost record has a pending status and effectivity date. Activation changes the status (to active) and effectivity date (to the activation date). Activating an item's standard cost record revalues existing inventory if costs change.
	Status	An item's active standard cost record is used for valuing inventory transactions. Pending item cost records are used in BOM calculations based on effectivity date.
	Cost	An item's cost is expressed for its inventory unit of measure. A manufactured item's cost can be calculated or directly entered.
	Other Fields	Miscellaneous charges for a manufactured item reflect the calculated amount of amortized constant costs.

Figure 5.3 Key Fields in an Item Cost Record

❖ *Costing Version.* A costing version contains cost records for standard costs or planned costs, as indicated by its costing type. The costing type also affects the calculation policies for a manufactured item's calculated cost, since standard costing principles must be enforced for standard cost items.

❖ *Site.* An item's cost record must be defined for each site that stocks the standard cost item. For example, an item purchased (or manufactured) at one site and transferred to a second site will require two item cost records, one for each site. The item's cost at the transfer site can be different, such as reflecting the increased costs associated with handling and transportation. Transfers between sites when an item's standard costs differ will generate a variance (termed a *cost change* variance).

❖ *Effective Date and Status.* The two fields concerning the status and effective date (also termed the activation date or from date) work together in tandem. The initial entry of an item cost record has a pending status and pending effectivity date. Activation changes the status to active, and the effectivity date to the actual activation date.

A standard cost item can only have one active standard cost record for each site, which will be used for valuing an item's inventory transactions at the site. The concept of one active cost record applies to the item regardless of the associated standard costing version. Activating an item's standard cost record will revalue existing inventory if costs change, and generate a variance (termed a *cost revaluation* variance).

Pending item cost records are used in BOM calculations based on the effectivity date.

• *Cost.* An item's cost is expressed for its inventory unit of measure. A purchased item's cost must be directly entered, whereas a manufactured item's cost can be calculated or directly entered.

• *Other Fields.* Miscellaneous charges must be included in an item's cost when the costing version contains standard costs. The primary rationale is that the miscellaneous charges for a manufactured item reflect the calculated amount of amortized constant costs, so that ignoring the miscellaneous costs would run counter to standard costing principles.

You can enter the item cost records and activate individual pending records (using the Item Price form), or activate all pending records within a costing version (using the Activate Prices form).

Txn Seq	Txn Date	Transaction Description	Record #	Key Fields for Item Cost Record					Cost	Data Maintenance Options
				Item	Costing Version	Site	Activation Date	Status		
1	7/7/08	Initially enter item's cost	#1	Part-1	Std-2008	Site-1	9/1/08	Pending	$10	
2	9/1/08	Activate current year's costs					9/1/08 Actual	Active		
3	11/15/08	Enter Item's cost for next year	#2	Part-1	Std-2009	Site-1	1/1/09	Pending	$11	Copy costing version
4	1/1/09	Activate next year's costs					1/1/09 Actual	Active		
5	2/5/09	Enter item's cost for new site	#3	Part-1	Std-2009	Site-2	2/15/09	Pending	$12	Copy costing version
6	2/14/09	Activate costs for new site					2/14/09 Actual	Active		
7	7/18/09	Enter item's simulated cost	#4	Part-1	Simulated-Cost	Site-1	1/1/10	Pending	$14	

Figure 5.4 Maintaining Standard Costs for a Purchased Item

Maintaining Standard Costs for a Purchased Item   The maintenance of a purchased item's standard cost involves the definition of item cost records within a costing version, as described in the previous section. The data maintenance starts with the initial loading of an item's cost prior to system cutover, and subsequent updates reflect a progression through time. Typical updates and the related item cost records for a single item number (Part-1) are illustrated in Figure 5.4 and explained below. The transaction dates and effectivity dates within Figure 5.4 illustrate the impact of time progression on maintaining an item's standard.

❖ *Initially Enter and Activate an Item's Cost.* The illustrations within Figure 5.4 reflect a cutover date of 9/1/08, so that the pending cost record for Part-1 must be entered beforehand (a transaction date of 7/7/08 in this example) and activated at the time of cutover (9/1/08). This first item cost record has been defined for the costing version Std-2008 and Site-1, with a cost of $10 per unit.

The item Part-1 has a purchase price trade agreement with its preferred vendor that reflects the same $10 cost for the 2008 calendar year, plus additional information about lead time and quantity breakpoints. This trade agreement information provides the item's default price on purchase orders, and requires separate data maintenance; it cannot be used to create item cost records.

❖ *Prepare an Item's Cost for the Next Period.* The illustrations in Figure 5.4 reflect an annual update of standard costs on January 1, so that the pending cost record for Part-1 must be entered beforehand (a transaction date of 11/15/08 in this example). This second item cost record has been defined for the costing version Std-2009 and Site-1, with a cost of $11 per unit. The item cost records can be directly entered or copied from existing data, as described in the breakout box on suggestions for copying item cost records. For example, the copy process can create new item cost records with costs increased by 10%.

❖ *Activate Item Cost Records for the Next Period.* You activate the item cost records within the costing version Std-2009 on the first day of the next period (1/1/09). The cost change for Part-1 will revalue existing inventory balances resulting in a cost revaluation variance.

❖ *Enter and Activate an Item's Cost for a New Site.* The illustration in Figure 5.4 reflects a new distribution center labeled Site-2 that will carry the same items as Site-1. These items will start to be transferred after 2/15/09. This third cost record for Part-1 is entered beforehand (a transaction date of 2/5/09 in this example) for the costing version Std-2009 and Site-2, and for a cost of $12. The copy function can be used as a short-cut approach for initially creating item cost records for Site-2 from the existing data for Site-1. The item cost records are actually activated on 2/14/09.

❖ *Enter an Item's Simulated Cost for BOM Calculation Purposes.* This illustration applies to manufacturing environments, where the item Part-1 will be used as a component and its costs will be included in BOM calculations. This fourth cost record is entered for the costing version Simulated-Cost and Site-1, with a pending effectivity date of 1/1/10 and a cost of $14.

In summary, maintaining the standard cost of a purchased item involves the creation and activation of item cost records across a time progression, as illustrated by the preceding examples.

Suggestions for Copying Item Cost Records

A copy function facilitates preparation of item cost records, such as preparing the next period's standard costs or preparing for a new site. The copy function (embedded in the Copy Costing Version form) focuses on the copy-to costing version, and there are two basic options for the copy-from source. You can copy the item cost records from a specified costing version, or copy the active item cost records regardless of costing version. The item cost records can be selectively copied (such as copying selected item numbers) to populate the copy-to costing version. The item cost records can also be selectively changed. For example, you can change the costs based on a factor or amount, change the site (thereby creating cost records for another site), or change the effectivity date (thereby creating cost records applicable to a future time period). The newly created item cost records have a pending status and can be manually maintained.[2] Costs for manufactured items need to be recalculated.

Purchase Price Variances   An item's standard cost provides the basis for calculating purchase price variances at the time of purchase order receipt (reflecting the difference with the purchase order price) and invoice entry (reflecting the difference between the purchase order price and invoice price). The Deviations in Cost Price report provides a detailed history of an item's purchase price variances. You can identify the need for changing standard costs by using the Standard Cost Evaluation report, which analyzes an item's historical purchase price variances and suggests a new standard cost.

Standard Costs for Manufactured Items and BOM Calculations

Standard costs typically apply to the manufactured items and purchased components in a standard product manufacturing environment. The standard costs for a manufactured item are defined by item cost records, just like a purchased item. The key fields within an item cost record (shown in Figure 5.2) and the use of these key fields to maintain an item's standard cost across time (illustrated in Figure 5.3) also apply to manufactured items. The key difference is that a manufactured item's cost can be calculated based on bill of material information and optional routing and overhead information. This section focuses on the use of BOM calculations to determine the standard cost of a manufactured item.

Preparing Item Information for BOM Calculations   BOM calculations use item master information about purchased components and manufacturing items, as described below.

---

[2] Several restrictions apply to the copy process. First, the copy process cannot create duplicate item cost records in the copy-to costing version. Second, planned costs can only be copied to another costing version that contains planned costs; they cannot be copied to a costing version that contains standard costs. Third, the copy process does not apply to cost records for cost categories and overhead formulas.

❖ *Information about Purchased Components.* Each purchased component should have an item cost record containing its standard cost, under the assumption that standard costs apply to all components. Each component should also be assigned a calculation group and a cost group. A purchased item's calculation group (aka *BOM Calculation Group*) defines applicable warning conditions in cost roll-up calculations. For example, a BOM calculation can generate warnings about a zero cost or a zero component quantity for the purchased item.

A purchased item's calculation group serves another purpose when calculating a parent item's planned costs, since it can be used to determine the source of cost data for the component. For example, the component's cost data can reflect purchase price trade agreements.

A purchased item's cost group provides cost segmentation in the calculated costs of its parent item, as explained in the separate breakout box about using cost groups to segment a manufactured item's calculated cost. The item's cost group can also be used in the assignment of G/L account numbers for variances.

❖ *Information about Manufactured Items.* Each manufactured item should be assigned a calculation group. The calculation group defines applicable warning conditions in BOM calculations, such as the lack of an active BOM version. You should also assign a standard order quantity when a manufactured item has constant costs. The item's standard order quantity for each site acts as an accounting lot size for amortizing constant costs, such as an operation's setup costs or a component's constant quantity. A subsequent section explains the amortization of constant costs for a manufactured item.

Using Cost Groups to Segment a Manufactured Item's Calculated Cost

Cost groups provide the basis for segmenting and analyzing cost contributions in a manufactured item's calculated costs, such as the cost contributions for material, labor, and overhead. Synonyms for cost group segmentation include cost breakdown, cost decomposition, and cost classification. Cost group segmentation serves several purposes.

– Segment costs for different types of material based on the cost group assigned to purchased items. Examples include ingredients and packaging material for a frozen food product. These cost groups represent direct material costs.

- Segment costs for different types of work centers based on the cost categories assigned to the work center and its operations. Examples include different types of labor and machines, and differences in setup versus run time. These cost groups represent direct manufacturing costs.
- Segment costs for different types of overheads based on the cost groups assigned to overhead formulas. These cost groups represent indirect costs.
- Calculation of routing-related overheads that reflect incremental costs for a routing operation.

A cost group type (of direct material, direct manufacturing, or indirect) assigned to each cost group provides supplemental segmentation for reporting purposes. It also constrains the ability to assign a cost group, such as constraining the assignment of direct material cost groups to items.[3] In addition, each cost group can optionally be assigned a behavior (of fixed or variable) for reporting purposes. Information about cost group segmentation for a manufactured item's calculated cost can be viewed on the Summary BOM Inquiry form, Cost Rollup by Cost Group form, and the Variance Analysis Statement report.

The cost groups serve another purpose when calculating a suggested sales price based on a cost-plus markup approach, since profit-setting percentages can be assigned to each cost group.

Preparing Cost Categories for BOM Calculations   Cost categories only apply to manufacturing environments using routing data or to project-oriented operations. Cost categories define the hourly costs for a work center and its related routing operations, and synonyms include labor rate codes and machine rate codes. The cost categories assigned to a work center will act as default values for its operations, as previously explained in Figure 3.4. The preparation of cost category information includes the assignment of a cost group to support cost segmentation, and to support routing-related overheads in a manufactured item's calculated costs. Different cost categories will be needed to support different purposes.

---

[3] A cost group type of Undefined means that a cost group can be assigned to items, cost categories, or overhead formulas. The assignment is not constrained. As an example, a cost group that represents an outside operation could be assigned to an item (the outside operation component) and to an overhead formula.

– Assign different hourly costs by work center, such as different costs for various types of labor skills, machines, or manufacturing cells.
– Assign different hourly costs for an operation's setup and run time.
– If applicable, assign piece rates by work center, or assign costs based on the output units from a work center.
– Segment different types of direct manufacturing costs in cost calculations, such as segmentation of labor and machine costs, based on the cost group assigned to cost categories.
– Provide the basis for routing-related overhead calculations, such as an hourly overhead amount for a work center.

A cost category requires additional information when production work applies to project-related time estimates and reporting. This additional information includes the assignment of a project category group (that supports a transaction type of hours), a line property (that indicates how reported hours will be charged to a project), and the hourly costs and sales prices associated with a project. Chapter 12 explains project-oriented operations.

Each cost category has its associated cost records within a costing version, similar to the item cost records for purchased items. The cost records can reflect site-specific costs or company-wide costs. The current active cost records are used for estimating production order costs, and for calculating actual costs based on the actual time (and associated cost category) reported against a production order. The current active cost record can be in specified in a costing version for standard costs or planned costs. Figure 5.5 summarizes the key fields in the cost record for a cost category.

The key fields for a cost category's cost record are similar to those of an item cost record, but there are several differences. These differences will be highlighted using an example of a labor rate code. The labor rate can be site-specific or company-wide, the labor rate can be different for a work center's run time and setup time elements, and the current active cost record for the labor rate code applies to the estimated and actual costs on production orders (regardless of the costing version of the active cost record). There is also a slight change in handling the cost record status, where activation of a pending cost record changes its status to current active, and also changes the status of an existing record (if any) from current active to previous active.

Preparing Overhead Formulas for BOM Calculations   The definition of an overhead formula supports the calculation of a manufactured item's overheads (termed *indirect costs*). An overhead formula can calculate

Field		Significance of the Field
Key Fields in Cost Record	Identifier	The identifier indicates the cost category (e.g., labor rate code)
	Costing Version	The costing version type can be standard cost or planned cost.
	Site	The cost record for a cost category can be site-specific or company-wide.
	Effective Date	Initial entry of the cost record has a pending status and effectivity date. Activation of the cost record changes the status (to current active) and effectivity date (to the actual activation date). If an existing record has a current active status, activation changes its status to previous active.
	Status	The current active cost record (regardless of costing version) will be used for valuing the estimated and actual time on a production order. Pending cost records are used in BOM calculations based on effectivity date.
Cost		The cost represents a work center's hourly cost (for setup and run time), or its piece rate cost (for output quantity), expressed in the local currency.
Other Fields		The cost group assigned to each cost category provides the basis for segmentation of direct manufacturing costs in BOM calculations.

Figure 5.5 Key Fields in the Cost Record for a Cost Category

material-related overheads or routing-related overheads. An overhead formula specifies a surcharge percentage to calculate material-related overheads, such as applying the percentage to the value of first-level components. An overhead formula specifies a rate amount to calculate routing-related overheads, such as adding an hourly amount to the setup costs or run-time costs for an operation. Each overhead formula has a unique identifier, and it must be defined as part of the Costing Sheet Setup form. After defining the identifier, you can maintain the cost records associated with the overhead formula.

❖ *Defining an Overhead Formula Within a Costing Sheet.* Setting up the costing sheet involves defining a format for displaying cost of goods sold (COGS) information about a manufactured item or a production order. The format (termed a *costing sheet*) segments material, labor, and overhead costs based on the cost groups assigned to items, cost categories, and overhead formulas. The definition of a costing sheet format is required to support overhead formulas.

The definition of a costing sheet format employs a tree structure with nodes.[4] In an example concerning overheads, you would add a node re-

---

[4] The costing sheet format typically requires intermediate subtotals when multiple cost groups have been defined, such as aggregating multiple cost groups pertaining to material costs. In this case, you add a total node to the tree, and then add related nodes for the multiple cost groups pertaining to material costs. You assign a unique identifier to the total node and to each cost group node. The unique identifier for each cost group node is typically assigned the same value as the identifier for the associated cost group, but you can assign a different identifier.

	Overhead Formula for Material-Related Overheads
Field	Significance of the Field
Node Identifier	The identifier indicates the overhead formula for a material-related overhead.
Node Type = Surcharge	Use a surcharge percentage to calculate an item's material-related overheads.
Node Subtype = Level	The percentage applies to the value of an item's first-level components ...
Calculation Basis	..that have a specified cost group. One or more cost groups can be specified.*
Applicability Rules Per Item = Yes	Allow definition of applicability rules within the cost record of the overhead formula so that the overhead formula will only apply to a specific item or group of items.
Cost Group of Parent Node	Define the basis for cost group segmentation of the calculated overhead cost.

	Overhead Formula for Routing-Related Overheads
Node Identifier	The identifier indicates the overhead formula for a routing-related overhead.
Node Type = Rate	Use a rate amount to calculate an item's routing-related overheads.
Node Subtype = Process	The rate amount will be added to the hourly cost for operation run time ...
Calculation Basis	... when its cost category has a specified cost group.*
Applicability Rules Per Item = Yes	Allow definition of applicability rules within the cost record of the overhead formula so that the overhead formula will only apply to a specific item or group of items.
Cost Group of Parent Node	Define the basis for cost group segmentation of the calculated overhead cost.

*The cost group must be identified in the costing sheet with a separate node identifier, so that you actually specify node identifiers rather than cost groups.

Figure 5.6 Embedded Costing Sheet Policies for an Overhead Formula

flecting an indirect cost group, and then add a related surcharge node (a child node) to specify the overhead formula identifier for material-related overheads. The definition of an overhead formula includes several fields that determine its behavior. These embedded policies within the costing sheet vary slightly for material-related and routing-related overheads, as displayed in Figure 5.6 and explained below. The embedded policies cannot be changed when maintaining the cost records for an overhead formula.

An overhead formula for a material-related overhead employs a surcharge percentage, as specified by a Node Type of Surcharge in the costing sheet setup. The percentage can be applied to the value of an item's first level components that have a specified cost group. Each overhead formula has an assigned cost group. You can optionally allow definition of applicability rules within the cost records for the overhead formula, so that an overhead formula (and specified percentage) only applies to a specific manufactured item or group of items.

An overhead formula for a routing-related overhead employs a rate amount, as specified by a Node Type of Rate in the costing sheet setup. The amount can be added to the hourly cost for run time (or setup time) when the operation's cost category has a specified cost group. Each overhead formula has an assigned cost group. You can optionally allow definition of applicability rules within the cost records for the overhead formula, so that an overhead formula (and specified amount) only applies to a specific manufactured item or group of items.

❖ *Key Fields in a Cost Record for an Overhead Formula.* You can maintain the cost records for each overhead formula, such as indicating the overheads for different sites, years, and manufactured items. Figure 5.7 summarizes the key fields in the cost record for an overhead formula.

The key fields for an overhead formula's cost record share some similarities to those of an item cost record, but there are several major differences. These differences will be highlighted using an example of a surcharge percentage for a material-related overhead. For example, the surcharge percentage can be site-specific or company-wide, and vary by type of manufactured item based on applicability rules. The current active cost record for the overhead formula applies to the estimated and actual costs on production orders, and the current active cost record can be specified in a costing version for standard costs or planned costs. There is also a slight change in handling the cost record status, where activation of a pending cost record changes its status to current active, and also changes the status of an existing record (if any) from current active to previous active.

Field		Significance of the Field
	Identifier	The identifier indicates the overhead formula for (1) material-related overheads or (2) routing-related overheads, aka surcharge percentage and rate amount. *
Key Fields in Cost Record	Costing Version	The costing version type can be standard cost or planned cost.
	Site	The cost record for an overhead formula can be site-specific or company-wide.
	Effective Date	Initial entry of the cost record has a pending status and effectivity date. Activation of the cost record changes the status (to current active) and effectivity date (to the actual activation date). If an existing record has a current active status, activation changes its status to previous active.
	Status	The current active cost record (regardless of costing version) will be used for calculating estimated and actual overheads on a production order. Pending cost records are used in BOM calculations based on effectivity date.
	Applicability Rule	The overhead formula can apply to a specific manufactured item, a subset of items (based on item group), or all manufactured items.
Overhead Cost	Surcharge Percentage	The surcharge percentage is used to calculate material-related overheads.
	Rate Amount	The rate amount is used to calculate routing-related overheads.

*The identifier actually represents the user-defined Code assigned to a Node (for a Surcharge or Rate) within the Costing Sheet. The term overhead formula identifier will be used for simplicity's sake.

Figure 5.7 Key Fields in the Cost Record for an Overhead Formula

Alternative Approaches to Manufacturing Overheads

Several approaches can be used to model manufacturing overheads. The approach for material-related overheads does not require the use of routing information, which makes data maintenance less complicated and also aligns with lean accounting principles. For example, an overhead formula can apply a surcharge percentage to the total value of first-level components.

The approaches for routing-related overheads require the use of routing information, which makes data maintenance more complicated. These approaches include:

❖ *Overhead Formula for Incremental Operation Cost.* An overhead formula can define an incremental overhead cost for an operation's run time or setup time costs, or its piece rate cost.

❖ *Overheads Based on Secondary Resources for a Routing Operation.* A secondary resource can represent a work center overhead, so that overheads apply to the time requirements for the primary resource.

❖ *Overheads Based on Output Units for a Routing Operation.* In cases where overheads can be tied to output units (rather than time), the cost category assigned to an operation's output quantity can indicate the overhead amount per unit.

Performing a BOM Calculation   The BOM Calculation form is used to calculate a manufactured item's cost, and generate an associated item cost record within a costing version.[5] The BOM calculation form can optionally calculate a manufactured item's sales price and generate an associated item sales price record within a costing version. These calculations are referred to as BOM calculations; other synonyms include cost roll-up calculation and sales price calculation. The nature of BOM calculations varies slightly depending on how you initiate them. The BOM calculation form can be initiated for a single manufactured item, or for multiple items within a costing version, as summarized in Figure 5.8 and described below.

---

[5] Note: A different type of cost calculation (termed an order-specific BOM calculation) is used in the context of a sales order, sales quotation or service order line item. A separate section covers order-specific BOM calculations.

BOM Calculation Information	Performing a BOM Calculation	
	For an Item	For a Costing Version
Item Identifier	Inherited	All items or selected items or where-used items
Costing Version	User specified	Inherited
Site	Inherited from costing version policy; Or manually enter the site and calculation date (if not mandated)	
Calculation Date		
BOM Version	Inherit active version for the site; override with an approved version	Inherit active version for the site
Route Version		
Calculation Quantity	Inherit item's standard order quantity (for a site); manually override	Inherit item's standard order quantity (for a site)
Calculated Cost	Generate an item cost record for the single item	Generate an item cost record for each selected item

(Key Fields in Item Cost Record)

Figure 5.8 Performing a BOM Calculation

❖ *BOM Calculation for an Item.* BOM calculations for a single manu-factured item can be performed using the *BOM Calculation for an Item* form. As shown in the middle column of Figure 5.8, this form inherits the item number, and you specify the relevant costing version. Other information can be inherited from the costing version policies (such as the site and calculation date), from the item's active BOM and route versions for the site, and from the item's standard order quantity for the site. Figure 5.8 displays the inherited information and the ability to override the information. For example, you can override the item's active BOM version with another approved version. As another example, the costing version may represent next year's standard costs with a mandated calculation date of January 1, which cannot be overridden.

❖ *BOM Calculation for a Costing Version.* BOM calculations for multiple manufactured items can be performed using the *BOM Calculation for a Costing Version* form. As shown in the right hand column of Figure 5.8, this form inherits the costing version, and you can optionally select items and employ the where-used concept.[6] Other information can be inherited

---

[6] The concept of where-used updates is motivated by the single-level cost calculation for standard costs, since an item's recalculated cost can impact higher levels within the product structure. This impact on higher levels can also be calculated by performing the BOM calculations for all manufactured items.

from the costing version policies (such as the site and calculation date), from the item's active BOM and route versions for a site, and from the item's standard order quantity for a site. Figure 5.8 displays the inherited information and the ability to override the information. As an example, the costing version may contain costs for a specified site so that the inherited site cannot be overridden.

Policies Affecting BOM Calculations   The nature of BOM calculations varies slightly depending on whether the calculations involve a costing version for standard costs or planned costs, and the policies that can be inherited from the specified costing version. These policies are explained below.

❖ *BOM Calculation Policies for Standard Costs.* BOM calculations with standard costs must be restricted by costing version policies because the restrictions ensure standard costing principles will produce accurate, consistent results. For example, these mandated restrictions mean that cost roll-up calculations are limited to a single level (termed a single level *explosion mode*), the source of a purchased item's cost data must be from the item cost records within a costing version, and that miscellaneous charges must be included in the unit cost of an item. Miscellaneous charges for a manufactured item reflect the calculated amortization of constant costs.

❖ *BOM Calculation Policies for Planned Costs.* BOM calculations with planned costs do not have to follow standard costing principles. This means you can optionally mandate a restrictive policy in the costing version, perform multilevel cost roll-up calculations, and the source of a purchased item's cost data can be from item cost records or from another source (specified by an item's calculation group, such as purchase price trade agreements).

❖ *Other BOM Calculation Policies.* BOM calculations generate an infolog containing warning messages[7] and other types of messages. Several policies determine whether these other messages will be included in the infolog. For example, the infolog message should display the fallback information (when using the fallback principle), and indicate which items did not get updated with cost calculations (when updating calculated costs for items with missing cost records).

---

[7] The warning messages reflect the applicable warning conditions defined within the Calculation Group assigned to items (as described in Chapter 3), and you can override these warning conditions when performing a BOM calculation. For example, a warning message can indicate a zero quantity component or the lack of an active BOM version for a manufactured item.

Amortizing Constant Costs for a Manufactured Item A manufactured item's constant costs reflect operation setup times and the components with a constant quantity (or constant scrap amount). The concept of an accounting lot size is used to amortize these constant costs in BOM calculations. The item's site-specific standard order quantity (for inventory) acts as the default value for the accounting lot size; the quantity may be greater to reflect a multiple. You can manually override this default value when performing a BOM calculation for a single item, but the specified quantity only applies to the parent item. However, you can also specify a make-to-order explosion mode for planned cost BOM calculations, which means that the specified quantity will act as the accounting lot size for all manufactured components.

The calculated amount of a manufactured item's amortized constant costs is termed *miscellaneous charges*. A manufactured item's miscellaneous charges are typically displayed as two fields identifying the total amount and the accounting lot size (termed the *price unit* field), as exemplified by the displayed data on the Item form. Activating a manufactured item's cost record updates this information on the Item form. However, the Item form does not display the miscellaneous charges as part of the item's unit cost. This approach to displayed information clearly identifies the impact of an item's constant costs, but it can become confusing since the miscellaneous costs are actually included in the item's cost record.

Calculating Costs for Items with Missing Costs The concept of a *missing cost* refers to a manufactured item without a pending cost record (for the relevant key fields). For example, when you prepare item cost records within a costing version for a new period (prior to activation), a pending cost may not yet exist for an item. A missing cost typically reflects a new manufactured item, or an item that requires recalculation because the pending cost record was intentionally deleted. BOM calculations can be performed for just the items with a missing cost record, thereby supporting a net change approach to cost calculations.

When attempting to update costs for items with missing costs, it may be useful to be notified (via the infolog messages) that an item already has a pending cost record thereby preventing the desired outcome of updating the missing costs.

BOM Calculations Using the Fallback Principle The fallback principle indicates an alternative source of cost data (for a BOM calculation) when it does not exist within the specified costing version. BOM calculations for item cost records within a single costing version employ a fallback principle of none. However, several situations can benefit from BOM calculations employing a fallback principle of using another costing version or the active cost records. The following situations illustrate use of the fallback principle with standard costs.

❖ *Two-Version Approach to Maintaining Standard Costs.* A costing version can contain the incremental changes to standard costs, such as pending cost records that represent new items or cost changes. The use of separate costing versions for incremental changes is commonly termed the two-version or n-version approach to maintaining standard cost data. In this situation, the fallback principle can identify the use of the active costs contained within other costing versions (the n-version approach), or within a specified fallback costing version (the two-version approach).

❖ *Simulating the Impact of Cost Changes on Standard Costs.* A costing version that represents next year's standard costs can contain pending cost records about selected cost categories, overhead formulas, and/or purchased material. For example, the entry of pending cost records can reflect the anticipated cost changes for critical purchased components and labor rates. In this situation, the fallback principle can identify the use of the current year's costing version, and the BOM calculation can create pending cost records for all manufactured items.

Simulations about the impact of cost changes are generally performed using BOM calculations with planned costs, where the fallback principle relies on standard costs. The BOM calculations can be multilevel (rather than single level), and the costs for purchased components can be based on purchase price trade agreements (rather than item cost records).

Converting Items to a Standard Cost Method

A standard cost conversion refers to changing an item's inventory valuation method from an actual costing approach to a standard costing approach. The conversion process involves performing a prerequisite inventory close, performing several steps during a transition period (defined by a transition start date and a planned conversion date), and performing the conversion and an associated inventory close. Figure 5.9 displays the typical timeline for a standard cost conversion, and highlights the seven steps in the conversion process.

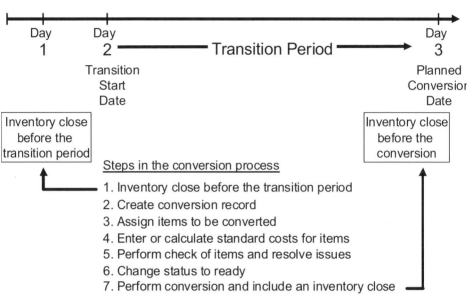

Figure 5.9 Overview of a Standard Cost Conversion

Figure 5.9 Overview of a Standard Cost Conversion

The duration of the transition period is defined by a transition start date and the planned conversion date. A transition period can be as short as a single day; Figure 5.9 illustrates a two-day transition period. The intended purpose of a transition period is to allow sufficient time to perform the seven steps (described below) in the conversion process. An item's inventory movements during the transition period are posted and valued according to the old inventory model.

Step 1: Inventory Close Before the Transition Period An inventory close must be performed before the transition period, since it settles an item's open transactions under the old valuation method. Figure 5.9 displays this inventory close on day 1. You can enter and post back-dated transactions (such as invoices) during the transition period so that you can close a prior period. The inventory close date must be one day before the transition start date, thereby ensuring a clean break with the old inventory valuation method.

Step 2: Create a Conversion Record Use the Standard Cost Conversion form to create a conversion record that also contains a user-defined identifier for a new costing version.

Step 3: Assign Items to be Converted   Identify the items that require conversion to standard cost.

Step 4: Enter or Calculate Standard Costs for Items   Enter each item's pending standard costs within the newly created costing version. An item cost record must be defined for each item and site. Use the BOM calculation to calculate a manufactured item's site-specific cost.

Step 5: Perform Check of Items and Resolve Issues   Perform a check of the selected items to identify issues that would prevent conversion, and then resolve the issues before performing another check. In terms of typical issues, an item's pending cost record must be entered for each site; an item cannot have open production orders or unposted inventory transactions; a service item cannot have a standard cost model; and the item's posting profile for the item must have a valid cost revaluation account. A separate report identifies the issues that would prevent converting the selected items to a standard cost inventory model.

Step 6: Change Status (of Conversion Record) to Ready   After the items have successfully passed the checks, you change the status (of the conversion record) to ready.

Step 7: Perform Inventory Close and Conversion   The inventory close can be included as part of performing the conversion on the planned conversion date, or performed as a separate step beforehand.

After successful completion of the conversion process, each item will have a standard cost inventory model and the item's standard costs will be activated. Subsequent inventory transactions will be valued at the item's standard cost. In addition, the system converts the item's physical inventory transactions during the transition period (for receipts and issues) to standard cost as per the conversion date. The system also converts the item's financial on-hand inventory to standard costs, and posts the value difference as an inventory revaluation variance.

You can analyze revaluation variances using the variance analysis report.

You can also analyze inventory value before and after the conversion date using the inventory value by inventory dimension report.

BOM Calculation of a Manufactured Item's Planned Cost

BOM calculations can be used to calculate a manufactured item's planned cost, where the costing version reflects a costing type of planned cost. One advantage of using planned costs is that BOM calculations can be multilevel rather than single level. A second advantage is the ability to designate the source of component cost data. There are two basic options on the source of component cost data.

-   Component costs based on item cost records within a costing version.
-   Component costs based on the source of cost data designated by the item's calculation group. In this case, the source of information can be the item's inventory cost (such as the item's actual cost or active standard cost), the item master information about the item's standard purchase price or inventory price, or the purchase price trade agreement information with the item's preferred vendor.

A BOM calculation with planned costs uses the cost records for cost categories and overhead formulas, and generates an item cost record within the specified costing version. This item cost record provides the starting point for viewing the cost calculation details, such as viewing the Complete BOM Calculation form. This item cost record provides reference information, and is typically never activated. Activating this cost record will only update the item master information about the item's inventory price.

Using the Component's Last Purchase Price in Planned Cost Calculations

The calculation of a manufactured item's planned cost can be based on the last purchase price for purchased components. As a prerequisite, each component item must have a policy to automatically update its standard purchase price with the last invoiced purchase order. This means that each purchase order invoice will automatically update the item's standard purchase price, and that the system will separately store this last purchase price. Hence, there are two different approaches for using the last purchase price in BOM calculations.

❖ *Use the Item's Standard Purchase Price as the Source of Component Cost Data in BOM Calculations.* The cost calculation group assigned to each component designates use of the standard purchase price, and BOM calculations employ the cost calculation group (rather than a costing version) as the basis for component cost data.

❖ *Copy the Item's Last Purchase Price into a Costing Version.* Using the Copy Costing Version form, you can "copy from" the stored data about the last purchase price and "copy to" a designated costing version for planned costs. The copy function creates pending *item purchase price* records within the copy-to costing version, which can be manually changed to pending *item cost* records. BOM calculations can then employ the costing version as the source of component cost data.

BOM Calculation of a Manufactured Item's Sales Price

BOM calculations can be used to calculate a manufactured item's suggested sales price based on a cost-plus markup approach or a rolled price approach.

Cost-Plus Markup Approach The markup reflects the profit-setting percentages assigned to cost groups, where a cost group has been assigned to each purchased item, cost category, and overhead formula. Each cost group can be assigned up to four sets of profit-setting percentages, labeled Standard, Profit 1, Profit 2, and Profit 3. Within the Profit 1 set, for example, a profit-setting percentage of 50% could be defined for a cost group assigned to purchased material, and a profit-setting percentage of 80% could be defined for a cost group assigned to a cost category for labor operations.

A BOM calculation generates a sales price record (rather than an item cost record) within a specified costing version.[8] The sales price record provides the starting point for viewing the calculation details, such as viewing the Complete BOM Calculation form. An item's sales price record primarily acts as reference information. However, activating an item's sales price record will update the item's standard sales price on the item master, which represents one option for an item's sales price (as previously described in Figure 2.5).

---

[8] The costing version must be able to contain item sales price records.

Rolled Price Approach   The rolled price approach only applies to a component. The BOM calculation uses the component's standard sales price (rather than its cost) to calculate the manufactured item's sales price. A policy within the calculation group assigned to an item (termed the *sales price model*) determines whether the component's sales price or cost-plus-markup will be used in a BOM calculation for a sales price.

Order-Specific BOM Calculations

An order-specific BOM calculation shares many similarities to a BOM calculation, but it reflects a different purpose and different capabilities. Figure 5.10 summarizes the major differences in terms of the primary purpose, the key outputs and inputs, and the secondary purposes. The following explanation focuses on the characteristics of an order-specific BOM calculation.

	BOM Calculation	Order-Specific BOM Calculation
Primary Purpose	Calculate the standard cost of a manufactured item or Calculate the planned cost of a manufactured item	Calculate the estimated cost and sales price of a custom product for sales order purposes
Key Outputs	Generate an item cost record within a costing version	Generate a calculation record containing the calculated cost and sales price; Transfer the calculated sales price to the order
Key Inputs	Information specified for BOM calculation Source of component's cost data within a costing version Source of labor rates and overhead formula within a costing version	Inherit information from originating sales order Source of component's cost data based on calculation code assigned to items Current active costs for labor and overheads
Secondary Purposes	Calculate an item's suggested sales price and generate an item sales price record within a costing version	Simulate an order's calculated sales price using a different set of profit percentages, a different manufacturing site, a different quantity, or a different date.
	Simulate an item's calculated cost using a set of item cost records, or using a source of component's cost data (when calculating planned costs)	

Figure 5.10 Order-Specific BOM Calculations

Primary Purpose   An order-specific BOM calculation is performed in the context of a sales order, sales quotation, or service order line item, typically for a custom product reflecting a customer specification. It calculates an estimated cost and sales price based on information for the originating line item. An order-specific BOM calculation has the exact same logic as a BOM calculation with planned costs using the items' calculation group as the source of component costs, an explosion mode of "according to BOM line type," and the current active costs as the fallback principle (for labor rates and overhead formulas).

Key Outputs   An order-specific BOM calculation generates a *Calculation Record* containing the calculated cost and sales price. It may be performed multiple times for a single order, such as simulating the calculated sales price using different sets of profit percentages, thereby generating multiple calculation records. The BOM Calculation Results form displays an item's calculation records. The sales price for a selected calculation record can be transferred to the originating line item.

An order-specific BOM calculation only applies to a sales context. It does not generate an item cost record or an item sales price record within a costing version.

Key Inputs   The key inputs for an order-specific BOM calculation initially reflect the values from the originating line item. These initial values include the ship-from site, ship date, order quantity, and the sub-BOM and sub-route (if specified). The initial values can be overridden. In particular, the site can be overridden to reflect a different manufacturing site, which may involve a different BOM version, route version, and costs for material, labor, and overhead.

The user can specify the desired set of profit-setting percentages, and an explosion mode (of multilevel or make-to-order). The explosion mode impacts the assumption of an accounting lot size for amortization of constant costs. In particular, a make-to-order explosion mode is also multilevel, and the order quantity determines the accounting lot size for all manufactured components (rather than each component's standard order quantity).

There are two critical inputs concerning an order-specific BOM calculation that differentiate it from a BOM calculation for standard costs.

❖ *Source of Component Cost Data.* The source of a component's cost data is determined by the Calculation Group assigned to each component item, such as using a component's purchase price trade agreement information.

The price agreements containing future date effectivity will be used for calculating costs for a future date. Pending item cost records within a costing version are not considered.

❖ *Costs for Labor and Overheads.* The cost calculations use the current active costs for labor and overheads. Pending cost records are not considered, so that you cannot use projected labor and overhead costs.

Secondary Purposes An order-specific BOM calculation has a few secondary purposes, such as simulations of an order's calculated sales price using different sets of profit percentages, a different manufacturing site, and a different quantity or date (which would affect usage of purchase trade agreement information). The retention of previous calculations (viewed on the BOM Calculation Results form) also supports comparisons of price.

BOM calculations have several secondary purposes, as illustrated in Figure 5.10. These secondary purposes include the calculation of an item's sales price, and simulations of an item's calculated sales price and cost.

Actual Costing

Actual costing provides different approaches for valuing an item's on-hand inventory based on periodic calculations termed *inventory closing and adjustment.*[9] An actual costing method typically applies to make-to-order or buy-to-order items, since the user can link a specific production order or purchase order to the sales order shipment, thereby identifying the item's actual cost of goods sold. An actual costing method involves several key concepts, as described below.

   – The value for an actual cost item can be entered on inventory journals for additions to inventory (such as a P/L Journal). This value initially defaults to the item's cost defined on the item master, but can be overridden. Activating an item's planned cost will update the value on the item master.

   – The anticipated cost for a manufactured item can be calculated using an order-specific BOM calculation (in a sales context), or using a BOM calculation with planned costs. This calculated cost reflects reference information, and is not used to value inventory transactions.

---

[9] The concept of continuously updating actual costs can eliminate the need for month end closing and adjustment. As an example, see **www.InventoryII.com** for more information about their add-on module for Dynamics AX.

- An item's issue transaction (such as a sales order shipment) will be valued at a running average cost as of the transaction date. The running average cost reflects the average of the financially updated transactions; it can optionally include physically updated transactions.
- The month end closing process will settle (aka *match*) the relevant receipt transactions to the issue transaction based on the item's inventory model, and adjust the item's issue transaction to the correct cost as of the closing date. The receipt transactions must be financially updated, such as an invoiced purchase receipt or an ended production order.
- The user can optionally link (aka *mark*) a specific receipt to a specific issue transaction, which will be used in month-end settlements regardless of the item's inventory model. Marking can occur before or after an issue transaction has been posted.

Dynamics AX supports several actual costing inventory models, as summarized in Figure 5.11. Each item must be assigned an inventory model group, which defines an actual cost inventory model and related policies. For example, the policy to prevent negative physical inventory should be enforced to avoid calculation problems in actual costing.

Inventory Model	Impact of Inventory Model on the Inventory Closing Process
Weighted Average	Issues will be settled against a summarized weighted average for the month
Weighted Average Date	Issues will be settled against a summarized weighted average for each day
FIFO	Issues will be settled against the newest receipts within monthly period
LIFO	Issues will be settled against the oldest receipts within monthly period
LIFO Date	Issues will be settled against the last receipts closest to the issue date
Basic Rules for all Inventory Models	An item's issues will be valued at a running average cost (as of the transaction date). The running average cost reflects the average of the financially updated transactions; it can optionally include physically updated transactions. The user can optionally link (aka mark) a specific receipt to a specific issue transaction.

Figure 5.11 Actual Costing Methods

An inventory closing is normally performed at month end. Each inventory model for actual costing has a slightly different impact on the inventory closing process, as shown in Figure 5.11. The inventory close process will settle issue transactions to receipt transactions based on the inventory model assigned to an item, and create adjustments to the value of on-hand inventory quantities based on financially updated receipts. These adjustments reflect corrections to the running average cost that was originally used to value an inventory transaction. An inventory close prevents users from posting inventory transactions to a prior period, and you can reverse a completed inventory close.

Prior to the inventory closing, you should identify open quantities (via the Open Quantities report) that reflect financial issue transactions that cannot be matched to a financial receipt. A related step identifies excessively high financial receipts that exceed an item's cost and user-specified deviation percentage (via the Investigation of Cost Price for Receipts report). You can then take action on the open quantities and deviations.

Case Studies

Case 25: Changing from Actual Costs to Standard Costs The All-and-Anything company wanted to change the inventory valuation method for several manufactured items from an actual costing approach to standard costing. As part of the seven step conversion process, the cost accountant used the Standard Cost Conversion form to create a conversion record and a new costing version. The pending standard costs for selected items were then calculated within the newly created costing version. After checking and resolving any issues, the cost accountant performed a standard cost conversion (along with an inventory close) on the planned conversion date, which updated the inventory model and activated the standard costs for the selected items.

Case 26: Calculate Item Sales Prices The Batch Process company wanted to calculate a suggested sales price for manufactured items based on a cost-plus-markup approach. The company had already been maintaining the current year's active standard costs for all items within a single costing version, and the active cost records for labor rates and overhead formulas, so that a single costing version could be used as fallback principle in BOM calculations. The sales manager defined the profit-setting percentages for cost groups associated with material, labor, and overhead, and also defined a separate costing version containing item sales price records. The sales manager then performed a BOM calculation for this costing version to calculate the suggested sales price using a specified set of profit-setting percentages. The resulting item sales price records were analyzed using the Complete BOM inquiry.

Case 27: Simulating Impact of Cost Changes   The Consumer Products company wanted to simulate the impact of cost changes on the calculated costs of manufactured items. The company had already been maintaining the active standard costs for all items within multiple costing versions, and the active cost records for labor rates and overhead formulas, so that active cost records could be used as fallback principle in BOM calculations. The cost accountant employed a separate costing version containing planned costs to define pending cost records (for selected items, labor rates, and overhead formulas) that represented the potential cost changes, and then performed a BOM calculation for this costing version to simulate the impact of these potential cost changes on the calculated costs of all manufactured items. The resulting item cost records were analyzed using the Complete BOM inquiry.

Case 28: Allocating Overheads Based on Material   The Distribution company performed final assembly of several products, and wanted to allocate overheads based on material (and avoid the use of routing information). An overhead calculation formula, for example, applied a surcharge percentage to the value of components in order to allocate overheads to these manufactured items. BOM calculations used the overhead formulas to calculate the cost of the manufactured items.

Case 29: Calculate a Sales Price for a Sales Quotation   The Equipment company wanted to calculate a manufactured item's suggested sales price for sales quotations, which could then be used to support price negotiation efforts. They wanted the calculated price to reflect a cost-plus-markup approach and the purchase price trade agreements as the source of cost data for purchased components (as defined by the cost calculation group assigned to each purchased item). As part of entering a sales quotation, an order-specific BOM calculation was performed to calculate the suggested sales price, which was then transferred to the sales quotation line item.

Case 30: Costing for Precious Metal Components   The Fabricated Products company manufactured make-to-order products from several types of precious metal components with purchase prices that could vary widely on a week-to-week basis. They wanted to immediately reflect new purchase prices of the precious metals in each product's cost and sales price. Using a standard cost approach, the standard cost of each precious metal was updated after a change in purchase price, and the manufactured items' costs (and suggested sales prices) were recalculated using BOM calculations. The cost changes revalued the existing inventory of components and products, but the company generally carried a minimum level of inventory.

Executive Summary

Product cost information supports valuation of an item's inventory transactions using a standard cost or actual cost method. Standard costs for items are maintained in a set of standard cost data (termed a costing version). Manufacturers can also maintain labor rates and overhead formulas in a set of cost data, and use BOM calculations to maintain the standard costs for manufactured items. In addition, the BOM calculations can be used for simulating projected costs or the impact of cost changes, or to calculate a suggested sales price. These simulations can optionally employ a set of planned cost data, which supports additional options in BOM calculations. As an example option, the source of cost data for purchased items can reflect purchase price trade agreement rather than the item cost records within a costing version.

With actual costing methods, an item's actual cost is not maintained in a costing version. An item's actual cost reflects financially updated receipt transactions (such as invoiced purchase orders) matched to issue transactions by an inventory closing process. For manufactured items, the actual production order costs reflect the active labor rates for routing operations and the overhead formulas, where labor rates and overhead formulas are defined in a costing version. Planned costs for manufactured items can also be calculated and maintained in a set of cost data. The BOM calculations can be used for simulating projected costs or the impact of cost changes, or to calculate a suggested sales price. With planned cost calculations, the source of cost data for purchased items can reflect their actual cost or purchase price trade agreement, or item cost records within a costing version.

An order-specific BOM calculation can be used in the context of a sales order, sales quotation or service order line item in order to calculate the estimated cost and sales price of a manufactured item, and optionally transfer the calculated sales price to the originating line item.

Several case studies illustrated product costing functionality, such as changing items from an actual cost to standard cost method, calculating item sales prices, simulating the impact of cost changes, calculating a sales price for a sales quotation, and costing for precious metal components.

Chapter 6

Sales and Operations Planning

A firm's sales and operations planning (S&OP) process starts with the definition of all demands for the firm's goods and services. It formulates *game plans* that drive supply chain activities to meet those demands. Hence, an effective S&OP game plan requires consideration of both demands and supplies. The nature of each product's game plan depends on the environment. The game plan may focus on stocked end-items in distribution and make-to-stock manufacturing environments. The game plan for a make-to-order manufactured product depends on the level of stocked components, the approach to defining product structure, and the need for direct linkage between production orders and sales orders. In this case, the game plan can be expressed as master schedules for stocked components and finishing schedules (aka final assembly schedules) for make-to-order items. Other considerations impact the nature of the game plans. For example, a multisite environment may require consideration of inventory safety stock and replenishment across a distribution network. Variations such as project-oriented and service-oriented operations also affect the game plans. The saleable products and services for many firms represent a mixture of environments.

The explanation of sales and operations planning consists of four sections about identifying demands, understanding planning calculations, common S&OP scenarios, and S&OP guidelines.

❖ *Identifying Demands*. Independent demands provide the logical starting point for formulating an S&OP game plan. The logic underlying planning calculations and demand-pull philosophies is built on chasing demands. Independent demands typically consist of sales orders or forecasts or a combination of both.

❖ *Understanding Planning Calculations*. The single term *planning calculations* refers to two tasks termed the *forecast scheduling* task and the *master scheduling* task. The forecast scheduling task calculates gross requirements based on forecasts to support long term planning of materials and capacity. The master scheduling task calculates net requirements to support day-to-day coordination of supply chain activities.

❖ *Common S&OP Scenarios*. Since the nature of an item's S&OP game plan depends on the environment, several common scenarios are used to illustrate considerations about demand and how to formulate a game plan. The scenarios represent several types of distribution and manufacturing environments.

❖ *Guidelines Concerning S&OP Game Plans*. The guidelines provide suggestions for improving the effectiveness of S&OP game plans.

An effective S&OP game plan results in fewer stock outs, shorter delivery lead times, higher on-time shipping percentages, a manageable amount of expediting, and improved customer service.

Identifying Demands

Sales orders identify actual demands. Actual demands drive all supply chain activities when visibility of the sales order backlog exceeds the cumulative lead time to obtain and ship a product. Lead time reduction efforts stemming from just-in-time philosophies can help companies produce to actual demand. However, actual demands must be anticipated in many situations such as selling a product from inventory or producing items from stocked components. One approach to stocking products in advance of sales orders involves a sales forecast, and the combination of sales forecast and sales orders defines demand for the saleable item. A second approach involves an order-point replenishment method, where the minimum quantity point represents forecasted demand over the item's lead time.

Sales Order Demand   A sales order line defines an actual demand for an item, expressed as a quantity, delivery date, and a ship-from site/warehouse. Another type of sales order—a subscription sales order for recurring sales—also defines actual demand. In addition, a sales quotation can optionally represent a demand when its probability exceeds a specified percentage. Chapter 7 provides further explanation of sales orders and sales quotations.

Sales Forecast Demand   A sales forecast defines an item's estimated demand, expressed as a quantity, date, ship-from site/warehouse, and forecast identifier. A sales forecast represents the desired inventory quantity on the specified date. A sales forecast can optionally specify an approved master BOM and routing for a manufactured item.

Each forecast entry for an item has a user-defined forecast identifier termed the *forecast model*. Using different forecast identifiers allows multiple sets of forecast data. Planning calculations are based on a specified set of forecast data. Multiple sets of forecast data often reflect various scenarios for simulation purposes, or forecast revisions based on changing market conditions. By retaining a set of forecast data, you can compare actual demand to forecast. A sales forecast for an item can also be associated with a specific customer or group of customers.

Some companies use the concept of a two-level forecast model. With a two-level forecast model, for example, the forecast identifier representing the company-wide forecast can be associated with several forecast identifiers representing regional forecasts. Each forecast entry has a forecast identifier corresponding to a regional forecast, so that the system automatically rolls up the company-wide forecast.

Several alternative methods can be used for entering forecasted demand, as described in the breakout box. For example, a repeating pattern approach can support daily projected usage rates while a group approach supports aggregate forecasts spread over multiple items based on mix percentages. In addition, forecasted demand can be manually entered or imported from another source, such as a spreadsheet or a statistical forecasting package.

Alternative Methods for Entering Forecast Data

Several alternative methods can be used as shortcuts for entering multiple forecasts for an item. These methods include a repeating pattern and a group of items, and the two methods can be used in combination.

Repeating Pattern A repeating pattern (termed an *allocation method*) results in the automatic generation of quantity and date entries, either as fixed or variable quantities per period. The repeating pattern approach can be used for forecasting an individual item or a group of items.

❖ *Fixed Quantity per Period.* The user specifies a fixed quantity, a period (such as month), and a starting and ending date. The planning calculations automatically generate a periodic sales forecast for the fixed quantity across the specified time horizon.

❖ *Variable Quantity per Period.* This method employs a user-defined template (termed a *period allocation key*) that spreads out a total quantity across several periods based on a mix percentage per period. The period allocation key, for example, could have percentages assigned to each month in a 12 month horizon, such as 5% in January, 9% in February, and so forth. This approach can be used to model a seasonal and/or trend demand pattern.

Group of Items (aka Planning Bill) A forecast can be defined for an item group rather than an individual item. This method employs a user-defined template (termed an *item allocation key*) that spreads out a total quantity across several items based on a mix percentage per item. This template is commonly called a planning bill of material, or a planning bill for short. The items must be assigned the same item group, and each template entry also defines the ship-from site/warehouse. For example, the template entries could define the mix percentages for shipping the same item from different sites/warehouses.

Handling the Combination of Actual and Estimated Sales Demand When using forecasted demand, the combination of sales orders and forecasts must be considered to avoid doubled-up requirements. Some companies manually maintain the sales forecast to correctly model the combined demand, where planning calculations do not employ any forecast consumption logic. However, the system supports two other approaches for automatically handling the combined demand. The approach to handling the combined demand is termed the *reduction principle* (also known as *forecast consumption logic*) for planning calculation purposes. The three forecast consumption approaches are described below.

❖ *No Forecast Consumption Logic.* Planning calculations add the two demands (stemming from sales forecasts and sales orders) for determining requirements. This approach applies to environments with no forecasted demand, or with a manually maintained forecast that accounts for the combined demand.

❖ *Forecast Consumption by Purchase/Sales Orders.* The forecast reduction principle of purchase/sales orders means that sales orders consume sales forecasts within each forecast period. The forecast period provides a logical time span (such as monthly) for comparing actual sales orders to sales forecasts within the period, and making assumptions about the combined demands for an item. For simplicity's sake a monthly forecast period will be used for further explanation.[1] In a given month, an item may have a single forecast or multiple forecasts; multiple forecasts typically indicate weekly, intermittent, or even daily demands that drive supply chain activities. Any sales order line item with a delivery date within the month consumes the sales forecasts within the month, starting with the earliest forecast and consuming forward. The sales forecasts within a given month can be over consumed; there is no carry-forward effect to consume forecasts within a future period. As time moves forward, an item's sales forecast becomes past due when the system date (in Dynamics AX) matches or exceeds the forecast date. Planning calculations ignore past due sales forecasts; there is no carry-forward effect within a forecast period.

It should be noted that a sales forecast can be entered for a customer or customer group, but the customer-specific forecasts are consumed by sales orders from any customer.

Sales forecasts are not consumed by sales quotations (when they are considered as demand). In environments primarily driven by sales quotations, one suggested approach would use the pipeline of sales quotations as an estimate of demand rather than sales forecasts.

❖ *Forecast Consumption Based on Reduction Percentages.* The reduction percentage approach ignores actual sales orders for forecast consumption purposes. It automatically reduces forecasts based on a user-defined template (termed a *reduction key*) of a reduction percentage by forecast period. This approach reflects the concept of a demand fence where planning calculations ignore forecasted demands within a specified time horizon from today's date, and the time horizon represents the sold-out backlog for an item. Let's say an item always has a sold-out backlog of one month and a partially sold-out backlog in the second month, so that 100% of an item's sales forecast can be ignored for the first month and 50% for the second month relative to today's date. The user defines these percent reductions in the reduction key assigned to the item, and different keys reflect the nature of a sold-out backlog for different items.

The second and third approaches to forecast consumption apply to stocked end-items and to make-to-order standard products with stocked

---

[1] A forecast period can be daily or yearly rather than monthly. For example, a daily forecast period might be used in conjunction with a daily repeating pattern, and a sales order line item only consumes a day's forecast.

components. In the latter case, the sales order backlog drives the near-term production of make-to-order items while the combination of sales forecast and sales orders (with future delivery dates) drive the procurement and production of long lead time items.

Statistical Forecasting and Demand Planner

The Demand Planner supports the development of a statistical forecast based on extracted data about an item's shipment history. It automatically determines the best fit with various statistical models to suggest a sales forecast. Projected quantities can be optionally overridden, and then used to automatically update a set of sales forecast data.

Purchase Forecast Demand A purchase forecast defines an estimated demand for a stocked component, expressed as a quantity, date, ship-to site/warehouse, and forecast identifier. A purchase forecast can optionally specify an approved master BOM and routing for a manufactured item. A purchase forecast is different from a sales forecast, and it requires consideration of forecast consumption logic to avoid doubled-up requirements. The three approaches to purchase forecast consumption are described below.

❖ *No Forecast Consumption Logic.* This approach applies to environments with no purchase forecasts, or with a manually maintained forecast that accounts for the combined demand.

❖ *Forecast Consumption by Purchase/Sales Orders.* The creation of a purchase order consumes the purchase forecast for a purchased item. In a similar fashion, the creation of a production order consumes the purchase forecast for a manufactured item. The previously described logic about the forecast period applies to a purchase forecast.

❖ *Forecast Consumption Based on Reduction Percentages.* This approach automatically reduces purchase forecasts based on a user-defined template of reduction percentages, as described above.

A purchase forecast can also be entered using an alternative method such as a repeating pattern or group of items. For example, a purchase forecast for a group of items represents a family planning approach for stocked components of a custom product. It should be noted that a purchase forecast can be entered for a specific vendor but the vendor-specific forecasts are consumed by purchase orders placed with any vendor.

Anticipating Demand Using Order Point Logic   An order-point replenishment method provides an alternative to forecasts when anticipating demand for stocked material. Order-point logic such as min/max suggests replenishment when an item's projected inventory balance falls below its minimum quantity. The minimum quantity represents estimated demand over the item's lead time. The system supports fixed or variable min/max quantities, such as variable quantities by month. In addition, the minimum quantity can be automatically calculated based on historical usage.

Anticipating Demand Variations Using Safety Stock   Many firms carry additional inventory to anticipate variations in customer demand, and meet customer service objectives regarding stockouts, partial shipments, and delivery lead times. The additional inventory is commonly called an inventory plan or safety stock. An inventory plan is typically expressed for items at the highest possible stocking level, such as saleable end-items that are purchased or manufactured to stock. A make-to-order manufacturer, on the other hand, typically expresses an inventory plan for stocked components.

An item's inventory plan can be explicitly expressed as a safety stock quantity when using a period or order-driven reorder policy. The system supports a fixed or variable safety stock quantity, and it can be calculated based on historical usage.[2] An inventory plan can also be implicitly expressed. An implicit inventory plan, for example, represents the extent to which a minimum order quantity exceeds typical demand over lead time. An order quantity multiple or maximum can also inflate the order quantity.

Other Sources of Demand   Visibility of all demands is critical to formulating effective S&OP game plans. Surprise demands can cause shortages that impact customer service or production, and result in expediting. Some sources of demand may need interpretation or alternative ways to express the demand, as illustrated in the following examples.

---

[2] The safety stock quantity (termed the *minimum quantity*) can be automatically calculated based on historical data, using either average issues during lead time or a desired service level reflecting the standard deviation. The calculation requires at least three months of historical data. The calculations are performed using the safety stock journal (also called the *item coverage journal*), as described in Chapter 2.

❖ *Customer Schedules.* Customer schedules represent a combination of sales orders (in the near-term) and forecast (in the longer term), and often require time-frame policies for proper interpretation.

❖ *Internal Sales Orders.* An internal sales order may be required to initiate production and/or procurement activities prior to obtaining the customer's purchase order. Once obtained, the designated customer can be changed on the sales order.

❖ *Customer Service Demands.* Customer service may require material for loaners, exhibition items, donations, replacement items and repairs.

❖ *Field Service Demands.* Field service may require spare parts for selling to customers, and for repair and field service projects. Chapter 14 explains service orders and the nature of field service demands.

❖ *Engineering Prototypes.* Prototypes may be built for internal or external customers, with requirements for material and production capacity. Procurement and production activity may also be initiated on new products with partially defined bills.

❖ *Quality.* Quality often requires validation lots or first articles, especially during ramp up to production lot sizes. Other quality-related demands can be embedded in planned manufacturing scrap, so that planning calculations identify the additional requirements for material and capacity.

❖ *Purchase Returns to Vendor.* Anticipated returns to vendor represent demands, as defined by return purchase orders that have not yet been posted as shipped.

❖ *Projects.* The demands associated with internal and external projects can be forecasted. An external project may also have project-specific sales orders or sales quotations, as described in Chapter 12.

Understanding Planning Calculations

The S&OP game plans can be expressed as master schedules for stocked items and a finishing (or final assembly) schedule for make-to-order manufactured items. These game plans drive coordination of supply chain activities based on planning calculations. The single term *planning calculations* refers to two major tasks termed the *forecast scheduling* task and the *master scheduling* task. Further explanation starts with the demands and supplies considered by the planning calculations. The separate tasks will then be explained, along with several guidelines for planning calculations.

Demands (Issues)	**Supplies (Receipts)**

Figure 6.1 content:

	Demands (Issues)	Supplies (Receipts)
All Environments	Sales Order Subscription Sales Order Sales Quotation	On-Hand Inventory Quarantine Inventory Purchase Order Planned Purchase Order Purchasing RFQ (Optional)
	Sales Forecast Purchase Forecast	
	Purchase Order Return to Vendor	Sales Order Return from Customer
	Transfer Order (Ship-from) Planned Transfer Order Requirement	Transfer Order (Ship-to) Planned Transfer Order Receipt
Manufacturing (Un-posted Inventory Journals)	Transfer Journal: Transfer-From Inventory Adjustment (Negative) Physical Count (Negative)	Transfer Journal: Transfer To Inventory Adjustment (Positive) Physical Count (Positive)
	Picking List Journal (Positive) BOM Journal for Component (Positive)	Picking List Journal (Negative) BOM Journal for Component (Negative) BOM Journal for Parent Item Reported-as-Finished Journal
	Component Requirement	Production Order Planned Production Order
Project	Project-Specific Forecast for Material or Time Project-Specific Sales Order Project-Specific Sales Quotation	Project-Specific Production Order Project-Specific Purchase Order

Figure 6.1 Sources of Demand and Supply

Sources of Demand and Supply

The sources of demand and supply are summarized in Figure 6.1. Some sources only apply to manufacturing or project-oriented environments. The previous section covered several sources of demand such as sales orders and sales forecasts, and how the system handles the combination of actual and estimated demand through forecast consumption logic.

The sources of demand shown in Figure 6.1 include un-posted inventory journals, component requirements stemming from production orders, and transfer order requirements. The sources of supply include on-hand inventory, quarantine inventory, and scheduled receipts reflecting purchase orders, production orders, transfer orders, and un-posted inventory journals. These sources of demand and supply are covered in future chapters, but are introduced now to understand the basics of planning calculations. Planning calculations can selectively include or exclude some of these sources of demand and supply.

Master Scheduling Task

The master scheduling task represents the primary engine for coordinating supply chain activities. As shown in Figure 6.2, the master scheduling task uses information about demands and

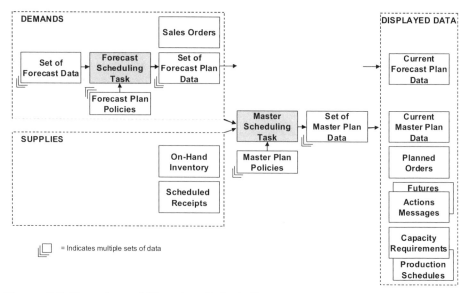

Figure 6.2 Overview of Planning Calculations

supplies and a set of master plan policies to calculate material and capacity requirements (termed a set of *master plan data* or *requirements data*). It also generates planned orders based on item planning data[3] and action messages to synchronize supply chain activities.

The master scheduling task includes finite and infinite scheduling logic for production orders, and vendor selection logic for planned purchase orders. It reflects the calendar of working hours assigned to each warehouse, customer, vendor, and work center. The master scheduling task employs a set of *master plan policies* to calculate a set of master plan data. For example, these master plan policies specify the selective consideration of demands and supplies. They specify the scheduling method and use of finite scheduling logic for planned production orders. They also indicate the selected set of forecast plan data and the forecast consumption approach.

The system supports multiple sets of master plan data and associated master plan policies for simulation purposes. The default set of displayed data reflects the company-wide policies for the current master plan and forecast plan.[4] Using this displayed data, the system helps coordinate supply chain activities through planned orders, suggested action messages, and analysis of capacity requirements.

---

[3] For more information, see the item planning data explanations for purchased items (Figure 2.2), manufactured items (Figure 3.6), and transfer items (Figure 13.4).

[4] These company-wide policies are embedded in the master planning parameters.

The master scheduling task generates suggestions about planned orders and existing orders, as previously summarized in Figure 2.4. Future chapters provide further explanation about using the suggestions for purchase orders (Chapter 8), production orders (Chapter 11), and transfer orders (Chapter 13).

Forecast Scheduling Task   The *forecast scheduling task* represents a second coordinating engine, as shown in Figure 6.2, when forecasted demands are applicable. It calculates forecasted demand (termed a set of *forecast plan data*) based on a set of policies such as a time horizon and the relevant forecast identifier. Forecast scheduling must be performed after changing forecast information so that the master scheduling task recognizes forecasted demands. Multiple sets of forecast plan data can be calculated, typically to reflect various scenarios for simulation purposes.

A set of forecast plan data represents gross requirements to support long term planning of materials and capacity, whereas a set of master plan data represents net requirements to support day-to-day supply chain coordination.

Considerations about the Master Scheduling Task   Explanations about an item's planning data (covered in Chapters 2 and 3) provided some baseline considerations for master scheduling logic. Additional considerations include the master plan policies, pegging information, realistic scheduling assumptions, vendor selection for planned purchases, and master scheduling with two sets of data.

❖ *Master Plan Policies.* The master plan policies allow the selective consideration of demands—such as forecasts and sales quotations—in planning calculations. Ignoring these demands provides one view of the minimally required activities to meet current sales orders. Other master plan policies ensure that the requirement dates associated with unrealistic sales order commitments are automatically updated based on projected completion dates. Another policy determines whether planning calculations for manufactured items with routing data are based on infinite or finite capacity planning.

❖ *Pegging Information about the Source of Demands and Supplies.* Analysis of planned orders and action messages typically requires pegging information about the source of demands and supplies. You can view single-level pegging (via a *Requirements Profile* form) and multilevel-pegging information (via an *Explosion* form).

❖ *Realistic Scheduling Assumptions for Planned Orders.* Several policies ensure that the master scheduling task generates realistic suggestions about planned orders. A realistic planned order, for example, reflects the item's lead time and a start date no earlier than today's date. A planned production order can reflect a variable lead time based on routing data, and optional consideration about finite material and capacity. When a requirement date cannot be met, the master scheduling task can suggest a projected completion date (termed a *futures* message).

❖ *Automatic Vendor Assignment for Planned Purchase Orders.* The suggested vendor for an item's planned purchase order can be based on purchase price trade agreement information, using either the lowest price or delivery lead time to suggest the vendor.

❖ *Master Scheduling with Two Sets of Data.* So far the explanations have focused on using a single set of data as the current master plan, since this is applicable to many environments. Some environments are better served by two sets of master plan data, where one set is dynamically updated by planned orders stemming from delivery promises on sales orders. The next paragraph describes this rationale in greater detail.

Considerations about Delivery Promises on Sales Orders   Realistic delivery promises for a sales order line item can be calculated during order entry using capable-to-promise logic. The delivery promise calculation generates planned orders when there are insufficient supplies for the end-item or its components. The planned orders immediately communicate the need for replenishment to meet the promised delivery date, and the order entry person can even generate actual production and purchase orders from these planned orders.

However, some sales order situations involve multiple checks of delivery promise information, and even deletion of the sales order when the customer is only asking about delivery promises or finds them unacceptable. These situations create difficulties for buyers and planners in determining appropriate actions for planned orders, especially when planned orders are constantly changing. One approach to handling this problem involves two sets of data termed the *static master plan* and *dynamic master plan.* The static master plan contains the results of the previous master scheduling task that generated suggestions about planned orders. The dynamic master plan starts with the same set of data, but is continuously updated by new sales order commitments. This approach insulates buyers and planners from planned orders stemming from delivery promise simulations. However, this approach assumes that the delayed communication of planned orders is acceptable (until the next master scheduling task generates a new set of data for the static master plan).

Common S&OP Scenarios

The nature of an S&OP game plan depends on several factors, such as the need to anticipate demand, the item's primary source of supply, and the production strategy for manufactured items. Consideration of these factors can be illustrated with several common scenarios. The first two scenarios reflect stocked end-items, while the next three scenarios reflect variations in a make-to-order production strategy. The first scenario illustrates a distribution environment with replenishment based on min/max logic, while the next four illustrate manufacturing environments employing forecasted demand. The scenarios also include a project-oriented environment and a multisite environment.

Scenario 1: Stocked End-Items Based on Min/Max   Most distribution environments carry inventory of purchased items in anticipation of actual demand, oftentimes based on min/max reordering policies. An item's minimum and maximum quantities can be fixed, or variable by time period to reflect seasonality and trends. The minimum quantity can be automatically calculated based on historical usage. This scenario focuses on min/max logic. Planning calculations suggest planned orders and action messages to coordinate supply chain activities. They also identify unrealistic situations via futures messages about the inability to meet a requirement date. Purchase orders can optionally be linked to a sales order, or drop-shipped from the supplier to the customer.

Scenario 2: Make-to-Stock Standard Product   The S&OP approach for a make-to-stock standard product is almost exactly the same as a distribution item, since it requires inventory to anticipate actual demand. Replenishment can be based on min/max logic, but this scenario focuses on using forecasted demand with forecast consumption by sales orders. As shown in Figure 6.3, demands consist of sales orders and sales forecasts. Sales orders consume sales forecast and drive shipping activities, and the combination of forecasts and sales orders drive the master schedule comprised of make-to-stock production orders.

Production and procurement activities are driven by existing and planned production orders. Planning calculations help formulate a realistic game plan by identifying potential material and capacity constraints. For example, action messages identify potential material constraints related to the end-item and its components. With scheduling based on an infinite capacity view-

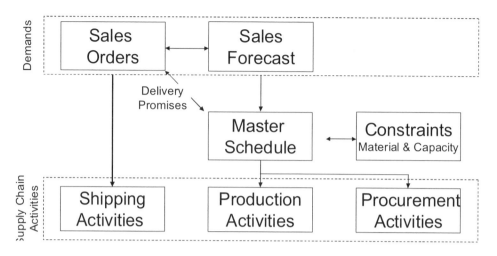

Figure 6.3 S&OP for a Make-to-Stock Manufactured Product

point, work center load analysis identifies potential capacity constraints in terms of overloaded periods. In overloaded periods, adjustments to available capacity (such as overtime and personnel transfers) or adjustments to loads (such as alternate routings) can help overcome the capacity constraint. With scheduling based on finite capacity and material, the action messages identify when delivery dates cannot be met.

Unrealistic situations in the supply chain often require changes to the master schedule or to sales orders. An analysis of an item's supplies and demands via pegging may be required to understand a situation and make the appropriate decision. The ability to make realistic delivery promises on sales orders helps ensure a realistic game plan and avoids excessive expediting.

S&OP Approaches for Make-to-Order Product

The game plan for a make-to-order manufactured item depends on the approach for anticipating demand of stocked components, the need for direct linkage between production orders and sales orders, and the approach to defining product structure.

Anticipating Demand for Stocked Components Several different approaches can be used to anticipate demand. One approach involves an order-point replenishment method for stocked components, while a second approach involves purchase forecasts. These approaches do not provide visibility of capacity requirements related to make-to-order items, nor do they take advantage of predefined bill/routing information for standard products. A third approach involves a sales forecast for end-items that drives replenishment of stocked components while sales orders drive final assembly of make-to-order items. This third approach involves consideration of forecast consumption logic to avoid doubled up requirements. A fourth approach involves sales quotations to anticipate demand, and generally requires a backlog of sales quotations to provide sufficient demand visibility.

Need for Direct Linkage   Production orders for a make-to-order product can be directly or indirectly linked to sales orders. For the end-item, the user establishes direct linkage by generating a production order from a sales order line item. The system automatically generates linked production orders for make-to-order manufactured components (when the component type is production) and linked purchase orders for buy-to-order purchased components (when the component type is vendor). Direct linkage was previously explained and illustrated in Figure 3.2.

Many make-to-order environments do not require direct linkage between production orders and sales orders, either for the end-item or for its components. Planning calculations account for indirect linkage in terms of the demand date and the scheduled receipt dates of supply orders.

Approach to Defining Product Structure   The predefined bill/routing information for a standard product represents one approach to defining product structure, as described in Chapter 3. The product structure for a custom product may be defined by option selection or a product configurator, as described in Chapter 4.

Scenario 3: Make-to-Order Standard Product with Direct Linkage
This scenario illustrates a make-to-order standard product built from stocked components. In particular, it involves sales forecasts to drive replenishment of stocked components, and direct linkage between the sales order and the production order. The make-to-order piece of equipment shown in Figure 6.4 provides an illustrative example. In this case, the equipment's predefined bill contains a make-to-order component (the base unit), a buy-to-order component (the outside operation for painting), a make-to-stock component (the extra control), and a phantom component (common parts). The predefined routing contains an operation to assemble the equipment.

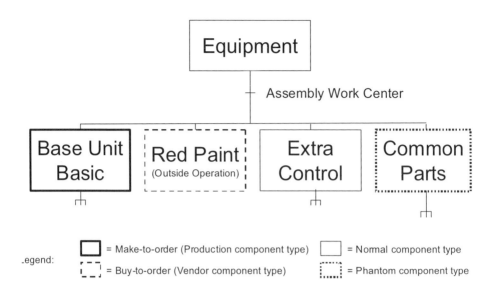

Figure 6.4 Example of a Make-to-Order Standard Product

The forecast consumption logic—via a manual, open order, or reduction percentage approach—ensures that only sales orders drive final assembly production orders. Direct linkage involves generating the production order from the sales order for the equipment. After generating the end-item's production order, the system automatically generates a linked production order for a make-to-order component and a linked purchase order for a buy-to-order component.

The sales order for a make-to-order standard product often requires a promised delivery date that reflects the bill and routing information. When calculating the promised delivery date, the user can also view the planned orders needed to meet the delivery date and optionally firm these orders. In this scenario, the S&OP game plan is expressed in terms of master schedules for stocked components and final assembly schedules (comprised of directly linked production orders) for the end-item and make-to-order components.

Scenario 4: Make-to-Order Standard Product with Indirect Linkage This scenario differs slightly from Scenario 3, since the production order for the end-item is not generated from the sales order so that it is indirectly linked to demands. The end-item's components also have a normal component type, so that the system does not generate linked production orders for the components. The critical issue involves forecast consumption logic, so that near-term sales orders drive the item's production orders and the sales forecast drives replenishment of long lead time components. With forecast consumption by sales orders or a reduction percentage, for example, the fully booked backlog of sales orders can drive near-term supply chain activities.

Scenario 5: Make-to-Order Custom Product with Component Forecasts This scenario involves a custom product built from stocked components, where replenishment of the stocked components is based on purchase forecasts. The custom product can be either a configurable item or a modeling-enabled item, where option selection automatically creates the configuration's product structure or the use of the product model automatically creates the master BOM/routing to build the custom product.

Independent demands for a custom product consist of end-item sales orders and purchase forecasts for stocked components. As shown in Figure 6.5, the purchase forecasts drive the master schedules for stocked components, whereas sales orders drive the finishing schedule for the end-item and any make-to-order components. Generating the production order from the sales order provides direct linkage between orders, and the system automatically generates linked production orders for make-to-order components.

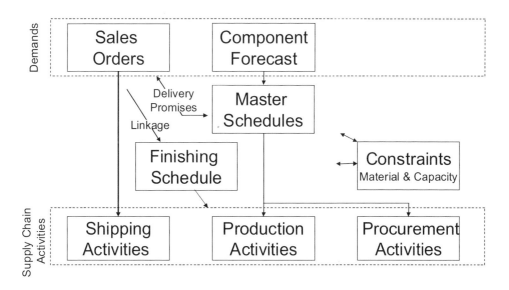

Figure 6.4 S&OP for a Make-to-Order Custom Product

Handling Partially Defined Make-to-Order Products

The definition of a product's BOM and routing information may be incomplete at the time of sales order placement. An incomplete design may reflect several conditions, such as rough quotes, evolving customer specifications, or requirements for further engineering design to specify part numbers and drawings. In many cases, procurement and production activities must be initiated for critical-path components before the design has been completed.

A basic decision must be made about the approach for maintaining the evolving product design. That is, the evolving design can be defined in terms of the master BOMs or the order-dependent bills for production orders. Planning calculations can use partially defined master BOMs and routings to help coordinate supply chain activities. A key step involves defining items for critical-path components, such as key subassemblies and long lead time purchased material, so that orders can be initiated. A critical-path manufactured item requires additional information about its bill of material. In this way, planning calculations can generate suggested action messages based on the evolving definition of product structure.

Scenario 6: Make-to-Order Product with a Backlog of Sales Quotations This scenario typically involves a custom product, where the backlog of sales quotations provides sufficient demand visibility to drive replenishment of stocked components. The purchased and manufactured components involving direct linkage will not be replenished until a sales quotation becomes a sales order, and you generate the associated production order.

Scenario 7: Project-Oriented Operation There are many variations of project-oriented environments for both internal projects and external projects, where external projects may be billed on a fixed price or a time-and-materials basis. However, a basic approach to S&OP game plans applies to all projects that involve forecasted and/or actual demands requiring coordination of supply chain activities. Chapter 12 provides more detailed explanations of project functionality, but an example will be used here to illustrate the S&OP approach.

The example involves a firm that sells and installs plumbing and electrical parts for commercial building construction sites. The external project consists of multiple subprojects reflecting the installation phases that must be scheduled to fit the dynamically changing progress of the building con-

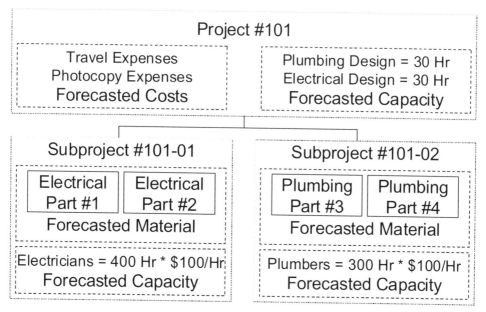

Figure 6.6 Example of a Project

struction. Each subproject has forecasted requirements for material and capacity. Figure 6.6 illustrates the forecasted requirements for two sub-projects involving electrical and plumbing installation.

This example involves two pools of skilled labor (electricians and plumbers) that are defined as work center groups, with the employees defined as work centers within each group. The parent project has forecasted capacity requirements for designing the installation, and forecasted costs for travel and photocopying. Each subproject has forecasted material and capacity requirements to perform the installation. For example, the electrical subproject has forecasted requirements for electrical parts and for the work center group of electricians.

The forecasted requirements provide visibility to coordinate supply chain activities related to capacity, material, and cash planning. Capacity planning, for example, can anticipate overloaded periods so that overtime and/or sub-contracted labor can be arranged. Changes to the construction schedule are reflected in updates to forecasted requirements. Project-specific sales orders for material consume the project-specific forecasts, and also provide a mechanism to ship materials to the site. In this case, the shipment trans-actions do not generate an invoice, since billing will be handled through project invoicing capabilities.

Scenario 8: Multisite Operation and a Distribution Network

There are two basic variations involving coordination of material movements between physical sites. One variation employs transfer orders to coordinate movements between sites in the same company, and the other variation employs intercompany orders to coordinate movements between sites in different companies. Chapter 13 provides more detailed explanations of this functionality, but an example will be used here to illustrate the S&OP approach.

The example involves a multinational firm that builds equipment in different manufacturing sites and stocks inventory at various distribution sites. As shown in Figure 6.7, manufacturing site #1 produces a base unit that must be transferred to manufacturing site #2 to produce the piece of equipment. Both sites are within the same company A so that transfer orders communicate the need for material movement. The equipment is sold to distribution site #3 within company B. After creating an intercompany purchase order in company B, the system automatically creates a corresponding sales order in company A.

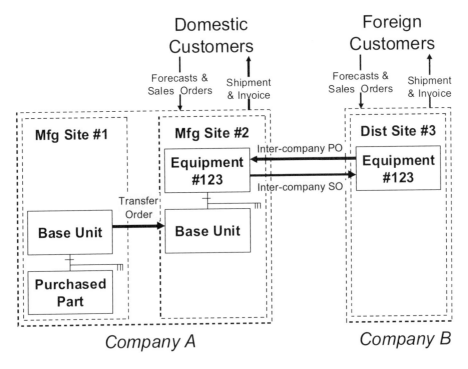

Figure 6.7 Example of a Multisite Environment

Company A sells the equipment to domestic customers while company B sells it the foreign customers. Sales forecasts for the equipment are defined for each company and site.

Guidelines Concerning S&OP Game Plans

Effective game plans lead to improved firm performance and bottom line results. Metrics include reductions in stock-outs, delivery lead time, missed shipments, partial shipments, and expediting efforts. Metrics also include improvements in customer service. The lack of effective game plans is typically cited as a leading cause of poor system implementation. The following guidelines provide suggestions for improving the effectiveness of S&OP game plans.

Minimum Planning Horizon for Each Game Plan   A saleable item's cumulative lead time represents the minimum horizon for a game plan, and additional months provide visibility for purchasing and capacity planning purposes. An additional 6 to 12 month planning horizon is typically recommended. This minimum planning horizon should be reflected in the item's time fences, such as the coverage and forecast time fences.

Reviewing and Updating Game Plans   The process for reviewing and updating each game plan should be embedded into the firm's regularly scheduled management meetings focusing on demands and supply chain activities. An agreed-upon game plan reflects a balance of conflicting objectives related to various functional areas, such as sales, engineering, manufacturing, purchasing, and accounting. Periodic revisions to game plans should be reflected in updated forecasts and promised delivery dates.

Primary Responsibility for Maintaining Game Plans   The person(s) acting as a master scheduler maintains the game plans and obtains management agreement. This role typically requires an in-depth understanding of sales and supply chain capabilities, as well as the political power to achieve agreed-upon game plans. The responsibility for providing sales order and forecast data typically belongs to the sales function, with a hand-off to the master scheduler. The primary responsibility for game plans should be reflected in the planner (and buyer) responsibility assigned to items.

Formulating Realistic Game Plans   Realistic game plans require identification of capacity and material exceptions that would constrain the plans, and then eliminating the constraints or changing the plan. Identification of material-related exceptions typically starts with suggested actions, while capacity exceptions are identified using work center load analysis. In many cases, a realistic game plan must anticipate demands and demand variations via forecasts and inventory plans for stocked material. Finite scheduling can also contribute to a realistic game plan.

Enforcing Near-Term Schedule Stability   Near-term schedule stability provides one solution for resolving many conflicting objectives, such as improving competitive efficiencies in purchasing and production and reducing exceptions requiring expediting. It provides a stable target for coordinating supply chain activities and removes most alibis for missed schedules. Near-term schedule stability can benefit from inventory plans and realistic order promises about shipment dates. It involves a basic trade-off with objectives requiring fast response time and frequent schedule changes. The critical issue is that management recognizes the trade-offs to minimize near-term changes. An item's freeze time fence represents one approach to support near-term schedule stability, since planning calculations do not suggest planned orders during the frozen period.

Making and Maintaining Realistic Sales Order Promises   Realistic delivery promises represent the key link between sales commitments and supply chain activities. The system supports delivery promises during order entry, and also through planning calculations that suggest delayed delivery based on projected completion dates. A critical issue is to reduce and isolate the number of sales order exceptions requiring expediting. One solution approach for meeting a delivery promise involves splitting delivery across two sales order line items with different shipment dates.

Executing Supply Chain Activities to Plan   Planning calculations make an underlying assumption that everyone works to plan, and the system provides coordination tools to communicate needed action. For example, it is assumed that procurement will ensure timely delivery of purchased material so that manufacturing can meet production schedules. It is assumed distribution will make on-time shipments because sales made valid delivery promises and procurement and production are working to plan. An unmanageable number of exceptions will impact this underlying assumption and the usefulness of coordination tools.

Reducing Exceptions That Require Expediting   The intent of near-term schedule stability, valid delivery promises and shipment dates, realistic game plans, and executing to plan is to reduce the number of exceptions to a manageable level. This improves the usefulness of coordination tools to meet the game plans.

Business Analytics and S&OP

The S&OP process translates business plans (expressed in dollars) into sales, production, and inventory plans (expressed in units), and requires management information about planned and actual results for each game plan. Business analytics—also known as business intelligence, data warehouses, and executive information systems—gives us one way to provide this management information in dollars and units. The data reflects summarized information with drill-down to more detail. The results are presented in a variety of formats—ranging from lists and tables to graphs and charts—for financial and operational metrics. For example, the set of sales forecast data provides the basis for planned sales while shipment history defines actual sales. Business analytics can also highlight key performance indicators about operational metrics, such as on-time shipping percentages, production performance, and vendor performance.

Case Studies

Case 31: S&OP Simulations   The All-and-Anything company required simulations to assess the impact of changing demands and supplies. Using multiple sets of forecast data to represent various scenarios, and a designated set of forecast data for planning calculation purposes, the management team could analyze the impact of changing demands on material and capacity requirements. For example, the planning calculations were first performed using infinite capacity planning to anticipate overloaded periods. After adjusting available capacity and consideration of alternate routings, the planning calculations were performed again using finite capacity and material to highlight unrealistic delivery dates.

Case 32:   Aggregate Forecasts by Item Group   The All-and-Anything company had thousands of stocked end-items, and wanted to minimize the effort to maintain forecasts for individual items. Items were grouped together for forecasting purposes, with a mix percentage assigned to each item, so that aggregate forecasts could be entered for each group of items. This approach reduced the number of forecasts to be maintained, from thousands of individual items to a few dozen groups.

Case 33: Common Component Forecast for Process Manufacturing   One product line within the Batch Process Manufacturing firm consisted of many end-items built to order from a common manufactured item. The bill of material for each end-item identified the common manufactured item and packaging components such as labels and bottles. In this case, the S&OP game plans for packaging components were expressed in terms of min/max quantities, while a purchase forecast was defined for the common manufactured item.

Case 34: Kanban Coordination in Consumer Products Manufacturing   The Consumer Products company was using a dedicated manufacturing cell for producing one product line. The cell's daily production rate (representing the mix of all items produced by the cell) provided the basis for daily rates for end-items and components, which were then used to calculate Kanban quantities and automatically generate Kanban cards for manufactured items.[5] Purchased components were kept in floor stock bin locations with bin replenishment based on electronic Kanbans to suppliers. They used an order-less approach to reporting production output with auto-deduction of component materials.

Case 35: S&OP Process Improvements   The Consumer Products company wanted to improve their sales and operations planning process using a collaborative planning tool. This tool enabled them to view past performance and time-phased projections of forecasts, bookings, orders, shipments, production plans and inventory levels. It supported what-if analyses in terms of unit volume, revenue and profits. It also provided structure to their S&OP process, such as tracking action items and measuring progress toward operational excellence.[6]

---

[5] See **www.eBECS.com** for additional information about their Lean Enterprise product for Dynamics AX. See **www.agilitybiz.net** for additional information about their Electronic Kanban product for Dynamics AX.

[6] See **www.oliverwight.com** for additional information about their sales and operations planning tool.

Case 36: Statistical Forecasting   The Distribution company used statistical forecasting to calculate future sales demand in monthly increments based on historical data. This required historical data about previous months (prior to cutover to Microsoft Dynamics AX). In addition to shipments, the historical data included customer returns, credit memos, and selected inventory adjustments. Further refinements included the requested shipment date (to give a true picture of demand patterns) in addition to the promised ship date. Statistical forecast information was also needed to drive purchase forecasts for stocked components, where the historical data reflected transaction history about usage rather than shipments.

Case 37: Planning Bills for Make-to-Order Custom Equipment
The Equipment company currently forecasts a group of stocked components for a configurable equipment item. Several customizations were being considered to extend the concept of planning bills. One customization involved adding a mix percentage field to each component in the bill of options for a configurable item. A second customization involved planning calculations so that forecasts for a configurable item would be exploded through the bill of options (and though the phantom, production, and vendor component types) to create purchase forecasts for normal component types. This planning bill approach would simplify the forecasting process, recognize planned changes in bills and routings, provide visibility of capacity requirements, and result in matched sets of stocked components.

Case 38: Manual Master Scheduling for Medical Devices   The Equipment company produced a line of medical devices that required a manually maintained master schedule to reflect the planner's decision-making logic about production constraints. The medical devices required an expensive outside operation for sterilizing a batch of multiple end-items. The scheduling considerations included a cost-benefit analysis about amortizing the fixed fee for sterilization over the largest possible batch weight subject to a batch weight maximum, while still building the product mix for customer demands and avoiding excess inventory. A manually maintained master schedule proved most effective for this case.

Case 39: Manual Forecast Consumption and Make-to-Order Products   The Fabricated Products company produced several standard products (such as wire harnesses and printed circuit boards) on a contract manufacturing basis for large customers. They only produced end-items to actual customer demand. The limited forward visibility of these sales orders meant that sales forecasts were used to drive replenishment of long lead time materials. The master scheduler avoided any confusion in forecast consumption logic by using a manual forecast consumption policy. He developed sales forecasts in a spreadsheet based on close coordination with the customers, and periodically imported the data as a "drop in forecast."

Case 40: S&OP for One-Time Products The Fabricated Products company designed, quoted, and built hundreds of one-time products to customer specifications. They used configurable items to model one-level and two-level custom products, and to define the unique bill and routing for each configuration. This detailed information provided the basis for calculating estimated costs and a suggested sales price for sales quotations. The sales quotation backlog was used as part of the S&OP game plans to anticipate material and capacity requirements.

Executive Summary

The ability to run the company from the top requires a sales and operations planning (S&OP) process that formulates an S&OP game plan for each saleable product. The nature of each game plan depends on several factors such as the visibility of demands, delivery lead time, and a make-to-stock versus make-to-order production strategy. The starting point for each game plan requires identification of all sources of demand such as sales orders and forecasts, and forecast consumption logic determines how the combination of these demands will drive supply chain activities. Planning calculations help formulate and analyze S&OP game plans, especially in using multiple sets of data for simulation purposes. Several scenarios illustrated how to formulate game plans for a distribution product and several types of manufactured products, as well as project-oriented and multisite environments. Special cases included a partially defined make-to-order product. Guidelines were suggested to improve S&OP game plans, such as how to formulate realistic game plans, enforce near-term schedule stability, and make realistic delivery promises. The case studies highlighted variations in S&OP game plans, such as S&OP simulations, Kanban coordination, planning bills, and statistical forecasting.

Chapter 7

Sales Order Processing

Sales orders capture demands for the firm's products and services. Sales orders comprise a key element in two larger contexts: the sales and operations (S&OP) game plan driving supply chain activities, and customer service across the customer relationship life cycle. The sales order often represents one step in the customer relationship, and may involve collaborative work in the sales channel as well as the supply chain.

Distributors and manufacturers focus on sales orders for material items. These orders may originate from one or more order streams, such as direct customer communication with order entry personnel, telemarketing, sales representatives, web-placed orders, and electronically transmitted customer schedules. Variations in sales orders can be expressed for individual line items, such as a direct delivery purchased item, or the configuration of a manufactured item. However, the basic structure of a sales order remains the same regardless of order stream and variation.

Information about customers and sales trade agreements provide the starting point for explaining sales order processing. The explanation of sales orders covers the variations for distribution and manufacturing environments, sales quotations, customer self service, returned items, and sales analysis. These topics are reflected in the following sections within the chapter.

1. Customer information
2. Sales prices and trade agreements
3. Sales orders
4. Sales order considerations
5. Sales order variations for manufacturers and distributors
6. Sales quotations
7. Customer self-service and the enterprise portal
8. Posting a sales order shipment and invoice
9. Customer returns and RMAs
10. Sales analysis

Customer Information

A subset of customer information directly relates to sales order processing, while other customer information such as contacts relates to other steps in the customer relationship. Each customer is defined in a customer master file by a unique identifier. Sold-to and bill-to customers require unique identifiers.[1] The customer master file defines information for sales order processing and other purposes such as sales analysis and accounting. Several data elements have particular significance to sales order management.

Preferred Ship-From Site/Warehouse   Each sold-to customer can have a preferred ship-from site/warehouse which acts as the default value in sales order header information.

Ship-to Addresses   A sold-to customer can have one or more addresses for delivery purposes, and a delivery address can be assigned to each sales order line item. When defining additional addresses, the user can designate one as the default delivery address and others as alternates. During sales order entry, the system displays the default delivery address but the user can select (transfer) an alternate to the order or create an order-specific delivery address. The user can optionally designate (move) the order-specific delivery address as customer master information.

Bill-To Customer and Invoicing Considerations   Each customer can optionally have a designated bill-to customer (termed the *invoice account customer*) that acts as a default on sales orders. The system supports a customer-specific numbering sequence for invoices. An invoice can be generated for each sales order or for multiple orders (e.g., with the same bill-to customer and currency) as a summary invoice.

Attributes Related to Pricing and Discounts   The sold-to customer determines applicable pricing and discounts for a sales order. Sales prices in trade agreements can be based on the *price group* assigned to the sold-to customer. Discounts in trade agreements can be based on three other groups

---

[1] The concept of a sold-to and a bill-to customer represents a basic viewpoint representative of many situations. The sold-to customer determines the applicable sales trade agreements, whereas the bill-to customer determines the applicable credit management policies. Each sold-to customer can have multiple delivery address (ship-to) locations, which determine the applicable sales taxes. More complex situations often require additional information, such as the corporate entity associated with various sold-to customers, or the end-user associated with a delivery address.

assigned to the sold-to customer—the *line discount, multiline discount*, and *total discount*.

Attributes Related to G/L Account Number Assignment

General ledger (G/L) account number assignments (such as revenue and cost of sales) are based on a combination of customer and item characteristics. For example, the revenue account can reflect sales based on customer group and item group.

Financial Dimensions for a Customer

The financial dimension(s) assigned to a customer provide a means to analyze sales by customer type. It can be used in conjunction with financial dimensions assigned to other entities, such as items, sales campaigns, and sales persons, to provide multi-dimensional sales analyses.

One-time Customers and Creating Customers During Order Entry

When initially entering a sales order, the sold-to customer can be created on the fly by indicating a one-time customer. The user enters the customer name and address information as part of creating the sales order, and the system automatically creates a new customer that is flagged as a one-time customer. Additional information defaults from an existing customer designated as the source of one-time customer information. The customer information can then be manually maintained, including the removal of the one-time customer flag.

Customer Hold Status

A customer hold status (termed the *stopped* flag) can prevent all transactions from being recorded, or prevent shipments to the customer. In addition, a stopped flag can be assigned to a sales order line item to prevent further transactions against the line item.

Language for a Customer

The language assigned to each customer determines which language version should be displayed on printed documents and other customer interactions. For example, the assigned language determines the language version for an item description on a printed packing slip or invoice.

Intercompany Trading Partner

Some enterprises have multiple companies defined within a single Dynamics AX instance, and trading between the companies. A sister company can act as a customer (or vendor) for intercompany trading purposes. The sister company must be set up as an end-point (in the Application Integration Framework) and associated with the relevant customer number Chapter 13 explains the setup information for intercompany orders and several scenarios for intercompany trading.

Customer Calendar of Work Days   Assigning a calendar to a customer and related delivery addresses enables delivery dates to reflect the available hours of operation (when using the delivery date control capabilities). The delivery dates are based on the company-wide calendar when a customer calendar is not specified.

Credit Management Policies   The bill-to customer can have no require-ment for a credit check, or a mandatory credit limit check with an associated credit limit amount. A company-wide policy (embedded in the A/R param-eters) defines the basis for credit limit comparisons, such as the customer's current balance, shipments not yet invoiced, and open sales orders. The user can check credit limit information during order entry, and the system prevents further transactions such as confirmations and shipments when the credit limit has been exceeded. A periodic task enforces a credit limit consistency check on open orders when the user changes the basis for credit limit comparisons.

Summarized Information   Summarized information about a customer can be viewed in several ways. A customer's statistics inquiry provides summarized data by monthly increments, such as the number and value of invoices and payments. Transaction detail can also be viewed by type of sales document, such as outstanding quotes, sales orders, and return orders.

Sales Prices and Trade Agreements

An item's sales price can be defined several different ways, as previously summarized in Figure 2.5. As one of these approaches, a sales trade agree-ment represents predefined information for selling products to customers, such as published list prices and/or discount schemes. An item's price and discount can be manually entered on a sales order, but trade agreements support automatic entry. There are several types of sales trade agreements that identify the sales price, line discount, multiline discount, and/or total discount. The different types can be used in combination with each other, such as defining the sales price and a discount. These trade agreements involve several considerations.

- Trade agreements for an item's sales prices and line discounts can represent either company-wide or site/warehouse-specific information, based on an item-related policy (embedded in the dimension group assigned to the item).
- The sales price trade agreement defines both a price and delivery lead time. Hence, a higher price may apply for faster delivery, or the delivery lead time could vary by ship-from site/warehouse.
- The sales price trade agreement optionally defines a miscellaneous charge, such as a surcharge for small order quantities or expedited delivery lead time. It is included in the net amount but not in the unit price for the item.

An additional consideration involves the system logic when there are multiple trade agreement entries that apply to a situation. Each trade agreement entry can optionally specify whether the system should search for other applicable entries. This concept of searching for applicable entries varies between sales price and discount trade agreements as described below.

- With sales price trade agreements, the system normally uses the most specific entry for price, such as using an item-specific price rather than a group-related price. With searching enabled, the system finds the lowest applicable price when multiple entries exist.
- With discount agreements, the system normally uses the most specific entry for the discount, such as using a customer-specific discount rather than a group-related discount. With searching enabled, the system uses all of the applicable discounts when multiple entries exist. For example, the system adds multiple line discounts together when multiple entries exist.

Sales Price Trade Agreement   A sales price trade agreement typically represents a company's predefined price book or the negotiated prices with a specific customer. Item pricing typically reflects one or more of the factors shown in Figure 7.1 and illustrated below.[2]

- Pricing by item and unit of measure, such as different prices per piece and per dozen.

---

[2] A set of company-wide policies (embedded in the *Activate Price/Discount* form within A/R setup) determines whether the system recognizes these factors.

Factor		Sales Price	Types of Discounts		
			Line Discount	Multiline Discount	Total Discount
Item	Item and UM	X	X		See item policy about Including item value
	Group of Items	N/A	X Line Discount Group*	X Multiline Discount Group*	N/A
	All Items		X	X	
Sold-to Customer	Customer	X	X	X	X
	Group of Customers	X Price Group	X Line Discount Group	X Multiline Discount Group	X Total Discount Group
	All Customers	X	X	X	X
Other Factors	Date Effectivity	X	X	X	X
	Currency Code	X	X	X	X
	Quantity Breakpoints	X	X	X	Order Value Breakpoint
	Delivery Days	X	N/A		
	Misc Charges	X			
	Policies	Price Group Policy: Price Includes Sales Tax			Item Policy: Include item value for total discount purposes

Note: Site or Warehouse-Specific Information / Company-Wide Information; N/A for Multiline Discount and Total Discount (site/warehouse-specific).

Figure 7.1 Sales Trade Agreements

- Pricing for a single customer, all customers, or a group of customers. The customer groups, for example, could represent wholesalers and retailers.
- Pricing by currency type, such as separate pricing for foreign sales.
- Pricing with date effectivities, for supporting annual price updates or seasonal price promotions. Price assignment reflects the order date on a sales order.
- Pricing with quantity breakpoints.
- Pricing based on delivery days.
- Pricing involves an additional miscellaneous charge, such as a charge for fast delivery, small order quantity, or freight.

Price trade agreements are expressed as one or more entries that identify the applicable factors. A simple pricing scheme that represents this year's list price, for example, would be expressed as one entry for each saleable item. Additional entries would be required for expressing prices based on a customer group, or for indicating other factors such as the effectivity dates and quantity breakpoints. Additional entries are also required for each site/warehouse when using site- or warehouse-specific pricing. Figure 7.1

illustrates the site/warehouse factor as a third dimension, since pricing can be company-wide or site/warehouse-specific.

Each entry within a sales price trade agreement requires a price and a price unit. Pricing reflects a specified UM and is normally expressed per unit, unless pricing must be expressed with more than two decimal places (such as expressing $.00123 as $1.23 per 1000 units). Each entry can optionally define a delivery lead time and miscellaneous charge.

During sales order entry, the system uses the trade agreement information to automatically assign an item's price using the lowest price of applicable trade agreement entries. The system also assigns the delivery lead time and miscellaneous charge associated with the price. The user can view available prices during order entry, such as viewing quantity breakpoints or future pricing to guide customer decisions.

Types of Sales Discounts in Trade Agreements   The types of sales discounts can be related to a single line item, multiple lines, the order total value, or a combination of these approaches.

❖ *Line Discount.* The line discount is expressed as a fixed amount or a percentage or both. In particular, the percentage discount can be expressed as a single value or as two values (e.g., using a 10% discount for both values results in a 19% discount). In the case where both a fixed amount and a percentage discount are applied, the system applies the discount percentage after reducing the price by the fixed discount amount. Line discounts often reflect one or more of the factors shown in Figure 7.1 and illustrated below.

  ○ Discounts for a single item, all items, or a group of items (based on the *Line Discount Group* assigned to relevant items). For example, the groups could represent different product lines.

  ○ Discounts for a single customer, all customers, or a group of customers (based on the *Line Discount Group* assigned to relevant customers). For example, the groups could represent large and small accounts, and the group code on a sales order defaults from the customer.

  ○ Discounts based on date effectivities, currency code (for foreign sales), and quantity breakpoints.

  A simple discount scheme involving a discount percent by customer group, for example, would require one trade agreement entry for each customer group. Note that a line discount can be company-wide or site/warehouse-specific, as shown in Figure 7.1.

❖ *Multiline Discount Based on Total Quantity.* The multiline discount reflects a discount based on total quantity for multiple line items. It is expressed the same way as a single line discount: as a fixed amount or a percentage or both. The trade agreement entries can reflect the factors shown in Figure 7.1, such as a discount that applies to a group of customers or a group of items. Two different group codes (both termed the *Multiline Discount Group*) can be predefined—one for items and one for customers—and then assigned to relevant items and customers. As shown in Figure 7.1, a multiline discount only reflects company-wide information, and can only be defined for a group of items or all items. The user must initiate calculation of multiline discounts on a sales order after all line items have been entered.

The combination of a line discount and multi-line discount can be handled different ways, as defined by a company-wide policy (embedded in the A/R parameters). A typical approach views the two values as additive. An alternative approach views the two percentages as multiplicative, or indicates use of the lowest value or highest value, or indicates use of only one of the values.

❖ *Discount (or Surcharge) Based on Total Order Value.* The total discount reflects a discount based on total order value. It is expressed the same way as a single line discount: as a fixed amount or a percentage or both. Expressing the fixed amount as a negative value represents a surcharge based on total order value. The trade agreement entries can reflect the factors shown in Figure 7.1, such as a discount with order value breakpoints that apply to a group of customers. Note that a different group code—the *Total Discount Group*—can be assigned to relevant customers. An item-related policy determines whether the system includes or excludes the item in calculating total order value. The user must initiate the calculation of the total discount on a sales order after all line items have been entered.[3]

Maintaining and Viewing Sales Trade Agreement Information

Information about sales trade agreements can be maintained directly on the relevant form (such as the sales price trade agreement form), or it can be prepared beforehand and then used to update trade agreement information.

---

[3] Alternatively, the total discount can be automatically calculated (based on a company-wide policy embedded in the A/R parameters).

❖ *Directly Maintain Trade Agreement Data.* You can directly maintain the sales trade agreement information by accessing it from the item, customer, or sales order forms, or from the group forms related to a line discount, multiline discount, or total discount group.

❖ *Prepare Data Beforehand.* Preparing data beforehand (using the Price/Discount Agreement Journal and its associated line items) offers several advantages in data maintenance. For example, you can create a new journal for preparing next year's sales price trade agreements, and then initially populate the entries with information about existing sales price agreements for selected items or customers. The information can then be manually maintained prior to posting the journal. In addition, you can perform mass changes to the entries (such as increasing the sales price a specified percentage or amount), or copy the entries in order to prepare price agreements for another item, customer, validity period, or currency.

Use the Sales Prices report to view sales price trade agreement information, or a subset of information based on the report's selection criteria (such as the selected items, customers, or currency). Use the Price/Discount List report to view all types of price and discount trade agreement information. Use the Price List report to view a comprehensive list of item sales prices, or the Customer Price List report to view the comprehensive list for each customer. Each report has selection criteria to view a subset of information.

Agreements about Supplementary Items   Some sales environments involve predefined agreements about supplementary items such as "buy ten and get an additional item free" which result in additional line items on a sales order. Supplementary items can also represent related items that should be sold together, or opportunities for up-selling or cross-selling. A supplementary sales item and quantity can be designated as mandatory or optional, and chargeable or free-of-charge. The rules may also include date effectivities, a minimum order quantity, and/or a one-time-only offer. The supplementary item can be tied to the sale of a specific item. Alternatively, it can be tied to one or more of the factors shown in Figure 7.2, such as the item group or customer group. Two different group codes (both termed the *Supplementary Item Group*) must be predefined—one for items and one for customers—and then assigned to relevant items and customers.

During the process of entering sales order line items, the user initiates a calculation that displays the applicable supplementary items. The items are

	Factor	Supplementary Item and Quantity	
		For Sales Purposes	**For Purchase Purposes**
Item	Item	X	X
	Group of Items	X Supplementary Item Group	X Supplementary Item Group
	All Items	X	X
Customer or Vendor	Single Partner	X	X
	Group of Partners	X Supplementary Item Group	X Supplementary Item Group
	All Partners	X	X
Other	Date Effectivity	X	X
	Order Quantity Minimum	X	X
Rules	Mandatory vs Optional	X	X
	Chargeable vs Free-of-charge	X	X
	One-time Offer vs Ongoing Offer	X	X
	Multiple freebies for large order qty	X	X

Figure 7.2 Supplementary Items

segmented into mandatory and optional (with user selection of the optional items), and acceptance results in additional sales order line items. For example, viewing and selecting the optional items can provide the basis for selling related products.

Agreements about Miscellaneous Charges Some sales environments involve predefined agreements about miscellaneous charges, such as handling charges for selected items or customers. These charges can be embedded in the sales price trade agreement information, or they can be specified separately as *auto-miscellaneous charges*. These auto-miscellaneous charges can be applied to an entire sales order or to individual line items, and expressed as a fixed amount, an amount per piece, or a percentage of value.

❖ *Order-Level Charges.* Charges related to the entire sales order can be defined for a single customer, all customers, or a group of customers (identified by the *Miscellaneous Charges Group* assigned to relevant customers). Examples of an order-level charge include order preparation costs for selected customers.

❖ *Line Item Charges.* Charges related to the sales order line item can be defined by customer and item, such as charges for a single item, all items, or a group of items (identified by the miscellaneous charges group assigned to relevant items).[4] Examples of a line item charge include a setup fee for producing selected items for a customer.

Sales Orders

Sales orders define demands and drive supply chain activities for material items. The basic structure of a sales order consists of header and line item information. As a reflection of this basic structure, the sales order number and line number uniquely identify a scheduled shipment. The sales order header identifies the sold-to customer, and optionally identifies a different customer for bill-to purposes. This customer information provides default values for the sales order header (such as the preferred ship-from site/warehouse). In a similar fashion, header information provides several default values when adding line items (such as the delivery date and delivery address). A delivery address can be assigned to each line item. Changes to header information can optionally mass-update line item information, with a prompt to confirm that mass update.

Sales Order Life Cycle   The life cycle of a sales order consists of four steps represented by an order status automatically updated by the system.

❖ *Open.* An open status indicates the order has been created.
❖ *Delivered.* All order lines have a delivered status.
❖ *Invoiced.* All order lines have an invoiced status. The significance of an invoiced status reflects several company-wide policies (embedded in the A/R parameters). For example, the policies determine whether the system allows changes to a fully invoiced order, whether the system automatically deletes a fully invoiced order, and whether the system retains information about deleted orders as part of the voided order history.

---

[4] Two policies (embedded within the A/R parameters) indicate whether the system recognizes auto-miscellaneous charges for the entire order and for line items.

❖ *Cancelled.* This only applies to a returned items order, where all order lines have been returned and a credit note generated.

An additional field (termed *document status*) indicates the last document printed for the sales order. The posting function is used to print a sales order document, including an order confirmation, picking list, a pro forma packing slip, and a pro forma invoice. It is also used to indicate shipment (termed *packing slip update*) and generate an invoice, and optionally print the associated documents.

Sales Order Line Item Life Cycle The life cycle of a sales order line consists of three steps represented by a line status automatically updated by the system.

❖ *Open.* An open status indicates the line has been created, and partial shipment or invoicing may have occurred.
❖ *Delivered.* The delivered quantity equals the order quantity. When using delivery tolerances, the delivered quantity can exceed the order quantity or the under-delivery can be flagged as closed during the posting process.
❖ *Invoiced.* The line item quantity has been completely invoiced, taking into account the over- or under-delivery considerations mentioned above. The significance of an invoiced status reflects the company-wide policies (embedded in the A/R parameters) about automatic deletion of a fully invoiced line item and whether the system retains information about deleted line items as part of the voided order history.

Over- and under-delivery delivery tolerances are expressed as a percentage, and the values assigned to an item act as defaults for the sales order line item.[5] However, a line item can be flagged as *ship complete* so that the system only allows delivery and invoice transactions that exactly match the order quantity. A line item can also be flagged as stopped to prevent any transactions, but this does not affect requirement calculations.

Historical Data Retention Information about line items and/or sales orders with an invoiced status can be system-deleted immediately or subsequently deleted (by a user-initiated process) based on company-wide policies. Another policy determines whether the system retains manually deleted sales orders as voided orders.

---

[5] Company-wide policies (embedded in the A/R parameters) indicate whether over- and under-deliveries will be allowed for sales orders.

Other Types of Sales Orders   The user indicates the sales order type when initially creating a sales order. In addition to a normal sales order, the order types include:

❖ *Journal (or Draft).* A journal sales order does not represent a demand. It is typically used to capture information early in the sales cycle, and the user changes the order type to sales order upon placement by the customer.

❖ *Subscription.* A subscription sales order represents a demand, and the system automatically recreates it after invoicing.

❖ *Blanket Sales Order.* A blanket sales order represents one form of a customer agreement that defines the item price (and discounts) based on an aggregate quantity. Each user-initiated release (for a specified quantity and date) creates a sales order that inherits the agreed-upon price, and represents a demand. A blanket order report identifies each release and summarizes the quantities ordered, shipped, and invoiced.

❖ *Item Requirement.* An item requirement represents a project-specific sales order, and must be created from a project. The sales order shipment does not require sales order invoicing, since invoicing (if required) is handled through the project.

❖ *Returned Order.* A sales order with a type of returned order is automatically created for an RMA (returned material authorization), and handles the arrival, receipt, and credit note for the returned goods (via a negative quantity line item). It also supports sending the returned item back to the customer. This chapter's section on customer returns and RMAs provides further explanation.

Sales quotations reflect a separate construct, and not a different type of sales order. A sales quotation can be confirmed, thereby generating a sales order with linkage back to the sales quotation. This chapter's section on sales quotations provides further explanation.

Sales Order Considerations

Variations to the basic sales order process reflect different ways of doing business with customers and different internal procedures. The following variations apply to all environments; a subsequent section covers additional variations that pertain to distributors and manufacturers.

Order-Related Text Many situations require textual explanations or additional descriptive information about the sales order and line items. Order-related text can be specified in several ways.

❖ *Carry Forward of Item Text to Line Item.* The item master allows each item to have an unlimited amount of descriptive text that automatically carries forward to the sales order line item, where it can be optionally overridden.

❖ *Document Handling Capabilities.* Documents containing descriptive text (defined as a document type of note) can be defined for the sales order header and/or each line item and flagged for internal or external purposes. The system can print the external notes on each sales document.

These note documents can be previously defined for customers and items but do not automatically carry forward to the sales order; they must be explicitly copied and pasted to the sales order header and lines. Other types of documents such as Word files, Excel spreadsheets, and images can also be defined.

❖ *Printing Descriptive Information.* The setup policies for A/R forms determine the extent to which each printed form includes descriptive information. For example, the printed packing slip can identify the external item number, the batch numbers of shipped material, and the note documents.

Sales Order Quantity The item's standard sales order quantity and UM act as default values when entering an order and can be overridden. The system provides a soft warning if the entered quantity exceeds the item's minimum or maximum sales order quantity, or does not match the item's multiple quantity for a sales order. When a partial shipment is anticipated, entering a separate "deliver now" quantity can simplify the posting process for deliveries. Partial shipments for a line item can be explicitly forbidden using the ship complete flag to indicate the delivery quantity must match the order quantity

Sales Order Dates for Shipment and Delivery A sales order line item has a requested ship date and a requested receipt date (aka the delivery date), where the difference represents the transportation time (termed *transport days*) to the delivery address. A sales order line item also has a confirmed ship date and confirmed receipt date, and the confirmed ship date drives planning calculations. The user can manually enter these confirmed dates, or the system will automatically populate these dates based on delivery promise calculations (as described in the breakout box). When these dates are left as empty, the system assumes the requested dates apply.

The ship date is affected by the concept of a sales lead time, which is the typical delay (expressed in days) between order entry and shipment. The sales lead time can be inherited from a sales price trade agreement, from the item information, or a company-wide default (in decreasing order of specificity).

The user can optionally enforce rules concerning the delivery dates (termed a *delivery date control* flag) on a given sales order and line item. These rules are explained below.

❖ *Order Entry Deadlines for Taking Sales Orders.* The concept of an order entry deadline means that orders received after a specified time are treated as if they were received the next day. A specified time for the deadline can be defined for each day of the week. You can define a deadline for each site and for a customer. You can view deadline information during order entry, and obtain warnings, on the Available Ship and Receipt Dates form.

❖ *Calendars.* Calendars can be assigned to the ship-from warehouse, the customer's delivery address, and the mode of delivery. These calendars can be used to constrain the ship date or delivery date. For example, a truck delivery may only occur on Tuesdays for a given geographic area and ship-from warehouse. The user can view available ship and delivery dates for a specified warehouse and mode of delivery.

❖ *Predefined Transport Days Information.* The transport days can be predefined to account for the combinations of ship-from warehouse, mode of delivery (such as air or truck), and the delivery address characteristics (such as the country, state, county, or ZIP code), so the system can automatically calculate a delivery date based on entry of the shipment date.[6]

The system provides a warning when the requested delivery date cannot be met, along with messaging about the reason(s).

---

[6] The transportation time is based on the ship-from warehouse. This means that a sales order line item that simply specifies a ship-from site does not have sufficient information to calculate the transportation time. In this case, each site can have a default ship-from warehouse (termed the *fallback warehouse*) for the purpose of calculating a transportation time.

Making Delivery Date Promises

The promised delivery date for each sales order line item can be calculated based on available-to-promise (ATP) logic or capable-to-promise (CTP) logic, and alternative supply options can be analyzed.

❖ *Available to Promise (ATP) Logic.* The promised delivery date for a sales order can be automatically calculated and assigned (based on ATP logic) during order entry. ATP logic considers on-hand inventory, scheduled receipts, and planned order receipts for the ship-from site and warehouse, and any existing reservations, within a specified ATP time horizon expressed in days.[7] If the requirement cannot be met, you can view the available to promise information to determine how much can be promised on the requested date, or when the full quantity will be available. The use of ATP logic can be specified on the sales order header or line item (as the basis for delivery date control).

❖ *Capable to Promise (CTP) Logic.* The promised delivery date for a sales order line item can be calculated based on CTP logic, and the projected date (termed the *futures date*) subsequently transferred back to the line item. The calculations consider the availability of on-hand inventory and scheduled receipts. When this is insufficient, the calculations consider the item's lead time to determine a valid promised delivery date. The calculations also suggest the planned order to meet this date; multiple planned orders may be necessary for a manufactured item and its components. The user can optionally firm the planned order(s) immediately. These calculations (termed an *Explosion* inquiry) must be user-initiated for each sales order line item, whereas ATP logic will automatically assign the shipment date as the user enters each line item.

Note: The concept of continuously checking capable to promise is embedded in the futures messages generated by the planning calculations. That is, the futures message warns when a sales shipment cannot be met, and identifies the projected delivery date.

❖ *Analyzing Supply Options for Making Delivery Promises.* The user can view alternative supply options (using the Supply Overview form) for a sales order line item. These options include inventory and scheduled receipts at different sites and warehouses, quarantined inventory, an

---

[7] A company-wide policy (specified in the A/R parameters) specifies the ATP time horizon, and a related policy determines whether planned orders will be considered as available supplies.

alternative item (if specified on the item master), and lead times to obtain the item from various sources.

Delivery Address by Sales Order Line Item   Each line item inherits the delivery address from the sales order header, and it can be overridden. When printing a document such as a picking list or packing list, a separate document can be printed for each delivery address. The separate documents correctly communicate which line items are being sent to the delivery address.

Tolerances for a Sales Order Delivery Quantity   With delivery quantity tolerances, the shipped quantity can be greater or less than the ordered quantity as long as it is with the specified tolerances. Over- and under-delivery tolerances are expressed as a percentage, and the values assigned to an item act as defaults for a sales order line item.

Default Ship-From Site/Warehouse for a Sales Order   The ship-from site and warehouse on a sales order line item normally defaults from the sales order header, which defaults from the sold-to customer. However, some cases involve an item-specific ship-from site/warehouse as the default value or even as the mandatory value.

Calculation of Sales Order Weight and Volume   The volume and net weight for each item is used to calculate the total for all line items on a sales order.

Reserving Material for a Sales Order Line Item   A reservation for an item's inventory can be made manually or automatically, and reservations can be made against an item's scheduled receipts.[8] With a manual approach, the user indicates reservations for specific inventory quantities and scheduled receipts.

Pricing and Discounting on Sales Orders   An item's price and discounts can be manually or automatically assigned on a sales order. For example, auto-assignment can reflect an item's standard sales price or sales

---

[8] The policy concerning reservations defaults from the sales order header, which defaults from the company-wide policy embedded in the A/R parameters. An additional policy determines whether reservations can be made against scheduled receipts.

trade agreements. A manually entered line discount can be expressed as a percent or an amount or both. A manually entered total discount can be expressed as a percent. Automatic calculation of a total discount or a multi-line discount requires a user-initiated function after entering all sales order line items. This chapter's section about sales prices and trade agreements provides further explanation.

Identifying an Alternate Item for a Sales Order Line Item   When an alternate item has been defined for an item, the system automatically suggests the alternative item during order entry and replaces the originally entered item number. An item-specific policy determines whether the system always suggests replacement or only when available inventory is insufficient to cover the ordered quantity.

Short-Cut Approach for Creating Multiple Line Items   A short-cut approach for creating multiple line items allows the user to view a user-defined subset of items, enter just the order quantity for desired items, and update the sales order. The user-defined subset of items reflects filters which can be saved and reused. The short-cut approach provides one means for reminders about selling related products.

Identifying Supplementary Items   Automatic calculation of supplementary items requires a user-initiated function after entering all sales order line items. Supplementary items provide one approach for reminders about selling related products, as described in this chapter's section about sales prices and trade agreements.

Mass Changes to Line Items Based on Changes to Header Information   Changes to selected fields in the sales order header can automatically update the same fields in the line items. Examples of selected fields include the ship-from site/warehouse, the delivery date, or the sales group for commission purposes. Each selected field and its automatic update policy can be identified as part of the A/R parameters for updating order lines.

Versions of a Sales Order   Posting a sales order confirmation results in automatic assignment of a version number. Each version is identified by the sales order number and a numeric suffix (such as -1 and -2). A sales order may be changed and the confirmation reposted in order to track versions of a sales order and communicate the changes to customers. The version number is displayed on a printed sales order confirmation. These historical versions can be viewed as part of inquiries about posted confirmations for a sales order. The system uses the existing sales order data (regardless of the assigned version number) for the purposes of the picking list, packing list, and invoice.

The existing sales order data can revert to a previous version via the *Copy-From Journal* function. You select from the displayed list of versions, and specify to delete lines from the existing order, so that the existing sales order data gets updated. You can optionally repost the sales order confirmation to assign a new version number.

Creating a Sales Order via the Copy Function
A copy function (termed *Copy From All*) can be used to create line items from an existing sales order. For example, the user can select the desired sales order and the desired line item(s) from a displayed list of all existing orders. You can also select from versions of sales orders, or from sales quotations, packing lists, and invoices. The user indicates how to update the existing order, such as appending information to the existing line items and recalculating prices for the new line items.

Using a Negative Quantity for a Sales Order Line Item
A line item with negative quantity represents a customer return and credit note. The item can be received against the sales order, and the value subtracted from the sales order invoice. The copy function can be used to automatically add line items with a negative quantity (via the option to *create credit note*). This copy function only works for previously invoiced sales orders, so that the original invoice price will be copied to the sales order. RMA processing involves the use of a sales order (with an order type of returned order) containing line items with a negative quantity. This chapter's section on RMAs provides further explanation.

Changing the Sold-To or Bill-To Customer on a Sales Order
Changes to the sold-to or bill-to customer can be made prior to posting shipments, but the changes have several impacts. For example, a change to the sold-to customer results in new delivery address information and typically a new bill-to customer. After changing the sold-to customer, the

user responds to system prompts about updating information that may be impacted by the change, such as prices and discounts that reflect the sales trade agreements with the new customer, or new delivery addresses.

Backorders in Sales   A backorder represents a sales order line item that is not yet delivered to a customer. Backorders can be viewed by item or customer in order to answer customer inquiries and help prioritize use of available inventory for picking and shipment.

Commissions for a Sales Order   A commission sales group (or sales group for short) identifies one or more sales reps. The sales group assigned to a customer acts as a default for a sales order, which then acts as a default for line items. The sales group represents a primary factor in calculating commission amounts for the sales order, along with the customer and products being sold. The calculated commission amount reflects a specified commission percentage times the sales order value (such as the gross revenue or net margin). Figure 7.3 illustrates these factors affecting commission calculations along with two scenarios. The first scenario can be defined by a single entry in the commission setup. It represents a single rep obtaining a 10% commission on all product sales to a given customer based on gross revenue value and this year's commission plan. An additional entry could define next year's commission plan. The second scenario represents a 10% commission split between two sales reps based on the type of product and customer. Multiple entries in the commission setup would be needed to define the various combinations of item groups and customer groups.

Commission calculations are normally based on the most specific entry related to a commission percentage, such as an entry for a specific item and customer rather than groups. With searching enabled, the system uses all of the applicable entries (when multiple entries exist) for calculating commissions. Commissions are calculated (with associated G/L entries) after posting a sales order invoice.

Month End Revenue Recognition of Sales Order Shipments Not Yet Invoiced   Certain month-end situations require revenue recognition based on shipments prior to actual invoicing. In this case, the shipment (recorded via the packing slip update transaction) can update a revenue account that will be cleared upon invoice generation. The *post physical revenue* policy (embedded in the Inventory Model Group assigned to the

			Scenario #1	Scenario #2
			Single rep obtains 10% commission for all sales to customer	Split commission of 10% based on type of product and customer
Factor	Item	Item		
		Group of Items (Commission Item Group)		X
		All Items	X	
	Sold-To Customer	Customer	X	
		Group of Customers (Commission Customer Group)		X
		All Customers		
	Sales Group*	Sales Group With One Rep (No Split)	100% for Rep #1	
		Sales Group With Multiple Reps (Split Commission)		60% for Rep #1 40% for Rep #2
Commission Percentage			10%	10%
Commission Rules		Value based on Revenue vs Margin	Revenue	Revenue
		Value based on Net vs Gross	Gross	Gross
		Date Effectivity	Current year's Commission plan	Current year's Commission plan
		Applicability Search One vs Multiple Entries	One Entry	Multiple Entries

*The sales group indicates the applicable sales reps and split commission information.

Figure 7.3 Commission Calculations

item) indicates that shipments should update the *packing slip revenue* account and a *packing slip revenue offset* account (defined in the Item Group assigned to the item).

Totals for a Sales Order   The system calculates several order totals, including revenue, cost and margin, discounts and taxes, and total weight and volume. Order totals can be displayed for order quantities, picked quantities, or shipped quantities. The total volume and weight can be used for truckload planning purposes.

Sales Order Variations for Manufacturers and Distributors

Sales order processing in manufacturing and distribution environments involves many of the above-mentioned considerations and a few additional ones. These additional considerations include custom products, using a cost-plus-markup approach to pricing, selling a kit item, and generating a production order linked to the sales order. An alternative approach to delivery promises can reflect the maximum quantity that can be produced from component inventory. Purchase orders can also be directly generated from a sales order, including direct delivery purchase orders. In addition, some situations such as equipment sales require installation or periodic maintenance of the equipment.

Handling a Custom Product A custom product can be defined using an option selection approach (for a configurable item) or a product configurator approach (for a modeling-enabled item) as described in Chapter 4.

Calculating a Manufactured Item's Sales Price via an Order-Specific BOM Calculation The user can perform an order-specific BOM calculation during sales order entry to calculate a manufactured item's suggested sales price, and then transfer the calculated price to the sales order line item. The Chapter 5 section about order-specific BOM calculations provides further explanation.

Viewing and Assigning the Item's Bill of Material You can view an item's multilevel bill information during order entry via the *Composed of Tree* inquiry. You can optionally modify the item's bill of material, which will update the master BOM information. In addition, you can optionally specify an item's approved-but-not-active BOM version and routing version on a sales order line item.

Selling a Kit of Material Items An item's bill of material can represent a kit of components, and the kit can be sold complete or as individual components.

❖ *Selling a Completed Kit.* A manufactured item can be flagged as a kit so that it can be priced, sold, and shipped as if it were completed. After posting the invoice, the system auto-deducts components based on the item's bill of material.

❖ *Selling the Kit Components.* During sales order entry, the user can view and select components (termed the *Explode BOM* function) for a specified line item. The system automatically adds a line item for each selected component, with pricing based on the component item and quantity. The original line item is displayed on the form but not on printed documents.

Generating a Production Order from a Sales Order A user can immediately generate a production order when the line item reflects a make-to-order manufactured product. As part of creating the production order, the user can view the item's bill and routing information, and override suggested values. For example, the assigned master BOM or routing can be overridden, or the production order number can be manually assigned to match the sales order number. The system automatically displays the production order form after creation, thereby allowing further data maintenance such as immediately scheduling the production order. The sales order line item is linked to the associated production order (and vice versa) as indicated by the reference fields on each order.

Checking the Maximum Possible Quantity That Can Be Produced from Component Inventory A customer sometimes asks "How many can you produce right away?" rather than asking about the delivery date for a requested quantity. An item's BOM inquiry (termed *maximum report as finished*) indicates the maximum possible quantity that can be produced from component on-hand inventory. The inquiry reflects a specified site/warehouse, the BOM version, and the logic for exploding requirements when shortages exist for a manufactured component. The screen displays the maximum quantity possible for the parent item, and also indicates which components (in the multilevel bill) constrain the ability to produce this maximum quantity. Several caveats apply to this inquiry: it ignores on-hand inventory of the parent item, and it does not consider reservations for the component inventory.

Generating Purchase Orders from a Sales Order You can immediately generate a purchase order for selected sales order line items. The suggested purchase order reflects the item's preferred vendor and applicable purchase trade agreements, and the order modifiers for the item's minimum, multiple, and maximum quantities. The process of creating the purchase order allows the user to view the item's approved vendors and trade agreement information, and override the suggested vendor. The system generates one purchase order for each group of line items to the same vendor. Each purchase order line item contains the reference to the associated sales order (and vice versa) to represent the linkage between orders. The material is reserved for the sales order. This approach requires separate transactions to receive the material and vendor's invoice, and then to record shipment and generate a customer invoice.

Generating Direct Delivery Purchase Orders from a Sales Order

You can immediately generate a direct delivery purchase order for selected sales order line items, just like generating a regular purchase order as described above. The delivery address is transferred to the purchase order, and a sales order shipment does not need to be recorded, since the purchased material is shipped directly to the customer. You still need to generate the sales invoice, and it reflects information about the quantity received and invoiced from the vendor.

Generating a Service Order for Installing the Sold Item   Some

situations such as equipment sales require installation of the equipment after it has been shipped. In these situations, you can create a service order (as part of sales order processing) to define the labor, materials, and expenses associated with equipment installation. Chapter 14 explains service orders.

The service order can be created before or after shipment/invoicing of the sales order, and the sales order line items provide the starting point for defining service objects. For example, a service object may represent a specific piece of equipment with an item number, a type of equipment, or a group of equipment. Creation of the service order involves three steps embedded in a wizard. As the first step, you must identify the related project and optionally identify a related service agreement. As the second step, you define the preferred date/time and technician for performing the service order to install the equipment. The third step involves identification of the service object(s) to be installed, and the optional identification of typical replacement parts (termed a template BOM) for each service object. These wizard steps result in the creation of a service order. Additional information must be added to the service order, such as the service task(s) and the estimated labor/material/expenses for each service task performed on a service object.

Generating a Service Agreement for Maintaining the Sold Item

Some situations such as equipment sales require periodic maintenance of the equipment after it has been shipped. In these situations, you can create a service agreement (as part of sales order processing) to define the periodic maintenance schedule and the associated labor, materials, and expenses associated with each maintenance visit. Service orders are subsequently generated based on service agreement information about periodic maintenance. Chapter 14 explains service agreements and service orders.

The service agreement can be created before or after shipment/invoicing of the sales order, and the sales order line items provide the starting point for defining service objects. Creation of the service agreement involves several steps embedded in a wizard. As the first step, you indicate whether information from an existing agreement will be copied (such as copying the service tasks and related labor/material/expenses), whether to create a new project (or use an existing project), and whether to create a new project contract (or use an existing contract). If a new project will be created, a second step involves definition of the project, such as the project description, project type, and project group. As the next step, you define the date range and preferred technician for the service agreement. The final third step involves identification of the service object(s) to be installed, and the optional identification of typical replacement parts (termed a template BOM) for each service object. These wizard steps result in the creation of a service agreement; they can also result in creation of a new project and project contract. Additional information must be added to the service agreement, such as assigning the service task(s) and the estimated labor/material/ expenses to each service object.

Sales Quotations

A sales quotation represents a key step in the life cycle of many customer relationships. A sales quotation can be converted into a sales order, or identified as lost or cancelled. The structure and life cycle of a sales quotation provide a starting point for further explanation about usage variations. Usage variations include the similarities with sales orders, the use of price simulations, the relationship between multiple quotations, and versions of a sales quotation.

Structure and Life Cycle of a Sales Quotation   The basic structure consists of a header and line item information. The header identifies the sold-to business account contact and related customer (if applicable).

Several aspects of the header information act as defaults for the line items, such as the requested ship date and probability of winning the quote. Each line item minimally specifies an item, quantity, ship date, price, ship-from site/warehouse, and a win probability.

The life cycle of a sales quotation consists of three basic steps (create, send, and disposition), with three possible dispositions (confirmed, lost, or cancelled), that are represented by five statuses.

❖ *Created.* The quotation has been created. It can be sent to or confirmed with the business relation contact.

❖ *Sent.* The quotation has been sent to the business account (via the *Send Quotation* update). The specified business relation cannot be changed. The quotation can be updated to a disposition of confirmed, lost or cancelled.

❖ *Confirmed.* The quotation has been converted into a sales order (via the *Confirmation* update), and all quote line items are converted into line items on the new sales order. The system identifies the link between the quotation and sales order.

❖ *Lost.* The quotation has been identified as lost (via the *Quotation Lost* update).

❖ *Cancelled.* The quotation has been identified as cancelled (via the *Quotation Cancelled* update).

The system allows changes to created or sent quotations, and creation of a customer from the specified business relation (via the *Convert to Customer* function). When updating the disposition of a quotation, the user can optionally record a win/loss reason code. Changes cannot be made to a quotation after it has been updated with a disposition.

Similarities and Differences with a Sales Order A sales quotation shares many similarities to a sales order, but there are also several differences, as described below.

❖ *Similarities.* The sales trade agreement information applies to quotations, and the user can calculate discounts and supplementary items. The user can define a custom product configuration, using either option selection for a configurable item or the configurator for a modeling-enabled item. The user can perform a BOM calculation and transfer the price to the quotation. The user can optionally employ delivery date control capabilities to the requested ship and delivery dates on a line item.

❖ *Differences.* A sales quotation can be defined for a business relation that does not have to be a customer. Each line item has an assigned probability that determines whether it will be considered as a demand by planning calculations. A promised delivery date cannot be calculated (via the *Explosion* inquiry). Previous quotes can be copied into a sales quotation, but previous sales orders cannot be copied into a quotation. The price simulation capabilities only apply to quotations.

Converting a Business Relation into a Customer   A customer can be created from the business relation specified on a quotation (via the *Convert to Customer* function). After creating the customer, the system displays the customer master form so that additional information can be entered.

Converting a Sales Quotation into a Sales Order   A sales quotation can be converted into a sales order (via the *Confirmation* update), and all quote line items are converted into line items on the new sales order. The system prevents conversion unless the business relation reflects a customer. The system identifies the link between the quotation and sales order.

Planning Calculations and the Sales Quotation Win Probability
Planning calculations can optionally include demands stemming from sales quotation line items with a win probability greater than a specified percentage. Treating these as demand makes sense in situations where the pipeline of quotations comprises 100% of the projected demand. Quotations do not consume a sales forecast. In situations where quotations and sales forecast are both considered as demand, the forecast may require manual adjustment to reflect the incremental demand not already in the pipeline of quotations and sales orders.

Price Simulations in Support of Price Negotiation Efforts   Price simulations can be used to support the salesperson's efforts to negotiate prices with the customer while still retaining visibility of the desired margins and contribution ratio. For example, the impact of a discount percentage, a discount amount, or a specified price can be evaluated. A price simulation can be performed for individual line items or for the entire quotation, and then saved as a scenario with a user-defined description. Multiple scenarios can be saved. The user can optionally apply a saved scenario to the quotation.

❖ *Price Simulation for a Line Item.* The user can enter a discount percent, a discount amount, and/or a specified price, and the price simulation displays the impact on margin and contribution ratio. Alternatively, the user can enter a specified margin (or contribution ratio) and the price simulation displays the impact on price. Applying a saved scenario updates the price, discount percent, and amount on the quotation line item.

❖ *Price Simulations for an Entire Quotation.* The user can enter a discount percent, and the price simulation displays the impact on margin and contribution ratio. Alternatively, the user can enter a margin (or contribution ratio) to view the impact on discount percentage. Applying a saved scenario updates the discount percent in the quotation header.

Relationship Between Multiple Sales Quotations Multiple sales quotations may be required in certain situations, such as quotes for different quantity breakpoints. Other examples would be quotes for multiple phases or for different groups of items such as basic versus optional. The user establishes the relationship by starting with a parent quotation, and then assigning the child quotation(s) using the *Alternative Quotations* function. The same function displays alternative quotations that have already been defined.

Versions of a Sales Quotation A sales quotation may be changed and then resent to the business relation in order to communicate the changes. The system automatically tracks each time a quotation is sent, and assigns a numeric suffix to the quotation identifier (such as -1 and -2) for each version. These historical versions can be viewed on the quotation inquiry and the Quotation Journal Inquiry. The system uses the latest version as the basis for confirming a quotation to create a sales order.

Sales Quotation Follow-Up Date and Expiration Date Each sales quotation has a follow-up date and an expiration date.[9] The dates provide reference information and the basis for selectively viewing sales quotations.

Mass Creation of Sales Quotations Using a Template Certain situations may require the mass creation of sales quotations, such as providing the same quote to several different contacts or customers. An initial

---

[9] The default values for the number of days until quotation follow-up and expiration are defined as company-wide defaults in the A/R parameters.

quote must be created and then designated as an active template (with a user-defined template name).[10] The periodic task for *Mass Create Quotations* can then be used with the specified template and a user-defined selection of business relations. The system creates a sales quotation for each business relation.

Deleting Sales Quotations Quotations are not automatically deleted by the system since win/loss analysis requires historical data. Periodic deletion of quotations should reflect the desired data retention policies. Use the Delete Quotations task to select quotations to be deleted based on criteria such as the status, creation date, and/or expiration date.

Customer Self-Service and the Enterprise Portal

One aspect of the Enterprise Portal involves the customer role, which is referred to as customer self-service. This customer role enables a customer to browse the product catalog, add items to a shopping basket, and create orders on-line. The shopping basket can include a modeling-enabled item (with an associated product model), so that the customer must complete the user dialogue to configure the custom product. The customer can add items to a shopping basket without ordering them, and then return at a later time to finish the order. Other features of the shopping basket can be defined as policies, such as enforcement of the sales order minimum, multiple, and maximum quantities, and displaying the customer's balance.

A guest role can also be defined, so that the guest can browse the product catalog without creating a shopping basket or order. The guest can also create a registration request to become a customer.

There are other roles within the Enterprise Portal. The internal sales role, for example, allows the web user to create and edit sales order information just like a normal user. Another role supports the internal consultant, allowing the web user to report hours on projects.

Posting a Sales Order Shipment and Invoice

Shipping and invoicing activities represent the completion of sales order processing, and different approaches can be taken to report shipping activity

---

[10] The planning calculations always ignore demands related to template quotations.

for material items. The basic approach focuses on reporting shipping activity against line items on an individual sales order, and is termed *posting the packing slip*. Information about the actual quantity shipped (and its bin location) can be entered for each sales order line item prior to posting. The posting transaction can also generate a pro forma invoice or an actual invoice to accompany the shipment. Other approaches to recording sales order shipments involve picking material prior to shipment, as described in Chapter 9.

The shipment quantity for a line item must match the order quantity to update the sales order line status. When using delivery tolerances, the delivered quantity can exceed the order quantity or the under-delivery can be flagged as closed during the posting process. Over- and under-delivery tolerances are expressed as a percentage, and the values assigned to an item act as defaults for the sales order line item. The system prevents posting when the delivery quantity exceeds either delivery tolerance.

A customer pickup represents slight variation of a sales order shipment and invoice. When the sales order's delivery mode represents a customer pickup, you can use the Pickup-Sales Order form to view these sales orders, record the shipment, and invoice.

Other approaches to recording sales order shipments involve a separate step for picking material before posting the packing slip. Chapter 9 explains the consolidated picking list approach and the order picking list approach for handling sales order shipments.

Customer Returns and RMAs

Customer returns generally require an authorization, termed a returned material authorization (RMA) number. In a simple situation, for example, the customer wants to return a defective product and obtain a credit. The company creates an RMA and provides the RMA number to the customer, who returns the item. The company subsequently records receipt of the returned item and creates a credit note for the customer. RMA situations can become more complex with variations in handling a returned item, its replacement, and the related financial transactions. Each variation involves different steps and considerations.

RMA processing builds on sales order functionality. Each RMA has an associated sales order (termed the *returned order*) for handling returns, and an optional second sales order (termed the *replacement order*) for handling replacements. Both sales orders have the same order number (but a different order type) with linkage to the originating RMA number.

❖ *Returned Order.* Every RMA has an associated sales order (with a sales order type of returned order) to only handle the arrival, receipt, and credit note for the returned item. Creation of an RMA automatically creates the associated returned order, which represents a mirror image of the RMA. Changes to the RMA information automatically changes information on the returned order; you cannot directly maintain data on the returned order.

❖ *Replacement Order.* An RMA can have a second associated sales order when a replacement must be shipped to the customer. This replacement order can be manually created for the RMA to support immediate shipment, or automatically created after an RMA line item (with a disposition indicating replacement) has gone through arrival/inspection and receipt. You typically assign an order type of *sales order* to the manually created replacement order, although another order type can be assigned (such as a blanket order).

This replacement order has all the functionality previously described for sales orders, which can be used to configure a custom product as the replacement item, to create a production order to repair a returned item, to create a direct delivery purchase order for sending the replacement from a vendor, or to support other purposes. These other purposes of a replacement order are explained in a subsequent point.

Further explanation will employ the terms *returned order* and *replacement order* for these two sales orders associated with an RMA. The explanation of RMA processing includes the use of quarantine orders (described in Chapter 10) to handle inspection of a returned item.

We'll start with a brief summary of dispositions and the structure of an RMA before covering the major RMA variations and basic steps for each variation. The major RMA variations reflect the use of a replacement order and the dispositions of an RMA line item. This section concludes by highlighting other variations in RMA processing, such as the different purposes of a replacement order and intercompany transactions.

RMA Disposition Codes and Return Reason Codes A user-definable RMA disposition code has an assigned action that indicates how to handle a returned item and possible replacement. You assign a disposition code upon arrival of the returned items; it can be reassigned as part of an optional inspection process. The key point of a disposition code, however, is the assigned action. There are four types of actions that apply to RMA processing (with or without a replacement order):

❖ *Credit Only*. This action indicates there will be no customer return; all other actions involve a customer return. For example, the items may be impossible to return, or are not worth returning because of their damaged condition.

❖ *Credit*. This action indicates that the returned item should be placed in inventory. For example, you can reuse the item immediately, or refurbish/repair the item to make it reusable.

❖ *Scrap*. This action indicates that the returned item should be scrapped; the receipt does not affect on-hand inventory balances.

❖ *Return*. This action indicates that the returned item should be sent back to the customer regardless of its condition.

There are two additional types of actions that only apply to RMA processing when use of a replacement order depends on the disposition of returned items.

❖ *Replace and Scrap*. This action indicates that the returned item should be scrapped, and that a replacement order should be automatically created after the returned item has gone through arrival/inspection and receipt. You must specify the replacement item after recording arrival/ inspection of the returned item. This action is not allowed when a replacement order was created for immediate shipment, since it would result in duplicate replacement efforts.

❖ *Replace and Credit*. This action indicates that the returned item should be placed in inventory, otherwise it is exactly the same as the return and scrap action.

The limited number of action types (six) means that you will need a minimum of six disposition codes. We will use just six disposition codes (one for each action type) in the following explanation, since these comprise the major variations enforced during RMA processing.[11]

You can also assign a user-definable return reason code to an RMA, thereby indicating the customer's reason for returning the item.[12] However, the return reason code does not affect the handling of returned items.

---

[11] The six dispositions help simplify the explanation, so we avoid saying "the disposition code and its related action type of credit (or scrap or return)."

[12] The user-definable return reason codes are also grouped together (into return reason groups), where the user-defined groups can assist you in assigning a reason code to an RMA.

Miscellaneous charges can be optionally assigned to a disposition code or a reason code. These miscellaneous charges can then be automatically calculated for the credit note associated with the returned item.

RMA Structure and Creation   The structure of an RMA consists of a header section and line items.

❖ *RMA Header Information.*   Header information includes the RMA number, and the associated sales order number that applies to the returned order and optional replacement order. The header information also includes the sold-to and bill-to customer, a deadline date, and optional reason code for the customer return.[13] The deadline date acts as the default value for each line item's expected receipt date. The deadline date can be used to justify cancellation of the RMA when items have not been returned beforehand. It does not prevent you from receiving returns after the date.

❖ *RMA Line Item Information.*   Each line item indicates the item, quantity, ship-to site/warehouse, and expected receipt date for the customer return. You can optionally describe a returned item with unlimited text, which may include a description of the item's damage and the desired disposition. You specify the sales price and the cost for each line item, and ultimately assign a disposition. Line item information can be copied from a previously invoiced sales order for the bill-to customer, which will copy the previous sales price and cost for the line item.

The life cycle for an RMA and each line item is reflected in two statuses: an RMA status and a RMA line status. These two statuses reflect the basic steps in RMA processing, starting with RMA creation and ending with a closed or cancelled RMA. The number of basic steps, and the applicability of each status, will differ for variations in RMA processing. Hence, the discussion of RMA status will be undertaken after reviewing the major variations.

Major Variations in RMA Processing   The three major variations in RMA processing reflect the use of a replacement order, since you can handle an RMA without replacement, with immediate replacement, or with replacement based on disposition of the returned item. Additional variations reflect

---

[13] The company-wide policies for a deadline validity period (expressed in days) and for a required reason code are defined in the A/R parameters.

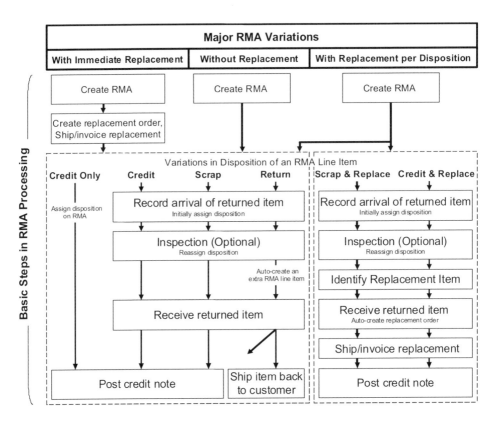

Figure 7.4 Basic Steps for RMA Variations

the disposition assigned to an RMA line item, such as credit, scrap, or return to customer. Figure 7.4 displays these three major RMA variations and the basic steps applicable to each variation.

With two of the major RMA variations (with immediate replacement and without replacement), each RMA can be assigned a disposition of credit only, credit, scrap, or return. Figure 7.4 displays these four applicable dispositions within a single box. The significance of each disposition is described below.

❖ *Credit Only*. A Credit Only disposition indicates there will be no customer return for the RMA line item. This disposition can only be assigned prior to recording any return activity. You post a credit note for the RMA line item using the associated returned order.

❖ *Credit*. The Credit disposition indicates the customer return will be placed in inventory and credited. You assign the disposition as part of recording arrival; it can be reassigned during an optional inspection process. You receive the customer return against the associated returned order, and subsequently post the credit note.

❖ *Scrap.* The Scrap disposition indicates the customer return will be scrapped and credited. You assign the disposition as part of recording arrival; it can be reassigned during an optional inspection process. You receive the customer return against the associated returned order, and subsequently post the credit note.

❖ *Return.* The Return disposition indicates the customer return will be placed in stock, and then sent back to the vendor regardless of condition. You assign the disposition as part of recording arrival; it can be reassigned during an optional inspection process. After completing the arrival (or inspection) step, the system automatically creates an extra line item on the RMA and the associated returned order, which will be used to send the item back to the customer. You receive the customer return against the associated returned order. You can then post the credit note for the returned item, and post the shipment and invoice for sending the item back to the customer. The credit note and invoice can be handled separately or in the same document.

As the third major variation, an RMA can have delayed generation of a replacement order based on the disposition of a returned item.[14] Figure 7.4 displays these two additional dispositions within a single box. The two dispositions involving replacement have the same basic steps, as illustrated in Figure 7.4 and explained below.

❖ *Replace and Scrap.* The Replace and Scrap disposition indicates the customer return will be scrapped and credited, and a replacement order will be automatically created by the receipt transaction. You assign the disposition as part of recording arrival; it can be reassigned during an optional inspection process. You identify the replacement item for the RMA line item after completing arrival/inspection. You can then receive the customer return against the associated returned order; the receipt automatically generates the replacement order for the specified replacement item. You can then ship and invoice the replacement item. In addition, you post the credit note for the returned order.

---

[14] You cannot have two replacement orders for the same RMA, so that immediate creation of a replacement order prevents a disposition involving replacement. This avoids a situation with duplicate replacement orders.

❖ *Replace and Credit.* The Replace and Credit disposition involves the same steps as a Replace and Scrap; the only difference is that the customer return will be placed into stock.

The basic steps may change slightly when you reassign a disposition code during the optional inspection process. For example, a scrap disposition on the arrival journal may be changed to a credit disposition (with no change in steps) or to a replace and scrap disposition (which requires additional steps).

RMA Status and Basic Steps   The status of an RMA and its line items are updated automatically as you perform the basic steps. Figure 7.5 displays the basic steps along with the associated status for the RMA and RMA line item. The status names reflect the steps that need to be taken as well as the steps already taken. An RMA line item status, for example, initially has an awaiting status that changes to registered, quarantine, or received based on actual steps taken for the returned item. Figure 7.5 also displays the related activities for each step. These activities involve the two sales orders related to an RMA: the returned order (labeled SO#1 in Figure 7.5) and the replace-

	Basic Steps in RMA Processing	Related Activities for the Step	RMA Status	RMA Line Status
1	Create RMA	Auto-create returned order (SO#1) RMA: Print RMA		Awaiting
2	Create replacement order for immediate sending	Create replacement order (SO#2a) SO#2: Print order confirmation	Created	
3	Record arrival of returned item	RMA: Print return acknowledgement		Registered
4	Inspection via Quarantine order	Use quarantine order to report good/scrap		Quarantine
5	Identify replacement item			
6	Receive returned item into inventory	SO#1: Print packing slip Auto-create replacement order (SO#2b)	Open	
7	Ship/invoice the replacement order	SO#2: Print the packing slip & invoice		Received
8	Post the credit note for the returned item	SO#1: Print the credit note		
9	Send item back to the customer	SO#1: Print the packing slip & invoice		
10	After posting the credit note or invoice	N/A	Closed	Invoiced
11	After canceling the RMA		Cancelled	Cancelled

Figure 7.5 RMA Status and Basic Steps in RMA Processing

ment order (labeled SO#2). The replacement order can be created immediately (SO#2a) or after disposition of the returned item (SO#2a). The basic steps provide the organizing focus for further explanation. The applicability of each step depends on the RMA variation.

❖ *Step 1: Create RMA.* You can directly enter RMA line items, or copy them from a previously invoiced sales order to the bill-to customer, and then print the RMA. You can assign a disposition of *credit only* to an RMA line item. Each RMA has an automatically created returned order to handle receipts and credit notes for the returned material.

❖ *Step 2: Create Replacement Order for Immediate Sending.* You can manually create a replacement order after RMA creation (prior to recording arrival of any line item), and add line items or optionally copy the existing RMA line items into the replacement order. You can print the order confirmation, and subsequently ship/invoice the replacement order.

❖ *Step 3: Record Arrival of Returned Item.* Returned items must first be reported through an arrival journal, typically by selecting the RMA line items on the Arrival Overview form to create the arrival journal.[15] Multiple RMAs and multiple RMA line items can be selected, thereby including them in a single arrival process. The creation of an arrival journal changes the RMA status from created to open, and the RMA line status to registered. You can print the return acknowledgment for the RMA.

You assign a disposition code to each returned item within the arrival journal line items. When the returned quantity is two or greater, you may need to split a line item to record different dispositions. You can optionally generate a quarantine order by indicating a quarantine warehouse and a quarantine management policy for the returned item. A quarantine order must be generated for items with a mandated quarantine policy.

❖ *Step 4: Inspection via Quarantine Order.* You can optionally reassign the disposition code on a quarantine order, and split the quarantine order quantity to indicate multiple dispositions. Chapter 10 explains quarantine orders. The creation of a quarantine order changes the RMA line status to quarantine.

❖ *Step 5: Identify Replacement Item.* When the disposition involves replacement, you must identify the replacement item and quantity for the

---

[15] Using the Arrival Overview form (to select and create an arrival journal) avoids the manual and error-prone process to enter the correct RMA references on the arrival journal.

RMA line item (after completing the arrival/inspection steps). One or more replacement item can be specified along with a desired quantity, and you can select the item's designated alternate as the replacement. The specified replacement item(s) and quantity will be included in the automatically-created replacement order.

❖ *Step 6: Receive Returned Item into Inventory.* Receive returned items into inventory by posting the packing slip for the returned order. When the disposition involved replacement, the receipt transaction also auto-creates the replacement order for the specified replacement item(s) and quantity. The receipt changes the RMA line status to received.

❖ *Step 7: Ship/Invoice the Replacement Order.* Use the replacement order for shipping and invoicing the replacement items, and printing the related documents.

❖ *Step 8: Post the Credit Note for the Returned Item.* Use the returned order for posting the credit note for the returned item.

❖ *Step 9: Ship Item back to the Customer.* A return disposition will automatically add a line item to the RMA (and its returned order) after completion of the arrival (or inspection) step, so that you can ship and invoice the return to the customer.

❖ *Step 10: After Posting the Credit Note or Invoice.* Posting a credit note (or invoice) changes the RMA line status to invoiced. The RMA status changes to closed after all line items have been invoiced. A closed RMA cannot be reopened or maintained.

❖ *Step 11: After Canceling the RMA.* An RMA can be cancelled at any time prior to recording arrival activity, and a canceled RMA cannot be reopened or maintained.

Purposes of a Replacement Order   A replacement order may simply be used to support immediate shipment of a replacement item to a customer. However, the replacement order has all the functionality previously described for sales orders, which can support a wide variety of RMA situations. The following examples highlight some other purposes of a replacement order line item. Hence, a replacement order with multiple line items can serve multiple purposes.

- Configure a custom product as the replacement item, such as configuring a modeling-enabled item.
- Identify the replacement components, such as exploding an item's bill of material to identify the components that should be sent to the customer.

   – Create a production order to repair a returned item. When creating the production order (linked to the replacement order line item), you can select an approved BOM/route version that reflects repair activity. After creating the production order, you can also specify the needed repair activity in the order-dependent bill/routing information, and issue the returned item to the production order. The calculated sales price provides one basis for charging repair activity to the customer.

As an alternative approach, repairs of a returned item can be managed using a service order, as described in Chapter 14. The service order approach typically applies to more complex repair activities, and employs project invoicing for charging the customer for repairs.

   – Create a direct delivery purchase order for sending the replacement from a vendor.

   – Identify supplemental items that should be included with the replacement item.

Handling Customer Returns from a Sister Company   When the customer represents a sister company, creation of the RMA (and its associated sales order for the returned item) will automatically create an intercompany purchase order within the database for the sister company. A second intercompany purchase order is also generated when you create a replacement order for the RMA. The RMA number is identified on both of these intercompany purchase orders. Chapter 13 explains intercompany orders in multisite operations.

Handling Replacement Orders That Involve Purchases from a Sister Company   A replacement order line item can involve a purchase from a vendor that represents a sister company, such as a direct delivery purchase order for sending the replacement item to the customer. Creation of the purchase order automatically creates an intercompany sales order within the database for the sister company (identified with the RMA number). Chapter 13 explains intercompany orders in multisite operations.

Estimated Arrival Date of a Customer's Returned Item   An RMA's deadline date acts as the default value for the estimated arrival date for an RMA line item; this date can be overridden to a later date. The deadline date (and estimated arrival date) can have a secondary purpose, since it can be used to justify cancellation of the RMA when items have not been returned beforehand.

Defining the Cost of a Returned Item   The cost of a returned item can be specified on the RMA line item. This value will initially default to the item's current inventory cost, or to the cost associated with a previous sales order when it is copied into the RMA line item. This cost will be used when recording receipt into inventory. The receipt will generate a cost change variance when there is a difference with an item's standard cost.

Defining the Credit Amount for a Returned Item   The credit amount for a returned item can be specified on the RMA line item. The associated sales order (with a type of returned order) uses this amount for subsequent posting of the credit note. The credit amount will initially default to the item's current sales price, or to the sales price associated with a previous sales order when it is copied into the RMA line item. The credit amount can be adjusted to reflect partial credit or no credit. When using a return disposition, you should consider the combined effect of the line items for a credit amount (for the returned item) and the invoice amount (for sending the item back to the customer).

Defining the Sales Price for a Replacement Order   The sales price on a replacement order line item can be specified. The value will initially default to the item's current sales price. It can be calculated using an order-specific BOM calculation for a manufactured item. The subsequent invoice amount for the replacement order should consider the credit note amount defined for the returned order. For example, the replacement order sales price may need to match the credit note amount.

Defining the Ship-From Site/Warehouse for a Replacement Order
The ship-from site/warehouse can be specified for each replacement order line item; these can differ from the ship-to site/warehouse for the RMA line items (and inherited by the associated returned order line items).

Miscellaneous Charges for an RMA   Miscellaneous charges can be specified for an RMA and its line items, which are inherited by the returned order (and optionally overridden). The miscellaneous charges can be automatically assigned based on the reason code (for the RMA) or the disposition code (for a RMA line item). For example, the miscellaneous charges could reflect a restocking fee associated with the reason code or with the disposition code.

Using Quality Orders in RMA Processing   A quality order can be used to report test results against predefined tests, and you can define rules for automatic generation of quality orders. In the context of RMA processing, for example, a quality order could be automatically created for returned items going though inspection (via a quarantine order), or for a replacement item prior to sales order shipment. The quality order results must be reported and validated, or the system prevents the next step in the process (such as the sales order shipment). Chapter 10 explains the use of quality orders, and their use with quarantine orders.

Analysis of Return Patterns   Return patterns can be analyzed using several predefined reports and their report parameters. The return volume report provides a frequency count of RMA reason codes, or of RMA line item disposition codes, in monthly increments over a specified time interval. The statistics ranking report provides a ranking of customers or items based on frequency counts of RMAs over a specified time period. The return cycle time report calculates the elapsed days for handling RMAs (with a breakdown by reason code) or RMA line items (with a breakdown by disposition code) over a specified time interval.

Sales Analysis

Requirements for sales analysis information vary significantly between firms and decision makers within a firm. Dynamics AX includes a number of standard sales analysis inquiries and reports, as illustrated below. Each company tends to develop customized reports to meet their unique requirements.

Sales Analysis for Individual Sales Quotations and Orders   The summarized data for a sales order or quote include calculated totals for revenue, cost, margin, and contribution ratio.

Sales Analysis for Individual Customers   The statistics window for a customer displays period totals for invoices and payments, including the number and value. It also displays information about the last invoice and payment. The Customer Turnover report displays the total value of sales orders or invoices by customer. The Top Customers report displays total revenue, margin, and quantity for each customer, with optional sequencing based on any of the three totals. A pivot table inquiry provides multidimensional sales analysis, such as sales by item group and customer group.

Sales Analysis for Individual Items   The statistics window for an item displays period totals for purchases and sales, including the number of orders, quantity and value.   It also displays information about the last purchase order and sales order.

Sales Analysis by Customer and Item   The Customer/Item Statistics report summarizes the items sold to each customer (in terms of quantity, revenue, and margin) over a specified date range, and optionally provides a comparison with another date range.   The Item/Customer Statistics report displays the same information for customer sales grouped by item.   The Business Statistics inquiry summarizes the sales units and revenue by type of item and customer, in tabular and graphic format.

Data Warehouse and Sales Analysis   Sales analysis often requires summarized data for large volumes of detailed transaction data.   This data summarization requires periodic data extractions into a data warehouse. Dynamics AX includes an installation wizard and population tools to support out-of-the-box data warehouse functionality with minimal technical expertise and implementation effort.   The cubes within the data warehouse reflect several business areas, including customers, sales, inventory, vendors, purchasing, and general ledger information.   They also reflect the financial dimensions employed within Dynamics AX.   A number of predefined reports are based on an analysis of best practices, and end-users can easily develop ad hoc customized reports—presented as graphs, maps, charts, and objects.

Case Studies

Case 41: Automotive Tire Outlets   A firm specializing in automotive tires required customized sales order processing to match the business processes at their outlets.   The typical customer contact starts with a telephone inquiry about the options, pricing, and availability about a given tire type, and proceeds through several steps including a quotation, sales order, work order, and invoice.   As part of the customizations for the quotation process, the system displayed alternative items with availability, pricing, and profitability along with highlighting to steer the customer's decision toward corporate promotions and higher margins. The system also suggested additional sales order line items about related services (such as tire installation and balancing) and indicated prior business with the customer.   The quotation could be converted to a sales order and a work order with scheduling based on tire availability. When inventory was unavailable at the local outlet, the system checked availability across all outlets and recommended an inventory transfer, or generated a purchase order to the tire manufacturer. Many of the customizations represented work simplification and advanced decision support, with extensive prototyping to ensure ease-of-use, user acceptance, and security considerations.

Case 42: Commissions and Rebates The All-and-Anything company required sophisticated compensation schedules for periodic payment of sales commissions, and for rebates to customers. Commissions are determined on the basis of margins, with selection criteria tied to territories and to the sales groups assigned to sales order line items (for handling split commissions). Commissions accrue over time until the original invoice is paid, and credit memos and returns must be accounted for. Different requirements applied to the calculation of rebates to customers, so that flexibility was critical to the solution.[16]

Case 43: Reserved Material by Batch The Batch Process manufacturer produced batch-traced items with batch attributes that affected usage suitability. Each customer specified acceptable values for these batch attributes during sales order entry, and the applicable batches were reserved. Customizations helped to automate this business process. First, batch attributes were defined by product category and each item was assigned a product category. Second, attribute values were assigned to batch numbers of saleable end-items. Third, a profile of acceptable values for these batch attributes could be defined during sales order entry. Finally, the available-to-promise calculations were customized to identify existing batches with applicable batch values, and to optionally reserve the material for the sales order.[17]

Case 44: Mobile Order Entry via Hand-Held Devices The Consumer Products company had field sales representatives that wrote orders on paper forms that were faxed to the home office for manual rekeying. This manual system was replaced with hand-held devices (with a built-in bar-code scanner) that allowed sales reps to enter quotes, orders, and invoices, and

---

[16] See **www.RedMaple.com** for additional information about the Advanced Compensation capabilities.

[17] See **www.Fullscope.com** for additional information about their add-on modules to support process distribution and process manufacturing environments.

print them via a portable printer. At headquarters, the sales documents were seamlessly and automatically posted into Dynamics AX during each user's synchronization. The solution increased order efficiency and reduced errors, and allowed the average order size to grow significantly.

Case Study 45: RMAs for Serialized Items The Consumer Products company required RMA processing on customer returns of their serialized electronic items. Each serialized number had a 12 month warranty period (from date of sale) for free replacement. The customer identified an item's serial number when requesting an RMA, which was used to verify the applicability of its warranty period. The customer shipped the returned item after receiving an electronic copy of the printed RMA. Items were shipped to a repair facility, which verified the serial number and sent a free replacement (when it was within warranty) or charged for the replacement (when it was not within warranty). The repair facility assigned a disposition to each returned item during an inspection process, which determined whether the item was usable, scrapped, or repairable. A scrapped item could also be stripped down for reusing the high value components.

Case 46: Rules-Based Pricing The Distribution company employed several types of rules-based pricing when selling their consumer products to retailers. The approaches included a surcharge for a small order and discounts for a large order (based on total order value), as well as discount percentages and supplementary items based on total quantity ordered for different items within a product line. A miscellaneous charge was added to items requiring faster-than-normal delivery lead time.

Case 47: Drop-Shipments A hair-care distribution company had franchises selling products as part of their hair-care services. Each franchise sent orders for hair-care products to the corporate office, which then placed drop-ship purchase orders with various suppliers that manufacture the private label products. The business did not require a distribution center. The franchises paid the hair-care company, which then paid the suppliers.

Case 48: Tiered Pricing Based on Year-to-Date (YTD) Quantity The Equipment company required tiered sales pricing based on year-to-date quantities specified in a contract. For example, the contract price was $10 for a YTD quantity up to 999, $9.50 for 1000–1999, and $9.00 for a YTD quantity of 2000 or greater. A contract consisted of multiple line items, specifying the item, the contract period (expressed as from- and to-validity dates), and the price for each quantity breakpoint. The cumulative sales were tracked for sales orders linked to the contract, with a complete transaction history for each sales order line.[18]

Case 49: Sales Quotations and Collaborative Selling   The Fabricated Products company developed sales quotations for configured products that required collaboration with the customer, and with independent sales agents involved in the sales process. Collaboration involved lead tracking and quotation preparation, documents (such as CAD drawings and specifications), electronic signoffs, and ultimately commissions for the sales agents.

Executive Summary

Sales orders capture demands for the firm's products and service, and comprise a key element in the larger contexts of customer relationship management and the S&OP process. Customer information and trade agreements provide the foundation for processing sales orders. The trade agreements define the item sales prices for individual customers or customer groups, and may reflect pricing based on effectivity dates, quantity breakpoints, delivery days, unit of measure, and currency (for foreign sales). A case study highlighted tiered pricing based on year-to-date sales. Trade agreements can also define applicable discounts based on total order quantity or total value. Other forms of agreements can define supplementary items and miscellaneous charges (such as setup fees). In addition, pricing can reflect a blanket sales order or a confirmed sales quotation.

Sales quotations are required in many environments, oftentimes from business relations that are potential customers. You can perform price simulations in support of price negotiation efforts while retaining visibility of desired margins and contribution ratio. For example, you can evaluate the impact of a discount percentage or a specified price, and save the scenario for subsequent use. Planning calculations can optionally include demands stemming from sales quotations based on assigned win probabilities. This is especially helpful when the pipeline of quotations comprises a high percentage of demand. Sales quotations can be assigned a win/loss reason code

---

[18] See **www.RedMaple.com** for more information about their contract pricing module.

for sales analysis purposes, and you can convert sales quotations (and business relations) to sales orders (and customers).

One critical aspect of sales order processing involves the initial delivery promise (based on available-to-promise or capable-to-promise logic), as well as the on-going projections of your ability to meet a promised date. Another critical aspect involves customer self service via the Enterprise Portal. Other aspects include variations in sales order processing, such as the configuration of a custom product, a calculated sales price, a kit, a buy-to-order item, the direct delivery of a buy-to order item, a service order for installing the sold item, or a service agreement for maintaining the sold item. Variations in handling customer returns include the disposition of returned items and the need for sending replacement items.

Sales analysis provides critical management information, and multidimensional analysis can reflect factors such as the customer, product, and salesperson. Commissions for salespersons are automatically calculated. The case studies highlighted numerous variations in sales order processing, including commissions and rebates, mobile order entry, and rules-based pricing.

Chapter 8

Purchase Order Processing

A primary responsibility of procurement is to coordinate and execute the supply chain activities driven by the firm's S&OP (sales and operations planning) game plans. Purchased material represents the dominant concern in distribution environments and in many manufacturing environments. Procurement activities can significantly impact the firm's bottom-line performance in terms of reduced material costs and inventories, improved quality and lead time agility, and fewer disruptions stemming from stock-outs or delivery problems. In addition, purchases of indirect material often constitute a large proportion of procurement activities.

Purchase order processing represents a key business process within procurement. The extent of procurement activities to define sourcing and agreement information for a purchase order depends on the situation. For example, one-time orders for non-stock items may require a purchase requisition and a requisition approval process. Some cases warrant solicitation of purchase quotations via a request for quote (RFQ), and the vendor's reply to the quote defines the basis for creating a purchase order. Considerable effort may be expended on trade agreements for critical or frequently replenished material. The trade agreement information can be used in planning calculations to recommend a vendor (with the lowest lost or lead time) on planned purchase orders, and in cost rollup calculations for manufactured items.

Information about vendors provides the starting point for explaining purchase orders. The explanation of purchase orders covers the variations for distribution and manufacturing environments, variations in sourcing and agreement information (such as trade agreements, requests for quotes, and purchase requisitions), and variations in purchase order coordination, receiving, and returns to vendor. These topics are reflected in the following sections within the chapter.

1. Vendor information
2. Purchase orders
3. Purchase order considerations
4. Purchase order variations for manufacturers and distributors
5. Purchase prices and trade agreements
6. Request for quote (RFQ)
7. RFQ considerations
8. Purchase requisitions and approval process
9. Purchase requisition considerations
10. Coordinating purchasing activities
11. Purchase order receipts and receiving inspection
12. Returns to vendor

Vendor Information

A subset of vendor information is directly related to purchase order processing. Each vendor is defined in a vendor master file by a unique identifier. Buy-from and pay-to vendors require unique identifiers, and a buy-from vendor can optionally have one or more ship-from addresses. Several data elements have particular significance to purchase order processing.

Preferred Ship-To Site and Warehouse Each buy-from vendor can have a preferred ship-to site and warehouse that act as default values when manually entering a purchase order for the vendor.

Ship-From Addresses A vendor can have one or more addresses for the purpose of identifying the ship-from location. When defining additional addresses, the user can designate one as the primary ship-from address and others as alternates. During purchase order entry, the system displays the primary ship-from address but the user can select (transfer) an alternate to the order or create an order-specific ship-from address. Each line item can be assigned a ship-from address. The user can optionally designate (move) the order-specific ship-from address for updating the vendor master information.

Pay-To Vendor Each vendor can optionally have a different pay-to vendor (termed the *invoice account* vendor), which acts as a default on purchase orders.

Attributes Related to Pricing and Discounts   Agreements about purchase prices and discounts are typically defined for specific vendors. However, some environments involve pricing and discount agreements with a group of vendors. For purchase trade agreement purposes, the group identifiers assigned to a vendor include a price group and three discount groups: the line discount, multiline discount, and total discount groups. The buy-from vendor on a purchase order determines the applicable purchase trade agreements.

Attributes Related to G/L Account Number Assignment   General ledger (G/L) account number assignments (such as trade payables and purchase price variances) are based on a combination of vendor and item characteristics. For example, the trade payables account updated by a purchase order receipt can be based on the vendor group and item group assigned to the vendor and item respectively.

Financial Dimensions for a Vendor   The financial dimension(s) assigned to a vendor provide a means to analyze purchases by vendor type. They can be used in conjunction with financial dimensions assigned to other entities such as items to provide multidimensional purchase analyses.

One-Time Vendors and Creating Vendors During Purchase Order Entry   When initially entering a purchase order, the buy-from vendor can be created on the fly by indicating a one-time vendor. The user enters the vendor name and address information as part of creating the purchase order, and the system automatically creates a new vendor that is flagged as a one-time vendor. Additional information defaults from an existing vendor designated as the source of one-time vendor information. The vendor information can then be manually maintained, including the removal of the one-time vendor flag.

Vendor Hold Status   A vendor hold status (termed the *stopped* flag) can prevent all transactions from being recorded, or only prevent invoices from being entered for the vendor. In addition, a stopped flag can be assigned to a purchase order line item to prevent further transactions against the line item.

Vendor Calendar of Work Days   When purchase lead times are expressed in working days, the calculation of a purchase order start date and/or delivery date can be based on a specified calendar of the vendor's working days. The calculations use the company-wide calendar as the default when a vendor calendar is not specified.

Language for a Vendor The language assigned to each vendor determines which language version should be displayed on printed documents and other vendor interactions. For example, the assigned language determines the language version for an item description on a printed packing slip or invoice.

Intercompany Trading Partner Some enterprises have multiple companies defined within a single Dynamics AX instance, and trading between the companies. A sister company can act as a vendor (or customer) for intercompany trading purposes. The sister company must be set up as an endpoint (in the Application Integration Framework) and associated with the relevant vendor number. Chapter 13 explains the setup information for intercompany orders and several scenarios for intercompany trading.

Summarized Information by Vendor Summarized information about a vendor can be viewed in several ways. A vendor's statistics inquiry provides summarized data in monthly increments, such as the number and value of invoices and payments. Transaction detail can also be viewed by type of purchase document, such as outstanding purchase orders, receipts, invoices, and backorder purchase lines.

Purchase Orders

Purchase orders for material items define scheduled receipts and provide one means to coordinate supply chain activities. The basic structure of a purchase order consists of header and line item information. As a reflection of this basic structure, the purchase order number and line number uniquely identify a scheduled receipt. The purchase order header identifies the buy-from vendor and optionally identifies a different vendor for pay-to purposes.

Purchase Order Life Cycle The life cycle of a purchase order consists of four steps represented by an order status automatically updated by the system.

❖ *Open.* An open status indicates the order has been created.

❖ *Delivered.* All order lines have a delivered status.

❖ *Invoiced.* All order lines have an invoiced status. The significance of an invoiced status reflects several company-wide policies (embedded in the A/P parameters). For example, the policies determine whether the system allows changes to a fully invoiced order, whether the system automatically deletes a fully invoiced order, and whether the system retains information about deleted orders as part of the voided order history.

❖ *Cancelled.* This only applies to a returned items order, where all order lines have been returned and a credit note generated.

Note: An additional field (termed the *document status*) indicates the last document printed for the purchase order.

Receipts and invoices can be reported against a purchase order using the posting function, where the posting function can optionally print the related purchase order document. The printed documents include a purchase order confirmation, a receipts list, a packing slip, and an invoice. A pro forma version of each document can also be printed. You must indicate the vendor's packing slip number for an actual receipt (termed a *packing slip update*), and the vendor's invoice number for an actual invoice. The system can optionally prevent or warn about use of duplicate numbers for a vendor's packing list number and invoice number.[1]

Purchase Order Line Item Life Cycle   The life cycle of a purchase order line consists of three steps represented by a line status automatically updated by the system.

❖ *Open.* An open status indicates the line has been created, and partial receipts or invoices may have been entered.

❖ *Received.* The delivered quantity equals the order quantity. When using delivery tolerances, the delivered quantity can exceed the order quantity or the under-delivery can be flagged as closed during the posting process.

❖ *Invoiced.* The line item quantity has been completely invoiced, taking into account the over- or under-delivery considerations mentioned above. The significance of an invoiced status reflects the company-wide policies

---

[1] Company-wide policies (embedded in the A/P parameters) determine whether the system prevents, warns about, or ignores duplicate numbers for vendor packing slips and invoices.

(embedded in the A/P parameters) about automatic deletion of a fully invoiced line item and whether the system retains information about deleted line items as part of the voided order history.

Over- and under-delivery tolerances are expressed as a percentage, and the values assigned to an item act as defaults for the purchase order line item.[2] However, a line item can be flagged as receive complete so that the system only allows delivery and invoice transactions that exactly match the order quantity. A line item can also be flagged as stopped to prevent any transactions, but this does not affect planning calculations.

Historical Data Retention   Information about line items and/or purchase orders with an invoiced status can be system-deleted immediately or subsequently deleted (by a user-initiated process). Information about deleted orders can also be retained as voided orders.[3]

Other Types of Purchase Orders   The user indicates the purchase order type when initially creating a purchase order. The user can subsequently change the order type, such as changing a quotation to a normal purchase order. In addition to a normal purchase order, the order types include

❖ *Journal (or Draft).* A journal purchase order is typically used to capture information early in the purchase cycle for an expense item, where requirements are not driven by S&OP game plans. The user changes the order type to purchase order upon placement with the vendor. It does not represent a scheduled receipt.
❖ *Subscription.* A subscription purchase order represents a scheduled receipt, and the system automatically recreates it after invoicing. For example, it can be used to purchase a recurring service such as cleaning services.
❖ *Blanket Order.* A blanket purchase order represents a contract with an aggregate quantity and expiration date, where each user-initiated release (for a specified quantity and date) creates a purchase order that represents a scheduled receipt.

---

[2] Company-wide policies (embedded in the A/P parameters) determine whether over- and under-deliveries will be allowed for purchase orders.

[3] Company-wide policies (embedded in the A/P parameters) determine whether deleted purchase orders and line items should be retained as voided orders.

❖ *Returned Order.* When creating a returned order, you enter the vendor RMA (Return Material Authorization) number and the line items are expressed with a negative quantity. Line items can be manually entered, or the original purchase order information can be copied with an inverted quantity.

Purchase Order Considerations

Variations to the basic purchase order process reflect different ways of doing business with vendors and different internal procedures. For example, these variations may involve the use of textual explanations, delivery dates, pricing, and discounts.

Order-Related Text   Many situations require textual explanations or additional descriptive information about the purchase order and line items. Order-related text can be specified in several ways, such as text carried forward from the item master or document handling capabilities.

❖ *Carry Forward of Item Text to Line Item.* The item master allows each item to have an unlimited amount of descriptive text that automatically carries forward to the purchase order line item, where it can be optionally overridden.

❖ *Document Handling Capabilities.* Documents containing descriptive text (defined as a document type of note) can be defined for the purchase order header and/or each line item and flagged for internal or external purposes. The system can print the external notes on each purchase document.

These note documents can be previously defined for the vendor and items but do not automatically carry forward to the purchase order; they must be explicitly copied and pasted to the purchase order header and lines. Other types of documents such as Word files, Excel spreadsheets, and images can also be defined.

❖ *Printing Descriptive Information.* The setup policies for A/P forms determine whether each printed form includes descriptive information. For example, the printed purchase order can identify the external item number and the note documents.

Purchase Order Quantity and UM   The item's standard purchase order quantity and UM acts as default values when manually entering a purchase order. The system provides a soft warning if the entered quantity exceeds the item's minimum or maximum purchase order quantity, or does not match the multiple quantity for a purchase order. When a partial delivery is anticipated, entering a separate "receive now" quantity can simplify the posting process for deliveries. Partial deliveries of a line item can be explicitly forbidden using the "receive complete" flag to indicate the delivery quantity must match the order quantity exactly.

Delivery Date and Purchase Lead Time Each purchase order line identifies one delivery date that indicates the scheduled receipt for the purposes of planning calculations. However, the user can optionally enter another date—the confirmed delivery date—indicating when it will be actually delivered, and planning calculations use this confirmed date.

When manually creating purchase orders, the line item's delivery date initially defaults to the delivery date specified in the order header, plus additional days for purchase lead time. The system automatically calculates this purchase lead time using the applicable source of information.[4] The purchase lead time represents the turnaround time to receive the item after purchase order placement. It can be expressed in calendar days or working days. The expected turnaround time can optionally include a safety margin that represents the time to prepare a purchase order.

Rescheduling Assumption and Purchase Lead Time Purchase lead time is related to the concept of a rescheduling assumption within the planning calculations, where it is easier to reschedule an existing purchase order to meet an item's requirements (within the time horizon defined by the item's normal lead time) compared to the creation of a new purchase order. You should specify the company-wide policy about using purchase lead times as the basis for the rescheduling assumption (termed the *dynamic negative days* policy) in the master scheduling parameters.

The item's normal lead time represents the simplest basis for the rescheduling assumption. A more complex basis consists of an item-specific time horizon (termed the *negative days* policy within the item's coverage group) that represents the fastest possible turnaround for buying each item.

---

[4] As described in Chapter 2, an item's purchase lead time can be defined as site- and warehouse-specific (within the item's coverage data), as a company-wide default (with the item's default order settings), or as a site-specific default (within the item's site-specific order settings).

Purchase Order Delivery Considerations   Delivery considerations include default values concerning delivery tolerances, the ship-to site/warehouse, and delivery weight and volume.

❖ *Default Delivery Tolerances.* With purchase order delivery tolerances, the system allows the received quantity to be greater or less than the ordered quantity as long as it is within the specified tolerances. Over- and under-delivery tolerances are expressed as a percentage, and the values assigned to an item act as defaults for a purchase order line item.

❖ *Default Ship-to Site and Warehouse.* A default ship-to site and warehouse can be optionally specified for an item, as defined on the item's Default Order Settings form (to specify the default ship-to site) and the item's Site-Specific Order Settings form (to specify the default ship-to warehouse). A mandatory flag indicates the default ship-to site and warehouse must be used on purchase order line items. The mandatory flag especially applies to items that are only purchased and used at a single site and warehouse.

❖ *Delivery Weight and Volume.* The system uses the volume and net weight for each item to calculate the total for all line items on a purchase order.

Pricing and Discounting on a Purchase Order   An item's price and applicable discounts can be manually or automatically assigned on a purchase order. With manual assignment, for example, the line item discount can be expressed as a percent or an amount or both, while the order total discount can be expressed as a percentage. Automatic assignment can reflect the item's purchase trade agreements, or a source document such as a purchase requisition or request for quote, as explained in subsequent sections within this chapter.

Miscellaneous Charges on a Purchase Order   Miscellaneous charges such as freight can be manually entered for a purchase order. They can also be automatically assigned based on item master data or purchase price trade agreements.

An alternative approach termed auto-miscellaneous charges can be defined within the A/P setup information. The auto-miscellaneous charges can apply to the entire order and/or to line items. The charges can be defined as a fixed amount, an amount per piece, or a percentage of value. Charges related to the entire purchase order can be defined for a single vendor, all vendors, or a group of vendors (identified by the *Miscellaneous Charges* group). Charges related to line items can be defined by vendor and item. Item-related charges, for example, can be predefined for a single item or a group of items (identified by the *Miscellaneous Charges* group assigned to relevant items).[5]

Short-Cut Approach for Creating Multiple Line Items A short-cut approach for creating multiple line items allows the user to view a user-defined subset of items, enter just the order quantity for desired items, and update the purchase order. The user-defined subset of items reflects filters, and can be saved and reused. This short-cut approach employs the *create lines* function within the line item section of a purchase order.

Identifying Supplementary Items Automatic calculation of supplementary items requires a user-initiated function after entering all purchase order line items. Supplementary items provide one means for reminders about buying related products.

Mass Changes to Line Items Based on Changes to Header Information Changes to selected fields in the purchase order header can automatically update the same fields in the line items. Examples of selected fields include the delivery date and the ship-to site and warehouse. Each selected field and its automatic update policy can be identified as part of the A/P parameters for updating order lines.

Versions of a Purchase Order Different versions of a purchase order can identify the history of changes. The system assigns a version number each time you post a purchase order confirmation, where the version reflects a numeric suffix (such as -1 and -2) to the purchase order number. Hence, posting the confirmation after making changes to purchase order information will automatically track the history of changes. The version appears on a printed purchase order confirmation, and the historical versions can be viewed on the purchase order inquiry. The most recent version is used for the purpose of the receipts list, packing list, invoice, and planning calculations.

You can revert to a previous version via a copy function (termed the *Copy from Journal* function) on a purchase order. Select from the displayed

---

[5] Two policies (embedded within the A/P parameters) indicate whether the system recognizes automiscellaneous charges for the entire order and for line items.

list of versions, and specify to delete lines from the existing order, so that the existing purchase order data gets updated. After making the updates, you should repost the purchase order confirmation to assign a new version number.

Creating a Purchase Order via the Copy Function A copy function (termed *Copy from All*) can be used to create line items from a previously entered purchase order. For example, the user can select the desired purchase order and the desired line item(s) from a displayed list of all previous orders. You can also select from versions of purchase orders, or packing lists and invoices. You can indicate how to handle updates, such as appending line items and recalculating prices for the new line items.

Generating a Credit Note from a Purchase Order Some situations require creation of a credit note while in the midst of purchase order entry. One approach employs a negative quantity for the purchase order line item. When posting the receipt or vendor invoice, the system will subtract the value from the invoice and record an issue rather than a receipt.

A second approach (termed the *create credit note* function) acts like the copy order function, since the user must select the applicable order from the displayed list of the vendor's previously invoiced purchase orders. This requires historical information but supports access to the original information such as purchase price. Just like the copy function, the selected line item can then be added to the purchase order (with a negative quantity).

Changing the Buy-From or Pay-To Vendor on a Purchase Order Changes to the buy-from or pay-to vendor can be made prior to posting receipts, but the changes have several impacts. For example, changing the buy-from vendor may result in a new pay-to vendor. After changing the buy-from vendor, the user responds to prompts about updating information impacted by the change, such as prices and discounts that reflect purchase trade agreements with the new vendor.

Handling Purchases of Expense Items The purchase of an expense item requires entry of an item number on a purchase order line item, where the item number typically represents a category of expense items. The Chapter 2 section about item identification provided guidelines about item numbers for indirect material and expense items. After entering the item number on a line item, the user must indicate the appropriate G/L account number associated with the expense item.

Totals for a Purchase Order   The system calculates several order totals, including a total invoice amount and total weight and volume. Order totals can be displayed for order quantities or received quantities. For example, the volume and weight of order quantities can be used for truckload planning purposes.

Purchase Order Variations for Manufacturers and Distributors

Purchase order processing in a manufacturing or distribution environment involves many of the above-mentioned considerations and a few additional ones. These additional variations include purchase orders linked to sales orders or production orders, and subcontract manufacturing with purchases of outside operations.

Handling a Purchase Order Linked to a Sales Order   (Buy to Order)   A purchase order directly linked to a sales order can be generated by the user during sales order processing. When prompted for generating a purchase order, the user can accept the suggested quantity and vendor (the item's preferred vendor) or override the suggestions. The user can also indicate whether to use the item's order quantity modifiers (for minimum, maximum, and multiple) for the purchase order quantity. The system then generates a linked purchase order, where the reference field information identifies the linkage in each order and the system reserves the scheduled receipt for the sales order. Changes to the sales order or purchase order are not automatically updated in the linked order; changes must be entered manually.

Handling a Direct Delivery Purchase Order Linked to a Sales Order   The handling of a direct delivery (drop-ship) purchase order is very similar to the buy-to-order process described above. There are several key differences. First, the user initiates a different process during sales order processing, and the system automatically transfers the delivery addresses to the purchase order (including addresses by line item).   Second, changes to the sales order can update the purchase order, such as a change in quantity, prior to any receipt transactions. Finally, a sales order shipment transaction is unnecessary, since the purchase receipt (or invoice) automatically updates the shipped quantity. The sales order invoice must still be posted.

Buying Selected Components Within a Kit Item   An item's bill of material can represent a kit of components, and the user can view and select components (termed the *explode BOM* function) for a specified purchase order line item. The system automatically adds a line item for each selected component, with pricing based on the component item and a quantity reflecting the bill structure. The original line is displayed on the screen but not on printed forms.

Handling a Purchase Order Linked to a Production Order   When the bill of material for a manufactured item contains a buy-to-order component (identified by a component type of vendor), a scheduled production order for the manufactured item automatically generates a linked purchase order for the purchased component. The system assigns the component's preferred vendor (if defined) or the item's preferred vendor to the purchase order. The reference field information identifies the linkage in each order and the system reserves the scheduled receipt for the production order. Schedule changes for the production order can automatically update the schedule for the linked purchase order.

Handling a Purchase Order for an Outside Operation   An outside operation is modeled by a component in the bill of material, and represents one case of the vendor component type described above. That is, a scheduled production order for the parent automatically generates a linked purchase order for the purchased component. A separate section in Chapter 3 explained the guidelines for handling subcontracted production using an outside operation component.

Purchase Prices and Trade Agreements

An item's purchase price can be defined several different ways.[6] As one of these approaches, a purchase trade agreement represents predefined information for buying products from a vendor, such as a negotiated price and/or discount scheme. A purchase trade agreement is normally defined for an item's preferred vendor and alternative vendors. An item's purchase price and discount can be manually entered, but trade agreements support automatic entry. There are several types of purchase trade agreements that

---

[6] The different ways to define an item's purchase price were described in Chapter 2 and illustrated in Figure 2.5.

identify the purchase price, line discount, multiline discount, and/or total discount. The different types can be used in combination with each other, such as defining the purchase price and a discount.

Preferred Vendor and Alternative Vendors   An item's preferred vendor can be specified on the item master as a company-wide policy, or as a site- or warehouse-specific policy as part of the item's coverage data. The preferred vendor is identified on planned purchase orders generated by the planning calculations.   However, leaving the preferred vendor field blank enables the planning calculations to suggest the vendor for planned purchase orders based on the lowest price or lead time information within the purchase price trade agreements.

A drop-down list of an item's alternative vendors can be viewed for a planned purchase order. The alternative vendors reflect the definition of vendor item numbers (termed external item numbers) or purchase price trade agreement information.

Purchase Price Trade Agreements   A purchase price trade agreement indicates the purchase price for an item. The purchase price typically reflects one or more of the factors shown in Figure 8.1 and illustrated below.[7] The agreement also defines the delivery lead time and an optional miscellaneous charge. For example, a different purchase price or a miscellaneous charge could be defined for a shorter delivery lead time.

- Pricing by item and unit of measure, such as different prices per piece and per dozen.
- Pricing by currency type, such as separate pricing for foreign purchases.
- Pricing with date effectivities, for supporting annual price updates or seasonal price promotions. Price assignment reflects the order date on a purchase order.
- Pricing with quantity breakpoints.
- Pricing based on delivery days.
- Pricing that involves an additional miscellaneous charge, such as a charge for fast delivery, small order quantity or freight.

---

[7] A set of company-wide policies (embedded in the Activate Price/Discount form) determines whether the system recognizes these factors.

| Site or Warehouse-Specific Information | | | | N/A | N/A |
| Company-Wide Information | | | | | |

Factor		Purchase Price	Types of Discounts		
			Line Discount	Multi-line Discount	Total Discount
Item	Item and UM	X	X	N/A	See policy about Including item value
	Group of Items	N/A	X Line Discount Group	X Multi-line Discount Group	N/A
	All Items		X	X	
Buy-From Vendor	Vendor	X	X	X	X
	Group of Vendors	X Price Group	X Line Discount Group	X Multi-line Discount Group	X Total Discount Group
	All Vendors	X	X	X	X
Other Factors	Date Effectivity	X	X	X	X
	Currency Code	X	X	X	X
	Quantity Breakpoints	X	X	X	Order Value Breakpoint
	Delivery Days Misc Charges	X X	N/A		
	Policies	Price Group Policy: Price Includes Sales Tax			Item Policy: Include item value for total discount purposes

Figure 8.1 Purchase Trade Agreements

Price trade agreements are expressed as one or more entries that identify the applicable factors. A simple pricing scheme that represents a single purchase price, for example, would require one entry for each item purchased from the vendor. Additional entries would be required for defining next year's price, quantity breakpoints, and variations in the items' purchase UM. Additional entries are also required for each site and warehouse when using site- and warehouse-specific pricing. Figure 8.1 illustrates the site/warehouse factor as a third dimension, since pricing can be company-wide or site/warehouse-specific.

Each entry within a purchase price trade agreement requires a price and a price unit. Pricing reflects a specified UM and is normally expressed per unit, unless pricing must be expressed with more than two decimal places (such as expressing $.00123 as $1.23 per 1000 units). Each entry can also define a delivery lead time and miscellaneous charge.

When manually creating a purchase order, the system uses the trade agreement information to automatically assign an item's price using the lowest price of applicable trade agreement entries. The system also assigns the delivery lead time and miscellaneous charge associated with the price. The user can view available prices during purchase order entry, such as viewing quantity breakpoints or future pricing to guide purchase decisions.

There are several considerations with respect to purchase price trade agreements:

- Trade agreements for an item's purchase price and line discounts can represent either company-wide or site/warehouse-specific information, based on an item-related policy (embedded in the dimension group assigned to the item).
- The price trade agreement information includes purchase prices and delivery lead times, and planning calculations can suggest a vendor for planned purchase orders based on lowest price or delivery lead time.[8]
- The price trade agreement information for purchased components can be used for calculating the planned cost of a manufactured item, as described in the Chapter 5 section about BOM calculations with planned costs.
- The price trade agreement optionally defines a miscellaneous charge, such as a surcharge for small order quantities or faster-than-normal delivery. It is included in the net amount but not in the unit price for the purchase order line item.

An additional consideration involves the system logic when there are multiple trade agreement entries that apply to a situation. Each trade agreement entry can optionally specify whether the system should search for other applicable entries. The system normally uses the most specific entry possible, such as a vendor-specific purchase price rather than one associated with a vendor group.

Types of Purchase Discounts in Trade Agreements Purchase discounts are calculated after the line item prices have been identified on a purchase order. The discounts can be related to a single line, multiple lines, the order total value, or a combination of these approaches.

❖ *Line Discount.* The line discount is expressed as a fixed amount or a percentage or both. In particular, the percentage discount can be expressed as a single value or as two values (e.g., using a 10% discount for both values results in a 19% discount), and the system applies the discount

---

[8] A company-wide policy (embedded in the master planning parameters) determines whether planning calculations consider trade agreement information for planned purchases and whether the criterion should be lowest price or lead time.

percentage after reducing the price by the fixed discount amount. Line discounts often reflect one or more of the factors shown in Figure 8.1 and illustrated below.

○ Discounts for a single item, all items, or a group of items (based on the *Line Discount Group* assigned to relevant items). For example, the groups could represent different product lines. Two different group codes (both called the *Line Discount Group*) can be predefined —one for items and one for vendors—and then assigned to relevant items and vendors.

○ Discounts based on date effectivities, quantity breakpoints, and currency code for foreign purchases.

A simple discount scheme involving a discount percent by group of items, for example, would require one trade agreement entry for each group. Note that a line discount can be company-wide or site/warehouse-specific, as illustrated in Figure 8.1.

❖ *Multiline Discount Based on Total Quantity.* The multiline discount reflects a discount based on the total quantity for multiple line items. It is expressed the same way as a single line discount (as a fixed amount or a percentage or both). The trade agreement entries can reflect the factors shown in Figure 8.1, such as a discount that applies to a group of items. Two different group codes (both called the *Multiline Discount Group*) can be predefined—one for items and one for vendors—and then assigned to relevant items and vendors. The user must initiate calculation of multiline discounts on a purchase order after all line items have been entered.

The combination of a line discount and multiline discount can be handled different ways, as defined by a company-wide policy embedded in the A/P parameters. A typical approach views the two values as additive. However, you could specify the policy as use the lowest value or highest value, use only one of the values, or treat them as multiplicative.

❖ *Discount (or Surcharge) Based on Total Order Value.* The total discount applies to the total order value. It is expressed the same way as a single line discount: as a fixed amount or a percentage or both. Expressing the fixed amount as a negative value represents a surcharge. The trade agreement entries can reflect the factors shown in Figure 8.1, such as a discount with order value breakpoints. An item-related policy determines whether the system includes or excludes the item in calculating total order value for the purpose of a total discount. The user must initiate calculation of the total discount on a purchase order after all line items have been entered, or the total discount can be automatically calculated (based on a company-wide policy embedded in the A/P parameters).

Maintaining and Viewing Purchase Trade Agreement Information

Information about purchase trade agreements can be maintained directly on the relevant form (such as the purchase price trade agreement form), or it can be prepared beforehand and then used to update trade agreement information.

❖ *Directly Maintain Trade Agreement Data.* Access the purchase trade agreement information from the item, vendor, or purchase order forms, or for a specified group related to a line discount, multiline discount, or total discount.

❖ *Prepare Data Beforehand.* Preparing data beforehand (using the Price/ Discount Agreement Journal and its associated line items) offers several advantages in data maintenance. For example, you can create a new journal for preparing next year's purchase price trade agreements, and then initially populate the entries with information about existing purchase price agreements for selected items or vendors. The information can then be manually updated prior to posting the journal. In addition, you can perform mass changes to the entries (such as increasing the price a specified percentage or amount), or copy the entries in order to prepare price agreements for another item, vendor, validity period, or currency. The concept of preparing data beforehand is employed within the request for quotes (RFQ) business process, so that a vendor reply can be used to prepare purchase trade agreement information.

Use the Purchase Price report to view purchase price trade agreement information, or a subset of information based on the report's selection criteria (such as the selected items, vendors or currency). Use the Price/Discount List report to view all types of price and discount trade agreement information, or a subset based on the report's selection criteria.

Agreements about Supplementary Items

Some purchase environments involve supplementary items, such as "Buy ten and get an additional item free," which result in additional line items on a purchase order. Supplementary items can also represent related items that should be purchased together, thereby providing a reminder to the buyer. A supplementary purchase item and quantity can be designated as mandatory or optional, and chargeable or free-of-charge. The rules may also include date effectivities, a minimum order quantity and/or a one-time-only offer. The supplementary item can be tied to the purchase of a specific item. Alternatively, it can be tied to one or more of the factors shown in Figure 7.2 (in the previous chapter), such as the item group or vendor group. Two different group codes (both called the *Supplementary Item Group*) must be predefined—one for items and one for vendors—and then assigned to relevant items and vendors.

During the process of entering purchase order line items, the user initiates a calculation that displays the applicable supplementary items. The items are segmented into mandatory and optional (with user selection of the optional items), and acceptance results in additional purchase order line items. For example, viewing and selecting the optional items acts as the basis for buying related products.

Agreements about Miscellaneous Charges   Some purchase environments involve predefined agreements about miscellaneous charges, such as handling charges for selected items or vendors. These charges can be embedded in the purchase price trade agreement information, or they can be specified separately as *auto-miscellaneous charges*. These auto-miscellaneous charges can be applied to an entire purchase order or to individual line items, and expressed as a fixed amount, an amount per piece, or a percentage of value.

❖ *Order-Level Charges.* Charges related to the entire purchase order can be defined for a single vendor, all vendors, or a group of vendors (identified by the *Miscellaneous Charges Group* assigned to relevant vendors). Examples of an order-level charge include order preparation costs for selected vendors.
❖ *Line Item Charges.* Charges related to the purchase order line item can be defined by vendor and item, such as charges for a single item, all items, or a group of items (identified by the miscellaneous charges group assigned to relevant items).[9] Examples of a line item charge include a setup fee for purchasing selected items from a vendor.

Agreements Expressed as a Blanket Purchase Order   A blanket purchase order represents one form of a vendor agreement that defines the

---

[9] Two policies (embedded within the A/R parameters) indicate whether the system recognizes auto-miscellaneous charges for the entire order and for line items.

item price (and discounts) based on an aggregate quantity. Each user-initiated release (for a specified quantity and date) creates a purchase order that inherits the agreed-upon price. A blanket order report identifies each release and summarizes the quantities ordered, received, and invoiced.

Request for Quote (RFQ)

A request for quote (RFQ) provides a structured approach for soliciting and using purchase quotations. RFQs are oftentimes used as an extension of purchase requisition activities, or in the context of sourcing an item with a planned purchase order. Hence, the starting points for an RFQ can be a purchase requisition or a planned purchase order. In addition, an RFQ can be manually created with the intent of creating a blanket order or a single purchase order.

The RFQ business process consists of several basic steps to create an RFQ and handle the vendor-specific replies. The terms RFQ and vendor-specific RFQ represent two different yet related constructs within Dynamics AX. The RFQ construct has a unique identifier, and you create an RFQ to identify the item(s) to be purchased and the applicable vendors that should be sent RFQ information. By sending the RFQ information, you create a vendor-specific RFQ (with its unique identifier) for each applicable vendor, and the vendor can reply to the vendor-specific RFQ. Figure 8.2 displays these basic steps within the information flow for RFQs, and provides the organizing framework for further explanation.

The basic steps include (#1) creating an RFQ, (#2) sending the vendor-specific RFQs to obtain reply information, (#3) receiving a reply for a vendor-specific RFQ, (#4) accepting or rejecting a reply, and (#5) the automatic actions for an accepted reply.[10] The starting point for creating the RFQ impacts the first step and the last step, such as creating the RFQ from a purchase requisition and then automatically updating the purchase requisition based on an accepted vendor reply. In addition, the information flow may include the optional steps (labeled #4a and #5a) to update purchase trade agreements with information that reflects a vendor reply.

Step #1: Create RFQ The critical information for an RFQ consists of the applicable vendor(s) and item(s), where the item information includes the

---

[10] The basic steps are reflected in the status of a vendor-specific RFQ (created, sent, received, accepted, and rejected).

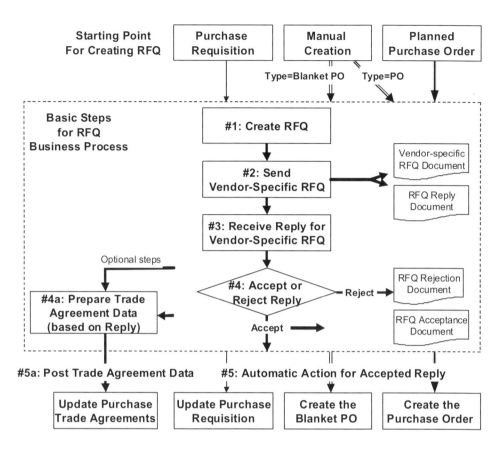

Figure 8.2 Information Flow for Purchasing RFQs

item identifier, quantity and unit of measure, delivery date, and the ship-to information. The starting point for creating an RFQ determines whether the item and vendor information will be automatically populated or manually entered. The starting points for creating an RFQ can be a purchase requisition or a planned purchase order, or an RFQ can be manually created.

❖ *Create an RFQ from a Purchase Requisition.* Information about the item and applicable vendor will be automatically populated based on information within the purchase requisition. The RFQ type is automatically assigned as purchase requisition, and the purchase requisition's status will be changed to pending RFQ.[11]

---

[11] The workflow configuration for a purchase requisition includes a task that represents completion of the RFQ information, so that you can create an RFQ prior to reporting the task as completed. This task may specify an automatic completion action after RFQ acceptance (which would update the RFQ reference information on the purchase requisition).

❖ *Create an RFQ Manually.* Information about the item(s) and applicable vendor(s) must be manually specified. The user also designates an RFQ type (as a purchase order or blanket PO) when manually creating the RFQ, which determines whether an accepted RFQ reply will automatically generate a purchase order or a blanket purchase order. Figure 8.3 displays these two RFQ types for a manually created RFQ.

❖ *Create an RFQ by Changing a Planned Purchase Order to an RFQ.* Information about the item and applicable vendor will be automatically populated based on information within the planned purchase order. The RFQ type is automatically assigned as a purchase order.

There are several caveats about changing (converting) a planned purchase order to an RFQ. Converting a planned purchase order to an RFQ will delete the planned order, and planning calculations can generate another planned purchase order unless RFQs are treated as a scheduled receipt (as specified in the Master Plan policies). This master plan policy should only be employed if there is a 100% probability that all RFQs for direct material will result in an accepted reply that generates a purchase order. In most situations, RFQs are only needed for some planned orders, such as a planned order for a new item, or for an infrequently purchased item. A suggested approach would be to manually create the RFQ (rather than convert the planned order to an RFQ), and to avoid the master plan policy of treating an RFQ as a scheduled receipt.

Step #2: Send the Vendor-Specific RFQs A vendor-specific RFQ will be created for each applicable vendor when you first send the information. When sending the information, you can optionally print an RFQ Reply document (for each applicable vendor) that specifies the desired information to be supplied by the vendor. For example, the desired information for each item may include the price, validity dates, and lead time. Sending information a second time can generate the printed document but does not create a new vendor-specific RFQ. However, if you subsequently add an applicable vendor to the RFQ, then sending the information a second time will create a vendor-specific RFQ for the additional vendor.

Step #3: Receive Reply for a Vendor-Specific RFQ You can manually enter the reply information for a vendor-specific RFQ, or automatically populate the reply (with information from the RFQ) and manually override values as needed. This information typically includes the purchase price, the discount percent or amount (if applicable), and the delivery lead time.

Use of the reply information differs slightly for the optional steps to update purchase trade agreements. For example, the quantity will be used for quantity breakpoints in preparing entries for the price agreement journal. That is, multiple RFQ line items for the same item can indicate different quantity breakpoints with different prices (rather than different purchases).

Step #4: Accept or Reject the Reply for a Vendor-Specific RFQ

You can accept or reject the reply information for a vendor-specific RFQ, and optionally indicate a user-defined reason for the decision for subsequent analysis purposes. When updating the accept/reject decision, you can optionally print an RFQ Acceptance or RFQ Rejection document to communicate the decision to the relevant vendor. Prior to the accept/reject decision, you can optionally request an updated reply, and view replies from multiple vendors for comparison purposes.

Step #5: Automatic Action for an Accepted Reply

Automatic actions are determined by the RFQ type assigned to an RFQ. The RFQ type reflects the starting point for creating an RFQ, as illustrated by the different types of arrows in Figure 8.2 and explained below.

❖ *RFQ Type of Purchase Order.* An accepted RFQ reply will automatically generate a purchase order, with a purchase order line item for each line item within the reply.

❖ *RFQ Type of Blanket Purchase Order.* An accepted RFQ reply will automatically generate a blanket purchase order, with a purchase order line item for each line item within the reply.

❖ *RFQ Type of Purchase Requisition.* An accepted RFQ reply will automatically update information for each requisition line item. This information includes the vendor, price, discount percent or amount (if applicable), and delivery date. The status of the purchase requisition will also be changed from pending RFQ to pending completion.

Optional Steps #4a and #5a: Prepare and Post Purchase Trade Agreement Information

The reply to a vendor-specific RFQ can serve as the basis for updating purchase trade agreement information, regardless of the accept/reject decision on the reply. The trade agreement information may consist of purchase prices or line item discounts, and information about lead times, miscellaneous charges, validity dates, and other factors. There are two steps to updating the purchase trade agreement information from a reply.

❖ *Step #4a: Prepare Purchase Trade Agreement Data (Based on the Reply).* The user creates a price agreement journal that contains an entry for each line item within the reply, which initially prepares the reply data in the necessary format.[12] For example, a reply line item may contain information about a purchase price and a discount percent, and the price agreement journal will contain two entries—one entry for the purchase price and a second entry for the discount percentage. The purchase price entries will reflect reply information about the price, unit of measure, currency, lead time, validity dates, and miscellaneous charges. In addition, the quantity will be treated as a quantity breakpoint within the agreement. The user can edit information within the trade agreement journal.[13]

❖ *Step #5a: Post the Purchase Trade Agreement Data.* The user posts the trade agreement journal, which updates the purchase trade agreement information.

RFQ Considerations

Usage of RFQs has several variations, such as creating an RFQ without an item number, creating RFQs for components of a manufactured item, and the use of copy and mass change functionality. There are also several reports and a transaction history for RFQs.

RFQs for Items Without an Item Number An RFQ is sometimes required for something that does not yet have an item number, where the item number will be assigned prior to completing the RFQ process. A line item on an RFQ normally identifies an item number, but a line type of *none* enables the user to indicate the desired purchase (without an item number) by entering information in the name, unit of measure, external item number, and text fields. The line item can be changed from none to an actual item number (on the RFQ or the vendor-specific RFQ) at any time prior to accepting the vendors reply. You cannot accept a vendor's reply unless an item number has been assigned.

---

[12] The identifier of the trade agreement journal represents the default defined in the A/P parameters.

[13] The reply information about a multiline discount will not be reflected in the trade agreement journal, so that the user must manually enter this information. A vendor reply with multiple line items that represent quantity breakpoints will be used to create multiple entries in the price/discount journal.

Create RFQ Line Items via Copying RFQ line items can be created by copying information from an existing RFQ or purchase order. The user can selectively identify one or more existing orders, and the line items, that should be copied. The copied line items can be added to the RFQ or replace the current information.

Mass Changes to RFQ Line Items Based on Changes to Header Information Changes in selected fields in the RFQ header can automatically update the same fields in the RFQ line items. Examples of selected fields include the ship-to site and warehouse, the delivery date, and the expiration date. An automatic update policy provides an option to prompt the user before making mass changes. Each selected field and its automatic update policy can be identified as part of the A/P parameters about requests for quotes.

Coordinating Follow-Up on Open RFQs Vendor-specific RFQs frequently require follow-up to ensure the vendor reply has been received prior to the expiration date. Use the Request for Quote Follow-up form to view all vendor-specific RFQs, and selectively filter the information based on the expiration date, vendor, item, or other attribute.

The Alert functionality (within Dynamics AX) provides another approach for coordinating follow-up efforts. For example, the alert notification can be generated when the RFQ expiry date has been reached, so that you can verify whether all of the replies have been received.

Viewing Transaction History Related to an RFQ The RFQ transaction history (viewed on the Request for Quote journal) contains a record for each vendor-specific RFQ that has been sent, received, accepted, or rejected. It also displays the reason for an acceptance or rejection if a reason was entered by the user.

RFQ Reports and Vendor Performance A vendor performance report indicates the ratio of accepted RFQs (and line items) versus the number sent, and also provides a frequency analysis of reason codes for acceptance and rejection. A report of previous RFQs (and their vendor-specific RFQs) can be viewed by item or by vendor.

RFQs for Components of a Manufactured Item When RFQs are required for the components of a manufactured item, enter the manufactured item on the RFQ and then use the Explode BOM function to view and select the components. The system automatically adds a line item for each selected component. The original line item is displayed on the screen but not on printed forms.

Considerations about Vendor-Specific RFQs Usage of vendor-specific RFQs has several variations, such as document formats and manual additions to vendor replies.

❖ *Defining the Format of a Vendor-Specific RFQ Document.* The printed RFQ document includes the item, quantity, and delivery date for each line item, and it can optionally include the unit price and net amount for each line item (by indicating your selection when sending an RFQ). However, you should use the RFQ Reply document to indicate the desired information to be supplied by the vendor. Another document (termed the RFQ Reply document) also specifies the desired information to be supplied by the vendor.[14]

❖ *Manual Additions to the Line Items on a Vendor-Specific RFQ.* Line items can be manually added to the vendor-specific RFQ. The line items initially reflect the line items specified on the RFQ. For example, the additions might represent alternative items, alternative units of measure, or additional quantity breakpoints for pricing purposes.

Purchase Requisitions and Approval Process

Purchase requisitions generally apply to many types of indirect materials, where procurement is triggered by a user request and involves an approval process before items can be purchased. However, a purchase requisition approval process sometimes applies to direct material items with requirements driven by S&OP game plans, such as sourcing a new item from a new vendor. The approval process employs the workflow management capabilities within Dynamics AX, where a predefined workflow template provides the framework for creating a workflow configuration that can be tailored to represent a purchase requisition approval process.[15] This explana-

---

[14] The desired RFQ Reply information can be specified as a company-wide default (in the A/P parameters about RFQs), and these defaults can be overridden for a given RFQ. In addition, policies within the A/P forms setup (for the RFQ) determine which types of note documents will be printed within the header and line items.

[15] Dynamics AX 2009 has two predefined templates that serve as the basis for creating a purchase requisition workflow configuration. One template applies to general purchase requisitions, and the second template applies to project-related purchase requisitions. These two templates share the same conceptual model consisting of a task, an approval process with one or more approval steps, and optional use of subworkflows.

tion focuses on the conceptual model underlying the out-of-the-box workflow template and the workflow configurations created from this template. It does not explain how to customize the template or create additional templates.

The workflow template for purchase requisitions contains an underlying conceptual model. Stated simply, the conceptual model consists of a task, and an approval process with one or more approval steps.[16] After you create a workflow configuration based on the workflow template, you define the nature of the task and each approval step through user-defined names and instructions. These names and instructions will be displayed to the end-users during the basic steps for submitting and processing a purchase requisition. In addition, the conceptual model consists of rules that need to be defined within the related workflow configuration. For example, the rules concerning an approval step include its conditions for use, assignment of the relevant approver(s), and time limits for completion. You define these rules for the task and approval steps within the workflow configuration to model your business process for handling purchase requisitions. Each time you create or modify a workflow configuration, the system automatically assigns a version number (e.g., version 1.0.0.0) so that you can track changes and flag the active version. The active version of a workflow configuration is automatically assigned to a submitted purchase requisition based on the rules concerning its conditions for use.

The information flow for a purchase requisition consists of five basic steps. The first two steps involve creating a purchase requisition and submitting it for approval. After submission, a workflow configuration defines and controls the next two steps related to task completion and approval. You perform these four basic steps using the Purchase Requisition form. A fifth step creates the purchase order for an approved purchase requisition. Figure 8.3 displays these five basic steps, and reflects the underlying conceptual model of a task, an approval process, and an approval step within the approval process.

Figure 8.3 also indicates the system-assigned status (in italics) that tracks the life cycle of a purchase requisition. The status changes as you perform each step (such as submitted, completed, approved), and also indicates remaining work (such as pending completion or pending approval). Canceling a requisition will reset the status to draft so that you can delete or submit it.

---

[16] The conceptual model also consists of optional subworkflows, as described in a later section. The concept of a subworkflow requires an understanding of the basic conceptual model within a workflow, so it would be confusing to discuss it at this point in time.

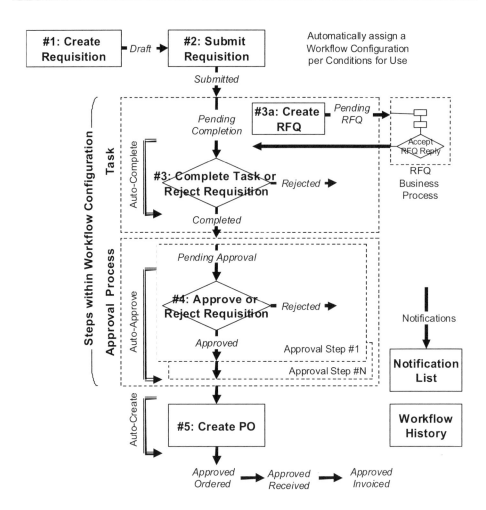

Figure 8.3 Information Flow for Purchase Requisitions

After submitting a purchase requisition (Step #2), it is possible to by-pass selected steps within the information flow. For example, you can define automatic actions within the workflow configuration in order to auto-complete the task (Step #3) and auto-approve an approval process (Step #4). As another example, an overdue task can be auto-completed, and an overdue approval process can be auto-approved. Conversely, the automatic actions and an overdue situation can result in auto-rejection. Finally, the system can auto-create a purchase order (Step #5) for an approved requisition. Figure 8.3 displays the automatic actions for these steps, and also displays the Notification List and Workflow History that apply to Steps #2 through #5. This section describes each step in more detail.

Step #1: Create a Purchase Requisition The person that creates a purchase requisition is termed the requisitioner. You can optionally designate a different requisitioner (using the *on behalf of* capability) when creating a requisition. The identity of the requisitioner (and their position within the organization) becomes important when an approval process reflects the organizational hierarchy. For example, information about the requisitioner's position and the associated report-to position provides the basis for assigning an approver that reflects the first-level manager or a higher-level manager of the requisitioner.

A purchase requisition consists of a header and line items, much like a purchase order. However, you can limit the items that can be entered on a requisition line item, as well as limiting the assignment of G/L accounts to an expense purchase, as described in the next major section concerning purchase requisition considerations about setup information.

Step #2: Submit the Purchase Requisition The system displays the anticipated workflow configuration (and submission instructions) that will be automatically assigned to the requisition when it is submitted. This assignment reflects the conditions for use embedded in each workflow configuration, and the information within a purchase requisition. For example, the assignment of a workflow configuration could be based on information concerning the ship-to address (such as a country-specific workflow), financial dimensions (such as a department-specific workflow), or items (such as a product-specific workflow). The user that submits a requisition is identified as the *submitted by* person, and the requisition status changes from draft to submitted, and then to pending completion.

Step #3: Report a Task as Completed A workflow configuration includes a single task, and task examples include creation of vendor information, verification of information completeness, and RFQ processing. The task is typically assigned to a user-defined role, where the role (such as a purchasing agent) reflects a user group containing one or more users. Other assignment options include assigning the task to a specified user or to a position within the organizational hierarchy. The assigned user must report the task as completed,[17] or it can be automatically reported as completed (based on conditions for auto-completion). The requisition status changes from pending completion to completion, and then to pending approval.

---

[17] When a task is assigned to multiple users, one user must "accept" the task before reporting it as completed. After one user accepts the task, it is no longer assigned to the other users and is removed from their work lists.

The conditions for auto-completion are embedded within the workflow configuration for the task. When a task involves verification of information, for example, the auto-completion could be based on entries of a suggested vendor and price for each line item. When a task involves RFQ processing, the auto-completion can be based on the system-assigned RFQ reference number.

A task can optionally have a time limit for completion. The time limit is typically expressed in a number of hours or days along with a specified calendar of working times. Alternatively, the time limit can be expressed as a number of weeks, or as a specified day and week (such as a Friday within the first week of the month). You can indicate the automatic action (to complete or reject the task) that should be taken if an overdue task exceeds the time limit.

Step #3a: Create a RFQ for the Purchase Requisition (Optional)
An RFQ can be generated for selected lines within a purchase requisition which results in a requisition status of pending RFQ. The RFQ must be generated prior to completion of the workflow task. The RFQ business process includes sending the vendor-specific RFQ to vendors, receiving each vendor's reply, and accepting or rejecting the reply. An accepted reply automatically updates the purchase prices and RFQ reference number on the requisition line items, and the requisition status changes to pending completion. A previous section discussed the purchasing RFQ business process in greater detail.

Step #4: Approve or Reject the Purchase Requisition   The approval process within a workflow configuration can contain one or more approval steps. A simple approval process might contain a single approval step and a specified user as the assigned approver. Alternatively, the assigned approver for an approval step can reflect the organization hierarchy or a group of users.

❖ *Approver Within the Organizational Hierarchy.* The assigned approver(s) can reflect a position within the organizational hierarchy, such as a specific position title or the first-level manager of the requisitioner. When an approval step is assigned to a higher level position (such as the second- or third-level manager), the required approval can be sequential (for each position within the hierarchy) or single. Alternatively, the relevant manager within a hierarchy can be automatically identified based on having an approval limit greater than the requisition amount, and the required approval can be single (for the relevant manager) or sequential (for all managers up through the relevant manager).[18]

❖ *Approver Within a Role (Group of Users).* This approach is termed a role-based approval, and the role represents a group of users. You pre-define each user group, and the users within a group, so that the user group can be specified in the workflow configuration for the approval step. A policy within the approval step determines whether approval can be made by a single user within the user group, or whether it requires approval from all users, a majority of users, or a specified percentage of users within the user group.

The assigned user(s) must report the approval step as approved or rejected. A single approval step cannot be auto-approved, but the entire approval process can be automatically approved. A typical auto-approve situation reflects a requisition amount that is less than the requisitioner's spending limit. The requisition status changes from pending approval to approved or rejected.

A more complex approval process will typically contain multiple approval steps. Several considerations apply to multiple approval steps.

❖ *Linear Sequence of Multiple Approval Steps.* The first approval step must be approved before the second approval step can be approved, so that the sequence of approval steps (specified within the workflow configuration) becomes important.

❖ *Limited Conditions for an Approval Step.* An approval step may or may not be required based on its conditions for use. For example, the requisition amount can act as a condition for use, where one approval step only applies to requisition amounts of less than $5000 and a second approval step only applies to requisition amounts of $5000 or more. Other examples of conditions for use include the financial dimensions (such as a department-specific approval step), the item (such as a category-specific approval step), or the address (such as a site-specific approval step).

Each approval step and the entire approval process can optionally have a time limit for completion. The time limit is typically expressed in a number of hours or days along with a specified calendar of working times. Alter-

---

[18] The concept of assigning an approver within an organizational hierarchy (based on their approval limit) is implemented via the stop condition for an approval step.

natively, the time limit can be expressed as a number of weeks, or as a specified day and week (such as a Friday within the first week of the month). You can indicate the automatic action (to approve or reject the requisition) that should be taken if the overdue step exceeds the time limit.

Step #5: Create a Purchase Order for an Approved Requisition

A company-wide policy (embedded within the A/P parameters) determines whether purchase orders will be automatically or manually created from approved requisitions. With a manual approach, use the *Release Approved Requisition* form (also called the *Create Purchase Order* form) to selectively designate requisitions that should be used to create purchase orders. A separate purchase order will be created for each vendor and currency within the requisition line items. The purchase order will inherit information from the requisition (such as the delivery address and attention information), and you can view the linkage between the purchase order and requisition. The requisition status changes from approved to approved-ordered. As you proceed with receipts and invoices for the purchase order, the requisition status continues to change, such as approved-partially received, approved-received, and approved-invoiced.

Notification List and Other Actions

A Notification List summarizes the purchase requisition actions that need to be performed by a user, such as completing a task or approving an approval step.[19] The Notification List form can be accessed in different ways,[20] so that the user can take action by going to the origin of the notification. The user can optionally mark a notification as read or unread, and delete the notification, to help organize their work activities.

The Notification List can optionally include notifications about other types of events related to a task or approval process.

❖ *Events Related to a Task.* The events include the completion or rejection of a task, a request for change, delegation to another user, and escalation of an overdue task. As part of the workflow configuration for a task, you indicate which events should trigger a notification, who should receive the notification, and the message that should be displayed.

---

[19] A user can modify the purchase requisition and perform actions only when a task is assigned to the user. In addition, a user cannot make changes to a purchase requisition when approving an approval step. If changes are needed, then you can request changes or cancel the purchase requisition.

[20] The Notification List can be accessed from the Dynamics AX tool bar (via View > Notifications) or from the message bar (when it indicates the existence of notifications).

❖ *Events Related to an Approval Process.* The events include the acceptance or rejection of an approval step, a request for change, delegation to another user, and escalation of an overdue approval step. As part of the workflow configuration for an approval process, you indicate which events should trigger a notification, who should receive the notification, and the message that should be displayed.

Workflow History and Audit Trail The Workflow History form displays a complete transaction audit trail with step-by-step status for a purchase requisition. For example, it displays when a task was assigned, who it was assigned to, and who reported it complete along with their comments. The workflow history for a specific requisition can also be viewed when a user needs to report action on it.

Example of a Purchase Requisition Approval Process

A workflow configuration can be tailored to reflect the unique aspects of a purchase requisition approval process, as illustrated in Figure 8.4. The approval process in this example is based on the amount and type of purchase.

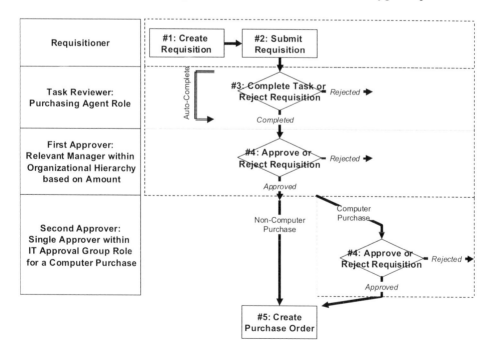

Figure 8.4 Example Approval Process Based on Amount and Type of Purchase

An employee (termed the *requisitioner*) initially creates and submits a purchase requisition. The task of reviewing it for completeness is assigned to a purchasing agent; it can be auto-completed if the information has been completed. The approval process involves a first approver that represents the relevant manager within the requisitioner's organizational hierarchy. The relevant manager is automatically assigned based on having an approval limit greater than the requisition amount. The approval process requires a second approver for computer-related purchases, where the second approver must be an employee within the IT Approval Group of users. The IT Approval Group ensures the requested computer meets the corporate guidelines. Approval of the requisition automatically creates a purchase order.

Purchase Requisition Considerations

The basic steps for handling purchase requisitions involve several setup considerations. Each step has unique setup information, as explained below. Additional considerations include the need for multiple workflow configurations for requisition approval, the use of subworkflows for modeling approval process variations, and the use of project-related purchase requisitions.

Setup Information for Creating a Requisition (Step #1)   The setup information impacting requisition creation can be grouped into several topics.

❖ *Limiting the Items That Can Be Entered on a Purchase Requisition (aka Product Catalog Items).* Purchase requisitions can be for any item, or limited to specified item numbers. These item numbers must be assigned to a product group within a hierarchy of product groups, where the top group is termed a product catalog. You can then identify this top group as a company-wide product catalog (within the A/P parameters). During creation of a requisition line item, the user can easily find and select the desired item number within the product catalog. The user cannot view or enter item numbers that are not within the product catalog.

An item's stopped flag for purchase orders (defined on the item's Default Order Settings) provides a second alternative to limiting items on a requisition. Purchase requisitions can be entered for all items except those with the purchase order stopped flag.

❖ *Creating a Requisition for a Category Item (aka Category Catalog Items).* The item number for a category item represents a category of non-stock or expense items, and descriptive text about the category item must be entered on a requisition to communicate what is being purchased. During creation of a requisition line item, the user can select the relevant category item (within a category catalog) and enter the appropriate descriptive text. To define a category catalog, a single category item must be assigned to a category group within a hierarchy of product groups, where the top group is termed a category catalog. You can then identify this top group as a company-wide category catalog (within the A/P parameters).

❖ *Limiting the G/L Accounts That Can Be Entered for Expense Items on a Purchase Requisition.* Limiting the G/L account numbers for a purchase requisition involves three steps. First, you define ledger account categories for types of expenses, such as office supplies and furniture. Second, you assign a ledger account category to the relevant G/L account numbers, such as the ledger accounts that represent different types of office supplies. Third, you identify the ledger account categories applicable to purchase requisitions (within the A/P parameters). You can then view and select from the applicable G/L accounts when entering a purchase requisition. You cannot enter a G/L account that is not applicable.

❖ *Enforcing an Item's Order Quantity Minimum, Multiple, and/or Maximum on a Purchase Requisition.* A company-wide policy (embedded within the A/P parameters) determines whether the order quantity modifiers will be enforced on purchase requisitions.

Setup Considerations for Submitting a Requisition (Step #2)
Several factors determine which workflow configuration will be assigned to a submitted requisition.

❖ *Selective Assignment of a Workflow Configuration Based on Conditions for Use.* The conditions for use (associated with a workflow configuration) can be based on information within the requisition header or line item, or about the employee originating the requisition. As noted in an earlier example, various workflow configurations may reflect country-specific, department-specific, or product-specific workflows. The conditions for use assigned to each workflow configuration must reflect mutually exclusive alternatives; otherwise the system cannot determine assignment when you submit a requisition.

❖ *Default Workflow Configuration.* The default will be used when the conditions for use do not result in the assignment of a workflow configuration.

❖ *Active Version of a Workflow Configuration.* Only the active version of a workflow configuration will be assigned. Modification of a workflow configuration will automatically result in a different version, and the relevant version must be flagged as active.

Setup Information Related to a Task (Step #3) The setup information impacting a workflow task includes the definition of user groups (roles) for role-based assignment of a task. In order to use role-based assignment, you must define a user group that represents the role (such as the purchasing agent role) and also assign one or more users to the user group.

The concept of organizational hierarchy may apply to the assignment of a task. It normally applies to an approval step, as described below.

Setup Information Related to the Approval Process (Step #4)
The setup information impacting a workflow approval process and its approval steps can be grouped into several topics.

❖ *Definition of the Organizational Hierarchy for Approval Step Assignment.* Positions must be defined, where each position has a report-to position that defines the organization hierarchy. A single position is assigned to each employee.

❖ *Definition of User Groups (Roles) for Role-Based Assignment of an Approval Step.* In order to use role-based assignment, you must define a user group that represents the role (such as the approvers for a given type of item, or for a given department) and also assign one or more users to the user group.

❖ *Employee Spending Limit for Purchase Requisitions.* You define a limit identifier for a spending limit related to purchase requisitions, and use it when setting up the spending limit for an employee. The employee's spending limit includes a specified currency and validity dates, and must be marked as active. A comparison between the requisitioner's spending limit and the requisition amount can be used in an automatic action to auto-approve a purchase requisition.

❖ *Manager's Approval Limit for Purchase Requisitions.* You define a limit identifier for an approval limit related to purchase requisitions, and use it when setting up the approval limit for a managerial employee. The employee's approval limit includes a specified currency and validity dates, and must be marked as active. A comparison between a manager's approval limit and the requisition amount can be used in assigning an approval step to a manager within the organization hierarchy, where the comparison is expressed as a stop condition. The relevant manager with the approval limit, or the sequence of managers through the relevant manager, will be assigned the approval step.

Need for Multiple Workflow Configurations   The need for multiple workflow configurations to model variations in business practices can be minimized by the functionality related to a task, the approval process and approval steps, and to subworkflows. Within an approval step, for example, the relevant approver (within the organizational hierarchy) can be assigned based on the approval amount, or approval can be assigned to a user group (with approval required by one or all users within the group). As another example, you can model some variations based on conditions for use associated with an approval step, such as conditions related to the item category or purpose of the purchase. These examples minimize the need for multiple workflow configurations to model variations in business practices. When using subworkflows within a workflow configuration, each subworkflow will require its own workflow configuration.

Using Subworkflows for Modeling Approval Process Variations
Subworkflows represent a modular approach to defining an approval process. Each module is represented by a separate workflow configuration (with a task and approval process). You assign the identifier of relevant configuration after adding a subworkflow to the primary workflow configuration. You also assign conditions for use to the subworkflow. A subworkflow can provide sequential or alternate workflow steps, as illustrated in Figure 8.5 and explained below.

❖ *Sequential Workflow Steps.* A subworkflow can be placed before or after the task or approval process within the primary workflow configuration.[21] The left side of Figure 8.5 illustrates the sequential steps for a subworkflow placed before the task, where the subworkflow represents the creation and approval of a new vendor. It is only performed when you require a new vendor (based on the conditions for use assigned to the subworkflow).

❖ *Alternate Workflow Steps.* Multiple subworkflows (with mutually exclusive conditions for use) can be placed within the primary workflow

---

[21] A policy assigned to the subworkflow (termed wait for subworkflow to complete) indicates whether its task and approval process should be treated as sequential steps.

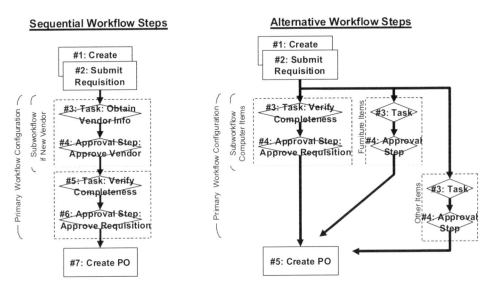

Figure 8.5 Using Subworkflows for Modeling Approval Process Variations

configuration to represent alternative workflow steps. The right side of Figure 8.5 illustrates two alternate paths, where one subworkflow only applies to computer-related purchases and the second subworkflow only applies to furniture-related purchases. The primary workflow contains the steps for other types of purchases.

The use of subworkflows and their associated workflow configurations provides greater flexibility in modeling variations in business practices. Effective usage requires appropriate assignment of the conditions for use. Effective usage also requires the appropriate text for the subject and instructions associated with each task and approval step, so that the end-user understands their job within the business.

Project-Related Purchase Requisitions and Workflow   A project-related purchase requisition and workflow are almost exactly the same as a general-purpose requisition. For example, the same basic steps and setup information apply to both types of requisitions. The three major differences reflect the unique functionality for projects, as described below.

❖ *Differences in the Workflow Template and Workflow Configurations.* A separate workflow template provides the starting point for defining workflow configurations about project-related purchase requisitions. Each workflow configuration must specify (within the conditions for use) whether it applies to a project-related or general-purpose requisition (when you employ both types of requisitions).

❖ *Differences in Creating a Requisition.* A project-related requisition must be created from the Projects form, thereby inheriting the appropriate project identifier. After creation, each requisition line item must be assigned a project category.

❖ *Differences in Creating a Purchase Order.* A project-related purchase order will be created rather than a normal purchase order.

Coordinating Purchasing Activities

A firm's S&OP game plans for saleable products and services provide the primary driver of purchasing activities for material items. The game plans define item demands that form the first step in every purchase cycle. Planning calculations synchronize supplies to meet these demands, as expressed through several coordination tools. The primary coordination tools consist of planned purchase orders and suggested action messages generated by planning calculations. The planned orders and action messages reflect the planning data for purchased material (described in Chapter 2) and the planning calculations (Chapter 6).

Suggestions for Planned Purchase Orders   The suggestions can be viewed on the *Planned Purchase Orders* form or the *Planned Orders* form. The displayed information typically represents the current master plan.[22] The user can also manually add a planned order. Purchase orders can be created from selected planned orders via a function termed *firming planned orders.*

❖ *Selecting and Firming Planned Orders.* You select planned orders via a marking check box. Planned orders can be viewed and optionally selected based on attributes such as the buyer, order date, and planned order status. You assign a status to planned orders (unprocessed, processed, and approved) to indicate those that have been analyzed, but this status only represents reference information. The form does not retain marked orders if the user exits before firming.

---

[22] The user can view information based on a selected set of master plan data or forecast plan data. For simplicity's sake the explanation focuses on the set of data representing the current master plan.

The firming function creates purchase orders for selected planned orders that have a specified vendor. The system creates single-line purchase orders unless the user indicates grouping preferences (via the firming dialogue when the user selects more than one planned order).[23] With grouping by vendor, the system can create multiline purchase orders from selected planned orders within a daily, weekly, or monthly period. An alternative grouping option can be based on the buyer, thereby segmenting purchase orders by buyer responsibility.

Execution of the firming function automatically deletes the selected planned orders, and creates a log for tracking which planned orders have been firmed and by whom.

❖ *Analyzing Planned Orders.* Buyers often need to understand the rationale and impact of a planned purchase order, and the system supports several analysis approaches.

- ○ Related action messages. The form displays action messages related to a planned order, such as expediting the planned order or delaying the delivery because of the projected lead time.
- ○ Understanding the sources of demand and supply. You can view single-level pegging information about the source of demand for a planned order. Additional inquiries display single-level pegging to all supplies and demands for an item (via a Net Requirements inquiry), and the multilevel pegging information about supplies and demands for a planned order (via an Explosion inquiry).

❖ *Editing Planned Orders.* The analysis efforts often lead to needed action, and several actions can be implemented on the planned orders form.

- ○ View and select from alternative vendors (via the selection list for the vendor field). Identification of alternative vendors reflects purchase price trade agreement information or vendor item information. The trade agreement information provides the basis for selecting a vendor based on purchase price, delivery lead time, quantity breakpoints, and effectivity dates.
- ○ Change quantity and/or delivery date for the planned purchase order.
- ○ Split the planned purchase order using a specified quantity and date.
- ○ Group together several selected planned orders for the same item, where the delivery date of the firmed order reflects the currently selected planned order.
- ○ Change the planned purchase order to a planned transfer order or production order to indicate an alternate source of supply.

---

[23] The default values for grouping preferences (when firming planned purchase orders) are defined as part of the master planning parameters.

○ Assign the planned order to an existing purchase order so that the firming process adds a line item to the existing order.
○ Convert the planned order to a request for quote.

Time Fences for Automatic Firming and a Frozen Period

The use of planned purchase orders is affected by two time fence policies regarding minimum turnaround time and automatic creation of purchase orders. These time fence policies are embedded in the coverage group assigned to an item.

Freeze Time Fence   The freeze time fence represents the shortest possible turnaround time to obtain material with a new purchase order, so that planning calculations will place planned orders at the end of the frozen period. An item's freeze time fence represents expedited delivery whereas the purchase lead time represents normal delivery.

Firm Time Fence   The firm time fence enables the system to automatically create purchase orders, thereby eliminating the effort to manually firm planned orders. However, automatic firming only works when planned orders have a suggested vendor (e.g., based on the item's preferred vendor or purchase price trade agreements). The system uses the company-wide grouping preferences to create multiline purchase orders, such as creating a multiline order for planned orders with the same vendor and within a weekly period. To be effective, the automatic firming time fence should be slightly greater than the item's purchase lead time and reorder cycle.

The firm time fence also applies to intercompany purchase orders, where automatically firmed-up purchase orders communicate requirements across a multicompany supply chain. In this case, an effective time fence must consider the desired visibility of intercompany requirements.

Action Messages   Planning calculations generate two types of action messages, termed *actions* and *futures*, as previously explained in Chapter 2 and illustrated in Figure 2.4. These messages are summarized below.

❖ *Actions Message.* An actions message indicates a suggestion to advance/postpone an order's delivery date, to increase/decrease an order quantity, or to delete an order. Suggested advancement of an existing order reflects the item's rescheduling assumption, so that the system suggests expediting rather than a new planned order to cover a requirement.

❖ *Futures Message.* A futures message indicates that the projected completion date for supply chain activities (based on realistic scheduling assumptions) will cause a delay in meeting a requirement date such as a sales order shipment.

Dynamics AX displays actions and futures messages on two different forms termed the *Actions* form and *Futures* form. Users cannot take action on these inquiry forms, but can readily access the relevant master table for the referenced order to indicate their action.

❖ *Actions Form.* The form displays the suggested date (and the change in days) for each postpone/advance message. It displays the suggested quantity (and the change in quantity) for each increase/decrease message, and just the change in quantity for each delete message. Each message identifies the referenced order.

❖ *Futures Form.* The form displays the affected order for each delayed message, along with the original and projected date (and the change in days). For example, the delayed date can apply to a sales order shipment or purchase order receipt.

Both forms support analyses of supply and demand information, such as the single-level pegging to all supplies and demands for an item (via a Net Requirements inquiry), and the multilevel pegging information about supplies and demands for a selected order (via an Explosion inquiry). Messages also apply to planned orders created by a previous planning calculation.

Purchase Order Receipts and Receiving Inspection

Receiving and vendor invoice activities represent the completion of purchase order processing. The basic approach focuses on reporting receiving activity against line items on an individual purchase order, and is termed *posting the packing slip*. Information about the actual quantity received (and its bin location) can be entered for each purchase order line item prior to posting. Another approach involves the use of an arrival journal to report actual receipts, and then the packing slip update, as described in Chapter 9.

Receiving Activities A receipt list can serve as a turnaround document for identifying inbound material and then recording actual quantities received. This turnaround document can help during the posting process in correcting the default values displayed for delivered quantities and locations. Alternatively, the data can be reported through a data collection system. The receiving process typically involves a single posting transaction for the packing slip, where information about actual material received can be entered for each line item prior to posting. In most situations, the vendor's invoice will be posted separately.[24]   In some situations, the receipt reflects the invoice, so that only the vendor's invoice should be entered without entering the packing slip information about the receipt.

The receipt quantity for a line item must match the order quantity to update the purchase order line status. When using delivery tolerances, however, the delivered quantity can exceed the order quantity or the under-delivery can be flagged as closed during the posting process. Over- and under-delivery tolerances are expressed as a percentage, and the values assigned to an item act as defaults for the purchase order line item. The system prevents the posting process when the delivery quantity exceeds either delivery tolerance.

Receiving Inspection Activities   Receiving inspection activities can be modeled using quarantine orders or quality orders or both. These constructs are summarized below. The "Quality Management" chapter provides more comprehensive explanations of quarantine orders and quality orders.

❖ *Quarantine Orders*. A quarantine order indicates that a received item must be inspected prior to usage, but does it not specify what to inspect. A quarantine management flag (embedded within the inventory model group assigned to the item) indicates a requirement for 100% inspection, and a purchase receipt will automatically create a quarantine order.

❖ *Quality Orders*. A quality order indicates that a received item must be inspected prior to the next step in the receiving process. It specifies what test to perform during inspection (along with the acceptable values for each test). It provides a means to record actual test results, and a comparison of actual test results against acceptable values, to determine whether the received material passes inspection. The need for receiving inspection via quality orders can reflect item- and vendor-specific policies.

---

[24] An item-specific policy can force separate steps for posting the packing slip and invoice. This policy is termed Receiving Requirement, and is embedded in the Inventory Model Group assigned to the item.

Three-Way Matching Between the Purchase Order, Receipts, and Invoice Three-way matching verifies that the invoice amount and quantity reflect the original order amount and actual received quantity. When entering an invoice, the system helps identify each price and quantity discrepancy, and the invoice can be saved or placed on hold. The invoice cannot be posted until you resolve the discrepancies, or mark the discrepancies as approved.

A company-wide policy (embedded with the A/P Parameters) indicates whether invoice matching will be used, and whether discrepancies must be approved.

Initial quantities for invoice entry can reflect receipt quantities. Receipts with unresolved receiving inspection issues, such as an open quarantine order or quality order, do not prevent invoicing. Identification of price differences can account for price tolerance percentages, which can be defined for a vendor, an item, or for the entire company.

Returns to Vendor

Returning material to a vendor typically involves a different type of purchase order (a type of returned order), but it can also be handled via a purchase order line item with a negative quantity.

Purchase Order Type of Returned Order When creating a purchase order, you designate the order type as returned order and enter the vendor RMA (Return Material Authorization) number. The line items for a returned order are expressed with a negative quantity. Line items can be manually entered, or the original purchase order information can be copied precisely (via the *Copy from All* function or the *Create Credit Note* function) with an inverted quantity. A user-defined reason code (termed *return action* code) can be specified for each line item. A scrap checkbox indicates the material does not warrant an actual return to vendor. After returning the item, the printed invoice reflects a credit note.

Negative Quantity for Purchase Order Line Item A line item with a negative quantity can indicate a return to vendor, rather than using a separate purchase order type of returned order. The additional line item typically reflects situations where quality or delivery problems require an immediate return, or an incorrect receipt quantity must be reversed.

Case Studies

Case 50:   Vendor Performance   The All-and-Anything company wanted to enhance vendor performance analysis beyond the standard reports for quantity and cost variances.   They wanted an overall score for each vendor based on the metrics described below, where the metrics reflected receipts during a specified time period.

* *Delivery Timeliness.* The scoring percentage reflected the number of on-time receipts divided by the total number of receipt transactions.   On-time receipts reflected the line item's confirmed date and delivery tolerances expressed in days.
* *Delivery Quantity.* The scoring percentage reflected the number of correct quantity receipts divided by the total number of receipt transactions. The correct quantity receipts reflected the line item's order quantity and delivery tolerances in percentages.   This metric required the ability to accept receipts outside of tolerances.
* *Quality.* The scoring percentage reflected the total good quantity divided by the total received quantity.   This metric required linkage between the reporting of good and scrapped material to the originating purchase order receipt.
* *Price.* The scoring percentage reflected a standard costing approach, with the total value of purchase price variances divided by the total value of received items.

Case 51: Conditional Release of Batch-Traced Material in Process Manufacturing   The Batch Process company purchased batch-traced material that required time-consuming compliance tests, and that could go into production subject to conditional release. As part of their customizations, they defined a batch attribute to identity status (such as a conditional release) that allowed usage, and prevented shipment of a batch-traced product comprised of batch-traced components with a conditional release.

Case 52: Buyer Action Messages   The Consumer Products company wanted to improve coordination of purchasing activities by enhancing suggested action messages. Building on the concept of buyer responsibility assigned to items and purchase orders, they extended the scope of suggested action messages to include follow-up on past-due receipt, suggested releases against a blanket order, and reviewing quotes and blanket orders about to expire.

Case 53: Supplier Coordination via E-Commerce The Distribution company wanted to improve coordination via several e-commerce initiatives with their suppliers of electronic components. The e-commerce initiatives included Biztalk and electronic marketplace capabilities. They communicated purchase order releases and changes to their suppliers, and received confirmations and changes from the suppliers. Automating these basic business processes improved coordination and reduced data entry errors and time. Additional capabilities included a common baseline of vendor performance metrics (such as delivery quantities/dates and tolerances), tracking of in-transit materials, and replenishment of vendor-managed inventory. These capabilities were frequently missing in the supplier's ERP system, so that the electronic marketplace provided supplemental benefits to the suppliers.

Case 54: Multiple Subcontractors The Fabricated Products company required several outside operations to produce an item. Several different contractors could perform each outside operation. Different levels in the bill of material defined each stage of manufacturing—one stage for each outside operation—and a production order was created for each stage. Each subcontractor was defined as a separate warehouse, so that supplied material and a completed item could be identified by inventory location. Material was shipped to the subcontractor performing the first operation, and auto-deducted based on reporting the production order as finished. The parent item was subsequently transferred to the warehouse corresponding to the next subcontractor. This approach allowed planning calculations to synchronize supplied material with the subcontractor performing each outside operation, and also minimized transaction processing about material movements between subcontractors.

Executive Summary

Purchased material represents the dominant concern in distribution environments and in many manufacturing environments. The supply chain activities for purchased material reflect demands stemming from the S&OP game plans for saleable products. Sourcing and agreement information can be defined, including the preferred vendor and purchase trade agreements about prices and discounts. Purchase quotations and requests for quotes can act as source documents for creating purchase orders. Planning calculations help coordinate procurement activities by communicating the need for planned orders and suggested changes to existing orders. The case studies highlighted variations in purchase order processing, including coordination of multiple subcontractors and vendor coordination via e-commerce initiatives.

Chapter 9

Inventory and Warehouse Management

Warehouse management involves the physical storage and movement of products within and between physical sites, as well as handling outbound and inbound shipments with trading partners. Various terms such as inventory management or distribution management are used to refer to these warehouse management activities, and responsibility for these activities may be assigned to one or several functional areas. For simplicity's sake further explanations use the terms warehouse management function and warehouse personnel.

The requirements for coordinating and reporting warehouse management activities vary from company to company, and between physical sites within a company. They also vary for different types of inventory transactions. Since we have already covered sales and purchasing, this chapter focuses on inventory transactions related to sales and purchase orders. Subsequent chapters explain the inventory transactions related to receiving inspection and quality management (Chapter 10), production orders (Chapter 11), projects (Chapter 12), transfer orders (Chapter 13), and service orders (Chapter 14). The requirements for handling palletized inventory are not included in these explanations.

The explanation of warehouse management starts with the basic functionality. This includes the definition of inventory stocking locations and basic warehouse management policies, as well as basic inventory transactions. Other warehouse activities include handling variations of arrivals and shipments. The shipment variations, for example, involve separate steps for picking material using either a consolidated picking list approach or an order picking list approach. The basic functionality and variations in business processes are reflected in the chapter's five major sections.

1. Basic functionality for warehouse management
2. Handling arrivals
3. Handling shipments
4. Consolidated picking lists for shipments
5. Order picking lists for shipments

Basic Functionality for Warehouse Management

Warehouse management functionality requires definition of inventory stocking locations and basic warehouse management policies. It also involves several types of basic inventory transactions, including adjustments, transfers, physical inventory counts, and cycle counts.

Sites, Warehouses, and Bins Each site has a unique identifier, and an optional financial dimension to support financial reporting by site. A site generally represents a physical site, and consists of one or more warehouses.[1] A site also provides the foundation for site-specific standard costs for items, and site-specific bills of material (BOMs), routings, labor rates, and overhead formulas for manufactured items.

Each warehouse has a unique identifier, and warehouse information includes its associated bin locations. The identifier for a bin location often reflects its coordinates (consisting of an aisle, rack, shelf level, and/or bin), but a different value can be manually assigned. Bin locations can be manually or automatically created. Automatic creation can be based on copying bin locations from another warehouse, or a process that creates bin locations for specified ranges of aisle, rack, shelf level, and bin numbers.

A warehouse is designated with a warehouse type of main; a main warehouse is also termed a default or normal warehouse. Two other types of warehouses may be needed to support inspections and transfers at a main warehouse.

❖ *Quarantine Warehouse.* Each main warehouse requires an associated quarantine warehouse when using quarantine orders to manage the inspection process. A quarantine warehouse has a separate identifier, a warehouse type of quarantine, and its own bin locations. Most situations will employ one quarantine warehouse for each normal warehouse. A minimalist approach would employ one quarantine warehouse per site.

---

[1] Each warehouse can only be associated with one site. A warehouse cannot be reassigned to a different site.

❖ *Transit Warehouse.* Each main warehouse requires an associated transit warehouse when using transfer orders to ship material from the warehouse. A transit warehouse has a separate identifier, a warehouse type of transit, and at least one bin location that always acts as a default. You need a minimum of one transit warehouse per site, which can be assigned to the main warehouses within the site. Alternatively, a transit warehouse can be defined for each main warehouse that acts as a ship-from location for transfer orders. The different transit warehouses provide more granular visibility of in-transit inventory. Chapter 13 explains the use of transfer orders in a multisite operation.

Several policies serve as the foundation for basic inventory transactions and warehouse management. These policies are defined for each warehouse, bin, and item, and include several stop transaction policies, as described in the following subsections.

Warehouse-Related Policies   A warehouse can have a default bin location that applies to all receipts, and a second default bin location that applies to all issues. These bin locations serve as a default when item-specific defaults are not specified. These default bin locations for a warehouse should only be specified when a single bin location makes sense, such as a single default bin location for a transit warehouse.

A warehouse can have a specified calendar, and optionally be designated as non-nettable (via the manual planning flag) so that demands and supplies are ignored by planning calculations.

Bin-Related Policies   A bin can be designated with a location type that affects usage by warehouse management transactions. The location types are an inbound dock, an outbound dock, a picking location, and a buffer. These location types are primarily used for palletized items. Given our focus on non-palletized items, we'll primarily use a location type of buffer for the inventory transactions covered in this section.

An unusable bin location can be identified as blocked. For example, the bin location may not be ready for use, or it may be undergoing repair.

Item-Related Policies   An item's inventory dimensions (embedded within the dimension group assigned to the item) determine whether site, warehouse, and bin must be specified on inventory transactions. They also determine whether batch numbers and/or serial numbers must be recorded for an item's inventory transactions. The negative inventory policies (embedded within the inventory model group assigned to an item) determine whether the item's physical inventory can be negative. With actual costing approaches (described in Chapter 5), a general guideline would be to prevent negative physical inventory, since this condition creates problems in calculation of actual costs. Negative financial inventory should be allowed, since this allows inventory usage after receipt but prior to financial updates such as posting a vendor's invoice for purchased material.

Items with standard costs must have an active item cost record in order to record inventory transactions. Chapter 5 explained standard costs and item cost records.

An item's inventory unit of measure determines how inventory balances will be maintained and displayed.

An item can have a default bin location within a warehouse—one for receipts and one for issues—that typically represents situations where the item is always stocked in the same location.

Stop Transaction Policies   The system can prevent selected inventory transactions for an item. Use the stopped flags to prevent all inventory transactions for an item, or to selectively prevent item transactions for (1) purchase orders, (2) sales orders, (3) intercompany purchase orders, and (4) intercompany sales orders. Transactions can also be stopped for a specified line item on a sales or purchase order, thereby preventing shipment or receipt. In addition, a company-wide policy optionally prevents inventory transactions during the process of cycle counting process or physical inventory (for items being counted).

Basic Inventory Transactions Within a Warehouse   The basic inventory transactions include inventory adjustments, transfers, and counts related to physical inventory or cycle counting. These basic inventory transactions within a warehouse are summarized in Figure 9.1 and explained in the following subsections. Other basic inventory transactions include arrivals and shipments, which will be covered in subsequent sections within this chapter. Other basic inventory transactions displayed in Figure 9.1 include quarantine orders (covered in Chapter 10), production orders (Chapter 11), and transfers to other warehouses in a multisite operation (Chapter 13).

Inventory Adjustments   Inventory adjustments represent one of the basic inventory transactions within a warehouse, as shown in Figure 9.1. They can

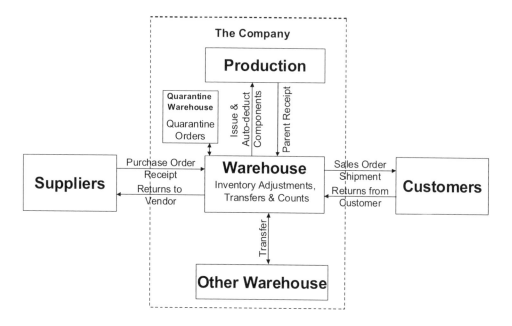

Figure 9.1 Basic Inventory Transactions

serve a variety of purposes, such as loading initial inventory balances, reporting inventory corrections, and reporting scrap. Inventory adjustment transactions can be recorded using either the movement journal or the profit/loss journal. The profit/loss journal employs a predefined G/L account number for an item's inventory adjustments, whereas a movement journal forces the user to specify this offsetting G/L account number for each inventory adjustment transaction.[2] The quantity can be positive or negative, and always reflects the item's inventory UM. Each adjustment minimally identifies an item, quantity, stocking location (site, warehouse, and bin), and the G/L account for offsetting the adjustment. The adjustment entries can be maintained and printed prior to posting the journal. Items with an actual costing method require an additional entry about the item's unit cost and possibly miscellaneous charges.

Inventory Transfers   Inventory transfers between stocking locations are recorded in an inventory transfer journal. Each transfer minimally identifies an item, quantity, and the old and new stocking locations (site, warehouse,

---

[2] A default value for the offset account number can be defined as part of the setup information for the movement journal. The predefined G/L account numbers for profit and loss are defined within the item group assigned to an item.

and bin). The transfer quantity is expressed as a negative, and always reflects the item's inventory UM. The transfer entries can be maintained and printed prior to posting the journal.

Inventory transfers reflect the immediate movement of material, without a requirement for tracking in-transit inventory. For example, an inventory transfer may be used to move material between two adjacent warehouses. Transfer orders should be used when in-transit inventory must be tracked. Chapter 13 explains the use of transfer orders in multisite operations.

An inventory transfer journal also supports the transfer of one variant of an item to another variant, as well as transferring one batch or serial number to another number, much like you would transfer inventory from one warehouse to another warehouse. Chapter 2 described the use of item numbers and variant codes (such as color and size) for item identification purposes.

Physical Inventory and Cycle Counting Physical inventories help ensure valid financial reporting of inventory value. Cycle counting can accomplish the same objective, and help identify the source of inventory errors. The counts for a physical inventory or for a cycle count are recorded in a counting journal. The user can manually or automatically create the journal lines identifying the items to be counted, print the journal as a turnaround document, and then record the counted quantity or the adjustment quantity for each journal line. Posting a counting journal updates the inventory balances. This represents a two-step counting process: one step to identify items in the counting journal and a second step to post the journal. A company-wide policy (embedded in the inventory parameters) optionally prevents inventory transactions during the counting process.

Automatic creation of journal lines can be based on one or more factors, such as a specified warehouse, a selected range of item numbers or item groups, or the items' cycle counting approach. An item's cycle counting approach (embedded within the *Counting Group* assigned to an item) typically reflects a periodic interval expressed in calendar days. In this case, the user specifies a "not counted since" date as the basis for automatically creating journal lines. A further refinement can eliminate any items with no inventory transactions since the last count. Alternatively, the approach can reflect a condition such as on-hand inventory reaching zero or the item's minimum quantity, since this approach minimizes the time and effort for performing a physical count.

Some companies employ a control group method in cycle counting, where the same items are counted every day to identify the sources of error immediately. Copying the journal lines from a previous counting journal into the new journal supports the control group method.

Some companies employ tags (with preassigned numbers) to conduct a physical inventory, typically with hand-written count information about the quantity and location. A separate tag counting journal can be used to record the tag numbers, tag status (used, voided or missing), and the count information, and then analyze missing tag numbers. This tag counting journal represents an approach to tag control. Posting it results in the creation of a counting journal (with journal lines for used tags), which must be posted to update inventory balances.

Dynamics AX Viewpoint of Inventory Transactions

The term *inventory transaction* normally refers to the physical movement of material, such as an inventory adjustment, receipt, or shipment. A purchase order and sales order are normally viewed as a scheduled receipt and shipment respectively. Dynamics AX employs a broader view of the term inventory transaction, since it creates an inventory transaction (with an associated inventory status) for various steps in purchase, sales, and production order processing. Figure 9.2 illustrates this broader viewpoint concerning the types and status of an inventory transaction. For example, the system creates an inventory transaction with an inventory status of "ordered" when the user creates a purchase order line item. This status changes to "received" after posting the vendor's packing list, and to "purchased" after posting the vendor's invoice.

Dynamics AX creates inventory transactions for posted and unposted inventory journals, as illustrated in the right-hand side of Figure 9.2. With the inventory movement journal, for example, a journal line item for a positive quantity (a receipt) represents an ordered line item prior to posting. Inventory transactions related to a BOM journal closely parallel those for a production order, since they both involve a parent item and its components.

The simplified viewpoint of inventory transactions in Figure 9.2 does not reflect all types of inventory transactions and statuses. A byproduct component in a bill of material, for example, would be shown as a component receipt with statuses of ordered and purchased. A return purchase order would have statuses of on order, deducted and sold. The system employs additional types of inventory status when using reservations and warehouse management transactions. With warehouse management transactions, for

Type of Inventory Transaction				
Purchase Order	**Sales Order**	**Inventory Journal***		
Receipt	**Shipment**	**Receipt**	**Issue**	

Status of Inventory Transaction	Ordered Create a PO line item	On Order Create a SO line item	Ordered Create a Journal Line	On Order Create a Journal Line
	Received Post the packing slip	Deducted Post the packing slip	Purchased Post the journal	Sold Post the journal
	Purchased Post the vendor's invoice	Sold Post the customer's invoice	N/A	

Production Order		**BOM Journal**	
Parent Receipt	**Component Issue**	**Parent Receipt**	**Component Issue**
Ordered Create a Production Order	On Order	Ordered Create a Journal Line	On Order Create a Journal Line
Received Post report as finished	Sold Post picking list	Purchased Post the journal	Sold Post the journal
Purchased Change Status to Cost Accounted or Ended	N/A	N/A	

▨ = Posting updates the inventory balance
*Inventory journals include Movement, Profit/Loss, Counting, Transfer, and Project Items journals.

Figure 9.2 Viewpoint of Inventory Transactions

example, the status of a purchase order receipt can be arrived and then registered (after posting the item arrival) before it becomes received (after posting the packing list), as illustrated in Figure 9.3. Additional illustrations of inventory status are shown in Figure 7.5 (for basic steps in RMA processing), Figure 9.5 (for basic steps in the consolidated picking list approach), and Figure 9.7 (for basic steps in the order picking list approach).

In summary, the inventory transaction audit trail displays both actual and anticipated receipts and issues. This audit trail includes batch and serial numbers when applicable. The user can view additional information about an actual receipt (or issue) concerning the physical and financial vouchers that identify the affected G/L account numbers and values.

Inventory Transaction Audit Trail and Inventory Balances You can view an item's transactions and inventory balances from the item master and from any form involving inventory transactions. You can specify the desired level of detail when viewing inventory balances, such as viewing inventory by warehouse versus viewing inventory for every bin, batch, and serial number. You can also view an item's inventory balances across multiple companies (when it has a company item number).

Handling Arrivals

Many inventory transactions represent arrivals into a warehouse, such as purchase orders and customer returns. An Arrival Overview form summarizes anticipated arrivals, and provides the starting point for reporting arrivals and updating orders with the receipt information. This section focuses on use of the Arrival Overview form for reporting purchase order receipts, and touches on other types of arrivals, such as customer returns (previously explained in Chapter 7) and transfer orders (Chapter 13).

Purchase Order Receipts   There are two basic approaches for reporting receipts against purchase order line items. The first approach involves a single receipt transaction (termed the *packing slip update*) against a purchase order, as previously described in Chapter 8. The second approach involves two transactions to initially record arrival and then to record the packing slip update.[3] This second approach typically employs the Arrival Overview form and involves four basic steps for handling arrivals. These four steps are shown in Figure 9.3 and explained below.

❖ *Step 1: Anticipate Arrival Activities.* The Arrival Overview form lists open purchase order line items that represent anticipated receipts, and also indicates line items requiring inspection via quarantine orders. Use filtering to highlight relevant line items, such as filtering based on the time window of expected deliveries (expressed as a number of days forward and back), the vendor, the ship-to site/warehouse, and the method of delivery. You can select relevant line items (or all items) to view the possible workload, expressed in terms of total quantity, volume, weight, and estimated handling time.[4] For example, selection of relevant line items may represent the anticipated arrival of a vendor's truck containing items scheduled for today's delivery.

---

[3] The use of an arrival journal can be mandated based on an item-specific policy (termed registration requirements) embedded within the inventory model group assigned to the item. The policy mandates that all receipts must be reported through an arrival journal.

[4] Each item's typical volume, weight, and arrival handling time (expressed in minutes or hours) can be defined on the item master.

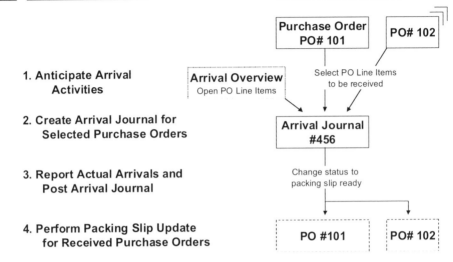

Figure 9.3 Handling Arrivals of Purchase Orders

❖ *Step 2: Create Arrival Journal for Selected Purchase Orders.* Use the Arrival Overview form to select relevant purchase order line items and create an arrival journal initially populated with the selected items and remaining order quantities.   Alternatively, you can manually create an arrival journal and its line items. Each line item within an arrival journal displays the expected quantity and the suggested bin location for the received item.[5]

You can optionally indicate the need to perform receiving inspection (via a quarantine order) on a given line item within an arrival journal. In this case, you must flag the quarantine management checkbox and place the item in a quarantine warehouse. A quarantine order must be generated for items with a mandated quarantine policy.

❖ *Step 3: Report Actual Arrivals and Post Arrival Journal.* Use the arrival journal to report actual receipt quantities and bin placement for each received item, and then post the completed arrival journal to register the material arrival. Posting the arrival journal also generates a quarantine order for each line item designated as requiring quarantine management. The arrival journal is now termed *packing list ready*, and the actual quantities and inventory placement cannot be overridden.

---

[5] The bin location on an arrival journal line item can initially default to the item's default receipt bin location within a warehouse (as specified in the item's setup information about warehouse items), to the warehouse's default bin location for receipts, or to the bin location specified in the setup information on the arrival overview form.

❖ *Step 4: Perform Packing Slip Update for Received Purchase Orders.* Record the vendor's packing slip number and post the *packing slip ready* arrival journal to update all purchase orders within the arrival journal. Alternatively, you can perform the packing slip update for individual purchase orders.

The displayed information on the Arrival Overview form can be tailored to support specific tasks, and you can save and reuse the tailored information. For example, the tailored information may consist of only purchase order receipts for a specified site/warehouse.

Customer Returns   Returned items must first be reported through an arrival journal, typically by selecting the RMA line items on the Arrival Overview form to create the arrival journal. Multiple RMAs and multiple RMA line items can be selected, thereby including them in a single arrival process. Each arrival journal line item must be assigned a disposition code, which determines subsequent processing steps as summarized in Figure 7.4 and its associated text. You can optionally generate a quarantine order by indicating a quarantine warehouse and a quarantine management policy for the returned item, and the disposition code can be reassigned on the quarantine order.

Transfer Orders   There are two basic approaches for reporting receipts against transfer order line items. The first approach involves a single transaction to post the receipt, as described in Chapter 13. The second approach involves two transactions to initially record arrival and then to record the receipt. This second approach employs the Arrival Overview form just like a purchase order receipt. That is, the Arrival Overview supports visibility of anticipated transfer order receipts, creation of an arrival journal for selected line items, registration of a completed arrival journal, and posting the transfer order receipt.

Handling Palletized Items   Some warehouse environments use pallets or containers for handling an item's inventory. The policy for palletized inventory is defined by the pallet inventory dimension assigned to an item. Several aspects of warehouse management functionality only apply to palletized items, such as rules about pallet put-away suggestions that account for bin location constraints, or the use of pallet transport orders to provide instructions to forklift drivers.

For palletized items, the arrival journal can indicate the creation of inbound pallet transports for communicating instructions to forklift drivers. Posting the arrival journal then triggers the creation of pallet transfer orders, with one or more pallets automatically identified (based on an item's pallet quantity). The suggested pallet placement also reflects pallet constraints of the bin locations.

Handling Shipments

Many inventory transactions represent shipments from a warehouse, such as shipments for sales orders and transfer orders. This chapter focuses on sales order shipments and briefly touches on transfer order shipments. There are three basic approaches for reporting shipments against sales order line items. The first approach involves the packing slip update for each sales order,[6] as previously described in Chapter 7. The other two approaches involve separate steps for picking the material prior to the packing slip update, either with an order picking list or a consolidated picking list.

The separate steps for picking the material involve three key constructs: output orders, shipments, and picking routes. The two picking list approaches differ significantly in how they handle creation of a shipment and picking route, and the assignment of output orders to a shipment and picking route. A brief introduction to these constructs provides the starting point for further explanation about the order picking list and the consolidated picking list approach to shipments.

Output Orders   Picking requirements for a sales order are communicated via an *output order* associated with each sales order line item. An output order (also termed an *inventory order*) has a unique identifier. It represents an authorization to pick the line item, and therefore provides a gateway for controlling picking and shipping activities. You can generate output orders from a sales order, either for individual line items or for all line items (via posting the picking list). You can also generate output orders for selected line items when using the Release Sales Order Picking form, which provides visibility of anticipated picking activities.

---

[6] The packing slip update approach has also been called inventory transaction picking. Items can be shipped without creating the output orders, shipments, and picking routes associated with the two picking list approaches.

Shipments   Output orders are grouped together to define the contents of a shipment from a specified site/warehouse. A shipment has a unique identifier, and at least one picking route for recording picking activities.

Picking Routes   A picking route consists of one or more output orders that need to be picked, and provides the basis for a printed picking list and reporting actual picking activities. A picking route has a unique identifier. After reporting material as picked, you can post the sales order packing list.

The term *picking list* has two different contexts within sales order shipments. The first context refers to the printed picking list for a picking route, and the terms picking route and picking list are often used interchangeably. The second context refers to the posting function for a sales order, where you post the picking list in order to create output orders that authorize picking activities.

Key Constructs for Transfer Order Shipments   The same constructs (output orders, shipments, and picking routes) also apply to the picking steps for transfer order shipments. For example, you can view anticipated picking activities on the Release Transfer Order Picking form, and generate output orders for selected transfer order line items. Output orders are grouped to gether to define the contents of a shipment, and a shipment has at least one picking route for printing a picking list and for reporting actual picking activities. After reporting material as picked, you can post the transfer order shipment.

With consolidated picking lists, transfer orders and sales orders can both be included in a shipment's contents, and separate picking routes will be created for the two types of orders. After items have been picked, different steps will be required to post the sales order packing slips and to post the transfer order shipments.

Consolidated Picking Lists for Shipments

The consolidated picking list approach employs the shipment construct as an organizing focus, and the assignment of output orders to define the shipment contents. The grouping of output orders, for example, may reflect the same ship-from site, shipment date, method of delivery, and/or customer. The assigned output orders can then be picked using a picking route and its associated printed pick list. The creation of picking routes reflects the *joint packing policy* (order, single customer, or all customers) assigned to the ship-

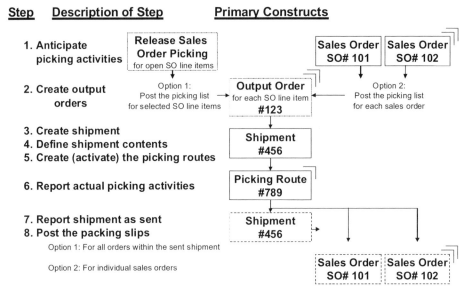

Figure 9.4 Consolidated Picking List Approach for Sales Orders

ment. That is, a picking list can reflect the output orders for a single sales order (similar to the order picking list approach), for a single customer, or for all customers. In this last case, the picked material for all customers can be separated at the outbound dock. The consolidated picking list approach consists of several steps. The basic steps are illustrated in Figure 9.4 and explained below.

Step 1: Anticipate Picking Activities The Release Sales Order Picking form provides visibility of anticipated picking activities, and displays open sales order line items that should be released for picking based on actual availability.[7] You can employ query criteria to limit the displayed information, such as limiting orders based on ship date, ship-from site/ warehouse, customer, or customer priority (termed the customer classification group). For example, the query criteria could reflect the subset of orders going to a certain customer on a given date. The displayed information can then be filtered. The displayed information indicates whether each line item can be delivered with available inventory, or whether you need to allocate inventory when it is insufficient. It also indicates expected receipts that are associated with production orders and transfer orders.

---

[7] The Release Sales Order Picking form does not currently display sales order line items when there is no inventory for the item. Those situations requiring shipment visibility prior to inventory availability will need a slight customization to display these line items.

Step 2: Create Output Orders (Authorize Picking)   There are two basic options for creating output orders, as shown in Figure 9.4. With the first option, they can be created from the Release Sales Order Picking form by selecting sales order line items (individually or in mass), and then posting the picking list. The posting process applies to the selected line items, and creates a single output order for each line selected. With the second option, you can post the picking list for individual sales orders to create an output order for each line item. In both cases, the posting process (for posting a picking list) does not generate or print a picking list; it only creates the output orders. As a variation of the second option, you can manually create an output order for an individual sales order line item (rather than for all line items via posting the picking list), thereby controlling which line items have been authorized for picking.

Step 3: Create Shipment   A shipment identifier must be created before you define its contents. You can create a shipment manually or with a *create shipment wizard*; the same information must be specified using either method.[8] We'll focus on the manual method for explanatory purposes. When creating a shipment identifier on the Shipment form, you specify a ship-from site and warehouse (as the source for picking material) and a bin location that represents the outbound dock for staging the picked material.[9] You also specify a joint packing policy that determines how picking routes should be created. This policy indicates whether a picking route represents the items for a single sales order, a single customer, or the entire shipment contents.

An additional policy (termed the *automatic additions status*) determines whether newly created output orders will be automatically added to the shipment. When you define a shipment and its contents, for example, you may want newly entered sales orders (and their newly created output orders) to be included in the shipment contents. In a typical scenario, you would define a shipment that represents a scheduled customer delivery from a given site, so that any newly entered sales orders would be automatically included in the shipment contents. The policy also indicates the point (within the

---

[8] When using the create shipment wizard, your first step is to specify the identifier of a shipment template. A shipment template consists of default settings that will be inherited by the newly created shipment, such as the default values for the ship-from site and warehouse. You typically define a shipment template for each major variation in shipment processing, so that it can be used with the create shipment wizard.

[9] As part of creating a shipment, you also specify the basis for reserving palletized items (termed the reservation sequence ID), which defines a warehouse-specific sequence for reserving pallets from picking, bulk, inbound, and outbound bin locations.

picking process) at which it still makes sense to automatically add output orders to the shipment contents. As a typical example, it makes sense to include newly created output orders prior to the creation of picking routes. It no longer makes sense to add output orders after you record the shipment as sent.

Step 4: Define Shipment Contents   After creating a shipment identifier on the Shipment form, you can view and select output orders to define the shipment contents, thereby assigning the corresponding sales order line items to the shipment. The displayed output orders reflect the ship-from site assigned to the shipment. You can view a running list of output orders assigned to the shipment.

Newly created output orders can be automatically assigned to the shipment contents when allowed by the automatic additions policy, as described above for Step 3.

Step 5: Create the Picking Routes   You create (aka activate) the shipment's picking routes from the Shipment form, where each picking route reflects various sales order line items. A shipment has one or more picking routes associated with it, as defined by its *joint packing* policy.[10]   For example, a joint packing policy of same customer will result in a separate picking route for each customer (containing the output orders associated with the customer). You can print a picking list for each picking route number. The printed picking list displays the items (and stocking locations) that need to be moved to the outbound dock, and can act as a turnaround document for reporting actual picking activities.

Step 6: Report Actual Picking Activities   You report the material actually picked for a specified picking route using the Picking List Registration form. The form displays the quantity and a stocking location for each item, which can then be confirmed or overridden as necessary. You may need to split a line in the picking route when recording quantities from two different bin locations or batch numbers for the same line item.

---

[10] The number of picking routes for a shipment is also affected by a company-wide policy (defined in the A/R parameters) about splitting the picking lists based on the customer's delivery address. That is, a picking route will be generated for each customer delivery address, and contain those output orders (within the shipment) that reflect the address on their sales order line item. An additional policy can be specified for splitting the packing slips (and invoices) based on customer address. You should use this approach when each customer delivery address requires separate attention for picking, packing, and/or invoicing.

You can optionally report a picking route as started; this provides reference information by updating the status of a picking route to started. You can optionally cancel a line item (or all line items) on a picking route. For example, you may want to assign the item to another shipment. Reposting the sales order picking list will generate another output order for the line item(s) associated with the picking route cancellation, which can then be assigned to another shipment.

Step 7: Report Shipment as Sent   The user indicates that a shipment has been sent on the Shipment form. At this time, the user can optionally create a bill of lading (for each sales order in the shipment) and print a shipment list (that displays all sales orders within the shipment). A sent shipment acts as the basis for posting the packing slip for all sales orders within the shipment.

Step 8: Post the Packing Slips   The last step involves two different options for posting the packing list, as shown in Figure 9.4. You can post the packing slips for all sales orders within a sent shipment, or you can post the packing slip for individual sales orders. The first option represents a mass update approach that simplifies transaction processing. Invoices must still be posted for the sales orders.

Policies for the Consolidated Picking List Approach   A given warehouse will typically have mandated usage of the consolidated picking list approach for all items, since this provides consistency in transaction reporting.   Some situations will only employ consolidated picking for selected items, or even for selected items at a selected warehouse.[11]

The consolidated picking list approach can be bypassed on a specific sales order by not creating output orders, and just posting the packing slip. However, you can prevent this bypass by mandating that items must go though a picking process, as defined by the picking requirement policy embedded in the inventory model group assigned to an item.

Attributes of bin locations can affect the sorting sequence to pick material. Sorting normally reflects the bin location coordinates, but a sort value can be manually assigned when coordinates do not reflect the optimal sequence. Bin locations can be grouped together (based on the area assigned

---

[11] The policy for mandated use of a consolidated picking list approach can be a warehouse-specific policy, an item-specific policy (specified in the Inventory Model Group assigned to the item), or an item/warehouse-specific policy (specified in the item's warehouse setup information).

to the bin); the area can be used in a picking list. The consolidated picking approach requires the definition of at least one outbound bin, with a location type of outbound dock.

Staging and Loading the Picked Material   A major variation in con-solidated picking involves the use of additional statuses (termed *staged* and *loaded*) to support additional functionality. For example, the picked material may be staged and then loaded on a truck (or in a container) before it can be reported as sent. The tracking policy assigned to each shipment (termed the Outbound Rule ID) determines whether you can use the additional statuses, and how they will be used. For example, you may want to enforce the rule that a shipment must be reported as loaded (on the truck) before it can be reported as sent.

You use the Shipment Staging form to view the whereabouts of ship-ments at the outbound docks, and to perform several functions that only apply to the shipment line items at a staged or loaded status.

  – Move a quantity of staged/loaded inventory to a different warehouse or bin
  – Load a quantity of staged inventory onto a truck
  – Unload a quantity of inventory from a truck (back to a staged status)
  – Unpick a quantity of staged inventory, so that it has to be picked again
  – Move the staged or loaded inventory to a different shipment

Moving inventory to a different shipment enables you to rearrange and consolidate the staged/loaded line items, so that they reflect the desired shipment contents.

Summary of Consolidated Picking List Approach   Each of the key constructs (output orders, shipments, and picking routes) has a life cycle represented by different statuses. The changes in status reflect the basic steps in consolidated picking. Figure 9.5 summarizes the basic steps for the con-solidated picking list approach, and depicts how each step changes the status of the key constructs. The figure also displays related activities for each step (such as posting the picking list to create output orders) and the optional steps.

#	Basic Steps in Consolidated Picking	Related Activities for the Step	Output Order	Shipment	Shipment Line	Picking Route	Picking Route Line
			Key Constructs				
1	Anticipate picking activity	Select items to be picked				N/A	N/A
2	Create output orders	Post picking list	Created			N/A	N/A
3	Create shipment	Assign site/warehouse and outbound bin	Created			N/A	N/A
4	Define shipment contents	Check for possible shortages / Assign policy on additional statuses	Handling, +Qty Registered	Registered	Registered	N/A	N/A
5	Create (activate) picking route	Print picking list	+Qty Activated	Activated	Activated	Activated	Activated
6	Report actual picking activities	Split line to report different bin locations [One line / All lines]	Ended, +Qty Picked	Picked	Picked	Started	Picked
		Optional: Report shipment as staged	+Qty Staged	Staged	Staged		Staged
		Optional: Report shipment as loaded	+Qty Loaded	Loaded	Loaded		Loaded
7	Report shipment as sent	Create bill of lading / Print shipment list	Ended, +Qty Completed	Sent	Completed	Completed	Completed
8	Post packing slips	Print packing slips / Print shipping labels					

⟍_____ **Status of Key Constructs** _____⟋

Figure 9.5 Summary of Consolidated Picking List Approach

The first two steps involve selecting items to be picked, typically using the Release Sales Order Picking form, and then posting the packing slip to create output orders, as indicated by the created status. The next two steps involve creating a shipment and defining the shipment contents, as indicated by the registered status. The steps also update the output order status and a related quantity field (such as registered). The fifth step normally involves creating (aka activating) the picking routes for a shipment based on its joint packing policy, as indicated by the activated status. The sixth step involves reporting actual picking activities on the picking list registration form, which results in a status of picked. Two optional steps can report a shipment as staged and loaded, where you use the Shipment Staging form to move an item's quantity to the next status. The last two steps enable you to report the shipment as sent, and then post the packing slip for all sales orders within the shipment. Alternatively, you can skip the seventh step and post the packing slip for individual sales orders.

Cancellation of a picking route line item, or cancellation of an entire picking route, results in a cancelled status; it also results in a cancelled status for the shipment line item and shipment.

The consolidated picking list approach introduces a level of complexity to system usage. The complexity factor reflects additional transaction processing, although a data collection system (as described in Case 58) can help. The complexity factor increases when there are frequent last-minute changes to sales order information, such as changing quantities/customers or deletions, since you may need to update the associated output orders, shipments, and picking routes.

Bill of Lading and Other Shipping Paperwork

A bill of lading can be automatically created by posting a sales order packing list or invoice.[12] It can also be created when reporting a shipment as sent, as illustrated in Figure 9.5. Some information pertaining to the system-assigned bill of lading identifier is automatically updated, such as the customer, sales order number, delivery address, and the shipped items and quantities. Other bill of lading information must be manually maintained, including each package type (such as carton), quantity and weight. Use the bill of lading form for data maintenance and document printing. A bill of lading can be manually created to support other types of shipments (such as office furniture), or to support a master bill of lading (such as shipments to a freight forwarder). After creating a bill of lading identifier, for example, the user must explicitly designate it as a master bill of lading and also assign the identifier to individual bills of lading associated with it.

Other shipping paperwork includes a packing list and shipping labels. The shipping labels reflect information that has been manually entered about how the items were packed into cartons. The user can indicate the number of packages (and associated weights and volumes) when posting the packing slip or invoice, so that the system can print a shipping label for each package.[13] Otherwise, the system assumes all items were packed into a single package.

Order Picking Lists for Shipments

The order picking list approach applies to a single sales order. It employs the same constructs (output orders, shipment, and picking route) as the consoli-

---

[12] A company-wide policy (embedded in the A/R parameters) determines whether the system automatically creates a bill of lading. Related parameters define default values for each bill of lading, such as the carrier and freight charge terms (prepaid, collect, or third party).

[13] A company-wide policy (embedded in the A/R parameters) determines whether the system creates shipping labels. The user can enter shipment specifications about packaging when posting the packing slip or invoice.

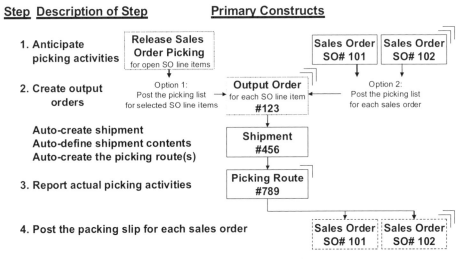

Figure 9.6 Order Picking List Approach for Sales Orders

dated picking list approach, but streamlines the process by auto-creating the shipment, shipment contents, and picking route when you create output orders for the sales order. The order picking list approach consists of several steps. The basic steps are illustrated in Figure 9.6 and explained below.

Step 1:   Anticipate Picking Activities   The Release Sales Order Picking form provides visibility of anticipated picking activities, as described in the previous section about consolidated picking lists.

Step 2:   Create Output Orders (and Auto-Create the Shipment and Picking Route)   The two basic options for creating output orders—posting a picking list for a sales order or for selected line items on the Release Sales Order Picking form—are just like the consolidated picking list approach. However, posting the picking list will also auto-create the shipment, shipment contents, and picking route for each sales order. Each shipment has a joint packing policy of a single order. An additional shipment and picking route will be generated for each additional ship-from site within the sales order line items.[14] Adding a sales order line item, and posting the picking list a second time, will create an additional output order, shipment, and picking route. You cannot manually add an output order to the shipment contents, and the automatic addition policy does not apply.

---

[14] The number of picking routes for a shipment is also affected by a company-wide policy (defined in the A/R parameters) about splitting the picking lists based on the customer's delivery address.

Step 3: Report Actual Picking Activities   You report the material actually picked for a specified picking route using the Picking List Registration form, just like the consolidated picking list approach. The form displays the quantity and a stocking location for each item, which can then be confirmed or overridden as necessary. You may need to split a line in the picking route when recording quantities from two different bin locations or batch numbers for the same line item.

You can optionally report a picking route as started; this provides reference information by updating the status of a picking route to started. You can optionally cancel a line item (or all line items) on a picking route. Reposting the sales order picking list will generate another output order for the line item(s) associated with the picking route cancellation.

Step 4: Post the Packing Slip for Each Sales Order   The last step involves posting the packing slip for individual sales orders.

Policies for the Order Picking List Approach   The order picking list approach applies to a warehouse and all items when you do not mandate use of the consolidated picking list approach. The order picking list approach can be bypassed on a specific sales order by not creating output orders, and just posting the packing slip. However, you can prevent this bypass by mandating that items must go though a picking process, as defined by the picking requirement policy embedded in the inventory model group assigned to an item.

Staging and Loading the Picked Material   A major variation in order picking involves the use of additional statuses (termed *staged* and *loaded*) to support additional functionality, as described earlier. The tracking policy assigned to each shipment (termed the Outbound Rule ID) determines whether you can use the additional statuses, and how they will be used.

Summary of Order Picking List Approach   Each of the key constructs (output orders, shipments, and picking routes) has a life cycle represented by different statuses. The changes in status reflect the basic steps in order picking. Figure 9.7 summarizes the basic steps for the order picking list approach, and depicts how each step changes the status of the key constructs. The figure also displays related activities for each step (such as posting the picking list to create output orders) and the optional steps.

#	Basic Steps in Consolidated Picking	Related Activities for the Step		Output Order	Shipment Line		Picking Route Line	
					Key Constructs			
1	Anticipate picking activity	Select items to be picked		N/A				
2	Create output order (for SO line items) Auto-create shipment Auto-define shipment contents Auto-create (activate) picking route	Post picking list Check for possible shortages Assign tracking id Assign policy on additional statuses Print picking list		Handling ·Qty Activated	Activated	Activated	Activated	Activated
3	Report actual picking activities	Split line to report different bin locations	One line	Ended ·Qty Picked	Started	Picked	Started	Picked
			All lines		Sent	Completed		Completed
		Optional: Report shipment as staged		·Qty Staged	Staged	Staged	Completed	Staged
		Optional: Report shipment as loaded		·Qty Loaded	Loaded	Loaded		Loaded
		Optional: Report shipment as sent						
4	Post packing slips	Print packing slips Print shipping labels		Ended ·Qty Completed	Sent	Completed		Completed

Status of Key Constructs

Figure 9.7 Summary of Order Picking List Approach

The first two steps typically involve selecting items to be picked using the Release Sales Order Picking form, and then posting the packing slip to create the output orders. This step auto-creates (aka activates) the shipment and picking route, as indicated by the activated status. The next step involves reporting actual picking activities on the picking list registration form. Reporting one line as picked changes the status of the output order (ended), and also changes the status of the shipment and picking route (started). The statuses change again after you report all line items as picked, and results in a sent shipment. However, three optional steps can report the shipment as staged, loaded, and sent, where you use the Shipment Staging form to move an item's quantity to the next status. The final step involves posting the packing slip for individual sales orders.

Picking List for Production Orders

The picking list for a production order (termed a picking list journal) represents an order-based approach to picking activities, but it differs significantly from the above-described approach for an order picking list. It does not employ the constructs of a shipment, picking route, and output orders to support picking activities.[15] The picking list journal involves additional considerations, such as the definition of components in the Production BOM, segmentation of the printed picking list based on the operation number assigned to components, component auto-deduction policies, and issuing additional components. Chapter 11 explains production orders and the related picking and receipt transactions.

Case Studies

Case 55: UPS Integration Most of the shipments at the All-and-Anything company were sent via UPS. Integrating the UPS capabilities into sales order and shipment processing meant that the user could shop for the best price and identify the estimated delivery date. The UPS tracking numbers were assigned to packing slips, with package tracking through the UPS Network.[16]

Case 56: Consolidated Picking List The shipping manager at the Batch Process company had several major customers with weekly scheduled truck shipments. The contents of a truck shipment reflected the assignment of multiple sales order line items, subject to the truck's weight and volume limitations. A consolidated picking list was used to pick the material and stage it prior to truck arrival. The staged material was then loaded onto the truck, and the loaded material was reported as sent when the truck departed. The packing slip update was then reported for all sales orders within the sent shipment, and invoices generated.

Case 57: ASNs and Bar-Coded Labels A key customer of the Consumer Products company required an advanced ship notice (ASN) and bar-coded shipping labels for each shipment. The shipping labels identified the cartons and pallets within a shipment. The ASN information included basic data about the shipment number and customer PO number(s) included in the shipment, as well as content data about the items (for a standard pack approach) or about the pallets, cartons, and items within cartons (for a pick-

---

[15] An output order can be created for a component within the Production BOM, but it prevents normal posting of the picking list journal.

[16] Several firms provide modules that support integration to UPS and other freight services. For example, see **www.nextinnovation.com, www.nmbsolutions.ca**, or **www.nextgeneration.com**.

and-pack approach). These represent the basic variations in the hierarchical data structure for the ANSI X-12 856 transaction for ASNs. The combination of ASN and bar-coded labels enables the customer to quickly and accurately process material receipts via bar-code scanning, and to anticipate incoming material for put-away purposes.

Case 58: Data Collection System   The Distribution company was considering implementation of an automated data collection system. A key requirement was the use of hand-held devices (such as the Microsoft Pocket PC) for recording all inventory transactions and bar-coded information. The devices also had to support label printing, inventory balance inquiries, and customization of the user interface.[17]

Case 59: Stockroom Action Messages   The warehouse manager for the Equipment company wanted to improve coordination of stockroom activities by providing suggested action messages. The customized window built on the existing functionality concerning receipts, quarantine orders, output orders, and picking documents that communicated needed stockroom action. It also identified new types of messages, such as the need to review past due picks and shipments, review receipts for items with shortages, replenish inventory in bins based on refill requirements, review auto-deduction errors, review lot expiration for stocked material, and perform cycle counts.

Executive Summary

Warehouse management involves the physical storage and movement of products within and between physical sites, and the handling of outbound and inbound shipments with trading partners. It requires the definition of sites, warehouses, and stocking locations, and accurate reporting of inventory transactions. These transactions include inventory adjustments, transfers, and cycle counting, as well as arrivals and shipments associated with purchase orders, sales orders, and transfer orders. An inventory status is assigned to actual and anticipated transactions for receipts and issues, as shown in an item's inventory transaction audit trail.

---

[17] Several firms provide data collection support for Dynamics AX. For example, see **www.rfsmart.com**, **www.dynamicssoftware.com**, and **www.nextinnovation.com** for additional information about their data collection capabilities.

You can plan warehouse personnel requirements by anticipating all arrival activities, whether they pertain to purchase orders, transfer orders, customer returns, production orders or other inventory transactions. When a vendor delivery arrives at the warehouse, for example, you can create an arrival journal that contains selected purchase order line items, and then report actual quantities and bin placements.

You can also plan picking requirements, such as picking material for sales order and transfer order shipments. When planning a scheduled shipment to a customer, for example, you can create a shipment identifier, assign the sales order line items to be shipped, and generate the consolidated picking list (or order picking lists) for the shipment's contents. You can then report the actual picked material, report the shipment as sent, and post the sales order packing lists. As an option, you can report the actual picked material as staged and then loaded onto the truck, or reassign the picked material to another shipment, prior to reporting a shipment as sent. The case studies included UPS integration, advanced ship notices, and data collection systems for handling warehouse transactions.

Chapter 10

Quality Management

The concerns of quality management typically extend across every aspect of supply chain management. This broad viewpoint of quality management, for example, ranges from the definition of item and product structure information through sourcing purchased material, actual production, sales shipments, and returns. These topics have been covered throughout the book. A narrower viewpoint focuses on some of the unique functionality required for quality management, and this chapter takes the narrower viewpoint.

Some aspects of quality management functionality are embedded in the definition of product structure information. For example, you can define quality factors in production processes (such as material scrap and operation yield percentages), and planned changes to routings and bills of material that reflect continuous improvements. Other aspects involve the definition and enforcement of materials management policies, such as batch/serial control, receiving inspection, product testing, and stopping replenishment or sales of obsolete items. Additional aspects include the coordination of quality resources to perform inspection and testing, and workflow management tools for structuring business processes. These topics are reflected in the following sections within this chapter.

1. Batch and serial tracking
2. Receiving inspection and quarantine orders
3. Product testing and quality orders
4. Quality problems and nonconformance reports
5. Coordination of quality management activities
6. Workflow tools

Batch and Serial Tracking

Quality management often requires enforcement of serial or batch tracking.[1] Two sets of policies define the quality management requirements for serial and/or batch tracking. The first set of policies indicates which items have tracking requirements; these are embedded in the dimension group assigned to an item. The second set of policies indicates how and when the batch or serial numbers are assigned; these are embedded in the number group assigned to an item.

Batch Tracking Policies Batch tracking is defined by the dimension group assigned to an item, where the inventory dimension includes the batch number. The batch number dimension has several policies that enforce batch tracking across all transaction types, and support unique requirements such as batch-specific costing and pricing.

A second set of policies (termed the *batch number group*) determines how batch numbers are created and when they are assigned to inventory transactions for received material. A batch number can be created manually or automatically, with pre- or post-assignment to the inventory transaction.

❖ *Manual Versus Automatic Creation.* Automatic creation allows specification of a batch number mask, such as a prefix and counter. The mask can also include the date, order number, and/or system-assigned lot ID.

Manual creation means that the user must manually predefine an item's batch number prior to using the batch number on an inventory transaction. The batch numbering mask does not apply. With purchase order receipts, for example, the manual creation approach allows the user to define an internal batch number that matches the vendor's batch number, and then assign it to the purchase order receipt.

❖ *Pre- Versus Post-Assignment Approach.* A pre-assignment approach means that one batch number must be assigned to the inventory transaction, such as assigning a batch number to a purchase order line. The system can automatically create and assign the batch number, or the user can do it manually.

A post-assignment approach only works with automatic creation. For example, the system automatically creates and assigns batch numbers

---

[1] Dynamics AX uses the term batch tracking rather than lot tracking, since the term *lot number* is used for internal identification of inventory transactions.

when posting purchase order receipts for the item. The system normally creates and assigns a single batch number for each transaction. However, the system can optionally support quality management requirements for fixed batch sizes, such as unique batch numbers for every 10 received when receiving a quantity of 50.

The attributes for each batch number include descriptive text, and a manufacturing date and expiration date. The system automatically creates these two dates based on the transaction date when using an automatic creation approach. The system supports expiration reporting based on the expiration date.

Batch tracking can serve other purposes. For example, batch numbers can be used for tracking inventory remnants, such as a partial roll of material returned to stock.

Serial Tracking Policies   Serial tracking is defined by the dimension group assigned to an item, where the inventory dimension includes the serial number. The serial tracking policies are almost exactly the same as the batch tracking policies, including optional support for serial-specific costing and pricing. One additional policy enforces inventory quantities of 1 for serialization purposes, otherwise a serial number acts just like a batch number. The primary difference with batch tracking is that an item's serial number does not have to be predefined prior to using it on an inventory transaction.

A second set of policies (termed the *serial number group*) determines how the serial numbers are assigned to the item's inventory. Just like batch tracking, these policies indicate manual versus automatic creation and pre- versus post-assignment of serial numbers. Each serial number also has attributes such as descriptive text and a manufacturing date.

The batch and/or serial numbers can be printed on sales and purchase documents based on the form setup policies. For example, the batch numbers can be printed on the sales order packing slip and invoice.

When using intercompany orders in a multicompany operation, the batch or serial numbers assigned to the shipped material (on the intercompany sales order) can automatically apply to the received material (on the intercompany purchase order). Chapter 13 explains intercompany orders.

Historical Information about Batch and Serial Numbers   Dynamics AX automatically builds batch- and serial-trace history based on receipt and issue transactions. Historical information can be viewed for a specified item, batch number, or serial number. In a manufacturing environment, the user can view forward or backward trace information using a multilevel indented bill format. Each entry in the indented bill format indicates a receipt or issue. For example, the batch number for a sales order shipment can be traced backward through the production order(s) to purchase order receipts. A receipt can also be traced forward.

Receiving Inspection and Quarantine Orders

An item's quarantine management policy (embedded within the inventory model group assigned to the item) enforces 100% inspection for all received material. After purchase order receipt, for example, the system automatically creates a quarantine order for the received quantity. A quarantine order can also be manually created for existing inventory, or selectively created when recording item arrival. A quarantine order prevents material usage until the inspection process has ended. Planning calculations view the quarantined material as immediately available.

Quarantine orders require the definition of a quarantine warehouse and the bin locations within this quarantine warehouse. A quarantine warehouse can then be associated with each normal warehouse that requires a quarantine order.

A quarantine order only applies to a single item and quantity, and consists of four statuses (created, started, report as finished, and ended). A manually created quarantine order has a created status, and the status can be changed to started. An automatically created quarantine order has a status of started. The optional report-as-finished status supports use of a separate put-away transaction.

❖ *Created.* A manually created quarantine order represents a directive to move material from the originating warehouse/bin to a quarantine ware-house/bin. The system does not prevent usage, and the quarantine order can be deleted.

❖ *Started.* The material has been placed in the quarantine warehouse/bin, and cannot be used until the inspection process has been completed. The inspection process can report material as scrapped (via the scrap func-tion), or as having inspection completed. You can split the order quantity in order to report a subset as scrapped or completed. The scrap function immediately reduces inventory and no further action is required. If material must be returned (such as a return to vendor), change the status to report as finished (or ended), and subsequently report the returned material.

❖ *Report as Finished.* This is an optional status to support a separate put-away transaction. By reporting inspection as finished, the system creates a separate arrival journal so the user can specify the put-away location before posting the journal. The user specifies the name of the desired arrival journal, such as the arrival journal for purchase receipts or the production input journal for production order receipts.

❖ *Ended.* The material can be used. The material is placed in the specified site, warehouse, and bin.

Manually creating a quarantine order will generate two inventory transactions: a scheduled issue for the normal warehouse (status of on order) and a scheduled receipt at the quarantine warehouse (status of ordered). Starting a quarantine order will deduct inventory from the normal warehouse and receive inventory at the quarantine warehouse. Reporting a scrapped quantity (with an immediate reduction in inventory), or reporting a good quantity and ending a quarantine order, will reduce the inventory in the quarantine warehouse. The nature of inventory transactions was previously illustrated in Figure 9.1.

The Quarantine Order form displays a list of existing quarantine orders, and provides the starting point for manually creating a quarantine order, reporting inspection results and status changes. It also serves as a dispatch list for inspection activities.

Since an item's quarantine management policy represents a requirement for 100% inspection of receipts, it should not be used for items with intermittent or as-required inspection. In these cases, you can selectively indicate the creation of a quarantine order when recording item arrival.

Quarantine Orders for Customer Returns

A customer return can be selectively placed on a quarantine order when recording arrival related to a Return Material Authorization (RMA). An RMA disposition code is initially assigned when recording the arrival, and you can reassign the disposition code on the quarantine order. The disposition code indicates what action should be taken with the returned item, such as returning it to stock, scrapping it, or sending it back to the customer. The quarantine order must be split in order to assign different disposition codes to subsets of the returned quantity. Ending the quarantine order will implement the action for the disposition code, such as scrapping the returned material. The logic associated with these RMA disposition codes only applies to quarantine orders for returned items. A disposition code entered for other types of quarantine orders does not have any effect, and is not recognized in the standard RMA reports about disposition codes. These disposition codes were previously explained in the Chapter 7 section on RMAs.

Product Testing and Quality Orders

Product testing entails the use of quality orders to report test results against a group of predefined tests. The explanation of product testing can be segmented into three areas: the definition of tests and test groups, the use of quality orders for reporting test results, and the rules for automatic generation of quality orders.

Tests and Test Groups There are two types of predefined tests—quantitative and qualitative—and one or more tests can be assigned to a group of tests.

❖ *Quantitative Tests.* Each quantitative test must be assigned a testing unit of measure, so that acceptable values can be assigned when it is included in a test group. A pressure test, for example, might use pounds per square inch (PSI) as the unit of measure. The units of measure must be predefined along with the desired decimal precision.

❖ *Qualitative Tests.* A qualitative test will have an associated test variable (and its enumerated outcomes) when you assign it to a test group. A taste test, for example, may have one test variable for sweetness (with possible outcomes of sweet, sour, and okay) and another test variable for color (with possible outcomes of dark, light, and okay). You designate whether an outcome represents a pass or failure of the test.

For both types of tests, you can optionally assign a test instrument and applicable documents that describe the test.

Tests are assigned to a group of tests (termed a *test group*), where the test group has a unique identifier.

❖ *Test Groups*. For each test group, you assign a sampling plan, an acceptable quality level (AQL), and an indication of whether the tests will require destructive testing of the sample. A sampling plan is used to calculate the sample quantity for a quality order, and it can be expressed as an absolute quantity or as a percentage. For example, a sampling plan of 10% for a purchase order receipt quantity of 500 would result in a sample quantity of 50. An acceptable quality level refers to the percentage of tests that must be passed. An AQL of 90%, for example, means that 9 out of 10 tests must be passed. Destructive testing will result in an inventory reduction of the sample quantity.

❖ *Tests Within a Test Group*. When assigning a test to a test group, you define the acceptable measurement values for a quantitative test, or the test variable for a qualitative test. Each test can be assigned a sequence number, validity dates, and documents. You can designate which test results should be included in a certificate of analysis report associated with a quality order. An individual test can have its own AQL, referring to the percentage of the sample quantity that must be passed, since test results can be reported for subsets of the sample quantity.

The test group assigned to a quality order provides the initial basis for which tests need to be performed. Tests can be added, deleted, or changed on the quality order.

Use of a Quality Order   A quality order defines the tests that need to be performed for an item and a sample quantity (aka test quantity) of its inventory. A quality order also defines the tests that need to be performed on an item's sample quantity related to an order, such as a purchase, sales, or production order. A quality order communicates the need to perform tests, and provides a mechanism for reporting results against the tests. You can manually create a quality order, or establish quality guidelines within each business process (such as a purchase order receiving process) for automatically creating a quality order. The next subsection explains automatic generation of quality orders.

After reporting the test results for every test within a quality order, you initiate a validation process that assigns a pass or fail status (based on meeting the overall AQL) and closes the quality order. When you try to perform the next step in the business process, an infolog warns you when the quality order has failed or has not yet been closed. In addition, you can optionally reopen the quality order and force the validation process to assign a pass status by accepting any error conditions.

You can view information about a quality order (and its test results) from multiple viewpoints. For example, the quality order can be viewed for the related batch number or from the related sales order, purchase order, production order or quarantine order.

You can optionally generate a certificate of analysis that displays the test results for a quality order. A certificate of analysis, for example, could be printed for a batch of material being shipped to a customer. The printed test results will only be displayed for designated tests within in the quality order.

You can optionally create a nonconformance report when a quality order identifies defective material. The nonconformance report provides the basis for further investigation, as described in a subsequent section about nonconformances.

Automatic Generation of Quality Orders You can define rules (termed *quality association records*) for automatic generation of a quality order for incoming or outgoing material. Each rule defines the set of tests, the acceptable quality level (AQL), and the sampling plan that apply to the automatically generated quality orders. Each rule also defines the event and conditions for automatically generating a quality order within an item's business process. The item's business process can be related to purchase orders, quarantine orders, sales orders, or production orders, but not transfer orders. These business processes for a quality order are shown in Figure 10.1 and described below.

Business Process (Reference Type)	Label of the event that triggers a quality order (Execution / Document)	The actual event that triggers a quality order	Warning on next step	Conditions — Site	Conditions — Item	Conditions — Other	Destructive test allowed
Purchase order	Before receipts list	Initial attempt to post receipts list	Yes	Site-specific or company-wide	Vendor or vendor group	N/A	No
	After receipts list	Post the receipts list	Yes				No
	Before packing slip	Initial attempt to post packing slip	Yes				No
	After packing slip	Post the packing slip	Yes				Yes
Quarantine order	Before report as finished	Initial attempt to report as finished	Yes		N/A		No
	After report as finished	Report the order as finished	Yes				No
	Before end	Initial attempt to report as ended	Yes				No
	After end	Report the order as ended	Yes				No
Sales order	Before picking	Initial attempt to post picking list	Yes	Item-specific, quality group-specific, or all items	Customer or customer group		Yes
	After picking	Post the picking list	Yes				Yes
	Before packing slip	Initial attempt to post packing slip	Yes				Yes
	After packing slip	Post the packing slip	Yes				Yes
Production order	Before report as finished	Initial attempt to report as finished	Yes		N/A		No
	After report as finished	Update the report as finished	Yes				Yes
Route operation	Before report as finished	Create production order	Yes		Work center or WC group		No
	After report as finished	Report the operation as finished	Yes				No
Inventory	None	None	N/A				Yes

Figure 10.1 Rules for Automatic Generation of a Quality Order

Figure 10.1 summarize the events (expressed in terms of the relevant document and execution timing) and the conditions for generating a quality order for various business processes (termed the *reference type*). In particular, it identifies the actual event that triggers automatic generation of a quality order. The conditions for generating a quality order can be site-specific or company-wide, and they can apply to a single item, a group of items (based on the quality group assigned to items), or all items. Other conditions depend on the business process, such as vendor-specific conditions for a purchase order or customer-specific conditions for a sales order. A quality order involving destructive tests can only be generated when inventory exists for the event, as shown in the right-hand column of Figure 10.1. The automatic generation of a quality order can be further described for each business process.

❖ *Purchase Order Process.* The generation of a quality order can occur before or after the posting of a receipts list or packing slip for the received material. A quality order that requires destructive testing can only be generated after posting the packing slip for the received material, because the material must be available for destructive testing. The need for a quality order can reflect a particular site, item, or vendor, or a combination of these conditions.

❖ *Quarantine Order Process.* The generation of a quality order can occur before or after reporting the quarantine order as finished or ended. A quality order that requires destructive tests cannot be generated for a quarantine order, because it is assumed that the quarantine order functionality will handle scrapping of the destroyed material. The need for a quality order can reflect a particular site, item, or vendor, or a combination of these conditions.

❖ *Sales Order Process.* The generation of a quality order can occur before or after the posting of a picking list or packing slip for the material being shipped. A quality order that requires destructive testing can be generated at any step. The need for a quality order can reflect a particular site, item, or customer, or a combination of these conditions.

❖ *Production Order Process.* The generation of a quality order can occur before or after reporting the production order's finished quantity. A quality order that requires destructive testing can only be generated after reporting production as finished. The need for a quality order can reflect a particular site or item, or a combination of these conditions.

When a production order contains a routing operation, the quality order can be generated before or after reporting the operation as finished. The need for a quality order can reflect a particular, site, item, or work center, or a combination of these conditions.

❖ *Inventory.* A quality order cannot be automatically generated for a transaction within an inventory journal (such as a profit/loss or counting journal) or for transfer order transactions. A quality order must be manually generated for an item's inventory quantity, and the selected test group determines what tests will be performed.

A rule must be defined for each variation in a business process requiring automatic generation of a quality order. The validity dates for a quality association record enable you to model planned changes in the business process.

Comparing Quality Orders and Quarantine Orders

Inspection requirements related to receipts and issues are often modeled with a quality order. There are several reasons. Automatic generation can reflect situation-specific conditions in various business processes, and a quality order indicates what should be inspected. A quality order provides a way to record test results and validate the results against the desired AQL. You can designate which test results are included in a certificate of analysis. A quality order prevents the next step in the business process until the test results have been reported and validated against the AQL.

Inspection requirements related to receipts can be modeled with a quarantine order. A quarantine order provides a way to report scrap, and it prevents usage until the quarantine order has been completed. An item's quarantine policy represents a company-wide mandate to perform 100% inspection of received material. A quarantine order can be selectively created when reporting the arrival of an item without a mandated quarantine policy. In many cases, a quality order should be used in conjunction with a quarantine order so that the inspectors know what should be tested, and the material cannot be used until completion of the quarantine order.

Quality Problems and Nonconformance Reports

A nonconformance report (termed a *nonconformance*) describes an item that has a quality problem, where the descriptive information includes the source and type of problem. The problem source is termed a *nonconformance type*. You assign a problem source and an associated problem type when you create a nonconformance.

Types of Problem Sources for a Nonconformance Report   There are five types of problem sources (aka nonconformance types) that can be assigned to a nonconformance report, and each type can have optional source information.

❖ *Customer Problem.* The source information about a customer problem can include the customer number, sales order number, or a lot number of a sales order transaction. For example, the nonconformance could relate to a specific sales order shipment or to customer feedback about product quality.

❖ *Service Request Problem.* The source information about a service request can include the customer number, sales order number, or lot number of a sales order transaction. For example, the nonconformance could relate to a specific sales order shipment or to a customer's complaint about item quality.

❖ *Vendor Problem.* The source information about a vendor problem can include the vendor number, purchase order number, or a lot number of a purchase order transaction. For example, the nonconformance could relate to a purchase order receipt or to a vendor's concern about a part that it supplies.

❖ *Production Problem.* The source information about a production problem can include the production order number or a lot number of a production order transaction. For example, the nonconformance could relate to a specific batch that was produced.

❖ *Internal Problem.* The source information about an internal problem can include the quality order number or a lot number of a quality order transaction. For example, the nonconformance could relate to the tests that are performed as part of a quality order or to an employee's concern about product quality.

Problem Types   The user-definable problem types provide a classification of quality problems for each nonconformance type. For example, the problem types for service requests could reflect a classification of customer complaints, whereas the problem types for an internal nonconformance could represent a classification of defect codes. A problem type can be authorized

for one or more nonconformance types (aka problem sources), as defined in the Nonconformance types form. For example, the problem type concerning a defect code could apply to all nonconformance types. You can change the nonconformance type assigned to a nonconformance, and this may require changing the problem type to a valid value for the new nonconformance type.

Use of a Nonconformance Report A nonconformance is initially created with an approval status of *new*, indicating that it represents a request for action. You can approve or refuse a nonconformance (which changes the approval status to *approved* or *refused*) to indicate that you will or will not take action on the nonconformance.[2] You can also close a nonconformance (as indicated by a separate check box) to indicate that you are finished with it, or reopen a nonconformance to indicate that further consideration is required.

Comments can be entered for a nonconformance by using the document handling capabilities. It is generally helpful to define a unique document type about nonconformances (by using the Document Type form) so that you can enter notes for the unique document type. You can then use the Report Setup form to define your policy about printing notes for the unique document type on the nonconformance report and tag.

A printed conformance report and nonconformance tag can be used to assist material disposition.[3] You can selectively generate reports and tags based on selection criteria, such as the nonconformance number, item, customer, vendor, or status that are associated with a nonconformance.

❖ *Nonconformance Report.* The nonconformance report displays identification information, such as the nonconformance number, item, and problem type. The report displays the related notes based on your report setup policies.

❖ *Nonconformance Tag.* The nonconformance tag displays identification information, such as the nonconformance number and item. The tag displays the related notes based on your report setup policies. The tag also displays the quarantine zone and type (such as restricted usage

---

[2] A user cannot approve a nonconformance unless the user has been assigned an employee identifier (via the User Relations form). The system tracks the nonconformance history in terms of the employees who changed the status.

[3] The printed nonconformance tag and report will display an assigned quarantine zone (along with information about unusable versus restricted usage) to guide handling of defective material. The zones may or may not correspond to inventory locations or work centers. Use the quarantine zones form to define zones that can be assigned to a nonconformance.

versus unusable) that you assigned to the nonconformance in order to guide disposition of the defective material.

Options for Nonconformance Reports There are several options for handling the business processes pertaining to a nonconformance report, such as corrective actions, the description of work, additional testing, and related nonconformance reports.

❖ *Corrective Action for a Nonconformance Report.* You can optionally define one or more correction for an approved nonconformance. A correction identifies what type of diagnostic should be performed, who should perform it, and a requested date and a planned date for completing the diagnostic. You predefine the user-defined diagnostic types, and assign one to a corrective action. Indicate that you have finished the diagnostic step by changing the status of a correction to end. The status can be reopened. Comments can be entered for a correction by using the document handling capabilities. It is generally helpful to define a unique document type about corrections (by using the Document Type form) so that you can enter notes for the unique document type. Use the Report Setup form to define your policy about printing notes for the unique document type on the correction report. A printed correction report displays identification information about the nonconformance and the related nonconformance notes, as well as the correction information (such as the diagnostic) and related correction notes. The report displays the related correction notes based on your report setup policies.

❖ *Description of Work for a Nonconformance Report.* You can optionally define one or more related operation for an approved nonconformance. A related operation describes the work that should be performed, expressed as a selected operation (from a predefined list of user-defined quality operations) and descriptive text about the reason for the work. After defining an operation, you can optionally define the miscellaneous charges, items, and time sheet labor hours that are required to perform the work. The calculated costs are shown for the related operation, and the total calculated costs are shown for the nonconformance. The calculated costs and the underlying detail (about items, labor hours, and miscellaneous charges) represent reference information, and they are only used within the quality management function.

❖ *Defining Further Tests about a Nonconformance Report.* You can optionally create a quality order from a nonconformance in order to identify the need for further tests. For example, a quality order may identify the need to test (or retest) the defective material. The newly created quality order displays the linkage to the originating nonconformance.

❖ *Defining Related Nonconformance Reports.* You can optionally link one nonconformance to another, or create a new nonconformance from an existing one. For example, the linkage can reflect the interconnection between quality problems.

Coordination of Quality Management Activities

Dynamics AX provides several coordination tools for quality management personnel, such as schedules, dispatch lists, and recommended actions.

Production Schedule for Quality-Related Operations
The production schedule and job list identify routing operations to be performed by a work center that represents quality resources. The quality resource may include a labor pool of inspectors, a burn-in area, or other resource under quality management control. This may require time reporting (or unit completions by operation) to correctly reflect progress against the routing, availability for the next operation, auto-deduction of material, and actual costs.

Dispatch List of Quarantine Orders
Each quarantine order identifies material placed into inspection or quarantine, but does not indicate what tests must be performed or a scheduled completion date. It may also identify a batch/serial number and the related order (such as a purchase or production order).

Dispatch List of Quality Orders
Each quality order identifies material that requires inspection, and the (remaining) tests that must be performed. It may also identify a batch/serial number and the related order (such as a purchase or production order).

Dispatch List of Nonconformances
Each nonconformance report (termed a *nonconformance*) describes an item that has a quality problem, where the descriptive information includes the source and type of problem.

Dispatch List of Corrective Actions (for a Nonconformance)
Each correction identifies what type of diagnostic should be performed, who should perform it, and a requested date and a planned date for completing the diagnostic.

Expired Batches   A batch that approaches or exceeds the batch expiry date can be identified by a printed report (termed the Date Items report), or by creating a cycle count journal of expired batches.

Workflow Tools

The workflow tool within Dynamics AX has two primary components: workflow templates and the configuration of workflows based on a workflow template.

Workflow Templates   Several workflow templates have been predefined for a subset of business functions within Dynamics AX, as illustrated in Figure 10.2. It is anticipated that future AX releases will include additional predefined templates, and that users will also create their own templates.[4] Development of workflow templates requires much the same type of developer skills as developing an AX form.

Workflow Configurations   Configuring workflows based on a workflow template requires no development skills. In a typical approval scenario, for example, a workflow must be configured for a transaction such as a purchase

Business Function	Example of a Predefined Workflow Template
Accounts Payable	Purchase Requisition Approval
	Project Purchase Requisition Approval
	Invoice Approval
Expense Management	Expense Report Approval
	Cash Advance Request Approval
Accounts Receivable	Customer Bank Remittance
	Customer Payment
General Ledger	Allocations
	Fixed Assets Budget

Figure 10.2 Examples of Predefined Workflow Templates

---

[4] Additional workflow templates have already been created by some firms. For example, see **www.RedMaple.com** for more information about their Workflow Templates module containing more than 50 additional templates.

requisition or an expense report. The user submits the transaction for approval, and the workflow configuration determines if anyone needs to approve it, notifies the relevant approvers (if automatic approval does not apply), and then tracks the approval steps.

The Chapter 8 section on purchase requisitions and approval process provided a detailed explanation of a workflow template and workflow configurations. This workflow template contained an underlying conceptual model consisting of a task and an approval process with one or more approver steps. It contained unique information (e.g., used in conditions) that reflected the context of purchase requisitions, such as the requisitioner and the requisition amount. The other workflow templates listed in Figure 10.2 also contain an underlying conceptual model that only consists of an approval process (and no task). Each of these templates has different information that reflect the context, such as the expense amount in the workflow template for expense report approval.

It is worth noting that Dynamics AX has an underlying workflow built into the transaction processing for each business process, such as purchase order or sales order processing. The basic nature of the transaction workflow within each business process can be shaped by various parameters and policies, and also facilitated by the prompts within a data-collection system. This transaction workflow concept can be augmented by user-defined workflow templates and configurations.

Case Studies

Case 60: Batch Attributes   A mining company produced and sold a mining product (coal), and employed batch tracking for all items from raw materials to finished goods. A quality template for each item defined the standard tests (and acceptable target values) for more than 50 batch attributes, such as the percentage of ash content and volatile matter. Actual values for each batch's attributes were determined by independent testing agencies. Prior to producing a blended coal product from different coal components, the quality manager could calculate the projected batch attribute values based on the weighted average of the component's batch attribute values.

Case 61: Regulated Environment for Process Manufacturing
The Batch Process company produced a pharmaceutical product with strin-

gent quality criteria concerning compliance to regulations and requirements for a validation audit. Starting with various lot-controlled ingredients, a batch was mixed, made into tablets, and then packaged in a bottle with a label. Each batch required a unique lot number. Tablets were treated as phantoms since production flows from the tablet machine immediately into packaging.

The quality criteria in this regulated environment impacted system usage in several ways. Systems security played a larger role, such as authorized access to update information about bills, batches, inventory dispositions, and transaction audit trails. It requires strict label control, conditional releases of lot-traced material, and lot genealogy for historical analysis purposes.

Case 62: Instrument Calibration The quality manager at the Consumer Products company required a schedule for instrument calibration based on usage and time factors, the tracking of instrument maintenance, and calibration warnings prior to instrument usage. Additional requirements included instrument certificate tracking and risk instrument notifications.[5]

Case 63: Inspection Frequencies The quality manager at the Distribution company required inspection rules about when and how often to perform inspection of incoming material. Some materials required inspection frequencies based on quantities or time factors or both, while other materials required inspection only on the first receipt from the vendor. Skip-lot logic was also required to meet inspection frequency standards for ISO 2859-1, NIST Series 6 and ANSI Z1.4.

Case 64: Quality Metrics The quality manager at the Equipment company required extensive metrics about inspection results, including pareto charting and variable control charts for test results about AQLs (acceptable quality levels) and defect codes. Additional metrics were needed for vendor delivery performance and sales order delivery performance.

---

[5] See **www.erpsolutions.biz** for additional information about their quality control applications that support instrument calibration, inspection frequencies, and quality metrics.

Executive Summary

A number of quality management concerns involve the enforcement of materials management practices, such as batch- and serial-control, receiving inspection (via quarantine orders), and required tests (via quality orders). A nonconformance report can identify a quality problem, and drive corrective actions and additional testing (via quality orders). Quality management can employ work flow tools to structure the completion of tasks and approvals within a business process. Dispatch lists can help coordinate quality resources to perform inspection and testing. The case studies included instrument calibration, inspection frequencies, and batch tracking in regulated environments

Chapter 11

Production Order Processing

Most manufacturing environments use production orders as the primary coordination tool for scheduling and reporting production activities. A production order is directly linked to a sales order for make-to-order products, or indirectly linked to demand for make-to-stock products. The production order for a make-to-stock product is typically generated by firming a planned production order, whereas you generate the production order for a make-to-order product from the related sales order. The production order for a make-to-order component (termed a *reference order*) will be automatically generated. Each production order goes through several life cycle steps.

Manufacturers may or may not employ routing data to model production activities. Routing data provides the basis for calculating a production order's lead time. The scheduling logic can optionally account for finite capacity constraints at work centers, and for block scheduling of operations with the same characteristics. An operation's work center can also indicate the warehouse source for picking the components required by the operation. Use of routing data typically involves reporting actual time and unit completions by operation, but auto-deduction policies can minimize the reporting efforts.

The explanation of production orders focuses on six major topics, as shown below.

1. Production order life cycle
2. Production order considerations
3. Production order scheduling
4. Reporting production activities
5. Coordinating production activities
6. Production order costing

Production Order Life Cycle

A production order has a unique identifier (termed a *production number*) that can be manually or automatically assigned; auto-assignment typically reflects a prefix and counter. The format for auto-assignment of production order numbers can be site-specific. Each production order identifies one manu-factured item along with the quantity, delivery date, and manufacturing site/warehouse.

A production order can be created by three different methods: manually entered, firming a planned production order, or created from a sales order line item. A production order is also automatically generated for each make-to-order component, as described in Chapter 3 and illustrated in Figure 3.2.[1] Each additional order (termed a *reference order*) is directly linked to the production order's component demand. A reference order can be auto-matically rescheduled and synchronized when the parent's production order gets rescheduled.

The life cycle of a production order consists of several steps represented by an order status.[2] The steps represent a linear progression that affects production order behavior, such as the ability to report actual production activities. Steps in the linear progression can be skipped; steps can also be reversed by resetting order status. Each step involves a user-initiated update task (and an associated dialogue) in addition to an order status. For example, changing order status from created to started involves a start task and an associated "start production order" dialogue. The production order life cycle first requires an understanding of these update tasks, since they provide the context for understanding order status. The types of update tasks and their significance are summarized in Figure 11.1 and explained below.

Create Order Task   The critical information in the create production order dialogue includes the item, quantity, delivery date, and manufacturing site/warehouse. The system assigns the active BOM version and routing ver-

---

[1] Automatic generation of reference orders only occurs after the parent's production order status is at least estimated.

[2] Those readers familiar with the production order life cycle in other ERP packages often ask for clarification about the differences. In Dynamics AX, for example, a planned production order represents a separate construct so there is no order status called planned. The process of firming a planned production order generates a production order with a designated order status such as scheduled or started; there is no order status called firmed or open. The started status (rather than the released status) indicates an authorization to report production activities. The reported-as-finished status means that the system ignores remaining component requirements and expected parent receipts, but additional transactions can be reported without reopening the production order. The order status can be reset at any time prior to ended status, and the system will automatically reverse all associated transactions.

		Significance of Update Task	Dialogue Default Values	Option to Include Reference Orders
Type of Update Task	Create Order	Initially create a new production order	No	N/A
	Estimate Order	Initially perform (if needed) to calculate material requirements Perform (if needed) cost-plus-markup calculation of a sales price Perform again (if needed) to recalculate costs based on updated information	Yes	Yes
	Schedule Order	Initially schedule material and capacity requirements Perform again (if needed) to reschedule order based on updated information	Yes	Yes
	Release Order	Perform (if needed) to print shop traveler of routing operations	Yes	Yes
	Start Order	Indicate started quantity (and selected operations) Perform again (if needed) to define the additional started quantity (and selected operations) Perform again (if needed) to indicate completion of all picking and/or all operations	Yes	Yes
	Report Related Activities	Print picking list and report material consumption via the picking list journal Report unit completions by operation via the report-as-finished journal Report time and unit completions by operation via the route (or job) card journal	N/A	
	Report as Finished	Report parent receipts, and optionally indicate completed order, picking, or all operations Perform again (if needed) to report additional parent receipts or indicate completed order Perform again (if needed) to indicate completion of all picking and/or all operations	Yes	N/A
	Costing	Initially perform to calculate actual costs to-date and optionally indicate ended order Perform again (if needed) to calculate actual costs to-date or indicate ended order	Yes	
	Reset Status	Change order status to created, thereby allowing deletion of production order Change order status, thereby reversing all associated transactions	Yes	Yes

Figure 11.1 Update Tasks for Production Orders

sion based on the manufacturing site and delivery date (or a user-specified BOM date if entered), but the user can manually override these with another version prior to creation. Once the order has been created, the order-dependent bill and routing initially reflect the specified BOM and routing versions, and they can be manually maintained. However, planning calculations do not recognize the requirements associated with a created order status.

Estimate Order Task   The estimate order task calculates the production order costs based on the order-dependent bill/routing and order quantity, and related cost information. For example, the labor and overhead costs reflect the current active cost records, as described in Chapter 5. A price calculation inquiry displays the production order's per-unit costs and a per-unit sales price.[3]

Schedule Order Task   When scheduling a production order (via a schedule order dialogue) using either of the two scheduling methods, the critical information includes the scheduling direction and several scheduling

---

[3] The calculated sales price can reflect a cost-plus markup approach (and a specified set of profit-setting percentages) or a rolled price approach or both, as described in the Chapter 5 section about BOM calculation of a manufactured item's sales price.

policies. The scheduling direction, for example, could be forward from today's date or backward from a specified scheduling date. The scheduling can optionally include consideration of finite capacity and finite material. A subsequent section provides further explanation of the two production scheduling methods and related policies. The schedule order task must be repeated after changing the order quantity or the order-dependent bill and routing.

The start and end dates for a production order cannot be manually entered, but the user can specify a desired delivery date for the order and then perform the schedule task with backward scheduling from the delivery date. The user can specify that a production order is locked, thereby preventing rescheduling by planning calculations and the use of the schedule order task.

Release Order Task   The release order dialogue can be used to print shop traveler paperwork (related to routing information) prior to starting production activities.

Start Order Task   Starting a production order quantity (via a start order dialogue) represents an authorization to start reporting actual production activities. The start order dialogue may be performed again when starting partial quantities or when starting selected operations. It can also be used to indicate completion of all picking activities or routing operations so that planning calculations ignore remaining requirements.

The reporting of related production activities (shown in Figure 11.1 for informational purposes) includes component material consumption as well as time and unit completions by operation. The started quantity can trigger auto-deduction of relevant components and operations. A subsequent section provides further explanation about reporting production activities.

Report as Finished Task   The report-as-finished task provides one approach for receiving production orders, expressed in terms of the good quantity and scrap quantity (termed *error* quantity). It can also serve as an auto-deduction trigger. The report-as-finished dialogue can indicate completion of all picking activities or routing operations so that planning calculations ignore remaining requirements. Indicating completion of the entire production order (via the *end job* flag) will change order status to reported-as-finished, which also results in remaining requirements being ignored. However, transactions can still be entered for the production order.

Order status will not change to reported-as-finished when transactions are missing unless the user indicates in the report-as-finished dialogue that errors will be accepted. Missing transactions may include expected parent receipts or remaining requirements for components and operations.

End Task   The end task calculates actual costs and changes order status to ended. The end dialogue also indicates how to handle scrap costs, either by allocating scrap costs to actual parent receipts or by charging them to a specified G/L account.

Under certain conditions the end task can be performed instead of the report-as-finished task (via the reported-as-finished flag in the end task dialogue). That is, it is assumed the quantity completed matches the quantity ordered, and the components and routing operations will be automatically auto-deducted.

Reset Status Task   A production order can be reset to a previous status, and you indicate the desired order status on the reset order dialogue. For example, order status may be changed to created to allow deletion, or changed to released from started so that the system automatically reverses all transactions about actual production activities.

Update Tasks and the Option to Include Reference Orders

Several update tasks for a production order have an option to include reference orders, as indicated in the right-hand column of Figure 11.1. The reference orders can be included in cost calculations, scheduling, releasing, and the authorization to start production activities. For example, the schedule order task can optionally include reference orders and even synchronize them. Resetting order status can apply to reference orders, and to optionally delete them. The update tasks can also be performed for a production order that represents a reference order.

Significance of Production Order Status   The update tasks provide a context for understanding the order status of a production order. The update tasks allow the user to skip steps, since the system automatically performs the intervening update tasks based on default values for each dialogue.

<table>
<tr><th colspan="3"></th><th colspan="7">Order Status</th></tr>
<tr><th colspan="3"></th><th>Created</th><th>Estimated</th><th>Scheduled</th><th>Released</th><th>Started</th><th>Reported as Finished</th><th>Ended</th></tr>
<tr><td rowspan="12">Significance of Order Status</td><td rowspan="3">Planning Calculations</td><td>Recognize Expected Parent Receipt</td><td colspan="5">Yes</td><td colspan="2">No</td></tr>
<tr><td>Recognize Component Requirements</td><td>No</td><td colspan="3">Yes</td><td>Yes*</td><td colspan="2">No</td></tr>
<tr><td>Recognize Operation Requirements</td><td colspan="2">No</td><td colspan="2">Yes</td><td>Yes*</td><td colspan="2">No</td></tr>
<tr><td colspan="2">Modify Order-Dependent Bill or Routing</td><td colspan="5">Yes</td><td colspan="2">No</td></tr>
<tr><td colspan="2">Copy BOM or Routing to Production Order</td><td colspan="2">Yes</td><td colspan="5">No</td></tr>
<tr><td colspan="2">Print Shop Paperwork for Routing Operations</td><td colspan="3">No</td><td colspan="3">Yes</td><td>No</td></tr>
<tr><td colspan="2">Print Picking List</td><td colspan="4">No</td><td colspan="2">Yes</td><td>No</td></tr>
<tr><td colspan="2">Report Actual Production Activities</td><td colspan="4">No</td><td colspan="2">Yes</td><td>No</td></tr>
<tr><td colspan="2">Ability to Delete Order</td><td>Yes</td><td colspan="5">No</td><td>Yes</td></tr>
<tr><td colspan="2">Perform Price Calculation</td><td colspan="5">Yes</td><td colspan="2">No</td></tr>
<tr><td colspan="2">Split Order Quantity</td><td colspan="5">Yes</td><td colspan="2">No</td></tr>
<tr><td colspan="2">Reset Order Status</td><td>No</td><td colspan="5">Yes</td><td>No</td></tr>
</table>

*Remaining component requirements ignored after reporting picking list as completed, and Remaining operation requirements ignored after reporting operation as completed

Figure 11.2 Significance of Production Order Status

For example, a user could manually create an order, and then start it.[4] As another example, the firming process can generate a production order with a scheduled status. The significance of each order status is shown in Figure 11.2.

The production order status determines whether planning calculations recognize expected parent receipts and requirements for components and operations. It also affects the ability to modify the order-dependent bill, print paperwork, report actual production activities, delete an order, perform price calculations, split an order quantity, and reset order status. In particular, Figure 11.2 indicates that production activities can be reported and transactions can be automatically reversed (via the reset order status task) up until the ended status.

[4] The ability to change from one status to another is defined within the production parameters.

Production Order Considerations

The basic production order information defines an item, quantity, delivery date and the manufacturing site/warehouse. Additional information includes the order-dependent bill and routing, the location for component material, and other factors.

Order-Dependent Routing   The order-dependent routing (termed the *Production Route*) initially reflects the master routing used to create the production order. The user can manually maintain the information and/or update it using the copy routing feature. The system does not recognize changes to the order-dependent routing until the user performs the scheduling task.

Order-Dependent Bill of Material   The order-dependent bill (termed the *Production BOM*) initially reflects the master BOM used to create the production order and the component date effectivities. The user can manually maintain the information and/or update it using the copy bill feature. The system does not recognize changes to the order-dependent bill until the user performs the scheduling (or estimation) task.

Location for a Component   A component's warehouse and bin location can be specified in the order-dependent bill, thereby indicating where the component should be picked from. The initial value for the component's warehouse reflects the source defined in the master BOM used to create the production order. For example, the warehouse may reflect work center consumption logic (as previously illustrated in Figure 3.3). The initial value for the component's bin location reflects the item's default bin location within the warehouse.

Splitting a Production Order   Splitting a production order results in a new production order for the specified quantity and delivery date. The split order quantity must be less than the originating order quantity. A started production order can be split, but only for a quantity that has not yet been reported as started. This approach avoids the complications associated with allocations of issued components and reported operation times to the split orders.

Production Order Lead Time   The system calculates a variable production lead time based on routing data, or it uses a fixed lead time when no routing data exists. An item's fixed production lead time (expressed in days) can be specified as a company-wide value, and overridden for a site/warehouse, as described in the Chapter 3 section about planning data for manufactured items. The calculation of a variable lead time reflects the order quantity, routing operations, available capacity, and scheduling method. A subsequent section covers the scheduling methods for production orders.

Prevent Order Rescheduling A production order can be flagged as locked to prevent rescheduling, and then unlocked when desired.

Reserving Components for a Production Order A component's inventory can be reserved for a production order line item. The user can manually specify the reserved material or use automatic reservations. Reservations can be made for batch- and serial-traced material as well as non-traced material. Reservations can also be made against scheduled receipts.[5]

Purchase Forecast Consumption by Production Orders A production order consumes the purchase forecast for a manufactured item (if specified) to avoid doubled-up requirements. The order's delivery date determines forecast consumption within a forecast period.

Identifying the Production Order Linkage to a Demand A production order can be directly linked to a demand, either a sales order line item or another production order's component. The system indicates direct linkage in the reference fields for a production order. In the same way, the reference fields for the corresponding demand (such as a sales order line item) indicate direct linkage to the production order. In contrast, a production order can be indirectly linked to demands via dates (the production order due date and the demand date), such as indirect linkage for a make-to-stock item. For example, a production order quantity may cover demands stemming from multiple sales orders. The system indicates indirect linkage with null values in the reference fields for a production order.

The significance of the reference type field can become confusing, since an additional system capability termed *marking* also employs the reference fields. A primary purpose of marking is to support cost tracking and reservations by linking receipt transactions to issue transactions. Marking automatically applies to a production order with direct linkage. It can optionally apply to production orders with indirect linkage. For example, the user can

---

[5] A company-wide policy (embedded in the inventory parameters) indicates whether reservations can be made for scheduled receipts of ordered material.

manually mark an existing production order so that costs can be tracked to one or more demands such as sales orders. As another example, the firming process for planned orders can assign marking to production orders and sales orders based on pegging information. In this case, the reference information for a production order satisfying multiple demands is null, whereas the sales order line items have reference information.[6] Marking does not provide direct linkage, but it can update the value of the reference type field. The dual use of the reference type field can lead to confusion. For simplicity's sake the explanation focuses on the significance of the reference fields related to direct linkage.

The Reference List inquiry for a production order identifies the linked reference orders.

Summarized Information   The summarized information includes estimated and actual costs for a production order. Access to detailed information includes actual component issues, parent receipts and routing operations, batch and serial tracking, and related linked orders (or reference orders).

Production Order Scheduling

Production orders with routing data can be scheduled using two different scheduling methods: a rough-cut method (termed *operations scheduling*) and detailed method (termed *job scheduling*). The term job scheduling may be confusing to those people that think of job as synonymous with a production order or project, but in this context job refers to the individual time elements within an operation. These time elements include setup, process, and transport time. Further explanation primarily uses the terms *rough-cut* and *detailed scheduling* methods to avoid potential confusion. The choice of a scheduling method involves several differentiating factors. In addition, each scheduling method involves choices about scheduling direction and finite scheduling logic.

Differentiating Factors for Choosing a Scheduling Method   The differentiating factors for choosing a scheduling method are summarized in Figure 11.3. The primary differences involve the scheduling focus, capacity planning and scheduling capabilities, and the time granularity.

---

[6] The firming process with marking has two variations— standard marking versus extended marking—that determine whether the reference fields indicate one-to-one or one-to-many relationships for marking purposes.

		Scheduling Method	
		Rough-Cut Method **Operations Scheduling**	**Detailed Method** **Job Scheduling**
Differentiating Factors	Scheduling Focus	Work Center Group	Work Center
	Capacity Planning	Aggregate (by Group)	Detailed (by Work Center) and Aggregate (by Group)
	Scheduling Capabilities		Interchangeable work centers within group* Alternate work center logic (Task Groups), Block scheduling via properties to minimize setups Selectively lock job and synchronize related activities Use of Gantt Chart
	Time Granularity	Schedule by date	Schedule by date and time
	Costing Capabilities	Average Time and Costs for Work Center Group	Specific Time and Costs for Work Center
	Printed Shop Traveler	Route Card	Job Card
	Reporting Operation Time and Unit Completions	Use Route Card Journal	Use Job Card Journal or Route Card Journal
	Computer Processing Time	Faster	Slower

*Selection of work center reflects the shortest possible lead time

Figure 11.3 Comparison of Scheduling Methods

❖ *Detailed Scheduling Method.* The detailed scheduling method (aka job scheduling) supports a work center focus with detailed and aggregate capacity planning, and several scheduling capabilities not supported by the rough-cut method. These scheduling capabilities include automatic assignment of a work center (within a group) based on shortest possible lead time, use of alternate work center logic, use of block scheduling to minimize setups, use of a Gantt chart, and time granularity for operation start/end times. Minor differences include the printed shop traveler, the approach for reporting operation time and unit completions, and computer processing time.

❖ *Rough-Cut Scheduling Method.* The rough-cut scheduling method (aka operations scheduling) should be used when routing data does not exist, or when simple production schedules by work center group are sufficient.

In summary, the detailed scheduling method should be used when the situation requires production schedules by machine, time granularity by hour, consideration of advanced scheduling capabilities, and both detailed and aggregate capacity planning. As a general suggestion, using just one method for all scheduling purposes will simplify system understanding, especially when reporting operation time via a single type of journal.

Variations in Scheduling Directions	Other Parameter	Applicability Operations Scheduling	Applicability Job Scheduling	Applicability Reschedule Planned Order*
Forward from today		Yes	Yes	No
Forward from tomorrow				No
Forward from an earlier planned start date				No
Forward from a specified schedule date	Specify a Schedule Date			Yes
Backward from a specified schedule date				Yes
Backward from the delivery date				No
Backward from the previously calculated end date				Yes
Backward from the calculated action date (requirement date)				Yes
Backward from the calculated futures date				Yes
Schedule according to last scheduling run				
Forward from a specified job	Specify a Job Identifier	No		No
Backward from a specified job				No
Forward from order date		No		Yes

*Planned orders are initially scheduled using backward scheduling from the requirement date.

Figure 11.4 Variations in Scheduling Directions

Scheduling Direction   Both scheduling methods support different scheduling directions. The basic scheduling directions are forward and backward as of a given date, such as the requirement date. Figure 11.4 summarizes the variations in scheduling directions for both scheduling methods. It also highlights the detailed scheduling method for locking a job (via a specified job identifier) and synchronizing upstream and downstream activities. Fewer options are available for rescheduling a planned production order.

Scheduling Options   Scheduling logic for individual production orders can optionally include finite capacity and finite material, the use of properties (for block scheduling purposes), and reference orders. Another option can exclude selected time elements, such as queue and transit time, to calculate the fastest possible production throughput.

❖ *Finite Capacity.* When a bottleneck work center has finite capacity, the scheduling logic ensures the scheduled loads do not exceed the available capacity. The system factors available working hours by an operations schedule percentage that limits loading.

❖ *Finite Material.* Scheduling logic requires on-hand inventory on the start date of the production order or the relevant operation (if applicable).

When there is insufficient inventory, scheduling logic uses the item's lead time to determine when it will be available. The components' availability date determines when the production order can be started.

❖ *Finite Property and Block Scheduling.* The finite property approach represents a form of block scheduling for grouping similar operations to minimize setup time, and performing them during a predefined block of time in the work center calendar.

❖ *Reference Orders.* The user can optionally schedule and synchronize reference orders related to the selected order, thereby synchronizing downstream (and upstream) orders via forward (and backward) scheduling.

Scheduling Method for the Master Scheduling Task   Each set of master plan policies determines whether planned orders will be scheduled based on detailed (job) or rough-cut (operations) scheduling methods. The system schedules existing orders automatically using the default scheduling method defined in the production parameters.

Reporting Production Activities

Several types of production activities can be reported against production orders. These activities include started quantities, component usage, and parent receipts, and also routing operation time and unit completions when routing data exists. There are several ways to report each activity as described below. Some of these approaches were described earlier in terms of the update tasks for a production order, but are included here for completeness sake.

Reporting Started Quantities   The started quantity defaults to the order quantity for all operations, but the user can override this in the start order dialogue. For example, the user can specify partial quantities or selected operations when there is a large order quantity or a multistep routing. Specifying a selected operation number also provides the basis for populating a picking list journal with a subset of the components (linked to the operation number). The started quantity can act as the auto-deduction trigger for forward-flushing material components and operations tied to the selected operations. In addition, the start order dialogue can be used to indicate completion of all picking activities and/or completion of all routing operations.

Reporting Material Usage   Component materials can be manually issued
or auto-deducted. Auto-deduction will be covered in a subsequent section,
so further explanation focuses on environments where all of the components
are manually issued. Manual issues are typically initiated based on a printed
pick list identifying the quantities and locations of components in the order
dependent bill. A picking list journal must be created in order to print the
picking list, where the journal lines identify components to be picked.

There are two common approaches for automatically populating the
picking list journal for manually issued components.

❖ *As Part of Starting a Production Order.* As part of the start order dialogue, the user can populate the picking list journal with all components
or the subset of components associated with the specified operation
number(s).[7] You can optionally generate a separate picklist associated
with each operation. Use the *complete picking list journal* policy to
include manually issued components. Do not use the *post picking list
now* policy since actual quantities and locations will be subsequently
entered on the picking list journal.

❖ *Extra Step to Automatically Create Journal Lines.* After starting a production order, the user creates the picking list journal via a "create lines"
dialogue. The dialogue specifies the basis for populating the journal
lines, such as all components with a remaining quantity required, or the
components associated with a specified operation number. The system
automatically creates a picking list journal and the journal line items after
finishing the dialogue.

A picking list journal and its line items can also be manually created,
typically in situations for issuing components not in the order dependent bill
or for handling returned components. Manually added journal lines represent
additional component issues (positive quantity) or returns to stock (negative
quantity), and do not reduce the remaining requirements for a component.

The printed picking list provides a turnaround document for recording
actual quantities and stocking locations on the picking list journal. Component quantity consumption can be reported in the item's base UM or other
authorized UM. The user can also indicate the component has been completely picked so that remaining requirements are ignored. The picking list
journal can then be posted to report material usage.

---

[7] The use of specified operation numbers does not require routing data, since the operation numbers are
assigned to components.

Definition of Remaining Requirements

A material shortage represents the remaining requirements for a component in the order-dependent bill for a started production order. The system ignores the components' remaining required quantity under several conditions: when a specific component has been flagged as completely picked; when picking for all components has been flagged as complete; when an operation linked to the material has been flagged as complete; or when the production order status becomes reported-as-finished. The system displays shortages on the Material Stock-Out List inquiry.

The remaining time requirements for a routing operation can also be ignored: when the operation has been flagged as complete; when the entire routing has been flagged as complete; or when the production order status becomes reported-as-finished.

Reporting for an Internal Operation   Reporting for an internal operation involves unit completions and/or operation time, and only applies to production orders with routing data. The system supports manual reporting and auto-deduction for internal operations. A subsequent section explains auto-deduction for routing operations, so that further explanation focuses on manual reporting.

❖ *Reporting Operation Time.* Operation time is reported on the route card journal for a production order.[8] Each journal line indicates the operation number, work center, time element (such as process or setup time), and actual hours expended. The route card journal provides several options for the user, such as overriding the basis for costing and indicating the employee performing the work. The user can optionally create a picking list journal from the route card journal; this may be useful when the operator is responsible for reporting component usage at the operation.

❖ *Reporting Unit Completions by Operation.* Units completions by operation are reported on the route card journal for a production order, and units can be reported without a time entry. Unit completions are reported

---

[8] The approach for reporting operation time depends on the scheduling method. The route card journal applies to production orders scheduled via either method, whereas the job card journal only applies to a production order scheduled via the job scheduling method. The two reporting approaches are similar. The job card differs slightly, since it also supports calculation of reported time based on specified start and end times. For simplicity's sake further explanation focuses on using the route card journal for reporting unit completions and operation time.

as a good quantity, with an incremental quantity for scrapped units and an optional reason code. The user can indicate the operation is completed so that remaining requirements are ignored. The route card journal provides several other options, such as overriding the basis for costing unit completions.

Reporting unit completions for the last operation has special significance. The good unit completions can optionally update parent receipts (by explicitly using the report-as-finished flag), where the warehouse and bin reflect production order information. Additional information may need to be recorded about batch and serial numbers based on the item's quality management policies.

The unit completions and processing hours provide one measure of progress against the routing operation. The system automatically calculates a completion percentage based on actual versus expected process hours as one indicator of remaining work, and this can be manually overridden. The completion percentage is used in planning calculations to calculate remaining work.

Labor Data Collection and the Shop Floor Control Module

The shop floor control module supports data collection for reporting unit completions and operation time via clock-in and clock-out registrations for specific production orders and operations. Based on this registration information, the system automatically accumulates the times and unit completions by operation, which can then be used to create line items in route card (or job card) journals. This functionality builds on the time and attendance capabilities within the module, and also supports preparation of payroll data from a single source of labor data.

Reporting for an Outside Operation Reporting for an outside operation reflects the Dynamics AX approach to handling subcontracted production. As described in the Chapter 3 section on subcontracted production, a purchased item with a component type of vendor represents the outside operation. The system automatically creates a linked purchase order after scheduling the parent item's production order. Reporting for an outside operation entails receipt (and a vendor invoice) of the purchase order. An additional step may be required to issue the component (via the picking list journal) when tracking the item's inventory.

An additional step or two is also required when using routing information to define the outside operation for scheduling purposes. After purchase order receipt, the outside operation should be designated as completed so that scheduling logic understands the remaining work. If the outside operation represents the last operation in the routing, reporting the unit completions can update the parent receipts.

Parent Receipts   Parent receipts refer to the reported-as-finished quantities of a production order.[9] Parent receipts involve identification of the good quantity, with an incremental quantity for scrapped units and an optional reason code. Parent receipts can be recorded three different ways.

❖ *Report-as-Finished Task.* This update task provides one method for reporting parent receipts when routing data does not exist. The user can also indicate the completion of all picking or of all routing operations, or completion of the entire production order. Only the report-as-finished task can trigger auto-deduction.

❖ *Report-as-Finished Journal.* This journal provides one method for reporting parent receipts when routing data does not exist. The user can also indicate completion of the entire production order.

❖ *Route Card Journal for Reporting Unit Completions at the Last Operation.* Routing data must exist, and the user must explicitly indicate a report-as-finished flag on the route card.

Reporting Parent Receipts in an Orderless Environment

Parent receipts can be reported in an orderless environment using the BOM Journal. The BOM journal works slightly differently than other journals, since the line items identify the parent item and its components. You initiate a separate form (termed the *report as finished* form) to identify the parent item being reported as finished and some additional data. This additional

---

[9] The term reported-as-finished has several contexts within Dynamics AX that can lead to confusion. These contexts include the update task for a production order, a journal for reporting unit completions by operation, report-as-finished flags when reporting production activities, and a production order status. Another context involves selling a kit item with auto-deduction of components after posting the sales order invoice. Hence, the term parent receipt is used for clarification purposes.

data enables the system to automatically populate the journal entries for the parent item and its components. The additional data includes the quantity completed, the BOM version, and an explosion policy. The explosion policy determines the basis of components used in producing the parent item, as described below.

* *Never Explode.* The underlying bills for manufactured components are never exploded, so that the components reflect the single-level bill. However, the system still explodes requirements through phantom components.
* *Always Explode.* The underlying bills for manufactured components are always exploded regardless of inventory availability, so that components only reflect purchased items.
* *Explode Only When Shortage Exists.* The explosion of underlying bills for manufactured components reflects available inventory.

It may be useful to review the system-generated journal entries—one entry for the parent item and one for each component—rather than posting immediately. The system explicitly flags each component and assigns a negative quantity; it assigns a positive quantity to the parent item.[10] Components are included regardless of their auto-deduction policy. The stocking locations reflect the default bins assigned to the items, which may need to be overridden. The BOM journal entries can then be posted.

Indicating Completion of a Production Order   The user can indicate completion of a production order using either the report-as-finished task or the report-as-finished journal, as described above. This changes order status to reported-as-finished. However, the system prevents changing order status when missing feedback or errors exist, as described below.

- All component quantities must be issued.
- Each operation must be reported as completed.
- Parent receipts must equal the good unit completions at the last operation.
- Parent receipts must be less than or equal to the quantity started.

---

[10] The bill of material journal cannot handle by-product components (displayed with a positive quantity); these should be deleted prior to posting.

The system provides warnings about these conditions. The user can override these warnings by using the accept errors flag on the report-as-finished task.

Auto-Deduction for Material Components An item's auto-deduction policy (termed the flushing principle) indicates whether a component should be manually issued, auto-deducted based on a start trigger, or auto-deducted based on a finish trigger. There are several differences between auto-deduction with the start versus finish trigger; these represent a forward-flushing versus backward-flushing approach.

❖ *Forward Flushing via Start Trigger.* The start order task automatically creates a picking list journal for forward-flushed material. This approach enables the user to review the journal prior to posting (to correct any mistakes). Alternatively, the start task can post the journal immediately without any review. The start task supports auto-deduction by specified operation, so that materials can be selectively auto-deducted during the production process.

❖ *Backward Flushing via Finish Trigger (Based on Parent Receipts).* The report-as-finished task records parent receipts, thereby acting as the trigger for backward flushing at the end of the production process. Backward flushing cannot be triggered when you report unit completions by operation. The report-as-finished task will automatically create and post a picking list journal for backward-flushed material, and you cannot review the journal prior to posting.

An item's flushing principle is assigned on the item master. It can optionally be overridden on a component in a master BOM, and subsequently overridden on the order-dependent bill.

Some situations may require an override of the components' auto-deduction policies so that you can correctly populate the lines within the picking list journal.

There are several methods to override the component auto-deduction policies:

❖ *Start Task.* The start order dialogue provides an option to override auto-deduction policies by indicating that all (or none) components should be auto-deducted.

❖ *Report-as-Finished Task.* The report-as-finished dialogue provides an option to override auto-deduction policies by indicating that all (or none) components should be auto-deducted.

❖ *Report-as-Finished Journal.* Using the automatic BOM consumption flag means that all components will be auto-deducted.

❖ *Route Card or Job Card Journal.* Using the automatic BOM consumption flag means that all components will be auto-deducted.

Auto-Deduction for Routing Operations Time expended at a work center (for process and setup time) can be manually reported or auto-deducted; likewise for unit completions. These represent three different aspects of a routing operation. A routing operation has three policies (embedded in the routing group) indicating whether each aspect must be manually reported or auto-deducted.

The auto-deduction policies for routing operations are slightly different than the ones for material, since they do not differentiate between forward- or backward-flushing. Hence, a fundamental decision is typically made about using either forward or backward flushing, so that auto-deduction does not result in doubled-up reporting.[11] The same triggers for auto-deducting material apply to auto-deduction for routing operations.

❖ *Start Trigger.* The start quantity and specified operation(s) determine how the system generates a route card journal, where journal lines identify the auto-deducted routing operation transactions. Policies embedded in the start order dialogue determine whether or not it is posted immediately. Reviewing the route card journal prior to posting allows the user to make corrections.

❖ *Finish Trigger.* The quantity of good plus scrapped items determines how many auto-deducted hours will be in the route card journal, and the journal is posted immediately without an option to be reviewed.

The system provides several methods to override the routing operation auto-deduction policies, some of which are described below.

---

[11] The decision about forward- versus backward-flushing is embedded in the *automatic route consumption* policy associated with the start order and report-as-finished tasks (and associated dialogues), where the policy is specified as never for one task. When using a backward-flushing approach, for example, the policy would be never for the start task and routing group dependent for the report-as-finished task. Conversely, the policy would be never for the report-as-finished task when using a forward-flushing approach.

❖ *Start Task.* The start order dialogue provides an option to override auto-deduction policies by indicating that all (or none) routing operations should be auto-deducted.

❖ *Report-as-Finished Task.* The report-as-finished dialogue provides an option to override auto-deduction policies by indicating that all (or none) routing operations should be auto-deducted.

Coordinating Production Activities

Planning calculations synchronize supplies to meet demands and provide several coordination tools. Chapter 6 explained planning calculations. The coordination tools consist of planned orders and suggested action messages, plus work center load analysis and production schedules when routing data has been defined.

Suggestions for Planned Production Orders Suggestions for planned production orders reflect the planning data for manufactured items described in Chapter 3. These suggestions can be viewed on the Planned Orders or the Planned Production Orders form.[12] The user can create production orders from selected planned orders via a function termed *firming planned orders*.

❖ *Selection of Planned Production Orders.* The form provides several methods to select planned orders. For example, orders can be individually marked or block-marked. Planned orders can also be viewed and optionally selected based on attributes such as the buyer, order date, and planned order status. You can assign a status to planned orders (unprocessed, processed, and approved) to indicate those that have been analyzed, but this status only represents reference information. The form does not retain marked orders if the user exits before firming.

❖ *Firming the Selected Planned Orders.* The firming function generates production orders for selected planned orders. The generated orders have an order status of scheduled, released, or started based on an item-related policy (embedded in the coverage group assigned to the item). The system automatically deletes the suggestion for a planned production

---

[12] The user can view information based on a selected set of master plan data or forecast plan data. For simplicity's sake the explanation focuses on the set of data representing the current master plan data.

order after execution of the firming function. It also creates a log for tracking which planned orders have been firmed and by whom.

The Planned Orders form provides one starting point for firming planned orders. An alternative approach starts from the Explosion form, oftentimes in the context of making sales order delivery promises (as described in Chapter 7).

❖ *Analyzing Planned Orders.* Planners often need to understand the rationale and impact for a planned order, and the Planned Orders form supports several analysis approaches.

○ *Related action messages.* The form displays action messages related to a planned order, such as expediting the planned order and delaying sales order delivery because of the projected completion date.

○ *Understanding the sources of demand and supply.* The form displays single-level pegging information about the source of demand for a planned order. Additional inquiries display single-level pegging to all supplies and demands for an item (via a *Net Requirements* inquiry), and the multi-level pegging information about supplies and demands for a planned order (via an *Explosion* inquiry).

○ *Calculate a projected completion date.* You can use the Explosion form to calculate a projected completion date (termed a futures date) for completing the planned production order quantity. As an option, you can also firm the planned orders for all components in the multi-level product structure.

○ *Understanding requirements for components.* The component requirements can be viewed along with action messages related to each component.

○ *Understanding requirements for routing operations.* The routing operations can be viewed along with the scheduled start/end dates for each operation.

❖ *Editing Planned Orders.* The analysis efforts often lead to needed action, and several actions can be implemented on the Planned Orders form.

○ Change quantity and/or delivery date for the planned production order.

○ Reschedule the planned production order using a specified scheduling method and scheduling direction, with optional consideration of finite material and capacity.

○ Split the planned production order using a specified quantity and date.

○ Group together several selected planned orders for the same item, with a total quantity for a single production order. The delivery date reflects the currently selected planned order.

○ Change the planned production order to a planned purchase order or transfer order to indicate an alternate source of supply.

Automatic Firming and a Frozen Period

The use of planned production orders is affected by two item-specific time fence policies regarding near-term schedule stability and automatic creation of production orders. These time fence policies are embedded in the coverage group assigned to an item.

❖ *Freeze Time Fence.* The freeze time fence provides one approach to support near-term schedule stability, since planning calculations will place planned orders at the end of the frozen period.

❖ *Firm Time Fence.* The firm time fence enables the system to automatically create production orders, thereby eliminating the effort to manually firm the planned orders. To be effective, the automatic firming time fence should be slightly greater than the item's production lead time and reorder cycle.

Action Messages   Planning calculations generate two types of action messages termed actions and futures, as previously explained in Chapter 2 and illustrated in Figure 2.4. These messages are summarized below.

❖ *Actions Message.* An actions message indicates a suggestion to advance/postpone an order's delivery date, to increase/decrease an order quantity, or to delete an order. Suggested advancement of an existing order reflects the item's rescheduling assumption, so that the system suggests expediting rather than a new planned order to cover a requirement.

❖ *Futures Message.* A futures message indicates that the projected completion date for supply chain activities (based on realistic scheduling assumptions) will cause a delay in meeting a requirement date such as a sales order shipment.

Dynamics AX displays actions and futures messages on two different forms termed the *Actions* form and *Futures* form. Users cannot take action on these inquiry forms, but can readily access the relevant master table for the referenced order to indicate their action.

Capacity Planning and Load Analysis Capacity load analysis is based on the production order routing data and available capacity. The user can optionally include or exclude loads stemming from planned production orders and projects (based on company-wide policies embedded in the production parameters). The nature of load analysis depends on three major factors: the scheduling method, the consideration of capacity limits, and the set of master plan data.

❖ *Scheduling Method and Load Analysis*. Rough-cut scheduling only supports load analysis for work center groups, whereas detailed scheduling supports load analysis of individual work centers as well as work center groups. Scheduling for all planned production orders is based on one scheduling method and capacity viewpoint, as defined in the master plan policies for the current set of master plan data. In contrast, scheduling for an individual production order can be based on a specified scheduling method and a finite capacity constraint.

❖ *Capacity Limits and Load Analysis*. Available capacity can be viewed as infinite or finite. An infinite capacity viewpoint means that scheduling of each operation's duration considers the available working hours at a work center, but an unlimited number of orders can be scheduled concurrently. This means load analysis can identify overloaded periods.

A finite capacity viewpoint means that only one order can be scheduled concurrently during working hours, and that scheduling logic considers existing loads. Scheduling logic only considers a finite capacity limit for work centers designated as having finite capacity.

❖ *Master Plan Data and Load Analysis*. Load analysis data can be viewed for a specified set of master plan data or forecast plan data. The current dynamic master plan acts as a default.

With these three factors in mind, load analysis can be viewed for a work center (or group) using a tabular or graphic format.

❖ *Tabular Format for Load Analysis*. The Capacity Load Inquiry provides a tabular format for load analysis of one work center or group. It displays total load hours in daily increments and automatically highlights overloaded days. The user can view detailed reference information about routing operations comprising a daily load. A separate form (termed Capacity Reservations) provides a tabular format about all routing operations for the work center.

❖ *Graphical Format for Load Analysis.* The Capacity Load Graphical Inquiry provides a setup dialogue that determines how to display load analysis information. For example, load information can be displayed in hours or percentages, and in specified increments (such as daily, weekly, or monthly) for a specified range of dates. These time increments represent the continuum of aggregate to detailed load analysis, and the percentage viewpoint can highlight overloaded periods.

Additional variations include displaying loads for a range of work centers, either as multiple graphics or as a single graphic with an accumulated load. Selected sources of loads can be excluded, such as loads stemming from planned production orders. The user cannot access detailed reference information about production order operations comprising a load.

The load analysis for a capacity-constrained work center can also identify over-loaded periods, since it is possible to schedule a production order without considering its finite capacity limits.

Production Schedules   The production order routing data provides the basis for creating production schedules by work center. The nature of a production schedule depends on the three major factors mentioned above: the scheduling method, the consideration of capacity limits, and the set of master plan data.

A production schedule identifies each production order's routing operations performed in the work center. It consists of the same detailed reference information as the load analysis drill-down, but is presented in a format more appropriate for communicating the needed action. In particular, it needs to provide visibility of production orders at various order statuses so that production personnel can finish those already started as well as anticipate those that need to be started.

Production schedules can be displayed in different formats, such as tabular or Gantt chart. Each firm tends to customize their production schedule to fit their operations, but a typical tabular format can be described. A production schedule in tabular format identifies work center operations in a priority sequence with the hottest operations listed first. The simplest sequencing rule is based on operation start (or ending) date and time.

Operation information includes the remaining units and time and the units completed. It may include other information that proves useful to the planner or production personnel, such as the prior and next operation, the expected operation scrap percentage, and the operation description. Much of the information may be identified on a production order traveler, thereby minimizing the need for including it in the production schedule. The Operations List Inquiry provides one example of a production schedule.

Coordination of Subcontracted Manufacturing Activities   Purchase orders provide coordination of subcontracted manufacturing activities. The Subcontractor Work form displays scheduled production orders with a linked purchase order that represents the subcontracted operation. The form displays information about purchase order status, and enables the user to update production order status via the start task and report-as-finished task.

When routing operations are defined for subcontracted work, the production schedule by work center and the Operations List can be used for coordination purposes. The Operations List displays production orders so that you can filter on the master operations associated with subcontracting, and optionally update production order status via the start and report-as-finished tasks. The capacity load analysis for an external work center reflects time specified in the routing operations.

There are four basic variations of coordinating supplied material: as a kit that is picked or transferred, or as stocked material at the subcontractor that is purchased or transferred. These variations were previously described in Chapter 3

Production Order Costing

A production order's estimated costs are initially calculated by performing the *estimate order task*, as described in this chapter's previous section on the production order life cycle. The nature of these cost calculations was previously described in Chapter 5; the calculated costs reflect the production order quantity and the production BOM/route rather than a master BOM/routing. The estimate order task may be used to recalculate estimated costs after changes, such as changes to components, to operations, or to active cost records for items, labor rates, or overhead formulas.

A production order's actual costs are automatically calculated based on reported activities, such as actual material usage and operation times. You can view detailed transactions about reported activities on the Production Posting inquiry for a production order. Several reports summarize reported activities for all current production orders, including the raw materials in process report, the work in process report (for routing transactions), and the indirect costs in process report (for overheads incurred).

You can analyze a production order's estimated and actual costs using the price calculation inquiry for the order, or using the Cost Estimates and Costing report. Cost information is shown for each component, operation, and applicable overhead formula.

Production variances are calculated after ending a production order for a standard cost item. The variances reflect a comparison between the reported production activities and the standard cost calculation for the manufactured item. The variances do not provide a comparison to the production order's estimated costs. Four types of variances are calculated: lot size variance, production quantity variance, production price variance, and production substitution variance. Figure 11.5 identifies these four variances that account for the difference between the production order's actual costs and the item's standard cost calculation.

You can analyze a production order's variances using the Production Variances inquiry or report. You can use the report options to view detailed variances by item/work center or by cost group, or to view summarized variances. The cost breakdown policy within the inventory parameters determines whether variances will be tracked by cost group. The Standard Cost

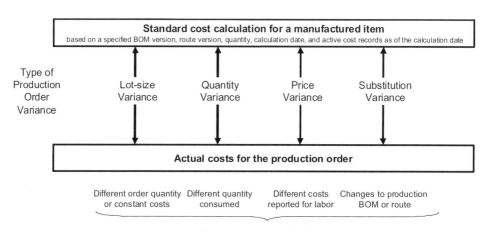

Figure 11.5 Types of Production Order Variances

Transactions inquiry provides another approach to analyzing production order variances. For example, you can identify the production variances associated with every production order for an item. In order to anticipate variances prior to ending a production order, analyze the detailed information provided on the Cost Estimates and Costing report.

Use the Variance Analysis Statement report to view production variances (and purchase price variances) during a specified time period, such as the current period or current year. Use the report options to view variances by item, production order, or cost group, with a summary or detailed breakdown of variances.

Case Studies

Case 65: Plant and Fleet Maintenance The All-and-Anything company had numerous machines and trucks involved in their manufacturing/ distribution business that needed scheduled and as-required maintenance. The manufacturer of each machine and truck provided suggested maintenance schedules and replacement parts. A separate group of maintenance personnel were responsible for purchasing and inventorying these replacement parts, and performing maintenance on the machines (in the production area) and on the trucks (in separate bays and in the field). Scheduled maintenance reflected the manufacturer's suggested schedules, which was typically based on utilization metrics (such as machine hours or truck miles) for actual and projected usage. The company wanted an integrated ERP system that could also support the maintenance tasks and the related time-and-attendance and payroll of maintenance employees.[13]

Case 66: Orderless Production The Consumer Products company produced and shipped several items within hours of receiving actual sales orders. Coordination of final assembly was based on non-replenishing Kanbans represented by each sales order, where the shipment transaction auto-deducted component materials. Some stocked components were manufactured to stock, based on replenishing Kanbans represented by empty containers. Reported completions (on the BOM Journal) triggered material auto-deduction.

---

[13] Several independent software vendors have developed Dynamics AX add-on modules that support plant and fleet maintenance. For example, see **www.annata.is** about their IDMS module, or **www.isoft-tech.co.za** about their AxMRO module.

Case 67: Customer-Supplied Material The Equipment company occasionally used customer-supplied material in production processes. They required identification of component requirements in the bill, visibility of scheduled receipts, a receiving process, and material tracking for customer-supplied material. The item number for each customer-supplied component represented a unique item and was valued at zero cost.

Case 68: Advanced Planning and Scheduling (APS) Integration The Fabricated Products company required APS capabilities to minimize setups and avoid additional equipment purchases for its line of extruded plastic products. Multiple extrusion machines produced plastic pipes of varying diameters and colors. Scheduling considerations included sequence-dependent setup time (based on pipe diameter and color), and machine capabilities for handling different products. Scheduling considerations also included machine-specific run rates, and secondary resources for tooling and skilled operators. To integrate an APS application, additional attributes were required for work centers (e.g., machine capabilities), routing operations (e.g., setup attributes), and calendars (e.g. available crew size by shift).[14]

Executive Summary

Production represents the distinctive competency of most manufacturers. A separate functional area known as production activity control is typically responsible for coordinating production activities. A production order represents the set of production activities to build a single item, and the item defines the source of information (such as the bill and routing) for what needs to be done. A production order can be linked to the source of sales order demand. Several considerations apply to production orders, such as the order status within the order life cycle, the order-dependent bill and routing, and the production order lead time. Production activities can be reported against started orders, such as picking material, reporting operation time, and receiving parent items. Coordination of production activities is based on suggestions for planned orders, action messages, and production schedules by work center. The case studies highlighted variations in manufacturing environments, such as customer-supplied parts and integration with advanced planning and scheduling (APS) capabilities.

---

[14] See **www.Preactor.com** for additional information about their Advanced Scheduler module.

Chapter 12

Project-Oriented Operations

Some manufacturing and distribution firms have project-oriented operations. These may be internally focused projects such as new product development or externally focused projects related to customers who may be billed on a fixed price or a time-and-material basis. In either case, a project typically requires a mixture of material, time (associated with human resources or machines), and expenses. The availability of material and time must be managed. These requirements also provide the basis for budgeting project costs and tracking actual costs, as well as the basis for invoicing for external projects. However, this chapter focuses on the supply chain aspects of project-oriented operations.

Three scenarios will be used to illustrate project-oriented environments. One scenario involves an internal project for new product development, while a second scenario involves an external project with multiple deliverables. A third scenario involves a project quotation for an external project. The definition of a project and its forecasted requirements provide the starting point for further explanation, as reflected in the following sections for this chapter.

1. Definition of a project
2. Forecasted requirements for a project
3. Reporting actual costs against a project
4. Considerations about using projects
5. Project quotations for external projects

Definition of a Project

A project is uniquely identified by a project number. Several key fields define the nature and characteristics of a project, including the project type and project stage. A project also entails the use of project categories and the optional use of a Work Breakdown Structure (WBS).

Project Type   A project is either external or internal. External projects require an associated project contact (for invoicing purposes) and customer. An external project may be created by a project quotation, and may involve project-specific sales orders for shipping items to the customer. In contrast, an internal project cannot be associated with a customer, produce customer invoices, be created by a project quotation, or have project-specific sales orders.

There are two variations of external projects.

❖ *Time and Material.* A time-and-material project is invoiced to the customer based upon the Work In Progress (WIP). The invoice recognizes both revenue and costs. The invoice amount can be calculated based upon the sales price for material and billable hours entered against the project, or a mark-up percentage applied to the costs. Invoices are generated via the invoice proposal process.

❖ *Fixed Price.* A fixed-price project is invoiced to the customer according to the commercial contract. Revenue is recognized on the project based on an assessment principle of either completed contract or a completed percentage. Revenue recognition is handled via an estimation process.

There are four variations of internal projects.

❖ *Investment.* An investment project helps budget and track costs against a unique activity that will be available to capitalize, such as the production of a fixed asset.

❖ *Internal.* An internal project helps budget and track costs against a unique activity that will not be available to capitalize, such as an engineering project.

❖ *Cost Project.* A cost project is the same as an internal project.

❖ *Time Project.* A time project supports time reporting about miscellaneous activities that do not impact the General Ledger. For example, it may be used to track vacation or illness, or for time reporting via the Shop Floor Control capabilities within Dynamics AX.

A project group must be assigned to every project. The project group defines the project type and controls posting to ledger accounts Most firms require more than one project group to support different project types or posting to different general ledger accounts.

A summary project represents another type of project, and is used to collect information about several projects for budgeting and reporting purposes.

Project Stage   The life cycle of a project consists of multiple stages, such as the three stages of created, in-process, and finished. You can optionally define up to eight stages along with user-defined stage names, but further explanation focuses on these three stages.[1] A basic rule is that the system enforces a linear progression through the project stages, and the user must indicate progression to the next stage. Several rules apply to each stage, as illustrated in Figure 12.1 and described below.

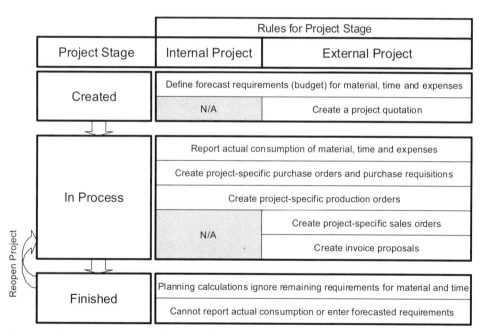

Figure 12.1 Summary of Project Stages

---

[1] The explanation focuses on the minimal number of stages for supply chain management purposes. Some firms may want additional stages for project management purposes. The additional stages can be selected from five predefined stages and three user-definable stages, and these stages can be renamed. The applicable stages must be defined for each project type (e.g., time and material projects) as part of the parameters form for projects.

❖ *Created.* The created stage is automatically assigned when you initially create a project. You can define forecasted requirements for material, time, and expenses at this stage, and optionally create a project quotation for an external project. Project transactions cannot be entered against the project. Planning calculations recognize forecasted material requirements, but do not recognize forecasted time requirements until they have been scheduled.[2]

❖ *In Process.* Project transactions can be charged to an in-process project. You can create project-specific production orders and purchase orders, and optionally create purchase requisitions and requests for quotes (RFQs) in support of these purchase orders. You can create project-specific sales orders for external projects, and also create invoice proposals.

❖ *Finished.* Project transactions cannot be charged against the project, and planning calculations ignore remaining requirements for forecasted material and time. A finished project can be reopened for further transactions by changing the project stage back to in process.

Subprojects for a Project Some projects require segmentation for costing or scheduling purposes, or to reflect project ownership within an organizational hierarchy. Subprojects provide one approach to segmentation. Each project can be a parent to one or more child projects, thereby supporting a multilevel parent-child hierarchy. A child project is termed a subproject. When forecasted capacity requirements are defined, scheduling logic assumes the child projects must be completed before the parent project. Aggregate costs—both budgeted and actual—can be viewed for a project and all of its subprojects.

The project number for each child project reflects the parent project number and a suffix, such as a parent project of "100" and a child project of "100-01". The naming convention for the suffix reflects a user-defined mask (such as "- ##") specified for the parent project.

Project Categories for Project-Related Transactions Project-related transactions such as forecasts and consumption of material/time must identify a project and a project category. A project category provides segmentation for reporting purposes including the integration with the General Ledger, and helps enforce several project accounting policies such as controlling the categories available to one project versus another. One or

---

[2] You perform a separate scheduling task for a project so that planning calculations recognize the forecasted time requirements associated with work centers such as machines or human resources.

more user-defined project categories must be defined for each type of project transaction (material, time, and expense). General guidelines for project categories include the following:

❖ *Project Categories for Material (Items).* The project categories typically reflect the nature of material, and often parallel the item groups assigned to items.

❖ *Project Categories for Time (Hours).* The project categories typically reflect the nature of project activities, such as two categories of design and testing for a new product development project. You can also define an hourly cost and sales price for each project category that will be used in budgeting and actual time reporting. Hence, different project categories may be defined to reflect differences in hourly costs and prices.

The project categories for time often parallel work center groups when projects involve production resources. Project categories related to production (also termed cost categories) were described in Chapter 5 for defining a work center's hourly rates, and for calculating a manufactured item's cost based on routing information.

❖ *Project Categories for Expenses.* The project categories typically reflect the nature of expenses, such as hire of equipment, airfare, lodging, and photocopying.

Several additional considerations apply to each project category. These considerations include the concept of a default line property and a category group, as described below.

❖ *Default Line Property.* The line property determines whether a transaction will be chargeable to the project, and whether the cost or sales price should be used as the basis for charging the project. It also determines whether the charged costs will be available for capitalization. The default line property assigned to a project category can be overridden at the transaction level.

❖ *Category Group.* The category group assigned to each project category provides the basis for aggregate reporting, and also the basis for default values when creating a project category. The default values can be overridden.

❖ *Requirement for Employee ID.* This policy determines whether an employee ID must be entered when reporting transactions for the project category, such as reporting actual time or expenses.

Work Breakdown Structure (WBS) for a Project   Each project can optionally have a WBS defined by activities within an activity tree. Forecasted requirements can then be defined by project, project category, and activity. In addition, a project's forecasted hours can be scheduled based on the sequence of activities. The activity tree assists integration with the work breakdown structure within Microsoft Office Project Server 2007 and Microsoft Project Pro.

Forecasted Requirements for a Project

A project's forecasted requirements for material and capacity provide the basis for a budgeted cost, and enable planning calculations to coordinate supply chain activities. Other types of forecasted requirements (such as expenses) are used for budgeting purposes but do not require supply chain coordination. Each forecasted requirement is assigned a forecast identifier; this approach allows different sets of requirements for simulation purposes.

Forecasted Material Requirements   The project's forecasted material requirements (termed *item budgets*) act just like a sales forecast, as described in Chapter 6. The forecasted requirement identifies an item, quantity, date, site/warehouse, a project category, and a forecast identifier. The forecast may specify an activity when the project has defined activities. The forecasted date is important, because planning calculations ignore past-due forecasts for material items.

The nature of the project determines which material items should be forecasted. With a project for an engineering prototype, for example, you could forecast the end-item (with components defined in its bill of material) or you could forecast the individual components. The bill of material information offers several advantages, such as time-phasing for component requirements and BOM calculations of the projected costs.

The concept of sales forecast consumption applies to forecasted material requirements for an external project, as described in Chapter 6. That is, a project-specific sales order consumes the project's forecasted requirement for an item. Sales orders that are not project-specific do not consume the project's forecasted requirements. A subsequent section provides further explanation of project-specific sales orders for reporting shipments related to external projects.

Forecasted Time Requirements   The project's forecasted requirements for time (termed *hour forecasts*) act similar to routing operations, as described in Chapter 3. Each forecasted requirement identifies the number of processing hours, the preferred work center/group, the project category, and a forecast identifier. The forecast may specify an activity when the project has defined activities. You can also assign a task group to the forecasted hours to support alternative work center logic.

After defining a project's time requirements, you must perform a scheduling task so that time requirements will be recognized by planning calculations. When performing the scheduling task, you specify the desired forecast identifier, the scheduling direction (forward or backward) and date, and the scheduling method (job or operation scheduling). You can also specify a sorting basis of project activities, so that scheduling logic reflects the sequence (and the linkage between activities) in calculating work center loads. You can optionally specify the use of finite capacity, and the scheduling and synchronization of reference orders.

The scheduling task assigns time requirements to work centers, and changes the dates for forecasted hours. For example, the scheduling task can assign time requirements to individual employees that represent work centers within a work center group. Planning calculations ignore past-due forecasts for capacity.

Forecasted Expense Requirements   The project's forecasted expenses represent an estimate of direct charges, segmented by project categories for direct charges. The system also supports several approaches to allocating direct costs, such as allocating a percentage over several categories or several time periods.

Budgeted Cost Based on Forecasted Requirements   The budgeted cost for a project reflects forecasted requirements for material, time, and expenses associated with a specified forecast identifier. The system automatically calculates a budgeted cost (and revenue) based on the cost (and sales price) specified for each forecasted requirement, and the user can optionally designate that a forecasted requirement should be excluded from budgeted costs. If forecast identifiers have been used to define multiple sets of forecasted requirements, then the system can calculated multiple budgeted costs. The project's statistics provide a summary of budgeted costs (and revenue) for a specified set of forecast requirements and date range.

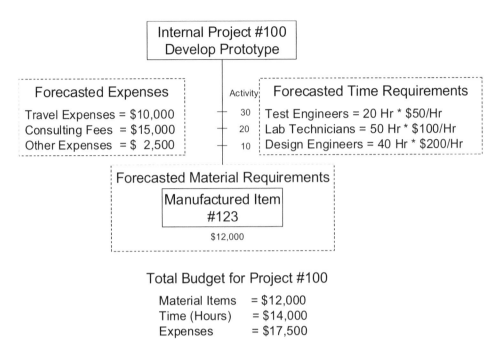

Figure 12.2 Forecasted Requirements for a Project

Scenario 1: Forecasted Requirements for a New Product Development Project

New product development often entails producing a prototype of the manufactured item, and additional costs associated with engineering time and related expenses. Figure 12.2 illustrates an internal project for developing a prototype. The project's forecasted material requirements consist of just one manufactured item, which has bill and routing information used in BOM calculations to estimate its cost. The project's forecasted time requirements include engineering time by three major groups of engineers: design engineers, lab technicians, and test engineers. Each work center group represents a pool of engineers with the same skill type, and consists of work centers that identify the relevant engineering employees. These time requirements are not included in the routing to produce the manufactured item. The project has forecasted expenses (such as travel and consulting fees) that will be incurred during prototype development.

Several project categories are also illustrated in Figure 12.2. For example, the expenses were segmented into three categories (travel, consulting fees, and other), the hours were segmented into three categories (design, lab, and test), and material only involved one project category (manufactured items). These project categories help segment budgeted and actual costs for analysis and reporting purposes. Figure 12.2 also illustrated the use of activities for the forecasted time requirements, where the activities were labeled 10, 20, and 30.

Scenario 2: External Project with Subprojects Subprojects often reflect segmentation of a project for costing or scheduling purposes. Figure 12.3 illustrates an external project for a firm that sells and installs plumbing and electrical parts for commercial construction sites. The two subprojects reflect the two major installation phases for electrical and plumbing parts, with forecasted requirements for material and time. The two work center groups represent the two pools of electricians and plumbers. The parent project defines forecasted capacity requirements for designing the installation, and forecasted costs for travel and photocopying. The same example was used in Chapter 6 to illustrate S&OP game plans for a project.

The number and structure of subprojects oftentimes reflect the organizational structure. Using Figure 12.3 as an example, there would be separate managers for plumbers and electricians, so that the subproject structure reflects their responsibility and reporting requirements. Information can also be accumulated for the general manager responsible for the entire project.

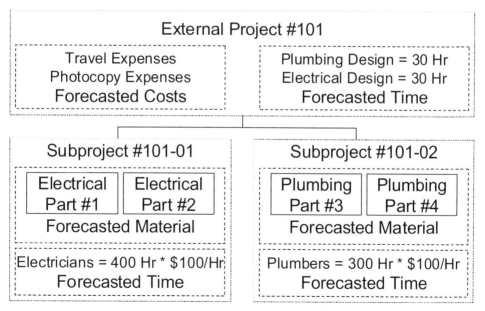

Figure 12.3 Subprojects for an External Project

Reporting Actual Costs Against a Project

Actual costs can be reported using several types of project-related transactions. The transactions can only be reported against an in-process project, and certain transactions can only be reported for external projects, as previously summarized in Figure 12.1.

Actual costs can be entered against a project using journals for the three basic project transactions: items, hours, and expenses. Actual costs can also be charged based on posted invoices for project-specific purchase orders.

Project Items Journal   This journal records the material issued to a project from Inventory. Each journal line indicates the quantity and stocking location of the item, and the associated project and project category. Each journal line represents an unplanned issue to a project, since it does not consume forecasted material requirements.

Project Hours Journal   This journal records the hours expended on a project. Each journal line indicates the hours and the associated project and project category (and project activity if applicable), and the relevant employee. The user can enter transaction text. You can use the Project Hours Journal form or a web journal for reporting time sheet entries. Web journals are typically used for employees who are remote or seldom use the system. Information entered on a web journal must be transferred to a project hours journal.

Project Expense Journal   This journal records costs charged to a project. Each journal line indicates the nature of the costs—such as a ledger entry or A/P invoice—using the field termed the offset account type. For example, a journal line for a ledger entry indicates the G/L account. Additional line item information includes the cost and currency, the associated project and project category (such as travel expense), the relevant employee (if applicable), and transaction text.

Project-Specific Purchase Orders and Posted Invoices   A project-specific purchase order can only be created from a project, and the posted invoice automatically updates actual costs for the project. The actual costs the quantity and price of the invoiced item, and the received material atically issued to the project. A project-specific purchase order has ct number in the purchased order header, and a project category o each line item.

Project-Specific Production Order   A project-specific production order can only be created from a project. The manufactured item must have an actual costing method so that actual costs for the ended production order will be recognized by the project.

Project-Specific Sales Orders for Recording Shipments to a Customer   A project-specific sales order is typically used to ship items to the customer site. It can only be created from an external project, using a manual creation approach. Alternatively, a project-specific sales order can be automatically created (to the customer on the project contract) for a project's forecasted material. It acts like a sales order in all respects except one: the invoice must be handled through the project invoice proposal.

The project number is identified in the sales order header, and each line item identifies the project category. As noted earlier, a project-specific sales order can consume the project's forecasted material requirements to avoid doubled-up requirements.

Considerations about Using Projects

Several considerations apply to project-oriented operations, such as changing project type, planning calculations, and the use of project MRP and project costing.

Changing a Project Type from Internal to External   A project sometimes starts as an internal project and then changes to an external project, or vice versa. Use the Change Project Group function to change the project type for the project.

Copying Forecasted Requirements to Another Set of Forecast Data   A separate set of forecast data may be required to model different requirements for a project. As a shortcut to entering the new data, one set of forecast data can be copied to another set (and then modified).

Using a Template to Create a New Project   A given project can be designated as a template, and then used by the Project Wizard when creating a new project. The wizard walks the user through several steps, such as specifying the new project number, the project contract, the start/end dates, and what information should be inherited from the template. Forecasted requirements (if any) are not copied to the new project.

Planning Calculations and the Forecasted Requirements for Projects Planning calculations can optionally exclude forecasted capacity requirements related to projects (as defined in the master planning parameters). The planning calculations also require information about whether forecast data should be used as demands, and which set of forecast data should be used (as defined in the policies for a forecast plan and a master plan). Planning calculations ignore forecasted requirements with past-due dates.

Project-Related Purchase Requisitions A project-related purchase requisition and workflow are almost exactly the same as a general-purpose requisition, as previously described in the Chapter 8 section on purchase requisitions. The same basic steps and setup information apply to both types of requisitions. The three major differences (described below) reflect the unique functionality for projects.

❖ *Workflow Template and Workflow Configurations.* A separate workflow template provides the starting point for defining workflow configurations about project-related purchase requisitions. Each workflow configuration must specify (within the conditions for use) whether it applies to a project-related or general-purpose requisition (when you employ both types of requisitions).

❖ *Create Requisition.* A project-related requisition must be created from the Projects form, thereby inheriting the appropriate project identifier. After creation, each requisition line item must be assigned a project category.

❖ *Create Purchase Order.* A project-related purchase order will be created rather than a normal purchase order.

Project-Related Requests for Quote (RFQ) A request for quote (RFQ) provides a structured approach for soliciting and using purchase quotations, as described in the Chapter 8 section covering RFQs. A project-related RFQ must be initiated from a project, and it involves the same basic steps. The basic steps include creating an RFQ, sending the vendor-specific RFQ to obtain reply information, receiving a reply for a vendor-specific cepting or rejecting a reply, and automatic generation of a project-urchase order for an accepted reply. In addition, you can update rade agreements with information that reflects a vendor reply.

Project MRP and Project Costing   Some manufacturing environments require project MRP and project costing capabilities. Generating a production order from a project-specific sales order provides the first step for project MRP since it establishes direct linkage between a production order and the project. The system automatically generates linked production orders for make-to-order components and linked purchase orders for buy-to-order components. These linked orders provide visibility of project-specific requirements, and project costing throughout the product structure.

A material item that can be shared between projects should be identified as a normal component, and with a period reordering policy. This approach enables planning calculations to generate one supply order for shared material to cover multiple project-specific demands. You can use the marking capabilities for the supply order (to link receipt transactions to issue transactions) thereby tracking actual costs for the shared material and supporting project cost considerations.

Project Quotations for External Projects

A project quotation often represents an initial step for defining an external project. It consists of line items defining the project requirements for material, labor, and expenses. It can be converted into a new project, linked to an existing project, or identified as lost or cancelled. When converting it to a project, the user can optionally create a project-specific sales order and sales forecasts for the line items. The structure and life cycle of a project quotation provide a foundation for covering variations in using project quotations.

Structure and Life Cycle of a Project Quotation   The basic structure consists of a header and line item information. The header identifies the sold-to business account contact and related customer (if applicable), the win probability, and the set of forecast data (termed the *forecast model*) for line item requirements. Several aspects of the header information act as defaults for the line items, such as the ship date. The line items can identify different types of forecasted requirements—for material items, hours, expenses, and fees—that will be involved in the project. For material items, the line item minimally specifies an item, quantity, ship date, and the ship-from site/warehouse.

The life cycle of a sales quotation consists of three basic steps (create, send, and disposition), with three possible dispositions (confirmed, lost, or cancelled), that are represented by five statuses.

❖ *Created.* The quotation has been created. It can be sent or confirmed to the business relation, but it cannot be updated to a disposition such as confirmed, lost, or cancelled.
❖ *Sent.* The quotation has been sent to the business account (via the Quotation update). The specified business relation cannot be changed. The quotation can be updated to a disposition of confirmed, lost, or cancelled.
❖ *Confirmed.* The quotation has been confirmed (via the Confirmation update). It can now be converted/linked to a project. After it has been converted/linked, the system identifies the link between the quotation and sales order.
❖ *Lost.* The quotation has been identified as lost (via the Quotation Lost update).
❖ *Cancelled.* The quotation has been identified as cancelled (via the Quotation Cancelled update).

The system allows changes to created or sent quotations, and creation of a customer from the specified business relation (via the *Convert to Customer* function). When updating the disposition of a quotation, the user can optionally record a win/loss reason code. Changes cannot be made to a quotation after it has been updated with a disposition.

Variations in processing project quotations reflect different ways of doing business and different internal procedures. The similarities with sales quotations will be covered first, followed by considerations for using project quotations.

Similarities and Differences with a Sales Quotation A project quotation shares many similarities to a sales quotation, as described below.

- A quotation can be created for a business relation that does not have to be a customer, and the business relation can be converted into a customer.
- You can specify material items in a quotation line item, and the sales trade agreement information applies to these items.
- You can calculate discounts and supplementary items.

- You can define a custom product configuration, using either option selection for a configurable item or the configurator for a modeling-enabled item.
- You can perform an order-specific BOM calculation and transfer the calculated sales price to the quotation.
- You can optionally employ delivery date control capabilities to the requested ship and delivery dates.
- A promised delivery date cannot be calculated (via the Explosion inquiry).

A project quotation is different than a sales quotation in several ways, as described below.

- A project quotation can specify line items for hours, expenses, and fees.
- The price simulation capabilities only apply to sales quotations.
- Sales quotations can be converted to sales orders; project quotations can be converted to projects. The process of converting to a project also provides an option to create project-specific sales orders and sales forecasts from the project quotation.

Scenario 3: Using a Project Quotation   A company generates project quotations for prospects and customers (business relations) that define the requirements for engineering time and a manufactured item. As illustrated in Figure 12.4, the quotation line items specify engineering hours and a manufactured item, along with the quantity and win probability. The manufactured item represents a custom product, where product structure information can be defined beforehand. The company sends a quotation, and confirms a winning quote (or indicates a lost or cancelled quote) along with a win/loss reason code for subsequent sales analysis purposes. A winning quote is then converted to a project, and a prospect must be converted to a customer beforehand. The system creates a project associated with the quote, and the user can optionally create the project's forecasted requirements (from the quotation line items) and a sales order. The sales order provides a mechanism for shipping the completed items to the customer, while invoicing is handled through the project capabilities. The work center for engineering hours must be specified once the quote becomes a project.

Since project quotations provide visibility of anticipated demand, planning calculations consider them as demand when the win probability

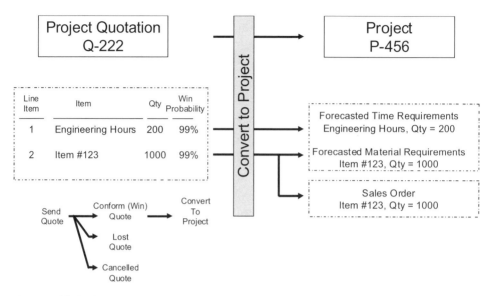

Figure 12.4 Using a Project Quotation

exceeds a specified percentage (such as 75%). Each project's forecasted requirements (and sales orders) are also considered as demand by planning calculations.

Converting a Business Relation into a Customer A customer can be created from the business relation specified on a quotation (via the *Convert to Customer* function). After creating the customer, the system displays the customer master form so that additional information can be entered.

Converting a Project Quotation into a Project A project quotation can be converted into a new project or linked to an existing project sales order (via the *Link/Transfer to Project* update), and all quotation line items are converted into line items on the project. The system prevents conversion unless the business relation reflects a customer. The system identifies the link between the quotation and sales order.

As part of the process, the user can optionally create a sales order for the quotation line item and/or a sales forecast. Figure 12.3 illustrates the creation of a sales order from the project quotation.

Planning Calculations and the Project Quotation Win Probability
Planning calculations can optionally include demands for items stemming

from a project quotation line item when it has a win probability greater than a specified percentage. However, the demands for hours are not recognized by planning calculations, since they are not yet assigned a work center.

Versions of a Project Quotation   A project quotation may be changed and then resent to the business relation in order to communicate the changes. The system automatically tracks each time a quotation is sent, and assigns a numeric suffix to the quotation identifier (such as -1 and -2) for each version. These historical versions can be viewed on the quotation inquiry and the Quotation Journal Inquiry. The system uses the latest version as the basis for confirming a quotation.

Relationship Between Multiple Project Quotations   Multiple project quotations may be required in certain situations, such as quotes for different quantity breakpoints. Other examples would be quotes for multiple phases or for different groups of items such as basic versus optional. The user establishes the relationship by starting with a parent quotation, and then assigning the child quotation(s) using the *Alternative Quotations* function. The same function displays alternative quotations that have already been defined.

Project Quotation Follow-Up Date and Expiration Date   Each project quotation has a follow-up date and an expiration date. The dates provide reference information and the basis for selectively viewing sales quotations.

Mass Creation of Project Quotations Using a Template   Certain situations may require the mass creation of project quotations, such as providing the same quote to several different contacts or customers. An initial quote must be created and then designated as an active template (with a user-defined template name).[3] The periodic task for *Mass Create Quotations* can then be used with the specified template and a user-defined selection of business relations. The system creates a project quotation for each business relation.

Deleting Project Quotations   Quotations are not automatically deleted by the system since win/loss analysis requires historical data. Periodic deletion of quotations should reflect the desired data retention policies. Use the Delete Quotations task to select quotations to be deleted based on criteria such as the status, creation date, and/or expiration date.

---

[3] The planning calculations always ignore demands related to template quotations.

Case Studies

Case 69: New Product Development Project The All-and-Anything company wanted to budget and track all costs associated with each new product development. An internal project was defined for a new product, with budgeted costs based on forecasted requirements for material, time, and expenses. Project categories for material, time, and expenses provided segmentation of the budgeted and actual costs. The activities associated with forecasted time requirements provided the basis for finite scheduling of critical resources. Project-specific purchase orders provided visibility of all purchased items. Detailed reporting of actual material, time, and expenses provided the basis for comparing actual costs to budget.

Case 70: Projects for Professional Services A division of the Consumer Products company provided several types of project-oriented professional services, such as services on installed equipment and engineering design services. Their requirements included seamless integration with Microsoft Project, approval procedures for purchase requisitions, web access for customers to report support issues, and time and expense reporting with web-based applications.[4]

Case 71: ETO Industrial Equipment The Equipment company manufactured engineer-to-order (ETO) custom products, and wanted to manage the engineering design time as well as the production of each large piece of equipment. Every custom product consisted of several basic subassemblies (such as a base, a tower, and a table) that were unique to each order, and engineering time was required to design the product structure of each subassembly. For each custom product, the company used a rules-based product configurator to automatically generate new items for the end-item and subassemblies, and assign routing data (based on templates) for production time as well as engineering time. This information enabled the firm to calculate an availability date (several months into the future) based on existing factory loads and current engineering commitments. The bill of material data was then entered as the engineers designed the subassemblies and end-item. Most components reflected existing item numbers, but the

---

[4] Several independent software vendors have developed Dynamics AX add-on modules that support professional service operations. For example, see **www.csginc.com** about their Professional Service Automation module, or see **www.DynamicsSoftware.com** about their Service Management module.

custom design often required new items to be designed and entered into the item master. The long lead time components were entered first to coordinate critical-path supply chain activities.

Executive Summary

Some manufacturing and distribution firms have project-oriented operations. These may be internally focused projects such as new product development or externally focused projects related to customers. The resource requirements for a project typically include material, time (associated with human resources or machines) and expenses. The forecasted resource requirements provide the basis for calculating a project budget, and for coordination of supply chain activities to complete the project on time and within budget. You can define multiple versions of the forecasted requirements (using different forecast identifiers), thereby supporting multiple project budgets. Each project budget has a calculated cost and sales price, which reflect the cost and sales price of each forecasted requirement.

A project is either external or internal. External projects require an associated project contract (for invoicing purposes) and customer. An external project may be created by a project quotation, and may involve project-specific sales orders for shipping items to the customer. In contrast, an internal project cannot be associated with a customer or be created by a project quotation. It cannot be used to produce invoices or have project-specific sales orders. Each project has a life cycle consisting of multiple user-defined stages, such as the three stages of created, in-process and finished. The rules for each stage determine what actions can be taken.

Some projects require segmentation for costing or scheduling purposes, or to reflect project ownership within an organizational hierarchy. Subprojects (aka child project) provide one approach to segmentation, and scheduling logic assumes the child projects must be completed before the parent project. Aggregate costs—both budgeted and actual—can be viewed for a project and all of its subprojects. Activities (aka work breakdown structure) provide another approach to segmentation. The activities can be assigned to a project, along with time requirements by activity. Scheduling logic accounts for the sequence of activities. Planning calculations can optionally exclude these capacity requirements.

A project's material requirements often involve project-specific production orders to produce an item, or project-specific purchase orders to obtain the material, so that costs flow directly into the project. Sourcing efforts for purchased material may involve a project-specific purchase requisition and a request for quote. These capabilities support project MRP and project costing. In particular, you can have a single production order (or purchase order) for an item shared between projects, and still track actual costs to the project via the marking capabilities.

Several scenarios illustrated the use of projects in manufacturing and distribution. One scenario involved an internal project for new product development and the production of a prototype. A second scenario involved an external project, and illustrated the use of subprojects to segment the work. The work segmentation also reflected the organizational responsibilities for different groups of employees. A third scenario involved the project quotations for engineering time and production of one-time products. The case studies highlighted project-oriented operations for new product development, professional services, and an engineer-to-order industrial equipment manufacturer.

Chapter 13

Multisite Operations

Many businesses involved in manufacturing and distribution have inventory at multiple physical sites. The multiple sites can serve different purposes. A site may reflect proximity to suppliers or customers, transportation or production cost considerations, or availability of raw materials and human resources. There may be political, technological, or competitive considerations for multiple locations. A site may represent an acquisition or internal growth, or it may represent a separate entity for financial reporting purposes.

The wide variety of multisite operations can be distilled into several basic variations. The simplest variation involves autonomous sites within a single company and AX instance, and no need for transfers between sites. Other variations require transfers between sites or companies within a single AX instance, which can be handled by transfer orders and intercompany orders respectively. In some cases, transfers may involve a sister company using a different AX instance or ERP system, which can be supported by the intercompany trade capabilities of the Application Integration Framework (AIF) within Dynamics AX.

The basic variations of multisite operations, and the prescriptions for solution approaches, provide a starting point for further explanation. The explanation of multisite operations consists of four sections.

1. Solution approaches for multisite operations
2. Transfer orders
3. Intercompany orders
4. Other multisite scenarios

When modeling physical sites in a multisite operation, you can use AX sites or AX warehouses or both. Chapter 9 explained sites, warehouses, and bin locations. In this chapter, we will use the terms *AX site* and *AX warehouse* when explaining system-specific functionality, and the generic terms of multisite and physical site (or site) for conceptual explanations.

Solution Approaches for Multisite Operations

The wide variety of multisite operations can be distilled into five basic variations. Several factors differentiate the nature of these multisite variations, such as the need for transfers between sites. Autonomous sites do not require inventory transfers. A distribution network, on the other hand, could be exemplified by a vertically integrated supply chain with transfers between manufacturing plants and distribution centers. The term distribution network refers to the need for transfers. Other distribution network examples include replenishment of a remote warehouse, space within a contract warehouse, a customer location (for stocking material prior to customer usage), a subcontract vendor location (for stocking supplied components or the completed parent), a customer service center, and delivery vans.

In addition to the need for transfers, other differentiating factors for multisite operations include the grouping of sites into companies, the AX approach to modeling physical sites, and the use of another AX instance or another ERP system by a sister company. Figure 13.1 summarizes how these factors influence the AX solution approach for supporting the basic variations in multisite operations.

		Basic Variations of Multisite Operations				
		Autonomous Sites without Transfers	Distribution Network in 1 company	Distribution Network in 2+ companies	Distribution Network with 2+ AX instances	Distribution Network with 2+ ERP Systems
Factors Affecting AX Solution Approach	Number of AX Instances	One			Multiple	Multiple ERP Systems
	Number of Companies (Legal Entities)	One		Multiple		
	AX Approach for Modeling Multiple Physical Sites	Use Multiple Warehouses, Multiple Warehouses with an AX Site, or Multiple AX Sites				
	Need for Transfers Between Sites or Companies	No	Transfers Between AX Sites or Warehouses	Transfers Between Companies		
	AX Solution Approach For Coordinating Material Transfers	N/A	Transfer Orders	Intercompany Purchase & Sales Orders	Handling Intercompany trade via the Application Integration Framework (AIF)	

Figure 13.1 Basic Variations of Multisite Operations

The prescriptive nature of Figure 13.1 identifies the AX solution approach for each multisite variation. Subsequent sections explain the use of transfer orders and intercompany orders. An explanation of the Application Integration Framework falls outside the scope of this book. Each section includes scenarios to illustrate variations in multisite operations.

AX Approaches for Modeling Physical Sites   The choice of an AX approach for modeling physical sites involves several considerations. The book's baseline model (described in Chapter 1) has focused on the use of multisite functionality within Dynamics AX, where each physical site is modeled as an AX site comprised of one or more AX warehouses. An additional option—multiple AX warehouses without an AX site—can be used when multisite functionality has not been activated.[1] Hence, there are three AX approaches for modeling physical sites: as multiple AX warehouses, as multiple AX warehouses with an AX site, and as multiple AX sites. Figure 13.2 summarizes these three AX approaches for modeling physical sites, which provide an organizing focus for further explanation. Figure 13.2 also summarizes the costing and production factors that differentiate the AX solution approaches.

❖ *Multiple AX Warehouses.* The use of multiple AX warehouses reflects a solution approach supported in previous versions of Dynamics AX; it does not take advantage of the AX multisite functionality. For example, this approach does not support financial reporting by warehouse, standard costing or calculation of overheads based on an overhead formula, and it does not fully support multiple manufacturing sites producing the same item. That being said, there are situations which employ this solution approach, as illustrated in Case 72.

❖ *Multiple AX Warehouses Within a Single AX Site.* This solution approach mirrors the above-described approach, and takes advantage of some of the AX multisite functionality. In terms of costing factors, for example, it supports standard costing and calculation of overhead costs, but does not support financial reporting by site.

❖ *Multiple AX Sites.* A solution approach using multiple AX sites provides several advantages compared to the other approaches, as illustrated in the

---

[1] The multisite functionality is active by default when you perform a fresh installation of Dynamics AX, and when you create a new company account after an upgrade to AX 2009. In both cases, you can deactivate the multisite functionality for a company account as long as you have not created a standard cost inventory model or a dimension group. In addition, the multisite functionality is inactive for all company accounts when you upgrade to AX 2009, although you can optionally activate the multisite functionality on a per company basis.

		AX Approaches for Modeling Physical Sites		
		Multiple AX Warehouses*	Multiple Warehouses Within a Single AX Site	Multiple AX Sites
Costing Factors	Financial Reporting By Site	No	No	A financial dimension can be assigned to a site, thereby supporting financial reporting by site
Costing Factors	Standard Costing	No	Supports standard costing	
Costing Factors	Standard Costing	No	An item's standard cost can vary by site	
Costing Factors	Labor Rates in Manufacturing	Supports labor rates	Supports labor rates with date effectivities and simulation capabilities	
Costing Factors	Labor Rates in Manufacturing	Supports labor rates	Labor costs (cost category costs) can vary by site	
Costing Factors	Calculation of Overhead Costs for Manufactured Items	No	Supports calculation of material- and routing-related overhead costs, and also supports date effectivities and simulation capabilities	
Costing Factors	Calculation of Overhead Costs for Manufactured Items	No	Overhead formulas can vary by site	
Costing Factors	Cost Calculations and Inquiries for Manufactured Items	Cost calculations and inquiries apply to the entire product structure		Cost calculations and inquiries only span a single site when its product structure spans 2+ sites
Production Factors	Manufacturing Plants Produce the Same Item	Partially supported by using different BOM and Route versions for the item		Fully supported by using a site-specific (or company-wide) BOM version and a site-specific Route version for the item
Production Factors	Other Production Considerations	N/A	N/A	A routing must be site-specific Work centers in a routing must be within same site Alternate work centers (within a task group) must be within the same site A BOM can be site-specific or company-wide BOM components must be from warehouses within the same site
Production Factors	Other Production Considerations			The warehouse location of auto-deducted components can be linked to the work center that requires the components

*The AX Multisite functionality must be deactivated

Figure 13.2 AX Approaches for Modeling Physical Sites

right hand column of Figure 13.2. In terms of costing factors, for example, it supports an item's site-specific standard costs, site-specific labor rates and overhead formulas, and financial reporting by site. One caveat involves the single-site considerations in the production factors and in the cost calculations/inquiries.

Similarities and differences in the use of AX sites and warehouses were previously illustrated Figure 2.1, which summarized company-wide versus site/warehouse information.

The scenarios throughout this chapter primarily reflect multiple AX sites. We'll start with two common multisite scenarios in a single company. The first scenario concerns autonomous sites, and the second scenario concerns a simple distribution network. The second scenario leads into the explanation of transfer orders for coordinating transfers between sites.

Scenario 1: Autonomous Sites Within a Single Company Autonomous sites do not require material transfers between locations, as illustrated in the left side of Figure 13.3 by two sites within the same company.

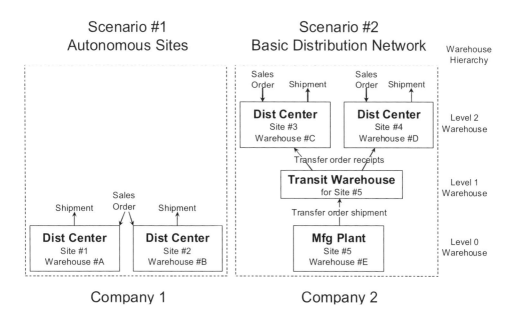

Figure 13.3 Multisite Scenarios for a Single Company

These physical sites could be modeled as AX sites or as AX warehouses. This scenario uses a unique AX site and warehouse for each physical site, such as Site #1 and Warehouse #A shown in the left side of Figure 13.3, with financial reporting by AX site. Sales orders can be taken for shipment from any site/warehouse, and purchase order line items designate the desired ship-to site/warehouse. A centralized accounting group handles accounting for all locations.

Company-wide information is defined for items, customers, and vendors, with site/warehouse-specific forecasts and planning data. The trade agreements about sales and purchase prices can be company-wide or site/warehouse-specific for a given item.

Scenario 2: Distribution Network Within a Single Company A simple example of a distribution network consists of a manufacturing plant supplying material to two distribution centers, as shown in the right side of Figure 13.3. The distribution network is reflected in the definition of a warehouse hierarchy, and in each item's site/warehouse-specific coverage planning policies. This planning data provides the basis for generating planned transfer orders to replenish inventory at the distribution centers. Purchase orders are delivered to any of the three sites/warehouses, and a centralized accounting group handles accounting for all locations.

Transfer Orders

Transfer orders support the coordination of supply chain activities for material flows between two sites/warehouses in the same company. A planned transfer order communicates requirements for moving material from one site/warehouse (the transfer-from location) to replenish inventory at another site/warehouse (the transfer-to location). Firming a planned transfer order creates a transfer order for actually recording the transfer. In addition, a manually created transfer order can be used to report unplanned transfers between sites/warehouses. Whether created automatically or manually, the transfer order represents a two-step approach to transfer material between warehouses. The two-step approach means that one transaction records the shipment and a second transaction records the receipt, with tracking of in-transit inventory in a transit warehouse.[2] A one-step approach can also be used, typically when a short transportation time does not require tracking of in-transit inventory. The one-step approach means that one transaction records the shipment, with automatic receipt of the shipped quantity.

Planning calculations use distribution requirements planning (DRP) logic to suggest planned transfer orders to meet demand based on site/warehouse-specific planning data. The following subsections explain the planning data for transfer items, the life cycle of a transfer order, variations in the transfer order process, and the use of planned transfer orders for coordinating transfer activities.

Planning Data for Transfer Items Planning calculations suggest planned transfer orders based on the item's site/warehouse-specific planning data. Some of the planning data reflects an item's company-wide policies, which can be overridden to reflect site/warehouse-specific policies. Figure 13.4 summarizes the planning data for transfer items, and highlights the company-wide versus site/warehouse policies as well the forms for data maintenance.[3] The figure also indicates one method for limiting replenishment. Further explanation covers each aspect of planning data within Figure 13.4.

---

[2] A transit warehouse must be assigned to each normal warehouse for tracking in-transit inventory shipped from the warehouse. Both the normal and transit warehouses must be within the same site. When inventory is also tracked by bin location, at least one bin must be defined for the transit warehouse (e.g., labeled the intransit bin). The bin location must be defined as the transit warehouse's default issue and receipt bin, since this bin location cannot be specified on a transfer order.

[3] An item's coverage data can be maintained by accessing it from the Items form, or from the Item Coverage Setup form. In either case, you can directly maintain the records, or use a wizard to create new records for selected sites/warehouses (which can then be directly maintained). Use of the Item Coverage Setup form provides several advantages, such as viewing items without any item coverage records, viewing a filtered subset of items, and deleting coverage data information.

		Company-Wide Policies	Site-Specific Policies	Site/Warehouse Coverage Planning Policies
Planning Data for Transfer Items	Relevant Inventory Dimensions For Coverage Planning Policies	Specify		
	Primary Source of Supply (Transfer)	N/A	N/A	Specify
	Preferred Refilling Warehouse			
	Coverage Code (Reordering Policy)	Specify Act as Defaults		Override
	Coverage Group (Set of Policies)			
	Default Order Settings — Transfer Lead Time		Override	N/A
	Order Quantity Modifiers for Transfers			
	Minimum Quantity	N/A		Specify
	Planner Responsibility	Specify		
Limits — Default Order Settings	Stop Transfer Activities for an Item	Specify	Override	N/A

Use Items form or Default Order Settings form   Use Site-Specific Order Settings form   Use Item Coverage form

Figure 13.4 Planning Data for Transfer Items

❖ *Relevant Inventory Dimensions for Coverage Planning Policies.* An item's replenishment logic concerning transfers can reflect a site, warehouse, or bin location viewpoint, as defined by its coverage planning policies (embedded in the Dimension Group assigned to the item). The book's baseline model assumes that sites, warehouses, and bin locations will be used, and that coverage planning will apply to sites and warehouses.

❖ *Primary Source of Supply (Transfer).* Replenishment based on transfers must be designated in the item's site/warehouse-specific coverage data, so that planning calculations generate planned transfer orders. The transfer policy (termed the *change planned order type* field) works in conjunction with the preferred refilling warehouse.

❖ *Preferred Refilling Warehouse.* The preferred refilling warehouse can be defined for transferring individual items to a warehouse (as part of each item's site/warehouse-specific coverage planning policies). Alternatively, it can be defined for a warehouse, so that it is assumed that all warehouse inventory will be replenished from one refilling warehouse unless specifically overridden. With the warehouse-level policy, you can specifically override an item's preferred refilling warehouse and/or primary source of supply (as part of the item's site/warehouse-specific coverage planning policies).

❖ *Coverage Code (aka Reordering Policy).* The item's coverage code represents a key part of the planner's decision-making logic about creating new transfer orders. The four reordering policies include min/max (time-phased order point logic), period (period lot-sizing logic), requirement (order-driven logic), and manual. These reordering policies were explained in Chapter 2 and summarized in Figure 2.3. An item's coverage code reflects a company-wide policy that can be overridden by site/warehouse.

❖ *Coverage Group (Set of Policies).* The coverage group assigned to an item contains the coverage code and other policies that represent a model of the planner's decision making logic about planned transfer orders and existing orders. An item's coverage group reflects a company-wide policy that can be overridden by site/warehouse.[4]

❖ *Transfer Lead Time.* The transfer lead time (aka transportation time) is expressed in days. It can reflect a warehouse viewpoint or an item viewpoint. The warehouse viewpoint defines the typical transportation time between a pair of warehouses, whereas the item viewpoint typically defines the transfer time as part of the item's site/warehouse-specific coverage planning policies. A subsequent subsection provides a more detailed explanation about these two viewpoints.

❖ *Order Quantity Modifiers for Transfer Orders.* Planning calculations suggest a planned transfer order quantity subject to order quantity modifiers for a minimum, maximum and multiple (for inventory). The system also provides a soft warning during manual creation of a transfer order when the user enters a quantity that does not meet these criteria.

❖ *Standard Order Quantity for Transfers.* The item's standard order quantity (for inventory) is used as a default when manually creating a transfer order. Transfer order quantities are always expressed in the item's inventory UM, and the system provides soft warnings to enforce the item's order quantity modifiers for minimum, multiple, and maximum.

❖ *Minimum Quantity* The minimum quantity represents an item's inventory plan or safety stock for a given warehouse. Chapter 2 explained the considerations about a minimum quantity, such as automatic calculation based on historical data, and the use of a variable minimum quantity by time period.

❖ *Planner Responsibility.* The concept of planner responsibility provides an organizing focus for communicating the need to synchronize supplies

---

[4] Chapter 2 explained coverage group policies for purchased material; these policies also apply to transfer items.

with demands. The concept of planner responsibility for transfer orders is often based on the buyer group assigned to the item. For example, planning calculations generate planned transfer orders identified with the buyer group, so that a planner can selectively view and mark planned orders for which they have responsibility.

❖ *Replenishment Limitations for a Transfer Item.*   Enforcement of replenishment limitations can stop transfers of an obsolete item.[5] The concept of a transfer stop flag is implemented via the field labeled the inventory stop flag. It can be specified as a company-wide policy, and optionally overridden for a specific site. The inventory stop flag means that an item's existing transfer orders cannot be shipped or received, and new transfer orders cannot be created for the item. It actually enforces even more restrictive limitations, since it prevents any further receipts or issues. The stopped flag does not impact planning calculations, so that planned orders will still be generated.

Structure and Life Cycle of a Transfer Order   The basic structure of a transfer order consists of header and line item information. The transfer order header identifies the ship-from and ship-to site/warehouse. Each line item identifies an item and quantity.

The life cycle of a transfer order consists of three major steps represented by an order status (termed *transfer status*) automatically updated by the system.

❖ *Created.* A created status means that line items can be added and data maintained on a transfer order. Two additional steps can be performed— to generate a picking list and to update picked inventory via the picking list registration—within the created status.[6]
❖ *Shipped.* All lines have been shipped.
❖ *Received.* All lines have been received. Information cannot be changed for transfer orders with a shipped or received status.

The posting function can employ a two-step process to report shipment and receipt of the transfer order line items. Posting the shipment can generate a printed Transfer Order Shipment form, while posting the receipt can

---

[5] A separate set of policies can be specified for sales order purposes (to stop or limit sales of an item) and for purchase order purposes (to stop or limit purchases of an item).

[6] The item's policy concerning picking requirements (embedded in the inventory model group assigned to the item) determines whether the picking list steps are mandatory or optional.

generate a printed Transfer Order Receipt form. Alternatively, you can employ a single-step process by indicating auto-receive when posting the shipment. The system automatically updates the *remaining status* for a transfer order line based on posted transactions, with the following possible values:

❖ *Shipping Updates.* The line has only been created or the line has not been completely shipped.

❖ *Receive Updates.* The line has been completely shipped but not yet completely received.

❖ *Nothing.* The line has been completely shipped and received.

Over- and under-delivery delivery tolerances (expressed as a percentage) can be specified for a line item.[7] A line item can be short shipped and flagged as closed, for example, thereby updating the remaining status to receive updates. Historical information about received transfer orders must be manually deleted.

Transfer Order Dates for Shipment and Receipt   The transfer order header specifies a shipment date and receipt date, along with the ship-from and ship-to site/warehouses and a mode of delivery (such as air or truck). The difference between the two dates reflects the transportation time (expressed in days) between the two locations. Each line item can also have a shipment and receipt date, and a mode of delivery.

The assignments of the shipment and receipt dates to a manually entered transfer order are affected by several policies. The *delivery date control* policy of *none*, for example, indicates that the dates will not be verified against calendars (for the warehouses and mode of delivery), nor will the dates reflect the typical transportation time between warehouses. Use of delivery date control will enforce rules concerning the shipment and receipt dates.[8] The system provides a warning when the shipment or receipt date cannot be met, along with messaging about the reason(s). The rules associated with delivery date control are explained below.

---

[7] A company-wide policy (embedded in the inventory parameters) determines whether over- and under-deliveries will be accepted on transfer orders.

[8] To enforce rules for transfer orders, the delivery date control policy should be defined as sales lead time or ATP (rather than a policy of none). A company-wide policy for the delivery date control policy (defined in the A/R parameters) acts as a default for a transfer order header, which can be overridden for the header and for the line items.

❖ *Lead Time to Process Order.* The concept of a sales lead time applies to a manually entered transfer order, and represents the minimum days to process the transfer order for shipment (after it has been entered into the system). With a sales lead time of 1 day, for example, a transfer order that is manually entered today will have a shipment date of the next day.[9]

❖ *Order Deadlines for Taking Transfer Orders.* The concept of an order deadline means that transfer orders entered after a specified time are treated as if they were entered the next day. A specified time for the deadline can be defined for each day of the week.[10]

❖ *Calendars.* Calendars can be assigned to the ship-from and ship-to warehouses, and to the mode of delivery between warehouses. These calendars can be used to constrain the ship date or receipt date. For example, a truck delivery between two warehouses may only occur on Tuesdays. The user can view available ship and delivery dates for a specified warehouse and mode of delivery.

❖ *Transportation Time Between Warehouses.* The shipment and receipt dates will account for transportation time between warehouses. This means that you can enter one date (say the shipment date) and automatically calculate the other date (such as the receipt date).

Transportation Time Between Warehouses   The transportation time between warehouses can be defined with two different approaches that reflect a warehouse viewpoint versus an item viewpoint.

❖ *Transportation Time Based on a Warehouse Viewpoint.* This viewpoint defines the typical transportation time between a pair of ship-from and ship-to warehouses. The transportation time must be defined for each warehouse pair when you have multiple warehouses. For each warehouse pair, you can optionally define the transportation time for different modes of delivery (such as truck or air), and mark one as the default mode of delivery.[11] This transportation time will be used in planned transfer orders, and in manually entered transfer orders with enforcement of delivery date control rules. Most situations will employ the warehouse viewpoint for defining transportation time.

---

[9] A company-wide policy for sales lead time (defined in the A/R parameters) applies to the transfer order header, whereas an item-specific sales lead time applies to each transfer order line item. The item-specific sales lead time for transfer orders can vary by site. A separate sales lead time applies to sales orders, as described in Chapter 7.

[10] The company-wide policies for each day's order deadline are defined in the A/R parameters.

[11] Planning calculations will use the transportation time associated with the default mode of delivery (if it exists) for the warehouse pair, or the typical transportation time between the warehouse pair (if a default mode of delivery does not exist).

❖ *Transportation Time Based on an Item Viewpoint.* This viewpoint supports an item-specific transportation time between a warehouse pair, thereby supporting unusual situations not handled by the warehouse viewpoint. You define this transfer time as part of an item's site/warehouse-specific coverage planning data, which also defines the primary refilling warehouse (aka the ship-from warehouse).

Planning calculations will use the transportation time associated with the warehouse viewpoint unless the item viewpoint has been defined.

Order-Related Text for Transfer Orders   Some situations require textual explanations or additional descriptive information about the transfer order and line items. Order-related text can be specified in several ways, such as documents attached to the header or line items of a transfer order, or the item's descriptive text on a line item. The Transfer Order Shipment and Transfer Order Receipt documents must be customized to print this information.

Recording a Transfer Order Shipment   A transfer order shipment can be recorded using the posting shipment function. As part of the posting process, it is common to display the line items (to allow editing) and request a printed Transfer Order Shipment. The user can indicate the shipped quantity for a line item, and optionally close it short (when under-delivery tolerances have been specified). Additional information can include a tracking number for the shipment. You can optionally indicate a one-step shipment/receipt process via the auto-receive flag, thereby eliminating the need for a separate receipt transaction.

There are two alternative approaches that involve a separate step for picking material prior to posting the shipment: the Consolidated Picking List approach and the Order Picking List approach. These two approaches were previously described in Chapter 9 for sales order shipments, along with an explanation of the related constructs of output orders, shipments, and picking routes. The same constructs and explanations apply to transfer orders with two major differences. First, you use the Release Transfer Order Picking form to anticipate picking activities and create output orders. Second, you post the transfer order shipment after completing picking activity (rather than posting the sales order packing slip).

Recording a Transit Order Receipt   A transfer order receipt can be recorded using the posting receipt function. As part of the posting process, it is common to display the line items (to allow editing) and request a printed Transfer Order Receipt. You can indicate the received quantity for each line item, and optionally indicate a scrapped quantity. The quantity shipped must be reported as received or scrapped.

An alternative for reporting transfer order receipts involves the use of an *arrival journal* and a two-step receiving process. An arrival journal consists of multiple line items that reflect different transfer order line items. Chapter 9 described the use of an arrival journal for recording receipts. An item-specific policy (embedded in the Inventory Model Group assigned to the item) determines whether the arrival journal approach is mandated or optional for receipt transactions.

The quarantine management policy does not apply to receipts related to transfer orders, so that a quarantine order (if needed) must be manually created after receipt, or created as part of reporting arrival. Quality orders cannot be automatically generated for transfer orders, so that a quality order (if needed) must be manually created after receipt.

When to Use the Transfer Journal Versus a Transfer Order

The transfer journal generally applies to inventory movements within a given physical site, as described in Chapter 9. It represents a one-step process for transferring an item to another location. The transfer journal offers a simple approach for recording unplanned transfers, especially with a short transfer time and no requirement for tracking in-transit inventory.

An unplanned transfer can also be handled via a manually-created transfer order, and you can optionally employ a one-step shipping process. Supporting documents can be printed, such as the Transfer Order Shipment document.

Using Planned Transfer Orders   A firm's S&OP game plans for saleable products and services provide the primary driver of transfer activities for material items. The game plans define item demands at a given site/warehouse. Planning calculations synchronize supplies at the sourcing warehouses to meet these demands, as expressed through several coordination tools. The primary coordination tools consist of planned transfer orders and suggested action messages generated by planning calculations.

Suggestions for planned transfer orders can be viewed on the *Planned*

Transfer Orders form or the *Planned Orders* form. A planned transfer order identifies the item's preferred refilling warehouse. The user can also manually add a planned transfer order. Transfer orders can be created from selected planned orders via a function termed *firming planned orders*.

❖ *Selection of Planned Transfer Orders.* You select planned orders via a marking check box. For example, orders can be individually marked or block-marked. Planned orders can also be viewed and optionally selected based on attributes such as the ship-from warehouse, buyer, order date, and planned order status. You can assign a status to planned orders (unprocessed, processed, and approved) to indicate those that have been analyzed, but this status only represents reference information. The form does not retain marked orders if the user exits before firming.

❖ *Analyzing and Editing Planned Orders.* Planners often need to understand the rationale and impact for a planned transfer order. For example, you can view action messages related to a planned order. You can also view single-level pegging information about the source of demand for a planned order. Additional inquiries display single-level pegging to all supplies and demands for an item (via a *Net Requirements* inquiry), and the multilevel pegging information about supplies and demands for a planned order (via an *Explosion* inquiry).

The analysis often leads to needed action, and several actions can be implemented on the planned orders form.

○ Change quantity and/or delivery date for the planned transfer order.

○ Split the planned transfer order using a specified quantity and date.

○ Group together several selected planned orders for the same item.

○ Change the ship-from warehouse, thereby indicating an alternate source of supply. You can view inventory availability at other sites to support decisions about changing the source of supply.

○ Change the planned transfer order to a planned purchase order or production order to indicate an alternate source of supply.

○ Assign the planned order to an existing transfer order so that the firming process adds a line item to the existing order.

Firming Planned Transfer Orders   The firming function creates transfer orders for selected planned orders. The system creates single-line transfer orders unless the user indicates grouping preferences (via the firming dialogue when the user selects more than one planned order). Grouping can be by date, week, or month.[12] With grouping by week, for example, the firming function can create multiline transfer orders containing planned orders between a warehouse pair.

Execution of the firming function automatically deletes the marked planned orders, and creates a log for tracking which planned orders have been firmed and by whom.

Planned orders can be automatically firmed, or automatically delayed to the end of a frozen period, based on time fence policies (embedded in the coverage group assigned to an item).

❖ *Firm Time Fence.* The firm time fence enables the planning calculations to automatically create transfer orders, thereby eliminating the effort to manually firm planned orders. The system uses the company-wide grouping preferences to create multiline transfer orders, such as creating a multiline order for planned orders within a weekly period. To be effective, the automatic firming time fence should be slightly greater than the item's transfer lead time and reorder cycle.

❖ *Freeze Time Fence.* The freeze time fence represents the shortest possible turnaround time to obtain material with a new transfer order, so that planning calculations will place planned orders at the end of the frozen period. The freeze time fence represents expedited delivery whereas the transfer lead time represents normal delivery.

Other Coordination Tools for Transfer Orders The action and futures messages provide one tool for coordinating transfer orders to meet company game plans. Planning calculations generate these two types of messages, as explained in Chapter 2 and illustrated in Figure 2.4.

The Transfer Order Release Picking form can be used to anticipate picking activities for transfer order shipments, and to create output orders for selected line items, when you employ a picking list approach. The Arrival Overview form can be used to anticipate transfer order receipts, and to create an arrival journal for selected line items.

Intercompany Orders

Trading between two companies involves a customer-to-vendor relationship. Intercompany orders can be used when both companies exist within the same

---

[12] The default values for grouping preferences (when firming planned transfer orders) are defined in the master planning parameters.

Dynamics AX instance. Intercompany orders require identification of the intercompany vendor in the buying company's database, and the intercompany customer in the selling company's database.

❖ *Intercompany Vendor.* Each sister company must be set up as an endpoint within the Application Integration Framework (AIF) and associated with the relevant vendor identifier. Additional setup information specifies the policies about how to handle intercompany purchase orders and value mapping, as described in the next subsection.

❖ *Intercompany Customer.* Each sister company must be set up as an endpoint within the Application Integration Framework (AIF) and associated with the relevant customer identifier. Additional setup information specifies the policies about how to handle intercompany sales orders and value mapping, as described in the next subsection.

Placing a purchase order with an intercompany vendor creates a corresponding sales order in the sister company, and vice versa. The purchase order header (or sales order header) indicates information about the corresponding intercompany order. The sales order shipment and then a purchase order receipt indicate the transfer. The system supports automation of the corresponding invoices and payments between the intercompany trading partners. The intercompany trading approach supports transfer pricing.

Purchase orders and sales orders were previously explained in Chapters 7 and 8 respectively, and intercompany orders have many similarities. This chapter focuses on the unique aspects of intercompany purchase orders and sales orders. Different scenarios representing different methods of creating an intercompany order provide the organizing focus for further explanation. For illustration purposes, we'll use a simple network comprised of a manufacturing company that supplies material to a distribution company, as shown in Figures 13.5 and 13.6. Each company requires setup information in order to process intercompany orders.

Setup Information for Intercompany Orders The intercompany capabilities require setup information. The following steps apply to the distribution company in the scenarios shown in Figures 13.5 and 13.6, so that it recognizes the manufacturing company as a vendor. It is assumed that the two companies have already been defined in the same Dynamics AX instance.

–   Create a vendor that represents the manufacturing company.
–   Create an intercompany trading partner identifier (termed an endpoint ID) that represents the manufacturing company, and assign it the relevant company identifier.
–   Designate the trading partner's role as a vendor (termed a constraint) and specify the vendor identifier.
–   Specify the authorized transaction (termed an action ID), which would be a purchase order in this case.
–   Define policies about the authorized transaction. These policies (termed action policies) can be used to model variations in trading practices. For example, the policies determine whether the purchase price can be edited on the intercompany purchase order. Other configuration policies include value mapping for key fields (such as item numbers and UM) that specify which values should be used. The value for item number, for example, is typically the company item but could be an external code. Some policies only apply to a given scenario, so that the scenario explanations will highlight the relevant policies.
–   Define the common item in the item master, and create a company item number and assign it to the common item. It will be a purchased item with a preferred vendor that represents the manufacturing company.

These same steps must be undertaken for the manufacturing company, so that it recognizes the distribution company as a customer. The only differences are the trading partner's role (customer), the authorized transaction (sales order), and the policies pertinent to a sales order. The common item will be a manufactured item.

Information about the manufactured item should include a standard sales price and/or sales price trade agreements that determine prices on the intercompany sales order and purchase order. This last point deserves repeating. Pricing information at the selling company normally dictates the price on the corresponding intercompany purchase order, unless policies within the setup information state otherwise.

Scenario 3: Manually Created Intercompany Purchase Order   A basic scenario consists of a manually created purchase order (in the distribution company) to an intercompany vendor (the manufacturing company). This results in an intercompany purchase order and automatic creation of an intercompany sales order at the manufacturing company. The system indicates the origin of each order as source and derived, respectively, since data maintenance is typically constrained for the derived order. Changes to the source order automatically update the derived order.

Several policies in the setup information apply to the intercompany sales order. One policy dictates the identifier for the corresponding sales order since it must be auto-assigned; it can match the source purchase order number or reflect the numbering sequence at the manufacturing company. Another policy determines whether users can edit the sales order price. Sales price information in the selling company normally dictates the sales (and purchase) price on the intercompany orders, and manual overrides can be prevented for control purposes. A related policy determines whether sales price trade agreements (at the selling company) can be used for pricing on the intercompany sales order.

The same process applies to a manually created sales order in the manufacturing company, where the customer is an intercompany partner (the distribution company in this scenario). This approach results in an intercompany sales order and automatic creation of an intercompany purchase order, where the respective origin of each order would be source and derived. Changes to the source order automatically update the derived order.

Scenario 4: Firming a Planned Intercompany Purchase Order

The sales and operation planning process, and the resulting game plans for saleable products, drive the planned purchase orders at the distribution company.[13] Firming a planned purchase order to an intercompany vendor will automatically create an intercompany purchase order and a corresponding intercompany sales order (at the manufacturing plant). The left side of Figure 13.5 illustrates scenario 4, where the first step (firm an intercompany purchase order) has been identified and the darker arrow indicates linkage to the intercompany sales order.

Creation of intercompany purchase orders provides visibility of demands to the manufacturing company. Hence, the minimum planning horizon must be considered in the game plans for the distribution company. It should exceed the cumulative lead time for manufacturing and transportation, as described in the guidelines concerning S&OP game plans. Automatic firming of planned purchase orders provides one approach for increased visibility of demands, where the firm time fence reflects the minimum planning horizon for the item.

---

[13] Previous chapters covered sales and operations planning (Chapter 6) and suggestions for handling planned purchase orders (Chapter 8).

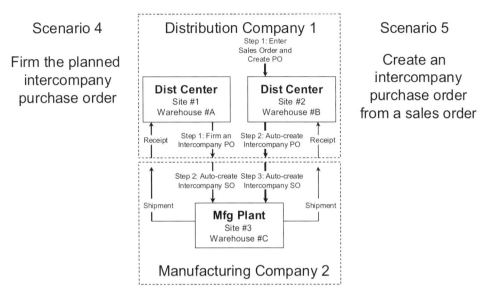

Figure 13.5 Distribution Network with Multiple Companies

Scenario 5: Create an Intercompany Purchase Order from a Sales Order

When entering a sales order in the distribution company, the user can manually initiate a function to create a purchase order linked to the sales order, as described in Chapter 7. This same process results in an intercompany purchase order when buying from an intercompany vendor (the manufacturing company in this scenario).[14] The right side of Figure 13.5 illustrates Scenario 5, where the first step (enter sales order and create purchase order) has been identified and the darker arrows represent the linkage to the intercompany purchase order and sales order. Changes on the originating sales order will automatically update the derived orders, such as changes to the quantity, delivery date, or delivery address.

A few policies in the setup information apply to this scenario. For example, one policy determines whether users can edit the purchase order price.

Scenario 6: Create a Direct Delivery Intercompany Purchase Order from a Sales Order

When entering a sales order in the distribu-

---

[14] The process can be automated based on a policy in the sales order header (termed the *autocreate intercompany order* policy), that defaults from the customer master policy. The system automatically creates the orders when you exit the form. This auto-creation policy should reflect the dominant trading practices with the customer.

tion company, the user can manually initiate a function to create a direct delivery purchase order linked to the sales order, as described in Chapter 7. This same process results in a direct delivery intercompany purchase order when buying from an intercompany vendor (the manufacturing company in this scenario).[15] The left side of Figure 13.6 illustrates Scenario 6, where the first step (enter sales order and create a direct delivery purchase order) has been identified and the darker arrows represent the linkage to the direct delivery intercompany purchase order and associated sales order. Changes on the originating sales order will automatically update the derived orders.

The sales order packing list at the manufacturing company indicates the ship-to address (for the end customer), and the bill-to customer (the distribution company). Posting the sales order shipment at the manufacturing company automatically updates information (in the distribution company) about the purchase order receipt and sales order shipment. Automatic updates also apply when posting the sales order invoice; no additional transactions need to be posted at the distribution company.

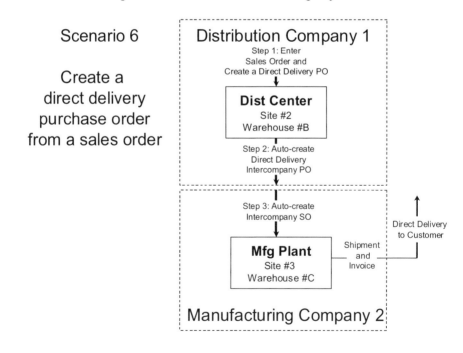

Figure 13.6 Direct Delivery for Intercompany Orders

<hr />

[15] The process can be automated based on a policy in the sales order header (termed the *autocreate intercompany order* policy). A policy in the sales order header must indicate that direct delivery can be used; this policy defaults from the customer master.

Several policies in the setup information only apply to direct delivery scenarios. For example, these policies determine whether to post and print the sales invoice automatically, since the vendor invoice acts as the trigger.

Scenario 7: Master Scheduling Across a Multicompany Supply Chain The sequence for performing the master scheduling task becomes important in a multicompany supply chain involving three or more companies. Planning calculations apply to a single company, which means the master scheduling task should first be performed for the top-tier company. This generates planned intercompany purchase orders that get automatically firmed (based on the firming fence) in order to automatically generate intercompany sales orders at the second-tier company. Master scheduling should then be performed for the second-tier company (and then the sequence of subsequent tiers, if any) in order to support DRP logic across the multicompany supply chain. This represents a simple scenario with a sequential cascade effect. More complex scenarios involve intercompany trading across companies in the same tier or between tiers, which requires multiple iterations of the master scheduling task to correctly support DRP logic.

The Intercompany Master Scheduling task performs a sequence of master scheduling tasks for companies in the supply chain. This requires setup information about each company's sequence number and designated set of planning data, as defined in the company's master planning parameters.[16] Some additional information is specified when performing the intercompany master scheduling task, such as the number of iterations to correctly support DRP logic in more complex scenarios. The additional information typically specifies regeneration calculations for the first iteration and net change calculations for subsequent iterations. This task can be started in any company, since setup information determines the sequencing.

Other Multisite Scenarios

The following scenarios illustrate additional variations in multisite operations. To summarize the previous variations, Scenarios 1 and 2 illustrated autonomous sites and a distribution network within a single company, and Scenarios 3 through 7 illustrated variations of intercompany orders between companies.

---

[16] Using different sets of planning data and the associated master planning policies for each set were described in Chapter 6.

Combined Invoice for Multiple Sales Orders   Normal processing generates one invoice for one sales order, but some customers require a combined invoice for multiple sales orders. This is termed a *summary update*. An automatic summary update can apply to all sales orders with the same bill-to customer and currency, and possibly other criteria such as the method of payment and sold-to customer. These criteria must be defined for individual customers, and a summary update designated upon invoicing. The concept of summary updating applies to other sales order documents such as packing slips. It also applies to purchase order documents.

Inventory Stocked at a Subcontractor Location   Inventory stocked at a subcontractor location can represent three different cases. Purchased components can be shipped directly to the subcontractor, material components can be transferred to the subcontractor from another site, and the finished item (built via an outside operation) can be stocked at the subcontractor. The manufactured item has a master BOM defining the supplied material and an outside operation component that defines work to be performed by the subcontractor. Chapter 8 explained the use of outside operation components to model subcontracted manufacturing.

One Manufacturing Plant Using Components from Another Warehouse   The warehouse source of components in a master BOM normally reflects the manufacturing location of the parent item, but the source can be a different AX warehouse within the same AX site. Three examples illustrate this situation. One example involves a manufacturing plant and a separate service parts location, where production orders in the service parts location use components stocked at the manufacturing plant. A second example involves a manufacturing plant with an adjoining raw material warehouse; components for production orders are issued directly from the adjoining warehouse. A third example involves a separate warehouse that represents floor stock inventory, with replenishment of floor stock inventory from the main stockroom. This third example is typically used to support material auto-deduction from floor stock inventory, and work center consumption logic (described in Figure 3.3).

Multiple Manufacturing Plants That Build Different Items   Manufacturing plants that build different products and subassemblies can be modeled as AX warehouses, since there is no requirement for site-specific BOM and routing information. Each manufactured item is only produced in one location, and the components in the master BOM indicate the relevant warehouse source of components.

Multiple Manufacturing Plants That Build the Same Item   Manufacturing plants that build the same products and subassemblies are normally modeled as AX sites, since you can define site-specific BOM and routing information.

Consolidated Financial Reports for Multiple Companies   Dynamics AX supports virtual company accounts such as the general ledger account numbers, and also consolidations of company accounts.

Centralized Engineering for Multiple Companies   One aspect of centralized engineering involves item master information.   Item master information is shared across all sites in a single company, but not shared across companies.   A multicompany operation may require new items in one company to be populated in the database for other companies.   Using the function to create items in other companies, a user can start from the item master in one company and then create the item in other target companies. The created item is typically assigned the same identifier, although it could be manually or automatically assigned a different identifier (e.g., based on auto-numbering in the other company).   A company item number must be created and assigned beforehand to the originating item number.   In addition, the trading partner information must be defined for the target companies, since this defines the value mapping for key fields such as UM.   The system provides a warning when a value does not exist in the target database (such as the UM value), and prevents creation of the item.

Case Studies

Case 72: Modeling Transfers via Production Orders   A coal company produced different grades of coal at multiple mines, and then railed this coal to multiple ports (where the item identifier for each coal grade was changed after receipt at the port) in order to be directly loaded onto waiting vessels for sending to customers.   When loading a vessel, each customer required a unique combination of coal grades to obtain their desired chemistry, as defined by a unique end-item number and its bill of material.   Each sales order line item specified an end-item item number.   The coal company wanted close coordination of trains and vessels to support direct loading, and finite scheduling to account for the bottleneck work centers associated with trains, train unloading, and vessel loading. Production orders (and associated routing data) provided the basis for finite scheduling, as well as tracking train batches and actual costs of purchased services from the rail and port vendors.

Case 73: Master Scheduling Across Companies The Batch Process company had a vertically integrated supply chain with multiple plants and distribution centers around the world. The manufacturing plants were located close to the source of raw materials, while the distribution centers were located close to the customers. Each location operated as a separate company. The intercompany trading partners were defined on the vendor master and customer master files, so that the transfers between locations were handled as intercompany purchase orders and sales orders. The intercompany master scheduling task ensured coordination across the multicompany supply chain.

Case 74: Home Furniture Outlets A Consumer Products company specializing in home furniture had multiple outlets grouped into various companies. Inventory replenishment was based on outlet-specific min/max quantities. As part of sales order processing, inventory could be checked within a given company's outlets or (if necessary) across all outlets. The system automatically created a transfer order for moving items within a company, or an intercompany order for moving items between companies. When inventory was insufficient, the user could generate a purchase order to the furniture manufacturer that was directly linked to the sales order.

Case 75: Van Deliveries of Dairy Products A Distribution company sold dairy products via van delivery to homes and businesses. Each van was viewed as a separate warehouse, with replenishment from the main distribution center based on transfer orders. An actual transfer was reported as single transaction using the auto-receive capabilities. Each van was equipped with portable computing to record actual sales, generate invoices and customer-specific reports, track and replenish inventory, and generate forecasted demands based on the latest customer information.

Case 76: Multiple Plants Build Same Item The Equipment company manufactured the same products in several plants that were modeled as AX sites. They defined a company-wide bill of material and a site-specific routing for each manufactured item. They also employed site-specific labor rates and overhead formulas, and site-specific standard costs for purchased material, in order to calculate site-specific standard costs for each manufactured item. S&OP game plans were defined for each product and site, and planning calculations coordinated supply chain activities for each site. Financial reports were generated for each site.

Executive Summary

There are many variations in multisite operations. The basic variations reflect requirements for material transfers between physical sites and how the sites are grouped into companies. A planned transfer order supports material coordination between two sites within the same company, whereas intercompany orders support material coordination between sites in different companies. The basic variations also reflect three options concerning the AX solution approach for modeling physical sites. Physical sites can be modeled as multiple AX sites or multiple AX warehouses with an AX site; they can also be modeled as multiple AX warehouses with multisite functionality deactivated. The advantages of activating multisite functionality include site-specific bills of material and routings, site-specific standard costs, and financial reporting by site.

Transfer orders support the coordination of supply chain activities for material flows between two sites/warehouses in the same company. A planned transfer order communicates requirements for moving material from one site/warehouse (the transfer-from location) to replenish inventory at another site/warehouse (the transfer-to location). Planning calculations use distribution requirements planning logic (DRP) to suggest planned transfer orders to meet demand based on site/warehouse-specific planning data. Firming a planned transfer order creates a transfer order for actually recording the transfer shipment, tracking the transit inventory, and recording the transfer receipt. The transportation lead time can reflect the delivery method (such as truck or air), as well as the relevant calendars for the delivery method and warehouses. The coordination tools include a summary of anticipated shipments and a summary of anticipated receipts. You can optionally employ a picking step prior to recording transfer order shipment, using either a consolidated picking list approach or an order picking list approach. Several scenarios illustrated variations in the use of transfer orders, including a distribution network of sites within a single company.

Intercompany orders support the coordination of supply chain activities for material flows between two sites in different companies within a single AX instance. Intercompany orders require identification of the intercompany vendor in the buying company's database, and the intercompany customer in the selling company's database. Item information must be defined in both companies, along with a company item number. Other setup information must be defined within the Application Integration Framework (AIF) to support intercompany orders. This setup information includes the definition of authorized transactions, and policies about the authorized transaction. For example, the policies define the value mapping for key fields (such as item number and UM) and the pricing basis. Pricing is typically based on the sales order price at the selling company. Several scenarios illustrated variations in the use of intercompany orders, including a simple inter-company purchase order, the creation of an intercompany purchase order from a sales order (entered in the selling company), and the creation of a direct delivery intercompany purchase order from a sales order (entered in the selling company). Another scenario explained master scheduling across a multicompany supply chain, which involves sequencing the master scheduling task to correctly reflect the hierarchy of companies within the supply chain. Transfers may also involve a sister company using a different AX instance or a different ERP system, which can be supported by the intercompany trade capabilities of the Application Integration Framework within Dynamics AX.

Additional scenarios illustrated other multisite variations, such as centralized engineering, consolidated financial reporting, and subcontracting. The case studies included home furniture outlets, van deliveries, and modeling transfers with production orders.

Chapter 14

Service Order Processing

Many manufacturers and distributors provide value-added services, often with field service personnel or internal service facilities. The most common examples reflect firms that sell and service equipment. Representative equipment includes computer products, home appliances, and industrial equipment. Illustrations within this chapter focus on equipment, with services performed by field service or internal personnel. These personnel will be referred to as service technicians; other titles include field service engineers, account managers, and service specialists.

A service order provides the basic tool for defining requirements and collecting actual consumption of material and resources. Common synonyms include a service work order or service call. Different examples of service orders reflect the differences between field service and internal service facilities.

– Field service examples include equipment installation, de-installations, upgrades, and preventive maintenance. These examples reflect scheduled activity, typically with predefined requirements for material and labor. Ad hoc examples such as equipment repairs or other emergency situations cannot be scheduled in advance, and resource requirements are difficult to anticipate. They often require response times in hours and minutes, and resource consumption gets reported after the fact. These services are performed by field service technicians that travel to the equipment location.
– Internal service examples include equipment repairs on a customer return or service work on a customer-supplied piece of equipment. These services are commonly performed by technicians within a repair department, or within a separate repair depot facility.

The materials required for performing service orders often represent a constraining factor. Too many service orders are not completed the first time because the right parts were not available. Service parts can be a large inventory investment. They tend to be slow moving, have short life cycles and highly variable demand, and high carrying and obsolescence costs. The same parts may also be needed for production or selling directly to customers. The people resources required for performing service orders can also be a constraining factor. These personnel often require advanced skill sets and experience. They cannot be easily hired and trained to meet overload situations, and extended periods of underutilization represents significant expense.

Effective management of service orders can help minimize the constraining factors associated with service parts and people resources, while supporting technicians with their day-to-day tasks. This chapter starts with an explanation of service orders, and covers the following major topics.

1. Service orders
2. Service order considerations
3. Supporting repair activity as part of a service order
4. Service agreements
5. S&OP considerations for service activities

Service orders involve supplemental capabilities for handling repairs. Service orders may also reflect the use of service agreements for defining periodic service activities. Several scenarios describe the use of service orders for equipment installation, repair, and periodic maintenance. The chapter concludes with suggestions about the S&OP game plans for equipment-related services.

Service Orders

Service orders build on the foundation of project information (described in Chapter 12). They can be characterized by their structure and life cycle, and by the types of line items on a service order.

Prerequisites of Project and Item Information   The use of service orders and service agreements builds on project functionality. In particular, each service order typically requires a separate project that defines the sold-to customer. This separate project can reflect an external project (such as time-and-material or fixed price) or an internal project (such as cost). Additional project information includes project categories, authorized employees, and the costs and prices for technician time.

– A project requires definition of project categories to segment activities related to labor hours, material, and expenses. A project category must be assigned to each service order line item.

– A project requires definition of the authorized employees that can report time against the project. An employee must be assigned for technician hours on a service order.

– A project requires definition of costs and prices related to time reported against the project. These costs and prices act as default values for technician hours on a service order.

A service order also requires an invoice project that defines the bill-to customer. One invoice project is typically required for each bill-to customer. Project accounting handles the generation of invoice proposals and invoices after posting a service order as completed.

Items must be defined for materials used on a service order. Items (and their associated bills of material) are also used to support the recording of repair history on a service order. Sales trade agreements define pricing for material on a service order.

Structure and Life Cycle of a Service Order   The basic structure of a service order consists of header and line item information. The service order header identifies the project and related sold-to customer, a delivery date, a brief description, and some optional information about the service to be performed.

❖ *Address for Delivering the Service.* This guides field service calls, but is probably unnecessary for internal repairs.

❖ *Segmentation/description of Service Tasks to Be Performed.* Each service task can have an extended description. Requirements for technicians and materials are associated with a service task.

❖ *Service Object(s) Being Serviced.* This provides some guidance for performing the work, and the basis for tracking repair history by service object.

❖ *Bill of Material for the Service Object.* This provides the basis for tracking changes to the service object, such as component replacement.

The life cycle of a service order consists of three steps represented by an order status (termed *progress status*) automatically updated by the system.

❖ *In-Process.* The order has been created. The system also assigns this status after a cancelled order has been revoked, or when the user reopens an order by adding a line to a cancelled or posted order.

❖ *Cancelled.* This indicates the user has cancelled the order.

❖ *Posted.* This indicates the service order has been posted to the project accounting journal for subsequent invoicing. At least one line item must be signed off as complete in order to allow posting. The system prevents changes to the service order, but additional line items can be entered (thereby reopening the order to an in-process status).

Situations requiring more detailed tracking of order progress (from in-process to posting) employ a second status termed *service stage.* For example, the user-defined service stages may indicate steps in the process, or convey situations such as waiting for parts. At least one service stage must be defined, which may be sufficient for simple situations.

Service order line items define the resources—the people, material and expenses—anticipated to be requirements for performing the service order on-site. They may also be added after the fact to define actual resources used on-site. A line item's life cycle consists of three statuses.

❖ *Created.* The line item has been created. The system also assigns this status after a cancelled order has been revoked.

❖ *Cancelled.* This indicates the user has cancelled the line or order.

❖ *Posted.* This indicates the line item has been posted. The line item must be signed off as complete in order to allow posting. The system prevents changes to the line item.

Types of Line Items on a Service Order   Service order line items define the resources that will be used on-site to perform the service. The line item information varies by type of resource (also termed *transaction type*).

❖ *Hours (Labor).* The line item specifies the technician's employee ID, the project category for hours, and the number of hours. Optional information includes descriptive text about the technician's work, the assignment to a service task and service object, and delivery date considerations.[1]

---

[1] The delivery date considerations include a specified delivery date, along with a time window (expressed as a range of dates) and time constraints (expressed as times for start after and/or end before) for performing the service. The time window provides the basis for grouping together service work that can be performed on the same date.

The user can optionally override the project-related labor rates for cost and price.

❖ *Item (Material).* The line item specifies the item number, quantity, site/warehouse and bin location, and the project category for material that is consumed on-site. Optional information includes an extended description of the item, the assignment to a service task and service object, and delivery date considerations.

Other material may be shipped to the customer site (from a site/warehouse), or shipped via a direct delivery purchase order. These materials (termed *item requirements*) must be defined separately. The shipment, or the purchase order invoice for the direct delivery, results in charges to the project. They are not entered as line items.

❖ *Expense.* The line item specifies the quantity, the project category for expenses, descriptive information, and the associated cost and price per unit. Optional information includes the assignment to a service task and service object.

Scenario 1: Service Order for Equipment Installation

A typical service order for equipment installation at a customer site is shown in Figure 14.1. The service order requires address information for the field service call. The user assigns a predefined service object (Equipment XYZ) to the service order, and attaches a copy of a predefined template BOM reflecting the equipment's bill of material. This copied information (termed the Service BOM) enables a technician to easily review product structure information should the installation require replacement parts. The user also assigns three service tasks (prep, install, and test) to the service order, and prepares detailed notes about each task. Finally, the user creates service order line items that identify the installation requirements for materials and the technician's time. Each line item can be associated with the relevant service task. Note that the installation requires two types of technicians (mechanical and electrical), and the line items are assigned to employees Joe and Sue.

The technicians report actual consumption of materials and time against the service order line items. If needed, the technician can specify additional item requirements that need to be shipped to the customer.

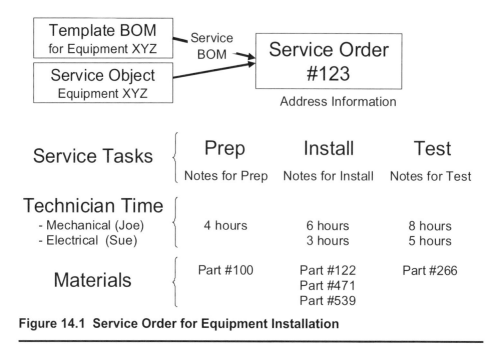

Figure 14.1 Service Order for Equipment Installation

Service Order Considerations

Variations to the basic service order process reflect different ways of doing business with customers and different internal procedures. These variations include shipping material to the customer, identifying the service object(s) and service tasks, progress tracking of service orders, defining response time requirements, and coordinating service orders via the dispatch board.

Material as a Service Order Line Item   This line item represents material consumed during the service order. It can be entered manually, or automatically created when recording repair history (such as recording a component replacement). The sales price reflects sales trade agreement information (if defined) or the item's standard sales price. It can also be calculated for a manufactured item using an order-specific BOM calculation; this calculated price can then be transferred to the line item. Chapter 5 explained order-specific BOM calculations.

Item Requirements for Shipping Material to the Customer
Material may be shipped to the customer site (from a site/warehouse), or shipped (from a vendor) via a direct delivery purchase order. These materials

(termed *item requirements*) must be defined separately on a service order. The shipment, or the purchase order invoice for the direct delivery, results in charges to the project. They are not entered as line items.

A project-specific sales order is created for item requirements; it contains a line item for each item requirement. The project-specific sales order consumes project-specific forecasts for material (if applicable). The project-specific sales order also acts as the starting point for creating a direct delivery purchase order.

Service Objects on a Service Order   A service object identifies an item that will be serviced. With equipment, for example, it could represent an item, a specific serial number of an item, a custom product configuration, a group of equipment, or a type of equipment. It can optionally refer to an item number. By defining a service object beforehand, it can be specified for the service order. One or more service objects can be specified on an order. Individual line items can optionally refer to a specified service object, thereby providing direction for the technician about what to work on. A service object must be specified in order to support repair functionality. The system automatically tracks all service orders performed on a service object.

Bill of material information about a service object is defined separately, first as a *template BOM*, which can then be attached to a service object specified on a service order. This is termed the *service BOM* after it has been attached. See the next section of this chapter on supporting repair activity as part of a service order for further explanation about template BOMs and service BOMs.

Using Service Tasks on a Service Order   Service tasks provide descriptive information about the work that needs to be performed. They also provide a method for segmenting work, especially with more complex service work.

❖ *Using Service Tasks for Descriptive Information.* Each service task has two sets of extended text for describing the work to be performed: one set for internal purposes and one for external purposes. The internal notes can provide comprehensive work instructions, whereas external notes can assist customer understanding. Many situations can employ just one set of notes.

❖ *Using Service Tasks for Segmentation of Complex Service Work.* An additional purpose of user-defined service tasks is to segment more complex service work into major phases (such as inspection, teardown, and rebuild for repairing an item). A simple service order may employ a single service task or none at all.

Communicating Service Requirements via Printed Paperwork A primary method for communicating service requirements consists of the printed paperwork for a service order. The standard paperwork is termed the *work description* for internal purposes, and the *work receipt* for external purposes. Effective internal paperwork helps deliver the service; it also acts as a turnaround document for reporting actual resource consumption. Effective external paperwork clarifies the expected services (beforehand) and the actual services delivered (afterward). Most firms will customize their paperwork, and several suggestions build on the standard information to make paperwork more effective

❖ *Standard Information.* The standard information consists of the service order line items in three groups: technicians, materials, and expenses. The materials group includes the additional item requirements being shipped to the site. Each line item indicates the assigned service object (thereby directing work to the right object) and service task (thereby grouping the line items into relevant phases). Extended text can be entered for the technician and material line items, but this typically reflects supplemental topics not covered in the descriptive information for service tasks.

❖ *Service Tasks.* Each service task has two sets of extended text for describing the work to be performed, as described earlier. Many situations can employ just one set, or just the extended text associated with technician and material line items. Service tasks also provide segmentation for complex service work.

❖ *Documents.* Documents can be attached to the service order header and line items, and incorporated into customized paperwork. For example, the documents could include schematics, installation guides, or user manuals.

❖ *Turnaround Document for Reporting Actuals.* The printed paperwork often provides the basis for hand-written notes about actual hours and materials, which the technician (or some other person) uses for computer data entry.

Create Service Order Lines via the Copy Function Copying provides a short-cut approach to creating service order line items. Line items can be copied from another service order (or service agreement), with an option to copy the information about service objects and service tasks. They can also be copied from a template service agreement, with the additional capability to copy selected line items from the template. The copy function adds line items to existing line items.

Detailed Progress Tracking of Service Orders Some situations require more detailed tracking of order progress between service order creation and completion. A separate status (termed *service stage*) can help track progress through user-defined stages. The stages may represent steps in the process, or situations such as waiting for parts. The user manually initiates an update to the next (or previous) stage, and the system prompts the user to select the desired stage (and optionally indicate a reason code).

Policies for each service stage determine whether order information can be modified or deleted, whether the user can cancel or post the order, and whether a reason code must be entered for changing the stage. For example, the reason code could indicate the reason for a cancelled service order. The company-wide stages and their policies are defined as part of setup information. At least one service stage must be defined, which may be sufficient for simple situations.

Reporting Actual Labor and Materials for a Service Order Consumption of actual labor and on-site materials is reported by posting the service order. The user must sign-off completion of one or more line items, or the entire service order, before it can be posted. The sign-off consists of a checkbox. The line items and quantities represent actual usage, so the user may need to update previously entered information prior to posting. Posting updates the project associated with the service order, and provides the basis for invoice proposals and invoices.

Other material may be shipped to the site (from a site/warehouse), or shipped (from a vendor) via a direct delivery purchase order. These item requirements are defined separately on a service order. The shipment, or the purchase order invoice (for the direct delivery), results in charges to the project. They are not entered as line items and posted.

Handling Service Orders Through the Enterprise Portal The Enterprise Portal provides access to service order information for service technicians. With this portal (termed the technician portal), service technicians can view and maintain their service orders and the related service object(s), tasks, and repair lines. They can also create new service orders, report actual labor, material, and expenses, and sign off a completed service order line item.

The Enterprise Portal also provides 24/7 customer access to service order and service agreement information. With this portal (termed the customer portal), the customer can view information about their planned and requested service orders, and initiate a request for a new service order. The customer's requested service order must then be transferred to a normal service order.

Defining Response Time Requirements via Service Level Agreements Service-oriented operations frequently have a response time requirement, such as responding within 4 hours after creation of a service order. A service level agreement defines the response time requirement, which can be expressed in minutes, hours, or days. A user-defined service level agreement is required for each response time requirement; it can then be assigned to a service agreement or a service order. Scheduling a service order beyond the required response time will result in a warning. Detailed reporting of actual time and task completion provides the basis for tracking performance against the response time requirement.

Coordinating Service Orders via the Dispatch Board A dispatch board provides the primary tool for coordinating technician time to perform service orders. The displayed information reflects in-process service orders with a line item defining labor requirements, an assigned technician, and an assigned service task.[2] The displayed information also reflects user-defined dispatch teams, with technicians assigned to a dispatch team in the employee master information.

The dispatch board provides a tabular format and a Gantt chart format for viewing service orders with labor requirements within a specified date interval. Service order information can be filtered and sorted in the tabular format, such as sorting based on the service date/time, service task, customer, or priority level. The Gantt chart format displays dispatch teams (and associated technicians) on the Y-axis, the date interval on the X-axis, and the current assignment of service orders. It supports drag-and-drop assignment of the technician and date/time; it also supports drill-downs about the related service order and service task. Both formats support the concept of dis-

---

[2] Service orders with a planned status are not displayed on the dispatch board; change the status to in-process to display the information. In addition, the dispatch board does not display time requirements unless the service order line item has an assigned task and technician. Note that a service task is also termed a service activity.

patching a service order, where a dispatched status indicates confirmation of the scheduled date/time and technician.

The dispatch board supports several functions for coordinating technician time to perform service orders, as illustrated below.

- Assign (or reassign) a preferred technician to a service order.
- Assign (or reschedule) a preferred date/time for performing the service order.
- Assign a dispatched status to indicate confirmation of the assigned technician and date/time to the service order.
- View undispatched service orders, and assign a dispatched status.
- View service level agreement information about required response time, and provide a warning when the assigned date/time is greater than the required response time.
- View the priority of a service order, with color coding (such as red, yellow, green) for priorities of high, normal, and low.
- Reverse changes to the dispatch board prior to saving the changes.
- Save changes to the dispatch board, which automatically updates service orders with the assigned technician and service date/time.

Management Reports about Service Orders   The standard reports include a customer schedule, a progress report, a margin report, and summarized data about hours consumption and order count. For example, the customer schedule coordinates activity by identifying the service orders being performed at a customer, along with the progress status, delivery date and time constraints, and associated service agreement (if applicable). The service order progress report provides similar information about each service order, with additional information about the service stage and reason codes. A service order margin report provides a summary of the sales, costs, and margin; it also provides a detailed breakout by line item.

Supporting Repair Activity as Part of a Service Order

Service orders are often used for coordinating and reporting repair activities. To support repair activities, you must add a repair line item (to the service order) to specify the service object being repaired. Additional information about the repair line item can help track repair progress, capture detailed information about the symptom/diagnosis/resolution, or track repair history against components.

A typical service order for equipment repair by internal technicians is shown in Figure 14.2. The user assigns a predefined service object (Equipment Type ABC) to the service order, and attaches a copy of a predefined template BOM reflecting the commonly replaced components on this type of equipment. This copied information (termed the Service BOM) enables a technician to easily identify component replacements, thereby creating repair history information. The user also assigns two service tasks (diagnosis and repair) to the service order.

The user initially creates a single line item for technician time to diagnose the problem. Additional items represent the estimated requirements to repair the equipment. The user can automatically add line items by using the service BOM to indicate the need for a replacement part. The user also creates a repair line for reporting information about the symptoms and diagnosis of the problem. After completing the repair, the user reports the actual consumption of time and material, and the problem resolution. This example depicts actual consumption of a part (Part #955) that was not included in the estimate.

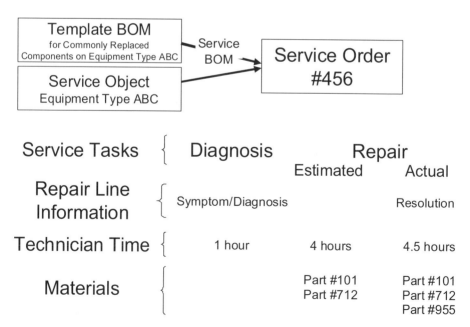

Figure 14.2 Service Order for Equipment Repair

The estimated requirements provide the basis for an estimated cost (which may require customer approval before proceeding); actual consumption provides the basis for actual costs. The system tracks repair history when the user reports the replacement parts against the service BOM; it also tracks information about the symptom/diagnosis/resolution.

Detailed Progress Tracking of Repair Activity   Some situations require more detailed tracking of repair activity. A separate status (termed *repair stage*) can help track progress through predefined stages. The stages may represent steps in the process, or situations such as parts ordered for shipment to customer. The user manually assigns and updates a repair stage to each service object being repaired. Repair stages are not required, and a repair stage does not have to be entered. The company-wide repair stages are defined as part of setup information.

Capturing Detailed Information about the Nature of Repairs
Basic information about repair history includes the service orders performed on the service object and some descriptive text. A structured approach can provide additional information about the nature of each repair, thereby assisting efforts to improve product design and customer service. Dynamics AX includes one structured approach using predefined categories to describe a repair problem in terms of the symptom, diagnosis, and resolution. The information reflects the two viewpoints of the customer and the technician.

❖ *Customer Viewpoint of the Problem.* This viewpoint consists of the general symptom (termed Symptom Area) and the specific problem (termed Symptom Code), along with information about when the problem occurs (termed the Condition) and descriptive text. As a simplistic example involving a car repair, the customer describes the general problem as the "engine will not start" and the specific problem as "it makes a clicking noise" under the conditions of "cold weather."

❖ *Technician Viewpoint of the Problem.* This viewpoint consists of the general diagnosis (termed Diagnosis Area) and specific diagnosis (termed Diagnosis Code), along with the suggested or actual resolution (termed Resolution). Continuing with the car example, the general diagnosis would the electrical system, the specific diagnosis is a dead battery, and the resolution would be to replace the battery. The technician can optionally enter a note with unlimited descriptive text about the repair.

A service object(s) must be assigned to the service order, and a repair line created, in order to report a problem. Information can be entered piecemeal or all at once. Definition of the predefined categories (for the symptom codes, resolutions, and so forth) typically requires expertise in the problem domain, thereby minimizing confusion when reporting a problem and when analyzing repair history.

Product Structure Data (Template BOMs) about Items to Be Repaired   The template BOMs represent a repository of product structure data about products that might be repaired, and each template BOM has a unique identifier. For example, a template BOM could reflect the bill for an item, a specific serial number of an item, or a simple list of commonly repaired components. A template BOM identifier (and its initial bill of material) can be created four different ways.

- Copy an item's BOM version .
- Copy the order-dependent bill for a finished production order. Information about serial or batch numbers is not copied.
- Copy an existing template BOM.
- Manual. Nothing is copied.

After creating the Template BOM, the component information can be manually maintained. Add components using drag-and-drop capabilities from item master information; these capabilities reflect the BOM Designer described in Chapter 3. A distribution item, for example, would require manual maintenance to define the components in its template BOM. A standard manufactured product would use the copy of the item's BOM version as the basis for components. A custom manufactured product would probably use the production order as the basis for components.

A template BOM provides the baseline for creating a separate service BOM; this service BOM can then be used to record repair history against the components. The system does not automatically update the template BOM based on changes to the service BOM.

Tracking Repair History Against Components Using the Service BOM   Once the Template BOMs have been defined, the definition of a service BOM consists of two steps: assign the service object to the service order and attach a template BOM. This creates a separate bill of material that can be maintained to track repair history against components. The system automatically tracks the repair history based on several changes to the components.

- Replace component with same item (via edit function), and optionally add the material usage as a service order line item.
- Change the component quantity (via edit), and optionally add the material usage as a service order line item due to an increase in quantity.
- Add a component (via drag-and-drop from the item master information), and optionally add the material usage as a service order line item.
- Delete a component.

When reporting a change to a component, the user can optionally generate service order line items to reflect material usage such as a replacement. Manual additions of service order line items do not update the repair history.

The two steps—assign a service object and attach a template BOM—must be repeated for each service order that repairs the item. Hence, the separate service BOM does not represent the cumulative changes caused by multiple service orders. For some situations, a suggested approach treats the service BOM (and associated template BOM) as a tickler list of commonly repaired components, thereby providing a prompt for technicians and a shortcut for reporting component changes. The repair history information gives a better idea about what components require replacement, and about potential design changes to reduce the amount of repairs.

Management Reports about Repair History The three aspects of supplemental functionality—repair progress, symptom/diagnosis/resolution information, and component changes in the service BOM—provide the basis for several management reports. These reports include repair history by service object, by service BOM and by technician (with details about each service order); and the frequency distribution of resolution by symptom and by diagnosis.

Service Agreements

A service agreement provides the basis for generating service orders, especially for periodic services. It specifies contractual details and a time period duration, along with the objects to be serviced and the tasks to be performed.[3] The information in a service agreement closely mirrors that in a service order, with additional information about how to generate service orders. We'll start with the structure of a service agreement, since this provides the basis for creating service orders.

Structure of a Service Agreement The basic structure of a service agreement consists of a header and line item information. The header identifies the project and a brief description, and five additional types of information about the service to be performed. The first three types of information (listed below) act as defaults for service orders created from the service agreement; the last two items provide constraints on creating service orders.

- Segmentation/description of tasks to be performed.
- Service object(s) being serviced.
- Bill of material for a service object. The user can manually maintain this service BOM after attaching a template BOM to the service object.
- Start and end dates. These constrain the dates for service orders generated from the agreement, or attached to the agreement after the fact.
- Grouping basis. This policy determines how line items will be combined into service orders generated from an agreement. For example, grouping can be based on line items for the same service object, task, or technician.

A service agreement has only two statuses: active and suspended. Service orders cannot be generated from or attached to a suspended agreement.

Service agreement line items define the resources—the people, material, and expenses—anticipated to be requirements for performing the service order on-site. A previous section covered the types of line items and the required information. A service agreement specifies additional line item information about a service interval and time window. The system uses this information when automatically creating service orders for the service agreement.

---

[3] A service agreement wizard can also be used to create a service agreement.

❖ *Service Interval.* The user-defined service intervals indicate when to perform the line item (daily, weekly, monthly, annually) and the frequency
(such as once per month).

❖ *Time Window.* This indicates the acceptable range of delivery dates, with
predefined values for the possible range. For example, the range could
be 1 day, 14 days, or within a month.

A service agreement line item has only two statuses: active and stopped.
Service orders will not be generated for a stopped line item.

Automatically Creating Service Orders from a Service Agreement

Service orders can be created from a service agreement. When using the
Create Service Orders function, the dialogue provides user options about the
time period (expressed as from and to dates), desired transaction types, and
selection criteria. It is typically performed for the entire service agreement.[4]
It generates service orders based on the time intervals for line items, and the
agreement's grouping basis for line items. For example, let's say the line
items represent requirements to perform monthly preventive maintenance on
a piece of equipment. All line items have monthly time intervals and the
same service object, and the service object acts as the grouping basis. If the
user specifies a six month time period, the system will generate six service
orders. The user must specify address information on the created orders
when they reflect field service calls.

The Create Service Orders function can be performed multiple times for
a service agreement, such as generating orders for different time periods.
The system understands when service orders have been generated, so that it
does not create additional orders (unless the orders have been deleted).

Using a Template Service Agreement

A template service agreement
provides a short-cut approach for copying line items into a service agreement
or service order. To create a template, start by creating a service agreement
and its line items, and then designate it as a template.[5]

For example, let's say we have multiple pieces of equipment requiring
monthly preventive maintenance, and we want a service agreement for each

---

[4] The create service orders function can also be performed for a single line item on a service agreement. For
example, this may represent sending a single technician to the site for a service call (per the service agreement).

[5] Assign a service template group to the service agreement in order to designate it as a template. The service
template groups are user defined. They typically reflect categories of service, such types of installations or field
service.

piece of equipment. A template would define the line items representing requirements to perform this preventive maintenance. We can then copy these line items into each service agreement, and add information about the service object.

Scenario 3: Service Agreement for Periodic Equipment Maintenance

A service agreement contains additional information about the service interval for each line item, so that service orders can be created automatically. This example builds on the first scenario, since the same piece of installed equipment requires periodic preventive maintenance. Figure 14.3 illustrates the service agreement line items for technician time (three line items) and material (five line items). Each line item has a specified service interval of monthly, quarterly, or annual. The service tasks (and related notes) reflect the names of the different intervals. Each line item is also associated with a service task and the service object.

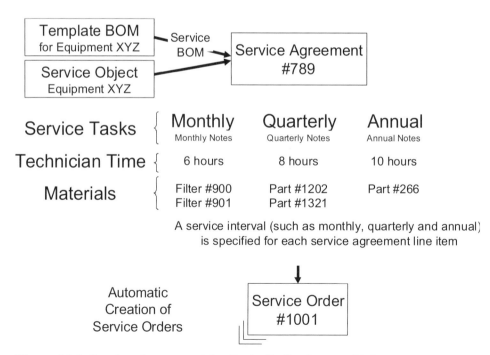

Figure 14.3 Service Agreement for Periodic Equipment Maintenance

Automatic creation of service orders for a one year time period would result in 12 monthly service orders. Using a grouping basis of service object, the monthly service orders would include relevant line items with quarterly and annual service intervals. The service tasks provide descriptive notes and segmentation about the monthly, quarterly, and annual activities.

A technician may report repair activities during a preventive maintenance call. In this case, the technician should report the replacement parts against the service BOM to build a repair history. The technician could also create a repair line for reporting information about the symptoms/diagnosis/resolution of the problem.

S&OP Considerations for Service Activities

The basic coordination tools for performing service orders consist of a customer schedule and a technician schedule. Anticipating the material and labor requirements will help minimize constraints while supporting technicians in their day-to-day tasks of performing the service orders. Anticipated requirements reflect a key aspect of the S&OP game plans for service activities. Several suggestions can guide the development of S&OP game plans.

Separate Warehouse for Service Parts This approach supports replenishment based on site/warehouse-specific coverage data, and possible use of site/warehouse-specific sales price trade agreements. It supports warehouse management practices that pertain to services and service parts, such as handling customer returns to the repair department, communication of shipping requirements, and default bin locations. Other unique requirements may include differentiation of new/used/repaired parts and customer-supplied parts.

Service parts inventory is stocked in delivery vans in some situations. These vans could be viewed as separate bin locations or separate warehouses.

Visibility of Service Order Requirements Planning calculations do not recognize the service order line items (for material and technician hours) as demands. This suggests a need for customization (as in Case 69), or an alternate approach to anticipated demands.

Anticipating Material Requirements Replenishment based on min/max quantities represents one approach to anticipate demands. In addition, the safety stock journal uses historical usage data to automatically calculate minimum quantities to meet a desired customer service level (such as 95%). Variable min/max quantities can support different demand patterns. Chapter 2 described this planning data for purchased material.

An alternative approach employs purchase forecasts to anticipate service order requirements. A planning bill (aka item allocation key) represents an additional tool, since it can reflect the mix percentages of anticipated parts. With equipment repairs, for example, the purchase forecast for the planning bill represents the number of units in the field that need to be repaired. Chapter 6 described the use of purchase forecasts and a planning bill.

Case Studies

Case 77: Planning Calculations for Service Parts The All-and-Anything company wanted to improve planning for their service parts inventory. They currently use a separate warehouse for service parts inventory, with items replenished based on min/max quantities. Most of the service parts demand stemmed from scheduled service orders with predefined material requirements (and technician requirements). They wanted to customize the planning calculations so that service order requirements were recognized as demands for material and work center capacity. This would provide visibility for stocking needed parts, and help anticipate overloaded periods for technicians.

Case 78: Repair Department The Consumer Products company had an internal repair department that charged customers on a time-and-material basis for repairing electrical products. Most products were received via returned item sales orders, and a repair technician established a service order (and a related project) for diagnosing and repairing each returned product. Repairs were undertaken after getting customer approval for the estimated repair costs, where the diagnosis defined the anticipated repair requirements (for material and technician time) as service order line items. Actual consumption was reported against the service order. Customers were billed through project invoicing for the diagnosis and repair costs.

Case 79: Installation Services The Distribution company sold industrial equipment and provided field services for subsequent installations. Each installation required a service order (and a related external project) that defined the service object and anticipated requirements for material, technician time, and expenses. Most installation requirements could be predefined via a template service agreement, and these were copied into the service order. The technician obtained the materials before going to the customer, and then reported actual consumption after making the field service call. Many calls identified a need for shipping additional materials to the customer, as defined in the item requirements for the service order.

Case 80: Equipment Maintenance Service The Equipment company sold industrial and medical equipment, and provided field services for performing periodic preventive maintenance. A service agreement defined each service object and service BOM. It also defined the anticipated requirements for material and technician time, along with the associated service interval information. For example, monthly requirements included filters and calibration tests. Each field service call often resulted in repairs, so that the technician reported the symptom/diagnosis/resolution information as well as the component changes against the service BOM. This repair history information provided feedback for improving the preventive maintenance efforts.

Executive Summary

Many manufacturers and distributors provide field services and/or internal service facilities. With equipment, for example, the field service personnel perform equipment installation, de-installations, upgrades, preventive maintenance, and emergency maintenance. Internal service examples include equipment repairs on a customer return or service work on a customer-supplied piece of equipment. A service order acts as the basic tool for defining resource requirements and reporting actual consumption of material, time, and expenses. A service agreement defines resource requirements with periodic service intervals (such as weekly or monthly maintenance intervals), which can be used to automatically create service orders to perform the periodic activities. The use of service orders and service agreements builds on project functionality for costing purposes, and for the purpose of invoicing external service work.

A service order typically identifies the equipment being serviced (aka the service object), and descriptive information about the needed services (aka service tasks). It also identifies the anticipated resource requirements—for material, technician time, and expense—for performing each service task on each service object. Each requirement is expressed as a service order line item, along with a specified project category. The project category for technician time, for example, determines an hourly cost and sales price; a related policy determines whether the transaction will be chargeable. These requirements are reflected in printed paperwork for internal and external purposes. Effective internal paperwork helps deliver the service; it also acts as a turnaround document for reporting actual resource consumption. Effective external paperwork clarifies the expected services (beforehand) and the actual services delivered (afterward). A dispatch board helps coordinate technician assignment and scheduling for service orders.

Material must be shipped to the customer site in some cases, which requires definition of a project-specific sales order to communicate and handle the shipping activities. This project-specific sales order can optionally generate a direct-delivery purchase order, so that material is shipped directly from a vendor.

Actual consumption of resources is reported against the service order line items. Technician sign-off for completed work provides the basis for invoice proposals and invoices. Service technicians can optionally use the Enterprise Portal to view and maintain their service orders, report actual resource consumption, and sign off a completed service order line item.

A service agreement specifies contractual details and periodic requirements, and provides the basis for generating service orders. The information closely mirrors that in a service order, such as the definition of resource requirements, service objects and service tasks. Additional information defines when to perform the periodic service.

The chapter included three scenarios illustrating the use of service orders for installing equipment by field service personnel, for repairing equipment by an internal repair department, and for managing periodic equipment maintenance with service agreements. Case studies covered additional illustrations, such as planning calculations for service parts.

Chapter 15

Summary

The starting point of this book is that supply chain management requires effective use of an integrated ERP system. Its central theme focuses on using Microsoft Dynamics AX for managing supply chain activities in manufacturing and distribution firms. Its target audience includes those individuals implementing or considering Microsoft Dynamics AX as their ERP system as well as those providing related services. The explanations address an overall understanding of how the system fits together to run a business, expressed in generally accepted terminology. This mental framework—in combination with hands-on experience, user documentation, and training courseware—can accelerate the learning process, and an overall understanding leads to more effective system usage.

Usage of any ERP system—including Microsoft Dynamics AX—is shaped by many design factors that make it easier (or harder) to learn and use. Many of the design factors related to Microsoft Dynamics AX have been covered in previous chapters. This final chapter summarizes the design factors shaping system usage. They are segmented into design factors related to the user interface, customization, system usage in distribution and manufacturing, and integration with other applications.

Design Factors Related to the User Interface

The user interface reflects a certified Windows application. It provides consistency across all screens that assist ease-of-learning and ease-of use. A few illustrations are provided below.

Navigation   Menus provide one means to navigate through Dynamics AX, and menus can be tailored. The system supports navigation via the mouse and short-cut keys. The user can also directly access information in other parts of the system (without using the menus) via the *go to main table* functionality.

Direct Access to Main Table Information Directly accessing the main table for a given field eliminates the need to navigate through the menus. During item master maintenance, for example, the user could access the main table for the Item Group field to create a new value. During purchase order entry, for example, the user can access the vendor master information.

Find and Filter Find capabilities can be based on any string of embedded text in a record identifier or its attributes. A filter limits the displayed records based on values in one or more fields, with sorting based on any field. The user can browse forward and backward through the subset. Filtering logic includes equal to, different from, greater than, less than, intervals, and wild cards.

Design Factors Related to Customization

Many firms need to tailor standardized functionality to model their distinctive business processes. The foundation technology for Dynamics AX makes customizations easier. For example, it integrates with anything that works in the Microsoft environment, such as Word, Excel, Outlook, telephony, and bar-code scanner applications. Its object-oriented technology provides a framework that significantly reduces the cost and complexity associated with custom programming and development. Dynamics AX includes an out-of-the-box Web portal interface. These represent unique capabilities that minimize customization efforts.

A critical issue with customization involves the ability to stay within the upgrade path for new releases of the ERP package. With other ERP packages, upgrading the customizations often becomes prohibitively expensive (or even impossible) so that the firm cannot take advantage of the new releases. There are many benefits to staying up-to-date with software releases. These benefits include staying abreast of technology developments, functionality enhancements, and leveraging the R&D expenditures by the software vendor and independent vendors. Dynamics AX provides several tools that simplify the upgrade process for customizations so that firms can stay within the upgrade path at minimal incremental cost. The following subsections describe some of the tools for customizing Dynamics AX and for upgrading customizations to new releases.

Isolating the Impact of Customizations via Version Layer Technology The version layers isolate the impact of customizations, making upgrades much easier and less costly. The layers correspond to the responsibility for code maintenance. For example, the first layer reflects core system development for the standard version maintained by Microsoft. Another layer reflects VAR customizations with responsibility by the VAR for code maintenance.

The significance of layer technology can be more easily understood in the context of an example. In this example, the company implementing Dynamics AX as its ERP system also installed a certified solution (the second layer) developed by an independent software vendor. The Microsoft partner providing implementation assistance modified this certified solution (via the sixth layer) and performed other customer-specific modifications (via the seventh layer). When upgrading Dynamics AX to a new release, the system identifies the differences between the current and new releases (at each layer). It isolates only those customizations requiring an upgrade, and each layer can be upgraded separately. This layered approach to program separation helps minimize the effort and costs for upgrading customizations.

Customizing Field Size via Extended Data Types The size of a field—such as the length of the item number or customer number—can be easily changed via extended data type functionality, and automatically updated throughout the system.

Customizations via an Integrated Development Environment The application software and development tools are tightly coupled together in an integrated development environment called MorphX. This approach eliminates the need (and costs) for additional development tools. It provides the advantages of a centralized code repository with the advantages of distributed applications using client server computing. For example, it eliminates the porting requirement to roll out synchronized changes to all production servers or client workstations. It also avoids integration issues such as conflicting software settings at individual workstations. By making changes easy, it can help improve the agility and flexibility of deploying IT applications.

Customizing Forms An end-user can tailor screen layout by selectively hiding, showing, and sorting fields, especially the display of applicable item and inventory dimensions. This provides a simple approach to customizing screen layout and the system remembers each end-user's preferences.

An end-user can also easily tailor printed documents such as a sales order confirmation using the form setup policies. The form setup policies for a sales order invoice, for example, can indicate printing of the customer item information, batch/serial numbers, document notes, and language-specific descriptions, and the system supports a separate invoice numbering sequence for each customer.

A Forms Designer supports the customization of forms (screens), such as changing field labels, rearranging fields on tabs, cursor movement between fields, and additional fields. The additional fields can represent changes to the Dynamics AX database or an auxiliary database. A Menu Designer supports the customization of menus.

Customizing Reports and OLAP   The development of customized reports typically represents a significant proportion of the initial and on-going implementation efforts. In addition, decision makers often require flexible ad hoc access to management information—preferably without the need for IT expertise and without the delays typically associated with IT's involvement in customized reports. The built-in report writer capabilities can simplify the development of customized reports, especially by anyone with skills analogous to an Excel power user. It includes a report writer wizard to help construct a customized report. The built-in OLAP (on-line analytical processing) capabilities can often eliminate the need for fixed reports, since they provide a data warehouse for supporting interactive information analysis.

Inherent Thin Client and the Application Object Server   The Application Object Server (AOS) within Dynamics AX provides inherent thin client functionality. A thin client engine eliminates the need for terminal emulation software and the associated hardware. It supports selective execution between the server and client workstation, and embedded data caching techniques to minimize bandwidth utilization for the telecommunication link. A workstation only requires one client software installation, and can be configured to operate as a thin client (via an AOS connection) or a fat client directly connected to the database. In addition, the AOS can operate as a clustered server to support redundancy without requiring extensive hardware infrastructure.

System Usage in Distribution Environments

The standardized functionality in an ERP system shapes its usage. Efforts to use the system should be guided by (rather than run counter to) its fundamental underlying design. This section reviews the major design factors affecting system usage in a distribution environment; the next section covers factors affecting usage in manufacturing environments. A distribution environment typically involves the purchase and sale of stocked material items. Major factors shaping system usage include item definition, variations in sales and purchasing, coordination of supply chain activities, warehousing, and multisite operations.

Item Definition The identifier for a purchased material item consists of an item number, or an item number and variant code for items with size/color variations. The system supports alternative identifiers for supporting sales, purchasing, bar coding, intercompany orders, and electronic documents. Other item information includes the following:

- Multiple units of measure for sales and purchasing purposes
- Extended text and documents such as Word files and images
- Physical dimensions such as weight and volume that can be used to calculate totals for a sales or purchase order
- Financial dimensions for business analytics purposes
- Quality management policies for enforcing batch and/or serial tracking, for enforcing inspection of received material, and for performing quality tests

Item Costing An item's cost provide the basis for valuing inventory transactions, and can be based on a standard costing or an actual costing method such as FIFO, LIFO, and weighted average. Miscellaneous charges such as freight or handling fees can be assigned to purchase orders and sales orders. An item's standard costs are site-specific, while an actual cost item can have company-wide or site/warehouse-specific costs, or even batch- and serial-specific costs.

Item Replenishment Item planning data provides the basis for item replenishment at sites, warehouses, and even bins. The basic replenishment methods include min/max, period lot size, and order driven. With the min/max method, the item's minimum and maximum quantities can be fixed or variable, where a variable quantity can be specified for user-defined time periods such as months. The minimum can also be automatically calculated based on historical usage. With the other replenishment methods, the minimum quantity represents the safety stock requirement. Order quantity modifiers (minimum, maximum, multiple) apply to the suggested order quantity.

The suggested vendor for a planned purchase order can reflect a company-wide preference, a site/warehouse-specific preference, or planning logic based on the lowest price or delivery lead time defined in the item's purchase price trade agreements. An item's replenishment method can also be based on manual planning.

Customers Different types of customers include one-time customers, intercompany customers, and customers requiring foreign currency and language-specific text.

Sales Orders A standard sales order defines actual demand for an item. Other types of sales orders include blanket sales orders that can be used to create standard sales orders. Sales orders can reflect intercompany sales, or customer self service via the Enterprise Portal. Sales order variations in distribution environments include

- Items shipped from stock
- Non-inventoried items such as services and fixed assets
- An alternate item automatically substituted for an ordered line item
- Purchased items reflecting a special order or drop shipment
- Project-specific sales orders
- Customer returns and RMAs, including the repair and/or replacement of the returned item
- Service orders to install the sold item, or service agreements for maintaining the sold item

Other sales order variations apply to distributors with light manufacturing, including

- Kits that are priced and sold as a complete item or as separate components
- Manufactured items built to order, with a production order linked to the sales order
- Manufactured items configured to order using option selection or a rules-based configurator, with a production order linked to the sales order

Sales quotations can be defined and converted into sales orders. In defining the pipeline of expected business, they can optionally act as demands based on their win-probability.

Sales order reservations can be manually or automatically assigned, with optional reservation of scheduled receipts.

Sales order delivery promises reflect available-to-promise or capable-to-promise logic, as well as applicable calendars.

Sales Pricing   An item's standard sales price and UM represent one approach to a predefined sales price. The standard sales price can be manually entered or automatically calculated. Automatic calculation can be based on a markup or contribution percentage applied to the item's inventory cost or purchase price. Other alternatives to sales pricing include the use of source documents such as sales quotations or blanket orders to create a sales order, and the use of sales trade agreements.

With a sales price trade agreement, for example, an item's sales price can reflect different factors such as customer type, unit of measure, quantity breakpoints, and date effectivities, as well as higher prices or a surcharge for shorter delivery lead times. Discounts off an item's sales price can be defined in sales trade agreements that reflect these same factors. Discounts can also apply to the total order quantity of multiple line items (such as items within a product group) and to the total order value. Other forms of rules-based sales pricing include supplementary items. Sales trade agreements can reflect company-wide or site/warehouse-specific sales prices for an item.

Sales Forecasts   Replenishment of stocked material can be based on sales forecasts. You can define multiple sets of forecast data, and also multi-level forecast models such as regional forecasts that roll-up to a company-wide forecast. An item's sales forecast can be expressed as individual quantities and dates, as a repeating pattern of a fixed or variable quantity per period (such as monthly), or as an item group forecast (aka planning bill) that spreads out a total quantity across several items based on mix percentages. An item's sales forecast can also be imported from spreadsheets or a statistical forecasting package. The system supports forecast consumption logic to avoid doubled-up requirements.

Sales Commissions   The system supports commission calculations for one or more sales reps, thereby supporting split commissions. The commission amount reflects a specified commission percentage times the sales order value (such as the gross revenue or net margin). Commissions can vary by type of customer, product, and date effectivity, with calculation after posting a sales order invoice.

Sales Invoicing The system supports a separate invoice for each sales order shipment, and also a summarized invoice for multiple sales order shipments. It also handles different payment terms, payment schedules, and payment fees.

Sales Analysis The system supports standard and ad hoc sales analyses. For example, the standard reports include totals for individual orders, customers, and items as well as sales analysis by customer and item. Other sales analysis approaches include business analytics, pivot tables, and data warehouses.

Vendors Different types of vendors include one-time vendors, intercompany vendors, and vendors requiring foreign currency or language-specific text.

Purchase Orders A standard purchase order defines a scheduled receipt for an item. Other types of purchase orders include quotations and blanket orders that can be used to create standard purchase orders. Additional types handle vendor returns, drafts, and subscriptions. Purchase orders can reflect intercompany purchases and purchases from one-time vendors. Several variations apply to purchase orders in distribution environments.

- Purchase of stocked material
- Purchased item reflecting a special order or drop shipment
- Purchase requisitions and approval process
- Request for quotes (RFQs)
- Project-specific purchase orders, requisitions, and RFQs
- Purchase of an expense item, fixed asset, or non-inventoried item
- Purchase of an outside operation linked to a production order
- Purchase of a kit that is priced and purchased as a complete item or as separate components
- Purchase of an item linked to a production order requirement
- Purchase of an item that must be configured to order

Purchase Prices An item's standard purchase price and UM represent one approach to a predefined purchase price. It can be manually entered or automatically calculated based on the last purchase invoice. Other alternatives to an item's purchase price include the use of source documents such a purchase requisition or blanket purchase orders, and the use of purchase trade agreements. With a purchase price trade agreement, for example, an item's purchase price can reflect different factors such as the unit of measure, quantity breakpoints, and date effectivities, as well as higher prices or a surcharge for shorter delivery lead times. Discounts off an item's purchase price can also be defined that reflect these same factors, as well as multiline and total discounts. Other forms of agreements can define supplementary items and miscellaneous charges.

Coordinating Procurement Activities   Planning calculations synchronize supplies to meet demands, and provide coordination via planned orders and suggested action messages.

❖ *Planned Purchase Orders.* Planned purchase orders reflect site/warehouse-specific planning data for an item. The suggested vendor can reflect advanced planning logic that considers purchase price trade agreement information about the lowest price or delivery lead time. The user can create purchase orders from selected planned orders, or use a firming time fence so that the system automatically creates the purchase orders.

❖ *Suggested Action Messages.* Planning calculations generate two types of suggested action messages termed actions and futures. An actions message indicates a suggestion to advance/postpone an order's delivery date, to increase/decrease an order quantity, or to delete an order. A futures message indicates the projected completion date will cause a delay in meeting a requirement date such as a sales order shipment.

Warehouse Management   Stocking locations are uniquely identified by a site, warehouse, and bin location. The system supports batch- and serial-tracking of an item's inventory. The system also supports inventory tracking for palletized items, such as a serialized container or pallet containing the same item.

An arrival overview provides visibility of all anticipated arrivals, such as purchase orders, transfer orders, and customer returns. You can record the arrivals associated with multiple orders, and then record receipts against specific orders. In a similar fashion, you can view anticipated picking activities for sales orders and transfer orders, and create consolidated picking lists or order picking lists to record the actual material picked and shipped.

With palletized items, the system supports coordination of forklift drivers for moving the material. The movement of received material, for example, can reflect directed put-aways. Movement within a warehouse can reflect bin replenishment policies, such as replenishing bins from a bulk storage area.

Multisite Operations   Dynamics AX supports different types of multisite operations, including autonomous sites within a company, a distribution network with transfers between sites, and intercompany trading. Transfer orders coordinate movement between sites and warehouses, and track in-transit inventory. Sales order line items indicate the ship-from site/warehouse, while purchase order line items indicate the ship-to site/warehouse. An item's prices and replenishment methods can be site/warehouse-specific.

Intercompany Trading   With intercompany trading, the purchase order in one company automatically generates the corresponding sales order in the supplying company. Planning calculations can be sequentially performed across a multicompany supply chain. Intercompany trading can also be supported when the trading partner is using another instance of AX or another ERP system.

System Usage in Manufacturing Environments

Manufacturing environments transform purchased materials into saleable items. In addition to the above-mentioned factors for distribution environments, the major factors shaping system usage include the definition of product structure for standard and custom products, variations in production strategy, project-oriented operations, and service-oriented operations.

Definition of Product Structure for Standard Products   Master bills of material (BOM) and master routings define product and process design, and are assigned to relevant manufactured items. A manufactured item can have multiple BOM and/or routing versions. Different versions may reflect planned engineering changes, different sites, different quantities being manufactured, or alternate formulations. Each master BOM and routing, and each assigned version, requires an approval to support subsequent use in planning, costing, and orders.

❖ *Bill of Material Information.* An item's bill of material can be company-wide or site-specific. Each component defines an item, a required quantity, a component type and other information such as the source warehouse, scrap factors, effectivity dates, and the corresponding operation number. The component type indicates whether a manufactured component is make-to-stock, make-to-order, or a phantom, and whether a purchased component is buy-to-stock or buy-to-order. The BOM Designer provides a graphical tool for bill maintenance. The component item's auto-deduction policy determines whether consumption is auto-deducted or manually issued. The component's required quantity can also be based on a calculation formula that employs measurement information about the component and its parent item. A manufactured component can optionally have a specified BOM version and/or routing version that should be used to produce the component.

❖ *Routing Information.* Each routing operation defines the operation number, the work center (or work center group), the time requirements and other information such as a scrap percentage and operation description. Each operation also specifies a master operation identifier that can optionally provide default values. Separate work center costs can be defined for an operation's setup time and run time, and for a piece rate.

Each work center belongs to a work center group, and has a calendar of working times. It can be designated as having finite or infinite capacity for scheduling purposes. For block scheduling purposes, a work center's calendar can indicate blocks of working time with a related property, so that similar operations are scheduled together to minimize setup times.

❖ *Order-Dependent Bill and Routing.* A production order has a separate order-dependent bill and routing that initially reflect the assigned master BOM and routing, and the user can manually maintain this information.

Scheduling Logic Based on Routing Information

A production order can be scheduled using forward or backward scheduling logic, with calculation of a variable lead time based on its routing information. The system supports several advanced scheduling techniques based on routing information. For example, the scheduling logic can assign a specific work center within a work center group or assign an alternate work center to shorten production lead time. Additional factors considered by scheduling logic include the following:

– Finite capacity

- Finite materials and the linkage of components to operation numbers
- Block scheduling (based on properties) to minimize setup times
- Primary and secondary resources required for an operation
- Crew size requirements
- Production quantity determines which BOM and routing version to use
- Production site determines which BOM and routing version to use
- Work center efficiency and loading percentage
- Cumulative scrap percentages in a multistep routing
- Parallel and serial operations
- Operation overlap
- Time elements for transit time and before/after queue times
- Remaining time for setup and run time
- Synchronization of reference orders linked to a production order

Planned Engineering Changes Planned engineering changes to an item's bill of material can be identified using three different approaches: the date effectivities for a component, the assigned master BOM (BOM version), and the specified BOM version for a manufactured component. Planned engineering changes to an item's routing can be identified using two approaches: the date effectivities for the assigned master routing (routing version), and the specified routing version for a manufactured component. With a date effectivity approach, the specified date on a production order determines which routing version, BOM version, and components will be used as the basis for requirements.

Custom Product Manufacturing The system supports two additional approaches for handling custom products manufacturing: option selection for a configurable item, and a rules-based product configurator for a modeling-enabled item.

❖ *Option Selection for a Configurable Item.* The user defines the product structure via an option selection dialogue. The master BOM defines a bill of options for a configurable item, consisting of common and optional components. The master routing defines common routing operations. The custom product can reflect a multilevel product structure, with option selection of items at each level and direct linkage between production orders.

❖ *Rules-Based Product Configurator for a Modeling Enabled Item.* The user defines the product structure via a user dialogue defined in a product model. After completing the user dialogue, the product model automatically generates a new master BOM and routing, and assigns these identifiers to the originating sales order or production order. It also assigns these identifiers to the modeling-enabled item, or to a newly created item number. The newly created item number can reflect a smart part number. The sales price can reflect a cost-plus-markup calculation based on components and operations, or a price calculation within the product model that reflects responses in the user dialogue. The custom product can reflect a multilevel product structure, with direct linkage between production orders.

Cost Calculations for a Manufactured Item   A BOM calculation function uses bill and routing information, and cost data about material, labor, and overhead formulas, to calculate the costs for a manufactured item. Overhead formulas can reflect material-related overheads and/or routing related overheads. The cost data for material, labor, and overhead formulas can be entered for future dates, so that projected costs can be calculated.

The calculation of a manufactured item's standard cost provides the basis for identifying production order variances. The calculation of a planned cost supports several types of simulation. For example, the simulation could reflect the last purchase price or the purchase price trade agreements for material items, and the projected labor costs and overhead formulas.

The BOM calculation can also calculate a suggested sales price for a manufactured item, using a cost-plus markup approach with profit percentages assigned to material, labor, and overhead. In a similar fashion, an order-specific BOM can calculate a manufactured item's suggested sales in the context of a sales quotation, sales order, or service order.

Production Strategy for Manufactured Items   Dynamics AX supports make-to-stock and various make-to-order production strategies, such as CTO and ETO environments. With make-to-order, the end-item's production order is directly linked to the sales order line item, and direct linkage also applies to the make-to-order manufactured components and the buy-to-order purchased components. Replenishment of stocked end-items or components can be based on order point logic or purchase forecasts, and safety stock can be used to buffer anticipated variations in forecasted demand.

Coordinating Manufacturing Activities Planning calculations synchronize production activities to meet demands, and provide coordination via planned orders and suggested action messages. Production schedules and load analysis by work center also act as coordination tools when routing data has been defined.

❖ *Planned Production Orders.* Planned production orders reflect site/warehouse-specific planning data for an item, the item's bill and routing information, and the scheduling logic. The user can create production orders from selected planned orders, or use a firming time fence so that the system automatically generates the production orders for an item.

❖ *Suggested Action Messages.* Planning calculations generate two types of suggested action messages termed actions and futures (as described earlier) to coordinate production orders.

❖ *Production Schedules and Load Analysis by Work Center.* The production schedule and load analysis represent the same information, and provide coordination at each work center. A Gantt chart can also be used to coordinate production.

Reporting Manufacturing Activities Several types of production activities can be reported against production orders. These activities include started quantities, component usage, and parent receipts. The activities also include reporting of operation time and unit completions when routing data exists. Auto-deduction can apply to material components and routing operations.

Lean Manufacturing Practices The system supports lean manufacturers with auto-deduction of material and resources, orderless reporting of production completions, daily production rates that reflect projected or historical usage, and constraint-based scheduling of manufacturing cells. Delivery promises also reflect the daily production rates.

Project-Oriented Operations Project-oriented operations involve forecasting requirements and tracking actual costs related to material, time, and expenses. External projects may also involve project-specific sales quotations and sales orders. The planning calculations can include the forecasted requirements for material and time, as well as demands stemming from the project-specific sales orders and quotations.

Service-Oriented Operations   Service orders provide coordination of field service and internal service personnel, and close integration with projects. Each service order defines the resource requirements—for material, labor and expenses—that serve as the basis for estimated costs. Materials can also be identified for shipment to the customer. Repair history can be recorded against the bill of material for items being serviced. Detailed information can also be recorded about the symptoms-diagnosis-resolution of repair problems. Actual resource consumption drives project accounting for invoicing purposes. Service agreements define resource requirements for periodic services, and provide the basis for automatically creating the service orders to perform the services.

Integration with Other Applications

The integration with other applications includes e-commerce, CRM, and accounting.

Integration with E-Commerce   E-commerce builds on the natural design of an ERP system since it provides electronic communication of basic transactions. Dynamics AX provides integrated e-commerce functionality in several ways, including Biztalk transactions and an enterprise portal. The enterprise portal expedites deployment using a role-based approach, such as roles for customers, vendors, service technicians, and employees. The customer role, for example, supports customer self-service so that customers can place orders and even configure custom products. Other roles support information retrieval and task performance by remote users, such as sales tasks to create new quotes, sales orders, and customers.

Integration with Customer Relationship Management (CRM)   The ability to manage customer relationships is fully integrated with standardized functionality for supply chain management. For example, the CRM activities can lead to sales quotations and sales orders. A campaign can be associated with a project so that all costs can be tracked by project.

Integration with Accounting and Human Resource Applications
The integrated applications include payables, receivables, general ledger, fixed assets, human resources, and payroll.

Concluding Remarks

When reviewing or learning any ERP software package, it is important to understand its underlying conceptual models and how it supports variations in business processes. It is easy to get bogged down in the details. Some of the key design factors that differentiate Microsoft Dynamics AX have been summarized above. These design factors influence how the system fits together to run a business, especially for managing supply chain activities in manufacturing and distribution.

Dynamics AX Terminology and Synonyms

System usage is shaped by several design factors. One of these factors is the terminology for window titles, field labels,and functions that describe system usage. This book's explanations used the Microsoft Dynamics AX terminology as much as possible, but sometimes employed generally accepted synonyms or alternative phrasing to clarify understanding. Several key terms such as posting, journals, and inventory transactions—are essential for explaining system functionality. This Appendix also includes a list of Dynamics AX terminology and synonyms.

Posting   A posting function must be performed before an inventory-related transaction updates the inventory balance and/or inventory value. Illustrations of inventory-related transactions include purchase order receipts, sales order shipments, production order issues, and inventory adjustments. The concept of posting allows multiple transactions to be entered and reviewed prior to updating the database. For example, the posting concept allows multiple inventory adjustments to be prepared and then a single user-initiated function (the posting function) updates the database. The posting function can be performed for a single transaction or a set of transactions, and represents a mass-update approach for a set of transactions. As a mass-update approach, the posting function provides immediate on-line notification of errors within the set of transactions. For example, an error dialogue indicates missing information about the inventory stocking location on a receipt transaction. Errors can then be corrected before performing the posting function again.

The posting function is also used to print paperwork related to inventory transactions, such as a receipt or shipment document. Since Dynamics AX employs a broader definition of inventory transactions (as explained below), the posting function also prints paperwork for purchase orders and sales orders and the related vendor invoices and customer invoices.

Journal The term journal is used in several contexts. A journal typically pertains to general ledger transactions, and a set of inventory transactions that impact inventory value are also termed a journal. Each line item in a journal represents one inventory transaction, and line items can be prepared and modified prior to posting. Journals used for different types of inventory transactions are shown in Figure A.1.

Journals are used for reporting other transactions in addition to inventory-related transactions. These transactions include reporting operation time against production orders (via the Route Card or Job Card Journal), and invoices and payments (via the Invoice Journal and Payment Journal). Several types of journals serve purposes unrelated to accounting, as illustrated below.

– Automatic calculation of item planning data for minimum inventory quantity (via the Safety Stock Journal).
– Creation of sales and purchase trade agreement information (via the Price/Discount Agreement Journal).
– Define absences in human resources (via the Absence Journal).

The term journal also refers to a potential sales order or purchase order, where the order type is journal rather than quotation. Changing the order type from journal to sales order results in an actual order.

Journal Name	Description of Inventory Transaction
Movement Journal	Inventory Adjustment
Profit/Loss Journal	Inventory Adjustment
Transfer Journal	Transfers between Stocking Locations
BOM Journal	Orderless Parent Receipt and Component Auto-deduction
Picking List Journal	Issue Components for Production Order
Route Card or Job Card Journal	Report Unit Completions at Last Operation for Production Order
Report as Finished Journal	Receive Parent Item for Production Order
Counting Journal	Physical Inventory Counts
Project Items Journal	Issue Material for a Project
Warehouse Management Item Arrival	Put-away Material after Purchase Order Receipt
Production Input	Put-away Material after Production Order Receipt
Picking List Registration	Pick Material prior to Sales Order Shipment

Figure A.1 Journals Related to Inventory Transactions

Inventory Transactions   The term inventory transaction normally refers to the physical movement of material, such as an inventory adjustment, receipt, or shipment. Dynamics AX employs a broader view of the term since it creates an inventory transaction (with an associated inventory status) for various steps in purchase, sales, and production order processing. See Figure 9.2 for further explanation of this broader viewpoint concerning the types and status of an inventory transaction.

Lot ID   The lot id represents an internal system-assigned identifier used for tracking every inventory-related transaction.   For example, the system assigns a lot ID to a journal line in an unposted inventory movement journal, and the posted transaction retains the same lot ID.

List of Terms and Synonyms   The following list of Dynamics AX terms and synonyms represents a mapping with commonly used terminology.

DYNAMICS AX TERM	SYNONYM or DEFINITION
Actions Message	Action message about existing supply orders
Automatic Route Consumption	Auto-deduction policies for a work center
BOM Calculation	Calculation of costs, sales price and net weight for a manufactured item
BOM Item	Manufactured Item
BOM Line	Component
BOM Linte Type	Component type (normal, phantom, production, vendor)
BOM Number	Identifier for a master bill of material
BOM Version	Master BOM assigned to a manufactured item
Calculation Group	Set of policies defining the source of an item's cost data in BOM calculations with planned costs
Capacity Unit	Run-rate per hour for a work center
Company Item Number	Item identifier for intercompany sales/purchases
Complete BOM	Costed multilevel bill
Configurable Item	Custom product with a bill of options, used in option selection process to define a unique bill and routing
Configuration Group	Option group for configuring a bill via option selection
Configure Item Dialogue	Option selection process
Corrective Action	Describes needed diagnostics for a quality problem
Cost Category	Labor rate code or machine rate code
Cost Group	Basis for segmenting an item's material, labor and overhead in cost calculations; basis for calculating an item's sales price using a cost-plus markup approach

DYNAMICS AX TERM   SYNONYM or DEFINITION

DYNAMICS AX TERM	SYNONYM or DEFINITION
Cost Price	An item's inventory cost
Costing Version	Set of cost data containing cost records about items, cost categories, and overhead formulas; set of data containing item sales price records generated by BOM calculations
Coverage Code	Reordering policy, such as min/max or requirement
Coverage Group	Set of item planning data policies
Coverage Time Fence	Planning horizon for planning calculations
Credit Note	Customer return; return to vendor
Dimension Group	Set of policies about item identification (Item Dimension) and inventory management (Inventory Dimension)
External Code	Item identifier for intercompany transactions
External Item Number	Vendor item, customer Item
Explode BOM function	Replace line item with the item's components
Explosion Form	Multilevel pegging information
Fallback Principle	BOM calculation policy about source of cost data if it does not exist in the specified costing version
Forecast	
– Item Allocation Key	Planning bill; group of items with mix percentages
– Period Allocation Key	Template for forecasting multiple periods
– Reduction Key	Basis for forecast periods, also an alternative approach to forecast consumption
– Reduction Principle	Forecast consumption logic
– Allocation Method	Repeating pattern to forecast a fixed or variable quantity
Forecast Model	Forecast identifier
Forecast Plan Data	Set of forecast data generated by forecast scheduling task
Futures Message	Action Message about projected completion
Indirect Cost Calculation Formula	Overhead formula for calculating material- or routing-related overheads for a manufactured item
Inventory Dimension	Inventory management policies for an item
Item Dimension	Basis for item identification (such as item number)
Item Name	Item description
Job Scheduling Method	Detailed scheduling method
Location	Bin location
Main Vendor	Preferred vendor for an item
Master Plan Data	Set of data generated by the master scheduling task

DYNAMICS AX TERM	**SYNONYM or DEFINITION**
Minimum	
– Purchase Order Quantity	Order quantity modifier for purchase orders
– Sales Order Quantity	Order quantity modifier for production orders
Minimum/Maximum Key	Pattern of time periods and multipliers for calculating a variable quantity for the minimum or maximum quantities
Minimum Quantity	Safety stock quantity
Modeling-Enabled Item	Custom product with an associated product model that provides a rules-based configurator
Negative Days	Time horizon for rescheduling assumption
Net Requirements Form	Single-level pegging
Nonconformance	Describes an item with a quality problem; the problem may require a corrective action
Non-Inventoried Item	Inventory dimension policies indicate no tracking of physical or financial inventory
Operation Scheduling Method	Rough-cut scheduling method
Operation	Master operation that provides default values when adding a operation to a routing
Packing Slip Update	Sales order shipment or purchase order receipt
Production BOM	Order-dependent bill for a production order
Production Number	Production order number
Production Order	Work order, manufacturing order
Production Route	Order-dependent routing for a production order
Profit-setting Percentage	Markup percentage assigned to cost groups for calculating an item's sales price using a cost-plus markup approach
Purchase Trade Agreement	Agreement about an item's purchase price, line discount, multiline discount, or total discount
Quality Order	Defines what should be tested; actual test results provide the basis for validation against AQL
Quarantine Order	Receiving inspection that prevents item usage
Reference Order	Production (or purchase) order linked to another production order
Report as Finished Quantity	Production order output or parent receipt quantity
Requirements Profile	Single-level pegging
Route Number	Identifier for a master routing
Route Version	Master routing assigned to a manufactured item
Safety Stock Journal	Calculation of minimum quantity based on historical usage
Sales Trade Agreement	Agreement about an item's sales price, line discount, multiline discount, or total discount

DYNAMICS AX TERM   SYNONYM or DEFINITION

DYNAMICS AX TERM	SYNONYM or DEFINITION
Scheduling Method	Detailed (job) or rough-cut (operation) scheduling method
Service Object	Identifier for something to be serviced, such as an item or a group of several items
Service Order	Service work order, service call
Service Task	Phase or segment of service work to be performed
Simultaneous Operations	Combination of primary and secondary resources for an operation number
Site	A physical site with financial reporting requirements
Standard Order Quantity	
– Inventory	Default value for production order quantity
– Purchase	Default value for purchase order quantity
– Sales	Default value for sales order quantity
Sub-BOM	Master BOM specified for a sales order or a bill component
Sub-Production Order	Production order directly linked to another order
Sub-Route	Master routing specified for a sales order or a bill component
Summary Bill	Total costs (and sales price) for a manufactured item segmented by cost group
Task Group	Alternative work center logic
Trade Agreement	Purchase trade agreement, sales trade agreement
Unit of Measure	
– Bill component UM	UM for bill of material component
– Inventory UM	Base UM for inventory costing and transactions
– Purchase Order UM	UM for purchase order line item
– Sales Order UM	UM for sales order line item
Warehouse	A physical site without financial reporting requirements
Work Center	Machine, person, tool or subcontractor
– Available Capacity	Working hours (times the work center head count)
– Work Center Capacity	Capacity per hour, such as concurrent tasks per hour

Index